Reinventing the Supply Chain Life Cycle

Reinventing the Supply Chain Life Cycle

Strategies and Methods for Analysis and Decision Making

Marc J. Schniederjans
Stephen B. LeGrand

Vice President, Publisher: Tim Moore
Associate Publisher and Director of Marketing: Amy Neidlinger
Executive Editor: Jeanne Glasser Levine
Editorial Assistant: Pamela Boland
Development Editor: Russ Hall
Operations Specialist: Jodi Kemper
Marketing Manager: Megan Graue
Cover Designer: Chuti Prasertsith
Managing Editor: Kristy Hart
Project Editor: Andy Beaster
Copy Editor: Keith Cline
Proofreader: Sheri Cain
Indexer: Cheryl Lenser
Compositor: Gloria Schurick
Manufacturing Buyer: Dan Uhrig

© 2013 by Marc J. Schniederjans and Stephen B. LeGrand

Publishing as FT Press

Upper Saddle River, New Jersey 07458
FT Press offers excellent discounts on this book when ordered in quantity for bulk purchases or special sales. For more information, please contact U.S. Corporate and Government Sales, 1-800-382-3419, corpsales@pearsontechgroup.com. For sales outside the U.S., please contact International Sales at international@pearsoned.com.

Company and product names mentioned herein are the trademarks or registered trademarks of their respective owners.

Printed in the United States of America

First Printing: November 2012

ISBN-10: 0132963876
ISBN-13: 9780132963879

Pearson Education LTD.
Pearson Education Australia PTY, Limited.
Pearson Education Singapore, Pte. Ltd.
Pearson Education Asia, Ltd.
Pearson Education Canada, Ltd.
Pearson Educación de Mexico, S.A. de C.V.
Pearson Education—Japan
Pearson Education Malaysia, Pte. Ltd.

Library of Congress Cataloging-in-Publication Data

Schniederjans, Marc J.
  Reinventing the supply chain life cycle : strategies and methods for analysis and decision making / Marc Schniederjans, Stephen Bert LeGrand. -- 1st Edition.
    pages cm
  Includes bibliographical references and index.
  ISBN 978-0-13-296387-9 (hbk. : alk. paper)
  1. Business logistics. 2. Strategic planning. I. LeGrand, Stephen Bert, 1962- II. Title.
  HD38.5.S346 2012
  658.7--dc23

                              2012034561

Contents at a Glance

Contents

About the Authors

Marc J. Schniederjans is the C. Wheaton Battey Distinguished Professor of Business in the College of Business Administration at the University of Nebraska-Lincoln and has served on the faculty of three other universities. Professor Schniederjans is a Fellow of the *Decision Sciences Institute* (DSI). His prior business experience includes owning and operating his own truck-leasing business. He is currently a member of the *Institute of Supply Management* (ISM), the *Council of Supply Chain Management Professionals* (CSCMP), the *Production and Operations Management Society* (POMS), and *Decision Sciences Institute* (DSI). Professor Schniederjans has taught extensively in operations management and management science. He has won numerous teaching awards and is an honorary member of the Golden Key Honor Society and Alpha Kappa Psi business honor society. He has published more than 100 journal articles and has authored or coauthored 18 books in the field of management. He has also presented more than 100 research papers at academic meetings. Professor Schniederjans is serving on numerous journal editorial review boards, including the *Journal of Operations Management* and *Production and Operations Management*, as well as on advisory boards. He is serving as an area editor for the journal *Operations Management Research* and is an associate editor for three other journals. Professor Schniederjans has also served as a consultant and trainer to a variety of business and government agencies, such as Dow North America, Ralston Purina Corporation, and the Ontario Hydro Electro Corporation.

Stephen B. LeGrand is the Vice President of Global Operations for the Irrigation Division of Valmont Industries, Inc. Valmont is the global leader in designing and manufacturing poles, towers, and structures for lighting and traffic, wireless communication, and utility markets and is a provider of protective coating services. Valmont also leads the world in mechanized irrigation equipment for agriculture, enhancing food production while conserving and protecting natural water resources. Stephen is responsible for operations of the division's mechanized irrigation product lines, with manufacturing in the United States, Spain, Dubai, Brazil, China, and South Africa, and with warehousing operations in Australia, Mexico, and Russia. He has been an operations professional for more than 25 years, with experience in M&A, managing manufacturing, supply chain management, and the recruitment and development of international professionals. Before joining Valmont, he served as the Director of Worldwide Operations for the Power Systems Division of the Kohler Company, where he led global operations in Singapore, China, France, India, and the United States. Stephen has a strong background in lean manufacturing, Six Sigma (DMAIC), supply chain management, quality, manufacturing engineering, production, customer service, and safety. Before joining Kohler Power Systems, he served as Operations Manager, Production and Inventory Control Manager, and Scheduling Manager for divisions of Newell Rubbermaid, gaining experience in acquisitions while helping manage operations in Mexico, Canada, the United States, United Kingdom, and France within the retail and B2B industries. Prior to his eight-year association with Newell Rubbermaid, Stephen's experience included 11 years in the defense electronics industry for Rockwell International and Hughes Aircraft companies, where he held positions in engineering, production, materials, and quality, producing radar systems for military aircraft (F-18, F-14, and F-15) and manufacturing *global positioning systems* (GPS) for handheld, vehicle, and missile (SLAM, TLAM) applications. He holds a Masters of Business Administration (MBA) degree from the University of Iowa in operations and earned a Bachelor of Science (BS) degree in industrial technology from the University of Northern Iowa. In addition, he has certification in Integrated Supply Chain Management from the University of Tennessee, *Certified in Production and Inventory Management* (CPIM) certification from the *American Production & Inventory Control Society* (APICS) and certification in technology from the *Society of Manufacturing Engineering* (SME).

Preface

Supply chains for the goods and services we consume or use impact all of us, every day. Business organizations realize that supply chains have become a strategy for success to better serve customers and improve their bottom line. How efficient and successful supply chains are is determined by how well they are managed.

To conceptualize what is involved in managing a supply chain, practitioners and scholars have explored a variety of paradigms. For instance, a supply chain may be viewed in the context of product life cycle stages (that is, Introduction, Growth, Maturity and Decline). Marketers have long used the product life cycle as a transformational process that can guide the movement of a product back up its life cycle, allowing the product to continue almost indefinitely. Guided by the stages of the life cycle, marketers can reinvigorate a product with innovations and new ideas to keep its demand growing and the product alive. Life cycling takes place in a variety of applications beyond its application to a product and can provide an interesting framework to study any type of business activity.

Supply chains, like the products and services they deliver, have life cycles. Supply chains need to be constantly reinvigorated and reinvented to keep them functioning, alive, and purposeful. The book you are reading organizes its content around the life cycling concept as it is related to the entire supply chain. The focus here is not the life cycle of a single product or service, but the life cycling of products, operations, processes, and procedures that collectively make up a supply chain. The purpose of this book is to provide a selection of topical knowledge that can help supply chain managers reinvent their supply chains and, in doing so, add to the life of the supply chain cycling process.

No single book can cover all the topics required to equip supply chain managers with total knowledge about a subject. The content in this book seeks to achieve three goals: (1) to provide basic text material on the practice and theory related to a select group of topics important in the management of supply chains, (2) to share experiential knowledge from executives through interviews to provide current thoughts on supply chain management, and (3) to make learning entertaining through the novelettes based on actual supply chain situations. To achieve these goals, this book is organized into 3 parts consisting of 22 chapters in total. In Part I, the basic text material of the book is presented in the first 13 chapters. These chapters cover a series of topics related to supply chain management, including, developing strategies; designing; staffing; managing; aligning; negotiating; outsourcing; social, ethical, and legal considerations; sustainability; building agility and flexibility; developing partnerships; risk management; and lean and other cost strategies. Each of these chapters begins with an outline to overview the organization of the chapter and a list of terms to hint at what follows in the content of the chapter itself. A short novelette follows this and is based on real supply chain managers' experiences in dealing with problems related to each chapter. The novelettes are a continuous story from the perspective of a Vice President of Operations and the management of an organization's operations, including the supply chain. These novelettes are followed in each chapter by a section designed for inexperience supply chain managers that covers prerequisite material. Also, a final section, "What's Next?" gives supply chain managers a look ahead based on current research about what the next three to five years may hold, again relating to the topic of each chapter.

Part II contains seven chapters. Each chapter contains an interview with a supply chain executive. These executives share their individual organization's approach to dealing with planning in the supply chain life cycles of their products or services. These interviews cover interesting strategies and tactics from small, medium, and large firms, as well as from manufacturing and service organizations.

In Part III, two additional novelette case studies are presented as a way of concluding the running novelette used in the first 13 chapters. Like the earlier novelettes in Part 1, they are based on the actual experiences of a supply chain executive.

This book has been written for supply chain practitioners, managers, executive, and CEOs, but any manager, and particularly those with operations responsibilities, will find its topics useful for helping to manage their supply chains. Engineers interested in the conceptual and strategic aspects of managing a supply chain may also find this book useful. One of the book's features for this audience is the "Prerequisite Material" section conveniently located in the beginning of each of the first 13 chapters. This material could be redundant for the experienced manager and so can be skipped or used as a review for managers who may need it. Also, the usual academic theory is almost completely absent from this book. Instead, we have drawn much of our material from recent trade publications of major supply chain organizations like the *Institute of Supply Management* (ISM). In addition, the fundamental analytical techniques that are usually distracting from the text material are not a part of this book. We have placed them in an accompanying workbook for those who want to learn more about the procedural aspects. The workbook is chiefly designed for undergraduate or graduate-level students majoring in supply chain management. The accompanying workbook provides a series of methodologies mentioned in the book and others that represent fundamental content in supply chain management. It also provides the educational pedagogy for use in college programs and support learning. Faculty adopters will also be provided with standard educational pedagogy (PowerPoints and a test bank).

We want to acknowledge the help of individuals who provided needed support for the creation of this book. First and foremost, we truly appreciate the generous time and effort given by the supply chain executives who shared with us their wisdom in dealing with supply chain management planning and decision making. Alphabetically, these executives include Brent Beabout, Senior Vice President of Supply Chain at Office Depot; Eddie Capel, Manhattan Associates

Executive Vice President and Chief Operating Officer; James Chris Gaffney, Senior Vice President Product Supply System-Strategy for Coca-Cola Refreshments; Mark Holifield, Senior Vice President of Supply Chain for The Home Depot; Yadi Kamelian, Vice President of Materials and Customer Service for Lincoln Industries; Mike Orr, Senior Vice President of Operations & Logistics for Genuine Parts Company; and Ronald D. Robinson, Director of Supply Chain Management for LI-COR Biosciences. We also want to acknowledge the great editing help we received from Jill Schniederjans. The book is now much less wordy than it might have been. Others who have contributed at the Financial Times Press include our very supportive executive editor, Jeanne Glasser Levine, and our consulting editor, Barry Render. They made the book a pleasure to write and worked with us to improve the final product.

While many people have had a hand in the preparation of this book, its accuracy and completeness are the responsibility of the authors. For all errors that this book may contain, we apologize in advance.

Marc J. Schniederjans and Stephen B. LeGrand

August 1, 2012

1

Developing Supply Chain Strategies

Terms

Aggregate planning

Bullwhip

Consensus planning

Core competency

Critical success factors (CSFs)

Customer value

Decline stage, life cycle

External environmental analysis

Growth stage, life cycle

Internal organizational analysis

Introduction stage, life cycle

Logistic management

Logistics

Maturity stage, life cycle

Mission statement

Operational planning

Product life cycle

Pull strategy

Push strategy

Push-pull boundary

Push-pull strategy

Stakeholder

Strategic planning

Supply chain

Supply chain life cycle

Supply chain management

Tactical planning

Third-party logistics (3PL)

Value

Value proposition

Vision statement

Novelette Introduction

In the first 13 chapters of this book, a fictional novelette related to the chapter's content is presented based on actual practices of experienced supply chain managers. These situational experiences can help explain problems and possible solutions to perplexing issues every supply chain manager faces. They represent real solutions to common problems. They are presented in first-person narrative from the perspective of a Senior Vice President of Operations Management responsible for supply chain management. This is a running novelette that builds from chapter to chapter with the same characters. The last two chapters of this book conclude with two larger problem situations, again using the same characters.

Novelette

My name is Bill, and I am the Senior Vice President of Operations for a firm that chiefly produces engines and engine parts for all types of applications: small engines for household appliances, medium-sized engines for automobiles and farm equipment, and large electrical generation engines for buildings. We also produce hardware products like tools. Our organization is divided into four different divisions: three are based on the size of the application of each engine; and a fourth division manufactures tools, hardware, and other construction materials. Each Division has its own Supply Chain Department, with a Supply Chain Manager as its head. The customer markets for our engines are global, and so is our sourcing for our supply chain. I am responsible for every aspect of production in all the Divisions and for the success of our supply chain that supports the production efforts.

Every day I come to work, there are usually adventures (what some of my colleagues would say are problems) waiting for me. Today is no different. It is the end of the business quarter, and we have just been given the financials and other operational measures, including those in the supply chain area. I have become increasingly aware that the focus of our organization-wide strategies does not seem to be impacting everyone in our organization the same way. As result, we do not achieve the success we have benchmarked for them. The reported results for the organization, as well as the supply chain department, at the end of the quarter makes this reality painfully clear. To address the problem, I called in the Vice Presidents of Operations for each of our divisions who report directly to me to inquire what might be done to move the organization forward toward achieving organizational and individual departmental goals. From the discussion it became clear that our firm does not presently do a very good job of communicating organizational goals down through the organization to everyone. People are simply not pushing in the same direction toward the goals that have been defined at the highest levels in the organization.

To attempt to resolve the lackluster performance, I got together with my peers (senior VPs in marketing, finance, information systems, and so on), and we clearly aligned and realigned organizational strategic goals that currently needed adjustment or a clearer definition. We then got together with the CEO and made sure she was onboard for the goals we articulated. Once all the organization-wide executives were onboard, we undertook a policy deployment program in the operations area. What this entailed was first meeting with each of the Division VPs of Operations and further delineating the organizational strategic goals into strategic goals for the operations area. From there, we took the operations area's strategic goals, which were longer term (of several years), and broke them down into specific and easy-to-define, one-year-interval tactical plans. Each yearly tactical plan was given measurable metrics or benchmarks as targeted yearly outcomes. These were viewed as *critical success factors* (CSFs) or "touchdown points" to achieve for the Operations Departments in each division. This effort streamlined and clarified tactics and expected outcomes that could be easily communicated between divisions and downward within each division.

I understood that communicating strategy, tactics, and operational planning requires more than a discussion on theory or procedure; it sometimes requires a very clear example or two. The VP of the

Small Engine Division (Alan) asked, "Bill, can you give me an example I can take back to my Supply Chain Department Head that will make sense to her?"

"Sure, Alan! One of your supply chain improvements could be in demand forecasting, where you are trying to improve your forecasting accuracy. Tactically, that might require you to have better trained salespeople to interact with customers to obtain point-of-sale information and glean what is needed to provide more accurate, aggregated forecast values. Better demand information reduces forecasting error. Accuracy in forecasting becomes a critical success factor for supply chain management because it avoids the waste of carrying excessive and burdensome inventory. Eliminating excessive inventory in the supply chain allows for a quicker response to customers. You also have fewer outages of stock with forecasting accuracy, which protects you from the competition. All of this backs up to organization-level goals of increasing value to customers and gaining more market share," I stated.

Alan nods and then asks, "Okay, that makes sense for the department heads; but given the shortage of time and the costs of training or retaining everyone, how far down the organization should we share the goals, tactics, and operational plans?"

I smiled and said, "Not everyone needs a training program; they just need information. Everyone down to the janitor should be given information on where they need to go and what they need to do to achieve their portion of the goals, tactics, and operational plans relative to their assigned duties. The more we communicate down the organization about where we are going, the better we will be able to all pull together to achieve what we seek to do in the short and long term."

1.1 Prerequisite Material

In this chapter and select chapters that follow, an introductory "Prerequisite Material" section seeks to acquaint less-experienced students of supply chain management with basic and elemental content and terminology. Experienced supply chain executives and managers might be tempted to skip this section in chapters where it is included, but they might instead want to use it as a review of basic concepts and terminology.

1.1.1 Logistics, Supply Chains, and Supply Chain Management

Logistics refers to the movement of things (that is, people, material, parts, finished goods, and information) in appropriate quantities and timing to meet the needs of an organization's *stakeholders* (that is, both internal stakeholders, like employees, and external stakeholders, like suppliers and customers). *Logistic management* seeks to manage the flow of manufactured products, services, and information through a business operation to the final customer. Complemented by logistics and logistics management, a *supply chain* represents a network of all processes, elements, and relationships that moves information, services, and materials, from their origins (for example, unearthed raw materials, supplier parts) through internal production in manufacturing organizations, delivery in service organizations, or external outsourcing vendors or supply partners for distribution networks to eventual consumers and beyond. As presented in Figure 1.1, a supply chain consists of a network of connected, independent suppliers, manufacturers/service organizations (usually many), distribution centers, retailers, and customers, which are all represented as nodes in the supply chain network. Some supply chains are less inclusive and are not concerned with upstream, multiple-tiered suppliers provide raw materials, downstream distributors, or retailers that market the product (for example, a commercial customer who receives goods directly from a manufacturer). Most firms today include a component of *sustainability* (that is, the desire to conserve resources and do no harm to the environment) in operations. (Chapter 6, "Sustainable Supply Chains," discusses sustainability in more detail.)

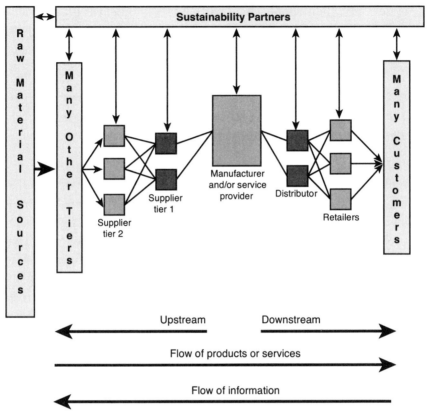

Figure 1.1 Simple supply chain network and flow diagram

Source: Adapted from Figure 5.1 in Schniederjans and Olson (1999), p. 70.

Generally, supply chains are divided into upstream (that is, various multiple levels of supplier tiers) and downstream (that is, finished product or service distribution and customers). Also, the flow of products travels downstream from suppliers to customers, while information about an organization's performance and customers tends to travel upstream through the supply chain.

Whereas logistics management provides a planning framework for supply chains, *supply chain management* builds linkages with various independent supply chain participants (for example, suppliers and customers). It is a management process that involves establishing and building trusting relationships. Indeed, supply chain managers seek to establish a relationship that is more of a partnership than just a transactional relationship involving the purchase of items from suppliers or the selling of items to customers. Supply chain managers working closely with their supply chain partners seek to deliver greater value to customers by reducing costs throughout the supply for all partners. Working with partners, supply chain managers seek many value enhancing objectives, but to do so requires planning.

1.1.2 Types of Organizational Planning: Strategic, Tactical, and Operational Planning

An overview of the typical organizational planning process is presented in Figure 1.2. *Strategic planning* usually involves issues that may significantly impact the organization from the external environment (for example, customers and competitors). It deals with issues such as what the firm wants to do in the future (for example, what industries or markets to explore), what businesses the firm wants to be in, and how to allocate the firm's total resources. Strategic planning also involves self-examination to determine resources and strives to move the organization toward longer-range strategic goals (for example, corporation growth in market share). The president of the firm and the board of directors usually undertake this planning. The outcome of this effort is a clear statement of long-term (for example, perhaps three or more years in the future) goals.

Tactical planning is the next step down from strategic planning efforts and deals with developing implementation approaches to achieve the strategic longer-range goals. It is the stage in the organizational planning process that breaks down longer-range goals into more immediate goals with greater detail. For example, in an organization where market share is a strategic goal, a tactic that would support this strategic goal might be to acquire a competitor in the next year or two to grow through acquisition. If a strategic goal is to become the most environmentally friendly organization in an industry, one supportive tactical goal might be to invest in or build a recycling facility in the next year or two. Chief operating officers, vice presidents, and general managers representing functional areas (for example, operations, finance, marketing) or divisions in an organization planning usually undertake this planning effort. The outcome of this planning effort is a set of intermediate goals that guide each of the functional areas or divisions over the next one or two years. These are more specific goals that take place within a fairly defined time horizon (for example, completing a building or a new production facility by a fixed date).

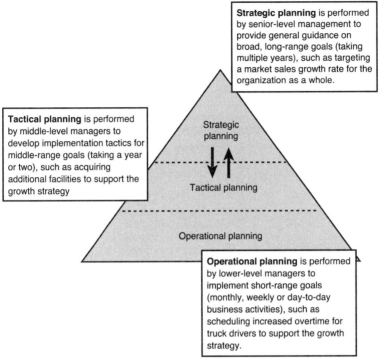

Strategic planning is performed by senior-level management to provide general guidance on broad, long-range goals (taking multiple years), such as targeting a market sales growth rate for the organization as a whole.

Tactical planning is performed by middle-level managers to develop implementation tactics for middle-range goals (taking a year or two), such as acquiring additional facilities to support the growth strategy

Strategic planning

Tactical planning

Operational planning

Operational planning is performed by lower-level managers to implement short-range goals (monthly, weekly or day-to-day business activities), such as scheduling increased overtime for truck drivers to support the growth strategy.

Figure 1.2 Organization planning stages

Source: Adapted from Figure 1.3 in Schniederjans et al., (2005), p. 37.

Operational planning is the final step in the organizational planning process that breaks down tactical goals into very detailed short-range goals for areas, groups, and individuals who make up the firm. All types of lower-level managers or supervisors throughout the organization undertake this planning effort. These short-range goals are very specific. Examples of operational plans include scheduling monthly, weekly, or daily production assignments for employees; arranging transportation scheduling for shipments to specific customers; and setting up purchasing order systems for parts.

1.1.3 Elements of Organizational Strategic Planning

Organizational strategic planning is a fairly common and consistent process undertaken more frequently when substantial change in an industry warrants reexamination of the direction a firm is strategically taking. The overall process of organizational strategic planning usually begins by reviewing a firm's *mission statement* (that is, a document defining broad objectives, like making profit) (see Figure 1.3). This is done to ensure the firm's strategic goals align with what it espouses in its mission statement.

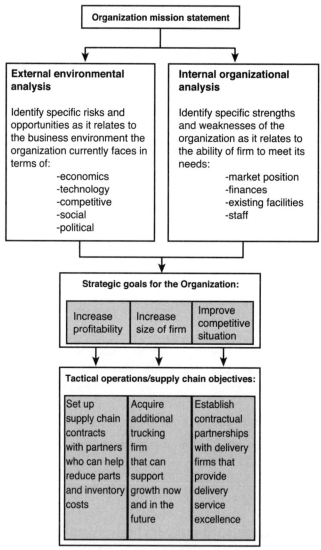

Figure 1.3 Organization planning stages

Source: Adapted from Figure 2.2 in Schniederjans (1998), p. 22.

The *external environmental analysis* examines the environment external to the organization (for example, competitor actions, new technology). This analysis seeks to determine possible risks and opportunities (for example, mergers and acquisitions, new supply chain partners) that might offer the acquiring firm an improved competitive position. This analysis helps provide answers to questions such as whether we are at risk from new competitors. If the opportunities are not greater than the risks, the analysis comes to an end and the firm does not pursue any changes in strategic plans. If the opportunities look more promising than the risks, an internal organizational analysis is undertaken.

An *internal organizational analysis* looks internally to identify strengths and weaknesses the organization may have in pursuing business plans. This analysis seeks to answer questions such as whether the organization has the finances, staff, and facilities to undertake opportunities identified in the external environmental analysis. If the answer is no, either the firm finds the resources it will need, or it does not take advantage of the opportunities. If the answer is yes, the firm initiates additional planning to define goals and align the organization's resources to achieve them.

The desired end result of these two analyses is a set of strategic goals that an organization can use to guide planning efforts. As shown in Figure 1.3, the organizational strategic goals can be broken down into tactical goals in functional areas such as operations/supply chain. Actually, the operations/supply chain executives (for example, vice presidents, general managers) usually develop function-level strategies that serve to guide tactical efforts. So, it is accurate to say that at each of the three planning levels (strategic, tactical, operational) strategies, tactics, and operational plans can be developed by organizational members to further detail and guide the organization to achieve its objectives.

Other possible outcomes of the organizational strategic planning process include the identification of critical success factors and core competencies. CSFs are a "must-have" set of criteria identified as critical for conducting business. They may be human, technical, financial, or resource, without which a firm believes it cannot be successful. CSFs are often identified during the internal organizational analysis, where organizational strengths are found. A related concept to CSFs is core competency. A *core competency* is what the firm can do better than its competitors. A core competency can be a CSF. An example of a core competency is the supply chain network that is more efficient than its competitors. Core competencies are often found during the internal organizational analysis where strengths are identified. Firms build on core competencies and try to outsource or improve noncore competencies.

1.2 Supply Chain Strategic Planning

"If you don't know where you are going, any road will get you there."

—*Lewis Carroll*

1.2.1 Positioning for Strategy Development: Understanding the Life Cycle of Products in Supply Chains

For an entrepreneur starting a new company with a single product or for seasoned supply chain executives with the responsibility of managing the flow of thousands of products, there will always be a need to plan for supply chains and develop strategies to develop, maintain, and end them. Where should a planner begin to develop a strategy for the supply chain? The answer depends partly on where the manager's product is located in its life cycle of its supply chain.

A *product life cycle* entails a single product's unit demand divided into four stages: introduction, growth, maturity, or decline based on customer demand (as shown in Figure 1.4). The *introduction stage* is where a product is introduced. Demand increases at a slow rate, while the product gains acceptance in the market. The *growth stage* is characterized by product demand that increases at an increasing rate.

The *maturity stage* is where product demand peaks and flattens out. The *decline stage* is where product demand increasingly decreases.

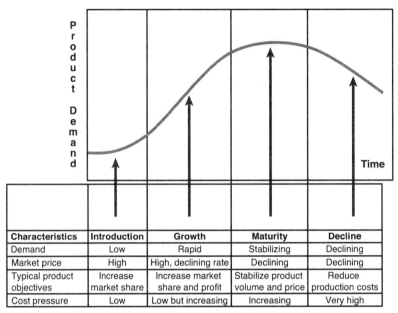

Characteristics	Introduction	Growth	Maturity	Decline
Demand	Low	Rapid	Stabilizing	Declining
Market price	High	High, declining rate	Declining	Declining
Typical product objectives	Increase market share	Increase market share and profit	Stabilize product volume and price	Reduce production costs
Cost pressure	Low	Low but increasing	Increasing	Very high

Figure 1.4 Product life cycle planning stages

The use of the product life cycle to plan a single product's supply chain is well documented in the literature (see Table 1.1) and continues to be a valid planning tool (as discussed throughout the remaining chapters).

Table 1.1 Select Research on Product Life Cycle and Supply Chains

Authors	Substance of Article
Amini and Li (2011)	Developed optimization model to examine the demand for products in supply chains in different stages of the life cycle.
Komoto et al. (2011)	Simulation study exploring how to reconfigure supply chains end-of-life products that are physically deteriorating and functionally obsolete.
Abo-Hamad and Arisha (2011)	Literature review study presenting an authoritative listing of optimization methodology to research life cycling in supply chains.
Quariguasi et al. (2010)	A study on life cycle design for closed-loop supply chains focused on sustainability.

Authors	Substance of Article
Atasu et al. (2010)	A strategy study of value added by remanufacturing products and the impact on product life cycle market demand disadvantages.
Fixson (2005)	Short product life cycles require consideration in supply chain strategy development and implementation.
Wang et al. (2004)	Life cycle product characteristics are related to supply chain strategies.

How can the position on the product life cycle be determined? Most experienced supply chain managers can answer this question by following demand forecasts. Today, statistical software not only forecasts demand but also projects trends that reveal life cycle stage behavior for individual products and product lines.

Once a product life cycle stage position is known, managers can use that information to better plan supply chain strategy within each stage of the life cycle. The life cycle position can help prepare managers for eventual changes that move a firm's supply chain planning efforts forward or backward in the life cycle by adapting or aligning strategies to fit the current market demand situation. The continual alignment or realignment of a supply chain is essential to be competitive. The supply chain activities used to create, maintain, and end a supply chain (or individual supply chains within a larger network) represent the *supply chain life cycle*. Managing the supply chain life cycle mirrors product life cycles. Like a product life cycle, the same strategies used in managing a supply chain life cycle are not as successful in differing stages because customer (and partner) needs change. Although many experienced supply chain executives can "feel the pulse" of demand within supply chains, it is better to know in advance using a life cycle approach of the direction and rate of change taking place or trending, to better lead supply chain planning for a product or a collection of products during each stage of a life cycle.

There are complicating factors to managing individual product life cycles in a supply chain network. For example, the aggregation of a product line or group of products produced and shipped through a supply chain network adds considerable effort to planning (see Figure 1.5). These products may have differing product life cycle timing and demand requirements but require an aggregated supply chain plan. Illustrated in Figure 1.6, the aggregated demand of a product line or group of products can create an aggregate product life cycle. When carried over the life of a firm, this figure represents the life cycle of both the firm and the supply chain. The impact of aggregation may also require a substantially different level (aggregated) of planning.

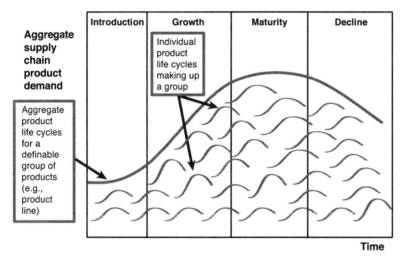

Figure 1.5 Relationship of product life cycles and their aggregation

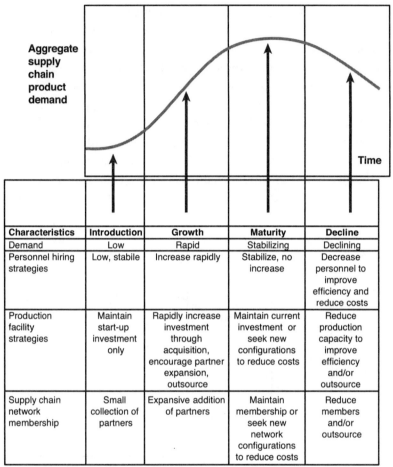

Characteristics	Introduction	Growth	Maturity	Decline
Demand	Low	Rapid	Stabilizing	Declining
Personnel hiring strategies	Low, stabile	Increase rapidly	Stabilize, no increase	Decrease personnel to improve efficiency and reduce costs
Production facility strategies	Maintain start-up investment only	Rapidly increase investment through acquisition, encourage partner expansion, outsource	Maintain current investment or seek new configurations to reduce costs	Reduce production capacity to improve efficiency and/or outsource
Supply chain network membership	Small collection of partners	Expansive addition of partners	Maintain membership or seek new network configurations to reduce costs	Reduce members and/or outsource

Figure 1.6 Aggregate life cycle supply chain planning

In Figure 1.7, the characteristics of this level of planning are considerably broader or more strategic in nature than the usual single product planning effort.

Throughout this book, references made to the product life cycle are used to illustrate how some global aspects of supply chain life cycles can be dealt with by managing product life cycle issues. It is the application of product life cycle strategies and methods that can help reinvent and revitalize a firm's supply chain life cycle.

1.2.2 Supply Chain Strategy Opportunities

Typical supply chain strategies might include building new supply chain networks to better serve customers or establishing recruiting programs to bring appropriate talent to a firm over an extend period of time. There are many possibilities for strategic objectives to be established and achieved. The key in strategic planning is to make sure the plan is aligned with the abilities of the firm and aligned to serve customers.

One approach for aligning a firm's strategies is through consensus planning. *Consensus planning* refers to a process where conflicting, functional organizational objectives and knowledge are intelligently reconciled to benefit all (McBeath, 2011). The steps in consensus planning are presented in Table 1.2. The steps in Table 1.2 seek to bring empowered decision makers together, motivating them to share forecasting information and weigh value with accuracy as a goal to reconcile functional differences. In doing so, it helps to align marketing with operations. It also reflects that planning efforts have very different timing requirements. Fast cycle planning compresses supply chain decision cycles so that rapid decision making can be initiated to avoid supply chain problems (like the *bullwhip effect* often caused by inaccurate forecasting resulting in excessive operational waste). Strategic planning is considered long-term planning, but for some organizations that time period could be months, not years. Likewise, tactical planning might be days instead of months, and operational planning could be minutes and not days.

Table 1.2 Consensus Planning Steps

Steps	Description
1. Reconciliation of forecasts	Identify and integrate demand and supply events between marketing and operations. Measure and reward/penalize forecasting accuracy. Use the latest forecasting technology to mathematically weight the differing forecasts used by marketing and operations to generate a more accurate forecast that is inclusive of all parties. Explore differing scenarios using forecasting tools that permit greater understanding between functional areas to encourage reconciliation efforts of all parties
2. Fast cycle planning	Rapid decision making cycles (for example, daily in some situations) based on current data. This step requires all relevant participants with authority to work together (ideally in the same room or technologically connected) to make resource decisions. Technologies to make communication and the sharing of information should be automated so that planning meetings can be called quickly to provide rapid response to environmental changes. Also, encourage and design information systems to channel fast cycle planning efforts up the organization to other stakeholders and upper management.
3. One-number planning	Coordinate procurement orders initiated in operations to match the marketing forecast demand, one for one. Marketing must agree to use what is purchased by operations to align supply with demand.

Source: Adapted from McBreath (2011).

Within each of the life cycle stages, many opportunities exist to develop strategies to overcome problems, improve efficiency, and achieve supply chain excellence for customers. The strategy generalities presented in this chapter are a good starting point, but considerably more detail is needed to understand the diversity of strategic issues that supply chain managers' face. The opportunities for strategic planning and decision making are as varied as the multitude of tasks supply chain managers are asked to perform. The content of this book focuses on many topical areas that require strategy development. In Table 1.3, supply chain strategy opportunities are briefly listed as they relate to the content and chapter locations within this book. You can use this table as a quick literature reference guide to specific content areas of study in supply chain planning.

Table 1.3 Supply Chain Strategy Opportunities

Life Cycle Stage	Strategy Opportunity	Description of Opportunity
Introduction	Designing supply chains	Improve efficiency of delivery to customer by designing or redesigning the distribution system (Chapter 2, "Designing Supply Chains")
Introduction	Staffing supply chains	Improve service to customers by having better trained and skilled staff (Chapter 3, "Staffing Supply Chains")
Introduction	Managing the supply chain network	Improve coordination among supply partners to save time (Chapter 4, "Managing Supply Chains")
Introduction	Managing costs	Keep costs low to improve profitability (Chapter 5, "Social, Ethical, and Legal Considerations")
Introduction	Performance evaluation	Identify and evaluate problem areas in supply chain network quickly, thus avoiding more costly correction problems (Chapter 6, "Sustainable Supply Chains")
Introduction	Social, ethical and legal considerations	Satisfy customers needs for social and ethical responsibility while working with government authorities to ensure regulation compliance (Chapter 7, "Aligning Supply Chains to Meet Life Cycle Customer Demands")
Growth	Aligning supply chains to meet growth in customer demand	Improve availability of product supply to customers in high-demand markets (Chapter 9, "Building an Agile and Flexible Supply Chain")

Life Cycle Stage	Strategy Opportunity	Description of Opportunity
Growth	Negotiating	Reduce costs and improve product quality in sourcing and purchasing decisions (Chapter 10, "Developing Partnerships in Supply Chains")
Growth	Building an agile and flexible supply chain	Improve responsiveness to shifts in customer demand (Chapter 11, "Risk Management")
Growth	Developing partnerships in supply chains	Build trust in the partnership relationships that can help reduce costs and provide for mutual learning for new product innovations (Chapter 12, "Lean and Other Cost Reduction Strategies in Supply Chain Management")
Growth	Risk management	Avoid costly mistakes in running a supply chain network and identify possible future threats (Chapter 13, "Strategic Planning in Outsourcing")
Maturity	Realigning supply chains to meet a maturing customer demand	Coordinate production and distribution to better serve retail and customer demand requirements (Chapter 15, "Interview with Mark Holifield of Home Depot")
Maturity	Lean and other cost reduction strategies in supply chain management	Develop strategies to reduce inventory and production costs throughout the supply chain network (Chapter 16, "Interview with Yadi Kamelian of Lincoln Industries")
Maturity	Sustainable supply chains	Develop new strategies to convert existing production waste into profit (Chapter 17, "Interview with Mr. Eddie Capel of Manhattan Associates")
Maturity	Managing costs and prices	Develop new strategies that seek to reduce costs, thus making products more price competitive (Chapter 18, "Interview with Ron Robinson of LI-COR Biosciences")
Maturity	Supply chain performance metrics	Control supply performance to reduce costs to improve customer demand (Chapter 19. "Interview with James Chris Gaffney of the Coca-Cola Company")

Life Cycle Stage	Strategy Opportunity	Description of Opportunity
Decline	Aligning supply chains to meet a declining customer demand	Develop strategies that seek to identify and discontinue infeasible products while maintaining products desired by customers (Chapter 21, "Novelette: So You Want to Build a Plant in a Foreign Country")
Decline	Outsourcing strategies	Develop strategies to outsource to other suppliers production effort that can be more efficiently handled outside the firm (Chapter 22, "Novelette: So You Want to Eliminate a Plant in a Foreign Country")

1.3 Critical Success Factors in Developing a Supply Chain Strategy

Every supply chain is unique, and the strategies needed for business success in one supply chain can be completely different in another. To deal with this diversity of application, criteria can be established to guide managers to identify areas within unique supply chains where strategic planning can be used to benefit the organization.

One approach to supply chain strategy development is to utilize CSF criteria in supply chains. CSFs can be used to identify relevant supply chain issues that would benefit from strategic planning efforts. One set of criteria was suggested by Slone et al. (2010). Although structured as steps in a proposed strategy development process (see Table 1.4), this set of criteria offers CFSs in the development of supply chain strategies. Any one of the five criteria could and should be used to develop strategies in an effort to continually enhance supply chain performance.

Table 1.4 Supply Chain Strategy Development Steps

Step in Supply Chain Strategy Development (That Is, CSF)	Description
1. Select leaders and develop supply chain talent.	Identify and recruit the right talent for the supply chains. Ensure that they have the right language, culture, and analytic skills to do their jobs and to lead others.
2. Stay current with supply chain technology.	Technology is always changing, and to be competitive in supply chain management, the latest technology must be acquired. This includes software, hardware, and tech training for staff and executives.
3. Avoid dysfunctional organization behavior that separates the functional areas within an organization.	Functional departments in an organization must work together as a team. Divisions within the Supply Chain department must also work together as a team. Discourage the "silo" or walled-up mentality of separating departments and encourage cooperation.
4. Encourage collaboration with supply chain partners.	Work to establish trust with supply chain partners and a genuine partnership between all supply chain partners, upstream and downstream.
5. Encourage project and change management.	Key to change a supply chain is both a willingness of managers to undertake change when needed (that is, develop an environment that fosters change) and to use project management as a tool to deal with specific problems and as a means to adjust the supply chain as needed.

Source: Adapted from Slone et al. (2010), pp. 40–51.

Relating the five CSFs back to the concept of a product life cycle, note that any of these five can be used at any life cycle stage. For example, consider the CSF of "selecting leaders and developing supply chain talent" from Table 1.3. Some executives are more efficient and successful at managing supply chains in growth stages, whereas others are more successful managing during the maturing stages. Optimizing a supply chain requires realigning talent to the life cycle stage of the supply chain. Alternatively, it requires executives be cognizant of the life cycle stage and to adapt its needs to the supply chain that supports it.

Another view of supply chain strategy CSFs is presented in Seuring (2009). In this research study, the author suggests strategy development in supply chains is a function of five criteria (see Table 1.5). These criteria are based on the types of decision areas that a typical supply chain manager has to deal with in the course of running the network. Other researchers advocate a similar listing of criteria for supply chain strategy development, such as product innovation, price and brand, value-added services, and relationships and experiences (Simchi-Levi, 2009, pp. 19–31). Whatever guiding paradigm a supply chain executive or manager chooses to use, CSFs can help identify areas for strategic planning and focus planning efforts.

Table 1.5 Supply Chain Strategic Decision Making Criteria

Decision Areas	Types of Decisions Related to Strategy Development
Products and services	Selection and introduction of products and services, performance goals in quality, speed, dependability, flexibility, and cost
Partnerships	Selection and development of relations with all types of supply chain partners
Plants and inventory	Plant structures, logistics, inventory policies
Processes	Organizations structure and production procedures
Planning	Information on product flow, sharing with partners, and controlling operations

Source: Adapted from Table 1 in Seuring (2009), p. 225.

1.4 Supply Chain Strategies

There are three primary supply chain strategies on which to structure processes to build a supply chain: push, pull and push-pull strategies (Simchi-Levi, 2008, pp. 188–195; Wincel, 2004, pp. 217–225). In a *push strategy,* the supply chain processes are initiated based on forecasts of anticipated customer demand. In a *pull strategy,* the supply chain processes are initiated by a customer order being placed. Combining the two, the push-pull strategy allows forecast demand considerations to drive the supply chain processes up to a point (called the *push-pull boundary*). After that point, push strategy process considerations are driven by customer demand.

Although the push strategy is classic business behavior, the advent of Japanese production methods (for example, just-in-time [JIT] management, lean management) fostered a pull strategy orientation for most manufacturing firms in the 1980s (Wincel, 2004, p. 217). Not all firms can use the pull strategy. Firms that produce complex products with long lead times, or whose customers value low prices (that is, cost minimization objective for the firm), are likely to find a push strategy more workable. However, customers less interested in cost minimization and instead value firms that focus on maximizing service levels and customer responsiveness are likely to find a pull strategy more workable.

Firms today find the push-pull strategy to be highly effective if they can find the right balance in the push-pull boundary. According to Arnseth (2011b), it is possible to balance how much pushing and pulling should be undertaken to optimize this strategy. Consider the push-pull strategy along the upstream and downstream of a supply chain. Everything upstream from the manufacturing or service facility might employ a push strategy (for example, long lead times and cost minimization efforts for extra raw materials to convert them into metal sheeting), while everything downstream might employ a pull strategy based exclusively on customer demand. To avoid or minimize the potential wastefulness of the pushing upstream inputs in manufacturing distribution systems, the push-pull boundary has to be determined as early in the supply chain network as possible for customer-focused organizations. Arnseth (2011b) has suggested three ways to determine the push-pull boundary. First, coordinate the amount of pushing or pulling to the firm's basic business model. If the firm is totally focused on customer responsiveness, the push-pull boundary will be located further upstream. Likewise, the more price sensitive customers are, the more the firm will seek greater lead times to reduce costs (that is, procurement by competitive shopping, developing less-expensive production systems), pushing the push-pull boundary downstream. Arnseth (2011b) also suggests that knowing inventory cost drivers (such as having cyclical, infrequent, or seasonal demand; low economies to scale; low purchasing power; and distance from the supplier) can all favor a push strategy. Alternatively, using a modular production process and outsourcing upsteam activities, a manufacturing organization could focus more on downstream customer demand requirements. All of these guide a demarcation of the push-pull boundary, where push strategy planning efforts end and the pull strategic planning efforts begin.

1.5 A Procedure for Supply Chain Strategy Development

There are always new supply chain executives being hired by existing firms, new firms creating supply chains, and executives launching a new strategic direction for supply chains that they manage. A strategy can be very limited to a specific domain in a supply chain (for example, acquiring new supply chain technology) or be very broad in nature impacting an entire supply chain (for example, a redesign of an entire supply chain network). Regardless of how much or how little a supply chain strategic plan might encompass, a procedure for guiding the development of a strategic plan is needed. In Figure 1.7, a proposed procedural plan leading to the development of supply chain strategies is suggested.

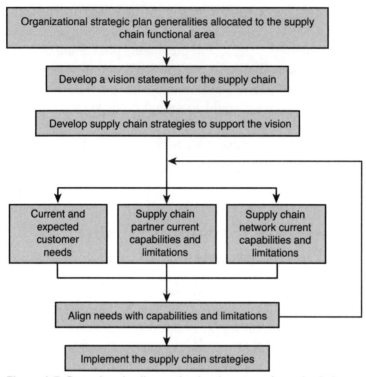

Figure 1.7 Procedure leading to the development of supply chain strategies

To begin, a supply chain executive officer or team of executives starts with broad, strategic organizational planning generalities and interprets them in terms of areas of responsibility within the supply chain management domain. To accomplish this and to aid in narrowing broad organizational objectives of the functional area, a supply chain executive could develop a vision statement to help others understand the general orientation toward a particular strategy development. A *vision statement* is used to define where a leader seeks to take the organization. A vision statement in supply chain management is a broad declaration defining the purpose of that functional area. It is a future-oriented statement reflecting the intentions of a supply chain executive in a role as a leader. A vision statement for a supply chain manager might be to seek an expansion in distribution management over the next couple of years to support an organizational strategic objective of market growth. The effort to generate a strategy involves translating the strategic organization goals down to the level of supply chain tactical planning. Once there, supply chain strategies to implement tactics could be developed. Figure 1.8 presents an example. To do this requires an understanding of current customer needs and the supply chain's capabilities and limitations for meeting those needs. Despite organizational strategy desires, a supply chain may not have the ability to achieve all proposed strategic objectives of a firm. Other factors such as organizational weaknesses or potential threats might dissuade a firm from considering all objectives. Most of these are actually eliminated during the organizational strategic planning process, but others are eliminated when the realities of supply chain limitations are revealed. In this case, revisions and alignments take place to either alter planning to meet customer needs or make revisions to enhance capabilities for meeting those needs (see alignment in Figure 1.7). Once the capabilities of the supply chain are in balance with current or expected customer needs, the supply chain managers can begin implementing supply chain strategies by developing detailed tactics that move the firm toward achieving objectives by modifying the supply chain network of partners.

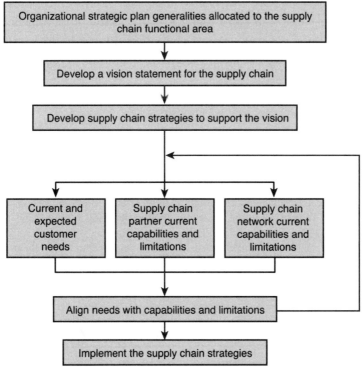

Figure 1.8 Example of procedure leading to the development of supply chain strategy and tactics

1.6 Starting Place for Strategy Development: Customer Value

Regardless of the outcome of any strategic planning process, the one certain and broad objective for any organization or supply chain is to seek greater value in everything. Therefore, value represents an appropriate venue for developing a supply chain strategy.

Value can be defined in terms of efficiency as the ratio of quality divided by price. Whether a supply chain partner is purchasing goods or services or selling them, the greater the ratio of quality to price, the greater is the value. Because the focus of most supply chains is to satisfy customer demand, there is a need to focus on *customer value* (that is, customer perception of what a firm offers in terms of products, services, and other intangibles). Based on perceptions, a customer typically employs various criteria to assess value. Primary dimensions of perceived value (see Table 1.6) can be used to develop supply chain strategies. It is not a coincidence that the dimensions of perceived customer value have some commonality to the CSFs found in the literature and based on experience. Just as it is important for a manager to build a speedy supply chain that returns profit to the organization quickly, speed is also valued by customers served by that speedy delivery system.

Table 1.6 Select Customer Value Dimensions

Value Dimension	Description	Supply Chain Roles
Relationships	The relationship between a firm and its customers that is acquired over time and builds toward trust. The stronger a positive relationship builds, the greater perceived value in the relationship.	Fulfilling downstream customer needs is a primary objective in supply chains. Building trusting relationship with customers and throughout the entire supply chain is essential to supply chain success.

Value Dimension	Description	Supply Chain Roles
Products	The product selection (for example, styles and colors) and its availability to customers. This includes a greater selection in quality, as well. The greater the product selection and availability, the greater the perceived value.	The supply chain makes available the quantity and quality of products where and when they are needed.
Prices	The price of the product relative to its perceived reputation as a quality or significant product to own. This considers cost advantages that help to lower prices and make the value increase. The greater the quality relative to price, the greater the perceived value.	Through skill with purchasing items from upstream suppliers and efficiency in logistics operations costs can be reduced and passed onto final customers with price reductions.
Innovation	Product innovation helps to define how advanced a product may be in the market and how long a product may last before becoming obsolete. The more innovative the product, the greater the perceived value.	Working with customers to learn their needs and suppliers who offer new ideas on product design and materials, supply chain managers can add innovation in delivery, packaging, and the product itself.
Product services	Additional services added on to the product to distinguish it from other competitors. The more additional services, the greater the perceived value.	Added services can include offering a variety of modes of distribution, enhanced timeliness of delivery, updating of product recalls, and post-purchase services.
Environmental impacts	Perception of product being environmentally friendly. The more environmentally friendly (that is, avoiding waste), the greater the perceived value.	Reducing environmental delivery costs of products, eliminating wasteful or environmental dangerous components and materials from products, and participating and supporting "green" production programs.

Source: Adapted from Fawcett et al. (2007), pp. 250–251; Simchi-Levi (2010), pp. 19–31.

Some firms formalize customer value in a proposition. A *value proposition* is a statement of what the firm considers is to be value to stakeholders (that is, partners or any members within a supply chain). A value proposition can also be viewed as a promise of what stakeholders will receive in terms of a product or service. It can be applied to entire organizations, divisions, departments, customers, products, and services. A procedure for developing a value proposition is presented in Table 1.7. Value propositions can also be expressed in terms of CSFs, like those listed in Table 1.6, but usually with more specificity. For example, Wal-Mart's "Everyday low pricing" is a customer value proposition that supports their organizational strategy of cost-efficiency. It is possible to have and utilize multiple value propositions to accommodate a wide variety of stakeholder perceptional needs.

Table 1.7 Procedure for Developing a Value Proposition

Ordered Steps in Procedure	Description	Example
1. Determine market.	Select the specific market (for example, customer related, organization related, employee related) that is being targeted for the value proposition.	Employees in the Supply Chain department
2. Determine products/services.	Determine which products or services are being offered to serve the specific market.	Health coverage
3. Determine what market values.	Based on market research or experience with the target market, assess what the market values in the product or service that is being offered.	Sense of well-being for employee and their families Confirms a caring organization
4. Determine customer benefits.	Assess the various benefits the target market derives from the existing products/services.	Reduced personal costs for heath care
5. Determine potential alternative products/services.	Explore alternative add-ons to the products/services that could be offered to enhance the benefits the target market derives.	Add dental coverage

Ordered Steps in Procedure	Description	Example
6. Substantiate resulting value proposition.	Confirm and document measurably the evidence to validate the value proposition from these steps.	Results of an employee survey on job satisfaction with heath care coverage

The value proposition can be used internally and externally to help direct a strategy focus regarding what the firm interprets to be of value to the customer. Internally, the analysis and results of the value proposition procedure can be used as a motivational device for employees to sell them on the concept of value and help focus efforts toward achieving product or service excellence. Externally, not everything that is collected in the value proposition procedure is shared. The resulting value proposition can be shared with external supply chain partners, customers, and suppliers. For these partners, the value proposition can used to promote areas of supply chain excellence that can be improved to reap benefits for the customer and, as an optimal outcome, build the loyalty.

1.7 What's Next?

As you look ahead in supply chain management strategic planning, trend information based on surveys can reveal where a supply chain organization will go. Monczka and Petersen (2011) undertook a comprehensive survey of supply strategy implementation to explore future opportunities. The strategies that appear to be "what's next" include those related to engagement of executives, vision-mission and strategic planning, commodity and supplier strategy processes, strategic cost management, procurement and supply organization structure/governance, human resource development, total cost of ownership planning, structuring and maintaining the supply base, measurement and evaluation of performance, and establishing supplier quality systems. These represent strategic areas viewed as important going forward toward 2015. Interestingly, when comparing these strategies in terms of recent implementation efforts, the gap between importance and actual implementation was significant. The results go on to suggest that Internet-based e-systems and available supply chain talent are viewed as critical enabling strategies. Growing in importance is environmental sustainability, though the survey commented that its development is not yet a major focus for many organizations. Each of these topics is discussed in the remaining chapters of this book.

2

Designing Supply Chains

Novelette

Terms

Collaborative planning, forecasting, and replenishment (CPFR)

Cross-functional

Electronic product code (EPC)

Enterprise resource planning (ERP)

Horizontal process network (HPN)

Materials requirement planning (MRP)

Matrix organizational structure design

Near field communications (NFC)

Radio frequency identification (RFID)

Silo problems

Supply Chain Council (SCC)

Supply chain network design

Supply chain operations reference (SCOR)

Unity of command

Universal product code (UPC)

Vendor-managed inventory (VMI)

Novelette

Having just attended a seminar at the annual *Institute of Supply Management* meeting, I was reminded of the importance of collaboration with supply chain partners. No sooner did I get back to my office than I found myself with inventory problems, chiefly due to a lack of collaboration with supply chain partners. What drives demand are customers, and market intelligence is what is used to know where our customers will lead. The marketing staff does a good job on general forecasting information, but the everyday demand in our stores for engine parts and other retail products we produced for retailers in our supply chain was lacking. Accurate forecasting is essential to maintain efficient operations and supply chains.

Jessica is the VP of the Tools, Hardware, and Construction Materials Division of our organization. Addressing me, she said, "Bill, marketing people do a great job of sharing the point-of-purchase information from our own retail stores. Unfortunately, the day-to-day stock outages we experience with many of the other external supply chain customers are not reported for many days. As you know, we have franchised stores and hundreds of other external customers that we don't always get much detail from in terms of their customer demand. In some geographic locations, our retail customers run out of stock and don't order any more until the end of the month. We serve tens of thousands of hardware and construction retail outlets that at any time can run out of our products and don't communicate that fact for days or even weeks due to their purchasing order policies and systems. We can't very well tell them how to order from us, so demand for our products goes unmet. We are losing business to our competitors when that happens. We need to do something and quick."

"Jessica, I have discussed this matter with the VP of Marketing and he suggested that the individual store variations in demand were probably due to in-store sales promotions and special pricing that store managers are allowed to run without approvals from their headquarters. This creates a short-term increase in sales of our products that we have not planned for," I replied.

"Bill, what has been happening in my Division is when their shortages are finally ordered, well after the event, the aggregated demand surge creates a bullwhip effect on my operation. That results in costly waste in my Division, and it is not something we can tolerate. We must come up with a better way to deal with this," said Jessica.

I have known Jessica for over ten years, and she is one of the best VPs we have. When she says move quickly, it's serious, not just for her Division, but for the other three that make up our organization. "Jessica, there is a better way, and it's through a more integrated approach of collaboration. We are going to design our demand management planning around a software system. There is a software system called *Collaborative Planning, Forecasting, and Replenishment* (CPFR) that can be used to fully integrate the actions of our retailing organization and those we partner with. Our computer system will be hooked up with our internal and external partners' computer systems. This integrated system will help us to share information, not just on customer demand on a near real-time basis but also information on when our partners are running product sales and beefing up demand in anticipation of a seasonal fluctuation or changes in customer preferences. This information allows us to undertake a closer collaboration with our partners to help them plan to have the products they need to keep their shelves filled, while at the same time helps us better understand what demand can be expected from those partners. Actually, we end up using cross-functional teams of our managers working with managers and owners to help identify where each can help the other in managing product demand," I explained.

"Bill, this sounds great, but getting buy-in from all of our retail partners, particularly the external ones, for linking up with our system and keeping them in the system may be a hard sell. What strategy will we use with those partners to sell this idea?" asked Jessica.

"Jessica, keeping their shelves filled means more money for them and more for us. This helps them give their customers what they want, when they want it. They will be motivated to participate by self-interest, and I think they and we will see that working in cross-functional ways will create a closer partnering relationship with our supply chain partners. I think the relationship will become so tight that our external customers will not think of doing business with anyone else," I answered.

"Bill, to implement this may I suggest bringing in our forecasting team, inventory team, production manager, and purchasing manager to represent our Division?" Jessica asked.

"Jessica, that is a great group, and they have to be brought together to work in unison, which is your job. It is important that each member is comfortable with the CPFR system and understand its inputs, outputs, benefits, and drawbacks before we can offer a program of integration to our supply chain partners," I said.

2.1 Prerequisite Material

As stated in the preceding chapter and in the remaining chapters in Part I of this book, this section is chiefly to acquaint less-experienced students of supply chain management with basic and elemental content and terminology. Experienced supply chain executives and managers might be tempted to skip this section in chapters where it is included, but they might instead want to use it as a review of basic concepts and terminology.

There are many different ways to design the organizational structure of a business. In a generic sense, all business organizations have to design the structure of functional areas or groupings (for example, marketing, operations). This leads to the designing of supply chain departments or divisions (for example, logistics, procurement), which in turn can lead to designing of the processes, which each performs (for example, production processes, delivery processes).

Organizational structures can be organized in many different ways. Typically, organizational structures center around functional areas, products, or regions (see Figure 2.1). The arrows in the figure define the direction of authority. The functional and geographical region designs are classically hierarchical, but can create the *silo problems* (that is, discourages communication between functional areas or regions). However, they provide better management control and make authority systems more delineated over a product design, where each product would have its own functional area (for example, finance) that may also have to report to a centralized department.

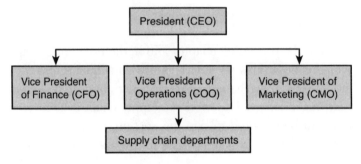

(a) Example of organizational structure design based on functional areas

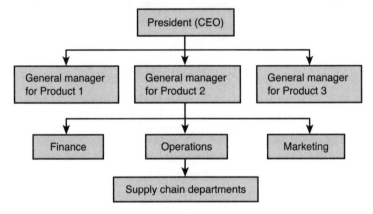

(b) Example of organizational structure design based on products

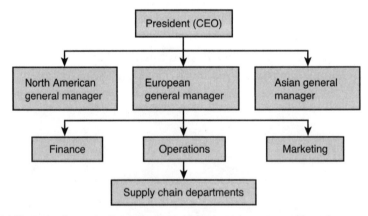

(c) Example of organizational structure design based on geographic regions

Figure 2.1 Organizational design structures

Similar to product design, organizations can also structure the design of business systems on the basis of individual projects. Figure

2.2 shows two typical project design structures. Project design structures can also be used within departments of an organization that might have a completely different organizational structure. In Figure 2.2(a), project managers have no activities or personnel reporting directly to them. Project managers, along with other department heads, act in a staff capacity to the general manager. In Figure 2.2(b), project managers have staff and functional line personnel reporting directly to them. Under this design, the project manager has full authority over the entire project, which permits faster response times for decision making. Unfortunately, this latter structure can lead to the silo effect, since separate functional areas are created under each project.

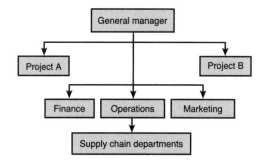

(a) Example of organizational structure design based on projects

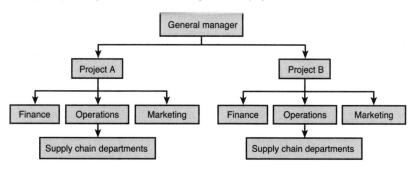

(b) Example of organizational structure design based functionally separated projects

Figure 2.2 Project-based organizational design structures

A *matrix organizational structure design* is a combination of a functional and project structure (see Figure 2.3). Although sometimes considered a project structure, it combines some of the best features of both. In Figure 2.3, the solid lines show lines of authority, which extend from the functional departments to each project group function. Once assigned to a group for a specific project, those functional staffers also report and work for the project managers (denoted as dashed lines in the figure). Matrix designs directly violate principles of *unity of command* (that is, reporting to only one supervisor) and can generate conflict in supervisory relationships, but research has shown for decades that a matrix design has higher levels of performance in dealing with complex and creative work environments (Ford and Randolph, 1992). They are able to achieve these positive outcomes because they encourage a greater degree of interaction and collaboration between functional areas than other organizational designs. From those interactions come new ideas, innovations, and improved efficiencies in operations.

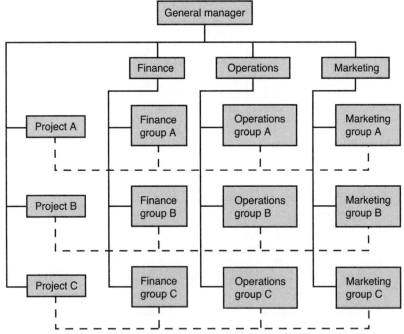

Figure 2.3 Matrix organizational design structures

Design considerations should also be viewed in the context of their application to the planning stages of the organization. At a strategic level, the hierarchy of the entire organization can be planned. Executives decide issues such as whether a product or geographic region design best serves the organization. At the tactical level, functional areas like operations can be planned. Here, the decision may be how departments (for example, logistics, production) should be structured to achieve better integration. Within the departments at the operational level of planning, design considerations might include project planning (for example, installing a software system for order taking) or undertaking supply chain initiative programs (for example, designing processes for manufacturing or distribution activities).

While designing a supply chain is generally considered to be a strategic planning process because it creates the environment under which all other forms of planning a supply chain are subordinated (Ganeshan et al., 1998, p. 849), it can be employed at any level of planning throughout the organization. The diversity of application necessitates managers to become aware of a variety of differing approaches to supply chain design to better fit the design needs with the design capabilities of the organization.

2.2 Design Consideration in a Firm's Supply Chain Organizational Structure

Every decision, plan, and person who works within a supply chain is constrained, limited, and influenced by the design of the firm's supply chain organizational structure. The design of the organizational and the supply chain organizational structures become pivotal components for creating and moving the strategic organization and supply chain objectives toward reality.

Different organizational designs can be used, but research and experience has shown successful supply chain organizations ideally seek and adopt structures that help them better serve customers. Therefore, supply chains are naturally inclined to seek out designs that aid interaction with customers and collaboration between partners to enhance operations, resulting in better customer service and profits for all stakeholders.

For organizations just beginning or facing the introduction stage of the product life cycle, upper management or chief operating officers (COOs) might suggest a matrix organizational structure. Matrix organizational designs are *cross-functional* (that is, allowing members of differing functional areas to work together as group or team on a project or program) and help end silo problems, thus encouraging interaction between functional areas. Figure 2.4 shows a matrix design that includes an organization's various product supply chains (perhaps broken down into separate supply chains by the customer). The authority (represented by the solid lines in the figure) is still retained by the functional areas and the general manager or supply chain executive. The dashed lines in Figure 2.4 represent an additional line of authority to individual supply chain managers, who are responsible for those customer's supply chains.

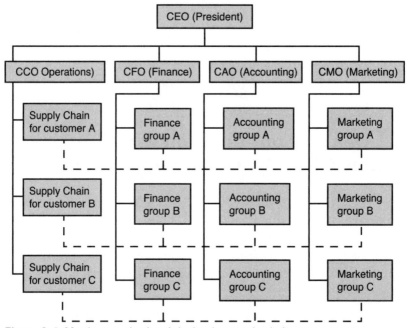

Figure 2.4 Matrix organizational design by supply chain customer type

Although matrix organizational designs have been used at the organizational level to restructure the entire business organization, they are also useful at other organizational levels, including supply chain departments. A supply chain executive (for example, vice president of operations) cannot always impact or alter organizational design structures, but may be able to structure the departmental supply chain organization to better accomplish its objectives. In Figure 2.5, a matrix design for a supply chain department is presented. Not all supply chains can be divided into customer groups or clusters. Rather than customer divisions depicted in the horizontal rows in Figure 2.5, other criteria can be used. Products can be used or geographic divisions (for example, North American markets, Asian markets) can be used to divide supply chain tasks into groups requiring differing internal supply chain resources (for example, logistics support). Matrix organizational designs were some of the first to encourage cross-functional behavior.

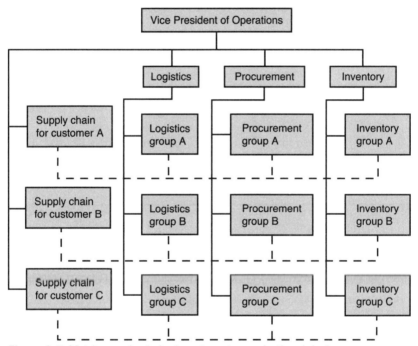

Figure 2.5 Matrix supply chain department organizational design

New supply-chain-related organization designs are being developed to better serve the cross-functional needs required in current supply chains. One example of an innovative organizational structure is referred to as a network design. A *supply chain network design* focuses on facility decisions related to establishing a supply chain network. Such decisions include the role of the facility (that is, what role and processes the facility will play in the supply chain network), where the manufacturing or service facility should be located, what capacity is needed to produce or store inventory, what markets the facility should serve, and the supply sources for each facility. Basically, a supply chain network design seeks to set up the network used within the supply chain system. The types of facilities to include in the network design and the roles they play in the supply chain network are often tied to strategic objectives (see Table 2.1).

Table 2.1 Types of Facilities Found in Supply Chain Network Designs

Type of Facility	Strategic Objective
Contributor	To serve markets near where it is located, but also assumes responsibility for production effort, process improvements, and product development
Lead	To create new products, processes, and technologies to serve the entire network
Offshore	To produce low-cost products for markets outside of the country where it is located
Outpost	To gain new knowledge or skills that exist within a particular region
Nearshore	To produce products in neighboring countries to lower transportation costs and overcome importing issues
Network	To anchor a logistics system in particular locations to achieve an efficient network of facilities
Server	To serve markets near where it is located and reduce costs by overcoming distribution costs (for example, tariffs)
Source	To produce low-cost goods that are the primary or only source for a limited number of products that serve the entire supply chain

Source: Adapted from Table 1.2 in Schniederjans (1998), p. 6.; from Table 1.2 in Schniederjans et al. (2005), p. 8.

Network designs can be used for many different organizational structure applications. For example, Procter & Gamble (P&G) designed an organizational planning structure, *horizontal process network* (HPN), that spans across the entire organization (Farasyn et al., 2011). The HPNs help define, manage, and execute work processes across all of P&G's business operating units. Each of the 11 planning processes in Figure 2.6 are spread over the 3 P&G business units, business services, and market organizations. To implement this design, P&G uses a team approach. HPN planning teams involve members of the business units, information technology managers, and other business and technical experts, including supply chain staff.

The teams work across business units dealing with issues such as the supply network planning. For example, sharing information about constraints, a team member working in another business unit might be able to identify surplus financial resources that would allow a new network facility to be acquired. In addition, sharing information helps educate members cross-functionally, engendering a holistic view of the entire organization. This design maximizes collaboration within the organization.

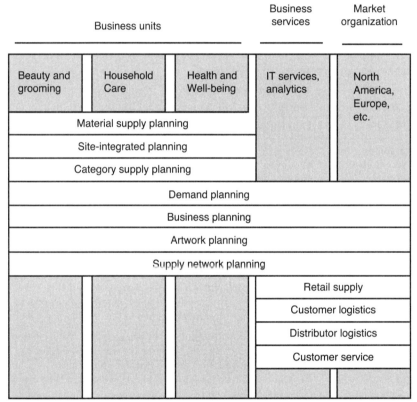

Figure 2.6 Procter & Gamble supply chain horizontal process network organizational design

Source: Adapted from Figure 1 in Farasyn et al., (2011), p. 68.

2.3 Approaches to Supply Chain Design

2.3.1 A Conceptual Procedure for Supply Chain Design

A step-wise conceptual procedure for designing supply chains is presented in Table 2.2. The idea behind this design procedure is to bring together critical elements of any supply chain (that is, customer, product, network, and processes) into collaborative efforts to create a supply that meets customer needs and organizational objectives. Clearly, the value proposition (discussed in Chapter 1, "Developing Supply Chain Strategies") is the critical success factor that drives designing efforts in this procedure.

Table 2.2 A Procedure for Designing a Supply Chain

Steps	Description
1. Identify the supply chain's end customer.	It is logical to begin at the end of the supply chain with customer groups or clusters instead of trying to design a supply chain to serve an infinite number of needs. Identifying specific customers for a unique supply chain facilitates the design effort and allows an organization to keep the focus on serving the specific customers. The focus is on the customer in this step.
2. Determine the supply chain's value proposition.	The value proposition (from Chapter 1) should be a function of what customers perceive as value in the product or service. Knowing precisely the features or characteristics that customers value permits design efforts to be focused on the products/ services. The focus is on the product in this step.
3. Determine the required relational needs for supply chain participants.	Identify the key participants in the supply chain. Determine what each needs to provide to serve the value proposition. Determine the best linkages in a possible supply chain network and what technologies are needed to establish the supply chain. The focus is on the linkages of supply chain participants and networks in this step.
4. Determine the critical success factors in delivering on the value proposition.	For the supply chain, determine the potential competencies required for the supply chain to be successful. Determine the new processes, timing requirements, and variability issues needed in the supply chain to achieve the value proposition objectives. In this step, process strategy (such as push, pull, and push-pull designs; see Chapter 1) is considered in the planning. The focus is on supply chain processes in this step.

Steps	Description
5. Draft an ideal supply chain design to support value proposition.	Based on the information about the customer, product, network, and processes, create a preliminary design for a supply chain that can achieve the value propositions. This involves defining the roles of each supply chain participant, their authority over their respective operations, and a declarative statement on any desired value-added roles that should take place over time. The focus in this step is to bring the information together from the other steps into a draft design of a complete supply chain.
6. Revise draft of supply chain design to develop final version of supply chain.	Continuous improvement of the draft design is needed to further optimize the final supply chain design. The focus in this step is on collaboration with supply chain participants to finalize a supply chain design that seeks to achieve value propositions that best serve the customers.

2.3.2 Life Cycle Approach to Supply Chain Design

Chapter 1 mentioned product life cycles as a means of identifying areas for strategic planning. Identifying a position on a life cycle helps managers detail design consideration strategies, tactics, and operational plans at every level of planning that they face. Figure 2.7 illustrates design-related strategies that can be considered using a life cycle approach.

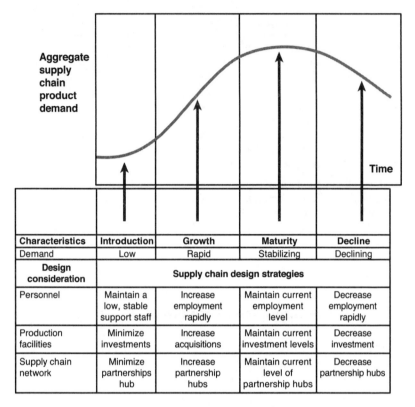

Characteristics	Introduction	Growth	Maturity	Decline
Demand	Low	Rapid	Stabilizing	Declining
Design consideration	**Supply chain design strategies**			
Personnel	Maintain a low, stable support staff	Increase employment rapidly	Maintain current employment level	Decrease employment rapidly
Production facilities	Minimize investments	Increase acquisitions	Maintain current investment levels	Decrease investment
Supply chain network	Minimize partnerships hub	Increase partnership hubs	Maintain current level of partnership hubs	Decrease partnership hubs

Figure 2.7 Design considerations and strategies during life cycle stages

2.3.3 Supply Chain Operations Reference Model

The *Supply Chain Operations Reference* (SCOR) is process focused and more ideally used for existing supply chains, although steps in this model can be adapted to create a new supply chain (http://supply-chain.org/companies/scor-helps-companies). It was developed by the *Supply Chain Council* (SCC) (http://supply-chain.org/scor), a global organization that seeks to apply advanced systems and practices in industry. SCOR is recognized chiefly as a diagnostic tool to find opportunities for improvement in existing supply chains, but in doing so, becomes an approach useful in designing and redesigning supply chains. The scope of the SCOR model includes customer interactions (that is, order entry to paid invoice) and all product transactions (that is, supplier's supplier to customer's customer). It uses processes, metrics, best practices, and technology to identify supply chain problems and enhance supply performance. It also helps in design issues related to customer service, cost control, planning and risk management, supplier and partner relationship management, and talent development. Table 2.3 relates design features and objectives to the types of diagnostic information that this model can provide.

Table 2.3 Examples of SCOR Model Diagnostics Information for Redesigning (or Designing) Supply Chains

Design Feature	Supply Chain Design Objective	Example of Design Diagnostic Information
Cost	Reducing supply chain total costs	Value-added productivity
Customer satisfaction	Enhancing product quality	Product returns
Customer satisfaction	Enhancing customer order fulfillment	Delivery commitment dates
Inventory	Avoiding waste in inventory days of supply	Inventory obsolescence
Timing	Enhancing order fulfillment lead time	Supply chain response and source cycle times

The SCOR model has evolved over the years, supporting design improvements related the SCC's view of a supply chain as a plan-make-source-deliver-return process. Table 2.4 provides summarizes one way to implement the model.

Table 2.4 Using the SCOR Model to Redesign (or Design) Supply Chains

Steps	Description
1. Analyze the competition.	Determine what is necessary to succeed in the competitive environment where the supply chain is to exist. This could apply to both a new supply chain that is being created or an existing one. An important element in the modeling process involves ensuring any critical success design factors in this step are measurable and that their application can be monitored for opportunities of continual improvement.

Steps	Description
2. Configure the supply chain.	Compare a draft of a new supply chain with an ideal configuration or compare an existing supply chain with an ideal configuration based on competitive needs. These configurations would include the supply chain networks, geographic locations, partners, and so forth. SCOR metrics, where they can estimated, can be used as a basis for these comparisons.
3. Align the supply chain.	Seeking to move the supply chains from a draft or existing design to the ideal design, align desired performance levels, practices, and systems (including information systems, distribution, and work flows).
4. Implement the supply chain.	Seek to implement the newly aligned design of the supply chain processes and systems with partners, people, processes, technology, and the organization.

2.3.4 Network Design

Chopra and Meindl (2001, pp. 314–316) suggested a supply chain network design for creating global supply chains. Today, most supply chains are global, and the framework presented by Chopra and Meindl (2001) considers many of the issues faced in any network design plan (see Figure 2.8).

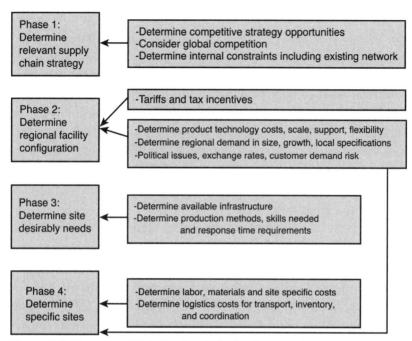

Figure 2.8 Chopra and Meindl network design framework

Source: Adapted from Figure 11.7 in Chopra and Meindl (2001), p. 314.

In Phase 1, the strategic positioning of the organization and the supply chain are considered. The organization's competitive strategy related to the supply chain (that is, where the firm wants to go in the future determined from the external organization analysis from Chapter 1) is added to the constraint realities (determined from the internal organization analysis from Chapter 1). Any global competitive risk factors are included to define the overall strategy for the network design.

In Phase 2, a preliminary regional facility forecast is estimated for customer demand in each country where the markets are important to the network design. Next, there is a need to determine, given network opportunities in the regional area, whether the impact of tariffs and taxes, political risks, potential exchange rate risks, and customer demand, needs, and risks is worthwhile. This is combined with a production technologies analysis that considers costs, scope of operation needs, and necessary support to keep the network functioning to meet strategic or tactical goals.

In Phase 3, the design effort focuses on selecting desirable facility sites within each region where facilities are to be located. Considerations for the existing regional infrastructure have to be considered in light of network needs. To build a viable supply chain network, infrastructure, including suppliers, warehousing facilities, transportation services, communication systems, and utilities, has to be in place. Also, for some networks the infrastructure requirements might include availability of a skilled workforce and the willingness of communities to work with supply chain managers.

Finally, in Phase 4, the specific locations for placement of network facilities are determined. This phase also involves consideration of the capacity allocations for each facility and network integration flexibility.

Although it is beyond the scope of this book to discuss the quantitative procedures used in network design, many useful methodologies can be employed to enhance the design location tasks (Chopra and Meindl, 2001, pp. 316–327). Some techniques, such as gravity location models, can be used to minimize distance between facilities and network optimization models (for example, methods such as minimum distance spanning tree, shortest route method) can be used to establish routing (Schniederjans, 1998, pp. 31–32). General modeling methods, such as mathematical programming models (for example, linear programming, the transportation method), can be used to allocate production capacity to each facility, locate demand requirements per facility, and set up manufacturing and warehouse facilities simultaneously (Schniederjans, 1999, pp. 103–117). Still, other methodologies, such as scaling, scoring, and ranking methods (for example, analytic hierarchy process) can consider qualitative information such as *critical success factors* (CSFs) and subjective facility location factors (for example, skill level of labor, quality of transportation system) (Schniederjans, 1999, pp. 45–101). For an extensive treatment of quantitative models useful in supply chain management design planning (and other supply chain planning applications), see Ganeshan et al. (1998).

2.4 Other Topics in Supply Chain Design

Before deciding on a supply chain design, many factors should be considered. Some will impact the structural design selection or creation, and others can be a constraint or a competitive advantage to be exploited as a benefit of the supply chain design (see Figure 2.9). These factors and many more are discussed throughout the rest of this book and allude to the diverse nature of supply chain design planning.

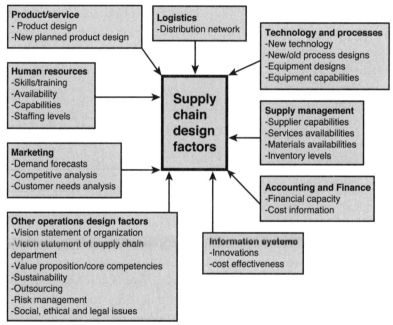

Figure 2.9 Select supply chain design factors

2.4.1 Change Management as a Design Flexibility Strategy

Supply chain departments are based on continuous change and adaptation to customer demand requirements. There is a need to establish a mindset that encourages change in organizations to keep them in a state of readiness for innovation. Many firms use *program* or *project management* as a means to introduce and manage organizational or operations change. (See Chapter 9, "Building an Agile and

Flexible Supply Chain," for more about program and project management.) For example, Van Arnum (2011) reported the use of project management principles in a pharmaceutical firm to achieve a cross-functional supplier integration of its outsource supplier network. Van Arnum also makes the point that project management should be viewed as an ongoing task for supply chain organizations. Firms not only need to use change management methods to undertake change through projects or program initiatives but should also use them frequently enough so that it becomes a philosophy of doing business and eventually becomes part of the organization culture. Changing the design of a supply chain should not be viewed as a threat, but as an opportunity to excel. The more project or program management is used in an organization to implement change, the more likely the firm's staff will find new and efficient ways to become flexible in making design changes. How much change is needed depends on the volatility in the supply chain and in partner industries.

2.4.2 Information System Design

The information systems technology hardware purchased for a particular organization design is largely determined by the software that runs the system at various levels within the organization. At the organizational level of design, information systems that run multiple functional areas (for example, *enterprise resource planning* [ERP]) involve the alignment of the organization's functional needs to the technology capabilities. Within a functional area like operations, other software (for example, *materials requirements planning* [MRP], focused on production materials planning) is integrated and aligned with the ERP system to serve objectives. Further down in the organization, departments (such as the supply chain department) have their own software applications (for example, *vendor-managed inventory* [VMI]) that monitor how suppliers are able to supply customer needs.

Integrating and aligning software is an important design requirement. Also, supply chain executives can use implementation as a design strategy to move their organizations toward becoming more collaborative. Using linkages between personnel in different functional areas, as well as different departments within those functions, to implement a software application, can help break down the organization silos and improve communication relationships.

Collaborative software applications can also help bring about collaborative efforts with external supply chain partners. CPFR is a software that requires the integrative work of suppliers with a manufacturing firm. This software helps trading partners work together to reduce forecasting errors and increase product availability by improving synchronization within a supply chain for inventory replenishment. In addition to building trust with supplier partners, this software is credited with reducing inventory and improving in-stock product availability (Fawcett et al., 2007, pp. 482–483).

2.4.3 New Technology: RFID

The use of new technologies can have a profound impact on supply chain design planning. For example, *radio frequency identification* (RFID) is being used in increasingly more applications, including in most supply chains (Beth et al., 2011, pp. 190–192). RFID is an umbrella term that refers to a family of various but related technologies, including *near field communications* (NFC) (that is, short-range technology permitting simple transactions, data exchange, and connections with smartphones and e-tablets) and *electronic product code* (EPC) used by retailers to retrieve product identification information that can be stored on the RFID tag. Unlike the revolutionary *universal product code* (UPC) number, RFID tags are unique in that they carry substantial reference information about pricing, manufacture dates, shipping destination, and so on. For supply chain management, this detailed information helps enhance traceability for product recall, inventory control, and product anticounterfeiting. Unlike the UPC number, which requires access to a mainframe to obtain additional information about a product, RFID tags contain information at the location where it is needed. By taking advantage of the RFID in the design of supply chain processes, planners allow greater decision making autonomy at the levels where the decisions are to be made, while impacting design considerations for information systems.

Patton (2011) suggests that tagging products well upstream in the supply chain will leverage advantages for all supply chain partners.

Handheld scanners used in combination with the RFID tags can allow for a quick check on large inventories without an extensive auditing process. The enhanced visibility provided by RFID can bring about substantial operations impact in terms of a reduction in suppliers running out of stock, elimination of shrinkage problems, and a reduction in shipping errors. At the same time, RFID can improve replenishment, improve order picking and packing accuracy, and allow for quick data entry into an organization's information system (thus improving response time in sharing this information internally and externally).

2.4.4 Design Innovation

Creating a flexible environment for change can invite and stimulate supply chain innovation. An important design consideration to enhance innovation with supply chain partners is to encourage the building of trust. As trust with supply partners increases, each is more willing to take risks in sharing innovative ideas without fear that information will be used against them by supply competitors or manufacturers. Although methods exist to assess the level of trust in an organization (Fawcett et al., 2007, pp. 359–361), what is important are the design elements that will lead to a culture encouraging trust to grow. Trust design elements that should be encouraged include a willingness to share information that could lead to innovation developments, building personal relationships with suppliers and making them friends rather than transactional business associates, and an assurance program that makes performance of partners transparent to all participants in the supply chain network. This last element helps to communicate the consequences of success and failure. In doing so, this becomes a motivational tool to encourage desired results and discourage poor performance.

How to initiate innovative idea development among supply chain partners can depend on how partners are recognized for their contributions to innovation. Yuva (2011) reported on a possible recognition system. Basically, suppliers can be segmented into groups based on their contributions of innovative ideas. Several segments (for example, gold, silver, bronze) could be established based on the number or quality of innovative ideas suppliers make available to the supply chain network. These segments and their value to the supply chain could be based on cost, availability, incoming quality, price, and delivery. Rewards to suppliers could include more and larger contracts.

2.5 What's Next?

According to the Aberdeen Group ("Globalization and...," 2011), there is a considerable trend toward redesigning sourcing geographies across multitier supply chain locations for discrete manufacturers. Future design efforts for all types of manufacturers and their supply chains are focused on the following:

- Improving internal cross-departmental systems, processes, collaboration, and integration
- Increased business-to-business collaboration
- Increased visibility into supplier processes and systems to maximize resource utilization
- Consolidating and redesigning and improving flow of sourcing geographically and through multitier network points

Fueling the value of design innovation, the survey revealed that investments in design and redesign ranked second in terms of providing a *return on investment* (ROI). Based on the survey results, the Aberdeen Group recommends supply chain design changes that streamline and optimize process steps with internal and external customers, embraces new collaborative visibility solutions and technologies, and enhances training and equipment to ensure personnel know how to use the new technologies and equipment.

3

Staffing Supply Chains

Terms

360-degree input

American Production and Inventory Control Society (APICS)

Career-path mapping

Career roadmap

Compensation

Council of Supply Chain Management Professionals (CSCMP)

Cross-functional succession

Ethnocentric

Executive search firm

Exit interview

Gap analysis

Geocentric

Global oriented

Home country national

Host country national

Institute of Supply Management (ISM)

Intercultural training

Job descriptive index (JDI)

Job satisfaction

Polycentric

Regiocentric

Sabbatical program

Third-party recruiter

Third-country national

Vice president of operations (COO)

Novelette

Organization growth is a common strategic goal for most organizations. Our Large Engine Division needed to grow, and our Board of Directors decided that an acquisition strategy should be undertaken to achieve this strategic goal. After an industry analysis was undertaken, a high-quality competitor was targeted for acquisition and subsequently acquired. Once acquired, the job of merging that new company into the current Large Engine Division was handed off to the organization's VPs, myself included. The size of the acquired firm's operations were as extensive as the entire Large Engine Division.

Merging operations of the new firm and the existing Large Engine Division operations was no small task. It created a very large division with the expected accompanying problems. As it usually turns out, the people who might be successful in a smaller organization do not always excel in larger organizations. The breadth of knowledge needed to run a larger operation, the skill sets required to handle the increased volume of business, and the psychological abilities to handle the stress in a higher-pressure operation are all critical success factors for personnel in merging two smaller organizations into one larger operation.

Pedro, the new VP of Operations for our Large Engine Division, came to see me unannounced shortly after the merger. "Bill, I have problem. Some of my long-time managers and some of the new managers we inherited in the merger are having problems running their respective areas of responsibility. I am finding myself running around putting out their fires, when they should be able to handle these problems themselves," explained Pedro.

"Pedro, sometimes in mergers, the size of a manager's responsibilities grows greater than his or her capabilities to handle the job. Being this is your first merger/acquisition experience, your staffing role will include making decisions on who stays in his or her current position, who is repositioned to a new position, and who we let go," I said.

"Bill, letting managers go, some of whom I have worked with for years, is not a very enjoyable experience," said Pedro.

"Pedro, staffing your organization is perhaps the most important critical success factor you face in your job. I think you should look at the job as helping people find a better vocation, one that they may enjoy more, rather than looking at it as terminating or changing their jobs. Many people just need a little push to help them realize that they can do better in a different job, and sometimes that is with another firm or internally in another area of our organization. We can help employees make transitions by having our human resource people help them relocate to a different job within or outside of our organization. For those currently leaving our company on their own volition, we should have exit interviews to learn what we can from them about improving what we do and how they view the way they have been treated. Some of what they say will matter, and some will not, but you may learn what they perceived was wrong and fix it," I pointed out.

"Thanks, Bill, that helps me, but what about those who want to stay in their current positions but are not quite handling their jobs?" Pedro asked.

"Pedro, let's deal with this by having the managers and other important personnel in your Division be tested by the psychology team from corporate headquarters to determine if they have the skill sets now needed to handle their enlarged responsibilities and can psychologically handle things. We can do a gap analysis to see differences between the desired skill sets and where they are lacking to learn what they need to bring them up to speed. Where there are gaps, you will have to ask them whether they are willing to undergo extra training and maybe if they are willing to go for *American Production and Inventory Control Society* (APICS) certification. Some will want to learn, and others will not, making your job of moving them easier. Given the connectivity of the supply chain to all the functional areas in your Division, learning about the supply chain is a good source of learning about everything we do. For those who are willing to learn more about our organization, consider asking them to switch positions with others in the supply chain area for a period of time. That exposure will help cross-train them, building in some flexibility, as well as a better understanding of your entire divisional needs," I commented.

"Bill, this is a major undertaking you are suggesting. I cannot do it overnight," Pedro explained.

"For sure, it may take you a year or more to fully integrate the new people on a career path and identify those who are not going to be able to work successfully in your new operation. Regardless of who stays and who leaves, it is important to treat everyone with respect. Someone we let go of today may come back to us in the future with skills and knowledge we will need," I surmised.

"What level of retraining for the staffers who stay with the firm should we undertake?" asked Pedro.

"One of the lessons I have learned is that by teaching staffers our way of doing procedures and processes, we standardize the employee's performance in much the same way we standardize component parts in our products. This allows us to transfer people within and between divisions with little retraining. You may want to consider borrowing some of the black belts and other staff from other divisions to help you orient and train your people. Time spent on this effort now will, through improved efficiency, pay back many times over in a relatively short period of time," I said.

"Bill, speaking of valued, enriched employees, we have a number of really key staffers who are so outstanding in their respective areas that we would like to promote them in an effort to keep them. Unfortunately, there are just not enough positions to permit the promotion, and in some cases these key people are just too valuable to the operation where they are to move them up in the organization. How do I keep these people happy in an effort to keep them where they are, even though they have earned by merit and deed a promotion to the next level, and they are capable of assuming that kind of position?" Pedro inquired.

"This is a difficult problem to deal with because you are actually holding people back. They may find advancement opportunities with competitors. There are two things that you can do: You can enlarge their responsibilities in that job situation, offering some psychological advancement that permits the employee growth in learning, and you can compensate them. It is also important that you are candid with these people and let them know how the organization values them. Tell your Department Heads to work closely with these key people and give them good coaching as a way of grooming them for future advancement. If people know they are valued and appreciated, it will go a long way to motivating them to stay with you. We want our organization to be a learning organization that grows people to have the skill sets to assume greater responsibilities when additional positions open up. We also want to let those, who for a period of time are held back know, that they have a future with the company that will include advancement as they continue to learn a broader base of skills and abilities to handle these jobs," I explained.

3.1 Prerequisite Material

This section is chiefly to acquaint less-experienced students of supply chain management with basic and elemental content and terminology. Experienced supply chain executives and managers might be tempted to skip this section in chapters where it is included, but they might instead want to use it as a review of basic concepts and terminology.

Jobs in supply chain management entail a wide spectrum of tasks and assignments. Staffing supply chain jobs requires finding talented people who will bring to the positions the right competencies and skills to overcome diverse challenges the organizations face in the global economy. Some of these competencies are listed in Table 3.1. There are, of course, many more, but these illustrate how staffing supply chain managers seek special individuals who are competent in many dimensions of social behavior.

Table 3.1 Staffing Competencies

Type of Competency	Description
Flexibility	Be able to work with differing people at any time and in any place in the world. Be open to new ideas, methodologies, and approaches.
Integrity	Be able to engender trust through honesty and high ethical values and conduct.

Type of Competency	Description
Resilience	Be self-reliant, creative, and enjoy taking on challenging issues.
Problem solver	Be able to conceptualize and solve multivariable, complex problems. Be able to handle ambiguity and uncertain and risk situations and enjoy problem solving.
Culturally sensitive	Be able to respect and be sensitive to differing value systems when working in differing cultures.

In any organization with a supply chain, basic jobs must be performed. Although titles may vary considerably from organization to organization, basic titles, responsibilities, and requirements are fairly standard for all organizations. To help conceptualize these positions, Table 3.2 describes a few of these positions.

Table 3.2 Types of Staffing Positions, Responsibilities and Requirements

Job Title	Responsibilities	Requirements
Vice President of Operations (COO)	Develop broad strategic goals in operations, providing the foundation for the supply chain department goals	Extensive experience in a variety of differing organizations
	Develop strategic and tactical objectives to implement the organizational goals	Extensive education of operations management
	Lead development of operations strategies	Extensive interpersonal skills
	Build relationships and direct integration with other functional areas	Extensive knowledge of processes, methodologies, and industry competitive behavior
	Supervise the supply chain directors and staff	
	Provide informational reports on organizational objective achievement status to president (CEO)	

Job Title	Responsibilities	Requirements
Director (supply chain)	Translate supply chain strategic goals into strategies for the departments in supply chain (for example, logistics, inventory, procurement) Build internal partnerships within departments and with other pier functional directors horizontally within the organization as needed Develop tactical objectives to implement the supply chain goals Supervise the supply chain managers and staff Provide informational reports on goal achievement status to COO	Extensive experience in specific department (for example, logistics, inventory, procurement) Extensive education in specific department subject area Extensive interpersonal skills Extensive knowledge in specific department processes, methodologies, and technology
Manager (supply chain)	Undertake projects to implement supply chain strategies and objectives within individual supply chain departments Supervise the subordinate supervisors and staff Develop tactical and operational objectives to implement department supply chain goals Provide informational reports on goal achievement status to directors	Some experience in a specific department (for example, logistics, inventory, procurement), activities and tasks Some education in a specific department activities and tasks Some interpersonal skills Some knowledge in choosing, developing, and implementing specific department processes, methodologies, and technology
Supervisor (supply chain)	Plan with managers tactics and operational plans to implement department goals and objectives Supervise subordinate personnel and staff Provide informational reports on goal achievement status to managers	Some experience and education in supervising personnel in specific department activities and tasks Some interpersonal skills Some knowledge in choosing, developing, and implementing specific department processes, methodologies, and technology

Some of the best sources for recruiting, staffing and education are provided by professional supply chain organizations. Three major professional organizations that provide education and employment support in the area of supply chain management are the *Institute of Supply Management* (ISM) (www.ism.ws/), *American Production and Inventory Control Society* (APICS) (www.apics.org/default.htm), and the *Council of Supply Chain Management Professionals* (CSCMP) (http://cscmp.org/). Collectively, they represent tens of thousands of supply chain professionals and educators offering certifications in supply chain management, including the content and requirements for staffing activities needed.

3.2 Staffing Supply Chains

3.2.1 Recruiting Strategies

Entry-level positions today should require a college degree in supply chain management. Recruiting these personnel involves establishing a college and university campus interviewing program. For organizations interested in recruiting entry-level employees, this might involve traveling to universities and working with student job placement departments or giving workshops on career opportunities where allowed by the campus. Developing a general *career roadmap* brochure explaining to the student what a career in supply chain management is about, what positions it can lead to, and how they can benefit is one useful tactic of the staffing strategy.

A more aggressive strategy is to build partnerships with specific universities where the supply chain organization can offer potential candidate students internships before they graduate. These internships can be either paid or not paid, and will offer the student an opportunity to gain experience in a real supply chain organization. They will also allow the firm to evaluate the student's potential for a future job.

Entry-level talent can also be located and recruited online with the variety of social networks such as Facebook or Twitter that allow for personal information to be made public. These are actually valuable sources of information. Much of what is available through these social networks is information that could not be requested under governmental laws restricting privacy.

For midlevel managers, recruiting can be efficiently performed with the help of major supply chain professional organizations. Major supply chain professional organizations, such as the ISM, CSCMP, and APICS, provide forums for job placement. They are general markets that act as conduits of candidate information and availability. All three organizations are actively involved in job placement, helping both the employee and employer to connect.

The midlevel and upper-level positions require more experience, which is a key factor in recruiting these employees. For supply chain executives within a firm, establishing a network of peer professionals that share information about employees can be a valuable and inexpensive way to identify candidates. Personal social networking can help find experienced personnel for midlevel and upper-level senior positions in supply chains. It goes without saying that job opportunities are still a function of "who you know" in an industry. A *critical success factor* (CSF) is to carefully review references (for example, who they are, what they say or not about criteria important to hiring firm). This information should be followed by interviews at all levels of responsibility in a department, functional area, and organization-wide. Each level of interviewers within an organization can bring unique perspectives and understanding to the recruitment process and selection.

Other recruiting for midlevel or upper-level senior supply chain management positions can be undertaken by professional recruiting organizations. Some of these include third-party recruiters or executive search firms. A *third-party recruiter* serves as an employment agency. It acts as an independent contact between the client company and the candidates. These recruiters tend to specialize in permanent, full-time, direct-hire positions or contract positions.

For supply chain executives, such as at the vice president level, *executive search firms* specialize in recruiting executive personnel. Executive search professionals typically have a wide range of personal contacts in the industry or field of specialty. They are knowledgeable in specific areas (for example, focusing research expertise in a limited field), such as supply chain management. Executive search professionals are typically involved in conducting detailed interviews and presenting candidates to clients selectively. They usually have long-lasting relationships with clients.

3.2.2 Evaluating Candidate Capabilities

Although certifications and degrees can be viewed as a general statement of the capabilities of personnel, there may be unique skills and competencies desired of the supply chain staff based on departmental needs. For example, being able to negotiate may be important for procurement employees, and being able to evaluate personnel is always important for candidate managers. A particular company's culture and philosophy of negotiating or evaluating personnel might require unique skills for new hires. To measure this, firms undertake skill assessments and diagnostic analyses to determine whether new hires possess the skills and competencies needed.

Flynn (2008, pp. 239–240) recommends a gap analysis to determine if employees need training for an additional or new skill or competency. *Gap analysis* is a tool that uses a survey method to measure the level of skills and competencies possessed by employees that are then compared to desired levels. Basically, a set of measures are taken of a desired set of skills. For supply chain personnel, Flynn (2008, p. 240) suggests this set of skills might include managerial skills (for example, project management, time management), interpersonal skills (for example, cross-culture communications, business ethics), analytical skills (for example, accounting, cost and price analysis), and commercial skills (for example, risk management, quality). A survey is given to new or existing employees that measures skill level by numeric responses (for example, 1 to 5 scale) to questions designed to reveal capabilities. These measures are then compared with a set developed by existing managers in the firm who excel at jobs in each area. The latter measures are the standard for comparison. The gap between the employee measures and the standard set from the managers reveals (if it exists) gaps between the employee's actual score and the manager's desired score and helps to specifically pinpoint the need for further training and competency development.

3.2.3 Retaining Employees

There are many CSFs that cause an employee to stay with or be retained by a firm. If not considered, CSFs can also become reasons why employees leave organizations. These CSFs include job satisfaction, compensation, work environment, and career succession opportunities.

Job satisfaction is the perception by employees of how fulfilling the tasks they perform are to themselves and their organizations. It is viewed as an emotional state resulting from the appraisal of one's job and attitudes toward the job. The more satisfied an employee is with their job, the more likely they are to be to want to keep their job.

Job satisfaction can be measured in many ways. The most common method for collecting data about job satisfaction is based on a numeric scale (for example, from 1, which represents agreement, to 7, which represents no agreement) with survey questions about job content, like "I am generally a happy person." A more standardized instrument for use in any firm is the *job descriptive index* (JDI), which has a specific questionnaire for measuring satisfaction along five dimensions: pay, promotions and promotion opportunities, coworkers, supervision, and the work itself. The scale used in this instrument has participants answer either yes, no, or can't decide (indicated by ?) in response to whether given statements accurately describe how they feel about the job.

Compensation and benefits are both very important in staffing retention. *Compensation* is the pay package of salary and benefits given to an employee for performing jobs. Salary is often a determiner of retention if it is out of line with peers or the market salary for a particular position. Benefits can be viewed as a part of an organization's compensation program. Benefits are where firms can be creative to encourage retention. Beyond providing compensation, firms can also include healthcare benefits, reimbursement for education, paid vacations, free travel benefits (for example, taking spouses on trips), flexible work hours, time off, and sabbaticals. Flexibility in structuring benefits can encourage retention.

The work environment is more than the physical locations where the employees work; it is also the psychological environment created by the organizations. Many supply chain managers are traveling more than working onsite in an office. The psychological environment is created by organization policies (avoiding rigidity in policies but seeking flexibility to seize opportunities), by upper management through their style of leadership (avoiding dictatorial styles but seeking styles that are supportive and nurturing), and by staff (seeking optimistic, energetic and communicative staffers who encourage the same from employee). Work environments that encourage a positive attitude about job content will be better able to retain like-minded people.

For many supply chain executives, career succession is as important as compensation or any other job-retention CSF. Knowing that advancement is possible in the future because of a clearly defined career succession program will encourage retention. Also, the knowledge of what career succession will bring in terms of future job satisfaction, compensation, and work environment will help foster an environment that encourages retention of employees. Everyone needs the hope that tomorrow will bring a brighter day, and for career-minded supply chain managers, hoping for better times tomorrow is what helps get them through rough times today. Mapping out a possible career path for employees and communicating it to them helps establish a personal interest perception (for the organization to the employee) that can be a strong motivator to stay with a firm. It helps them look ahead to opportunities and motivates them to want to stay in their jobs.

3.2.4 Terminating Employees

People who violate organization standards or fail to meet performance expectations may need to be terminated. Other reasons might include insubordination, theft, substance abuse, or physical violence. Ideally, the organization should have a formal process to exercise when a termination becomes necessary. The process has to comply with local, state, and federal laws. In foreign countries, the process may be easier or more complex, but regardless, the process of termination should be viewed as a serious event requiring care by and sensitivity to all involved.

In situations where large numbers of employees have lost jobs because tasks were outsourced to other organizations, many firms can negotiate with the outsourcer to hire the firm's employees to work for the outsourcer. In other situations, hiring freezes and retirements might prevent the need for major terminations when plant closings occur due to shifts in demand.

Whenever employees are terminated or let go, the organization should seek to undertake exit interviews. An *exit interview* is an interview conducted of the departing employee by the firm that is letting them go. Human resource staff members generally conducted these interviews. They seek to determine useful, perceptual, or factual information about why the employee is leaving the firm (either being fired or just leaving). Exit interviews can be conducted via paper and pencil forms, telephone interviews, in-person meetings, or online. Some employers choose to use a third-party human resource organization to conduct the interviews and provide feedback.

3.3 Global Staffing Considerations

3.3.1 Global Hiring Philosophy

In a very real sense, all supply chains today are global in scope, and staffing them offers managers incredible challenges and opportunities. One the first steps in staffing a global operation is to determine the type of individual a firm wants to recruit for global operations. There are different ways to categorize potential employees. One way is to look at candidates in the context of a firm's hiring philosophy. There are four different categories of potential employees to staff global operations, based on a firm's hiring philosophy: home country national, host country national, third-country national, and global oriented (see Table 3.3). The selection of a hiring philosophy represents a general guideline that can be used for all hires by a global firm regardless of the location, or it can be exercised based on the needs of the individual firm, the type of job, and willingness to trust the employees. Many factors can guide a global hiring philosophy selection, such as a firm's global strategies. For example, suppose that a U.S. firm has a low-cost objective for a new production facility that is being located in foreign country. Although most any of the four philosophies will apply, there may be some startup advantages of hiring a host country national or polycentric philosophy due to employees being familiar with the host country.

Table 3.3 Categories of Global Employees Based on a Firm's Hiring Philosophy

Category of Global Employee/Philosophy	Description
Home country national/ Ethnocentric	Recruiting employees under an ethnocentric philosophy means hiring employees who originate from a home country that is identified with the home base of the hiring firm. Some firms view their country of origin as their home country. This employee is familiar with and associated with the home country organization. For example, a person from the United States who views himself as a citizen of the United States being hired by a U.S. firm to work in Mexico.
Host country national/ Polycentric	Recruiting employees under a polycentric philosophy means hiring foreign nationals who live in the foreign country where the operations for the organization will be placed but works for a company whose origin is not from their own country. The foreign country acts as the host to the home country organization, and the employee lives in the foreign country (for example, a citizen from Japan working in Japan for a Chinese firm).
Third-country national/ Regiocentric	Recruiting employees under an ethnocentric philosophy means hiring foreign nationals who originate from a different country than either the home country or host country. This person is usually recruited from the same general region as the host country. For example, a person from France might be hired to work in a firm located in Germany but owned by a U.S. organization.
Global oriented/Geo-centric	Recruiting employees under a geocentric philosophy means hiring employees who can come from any country in the world and be located in any country to do their jobs.

Source: Adapted from Schniederjans (1998), pp. 37–38.

Why one type of employee would be selected over another rests largely in the advantages and disadvantages each hiring philosophy offers. Some of the advantages and disadvantages are listed for the home country national employee ethnocentric philosophy in Table 3.4, the host country national employee polycentric philosophy in Table 3.5, the third-country national regiocentric philosophy in Table 3.6, and the global-oriented geocentric philosophy in Table 3.7. In combination with other personnel information (for example, employee capabilities) and the organization needs, these philosophies can help in guiding a global hiring decision.

Table 3.4 Advantages and Disadvantages of a Home Country National Ethnocentric Hiring Philosophy

Advantage	Description
Potential loyalty	Home country nationals are more likely to have a cultural and personal identification with their own country than a foreign country. This can be an important consideration in operations where technology or production process secrets must be maintained and not shared with foreign nationals.
Improved communication	Home country nationals offer ease of communication between home country operations and home country personnel because of their understanding of the home country operation. This is important when orders from the home country must be translated and implemented quickly. The familiarity with home country operations will permit a quick response to home country orders.
Ease of staffing	Because the employee will be from the home country, the same host country staff and recruiting activities can be used domestically to recruit for the global operation (that is, no global recruiting costs necessary).

Disadvantage	Description
Lack of experience with foreign operations	A home country national recruited employee will tend not to be as knowledgeable in foreign locations as host nationals may be. Without an understanding of foreign culture, laws, and local production processes, this lack of experience can mean costly mistakes, legal problems, and disruption of facility operations. This disadvantage can also require costly training programs to be developed to help the home national get up-to-speed in the foreign country.

Disadvantage	Description
Communication problems with host nationals	There may not be adequate communication capabilities between the home nationals giving the orders and the host nationals receiving the orders. If the home national managers do not speak the native language adequately, their understanding of orders from the home country will be impaired because they might not be able to explain them to those host nationals who will actually do the work.
Repatriation problems	If home nationals or expatriates are unable to adapt to a foreign operation or its culture, they may have to be brought back to their home country. This would require expensive costs (that is, direct and indirect) of repatriating the employees.
Costliness of sending and retrieving personnel	Most expatriate programs require costly incentives to motivate home country personnel to go to foreign countries. When they return, they often require extensive and expensive retraining on home country operations to deal with changes that have taken place while they were living abroad.

Source: Adapted from Schniederjans (1998), pp. 39–41.

Table 3.5 Advantages and Disadvantages of a Host Country National Employee Polycentric Hiring Philosophy

Advantage	Description
Familiarity with host country	The host country national will be familiar with the country culture and ways of doing business in the foreign country. This should mean they will be more productive in the short term during their a startup period and during their long-term assignment with the firm.
Positive motivator for other host nationals	As the organization hires more host nationals, host national employees will be more likely to perceive the home country organization as valuing their contributions to the firm. This creates a perception that the foreign local personnel can participate in decision making concerning their operations as equals with home nationals.
Possible reduced cost of personnel	In operations where the bottom line is a driving factor, host nationals often are less costly in terms of salary, moving expenses, and benefits.

Disadvantage	Description
Lack of understanding of home country operations	The host country national will not be familiar with the home country organization culture or the home country operation. This can mean poor productivity in the short term.

Disadvantage	Description
Poor communication with home country operation	Host country nationals may not be familiar with accepted means or subtleties of communication with the home country operation. This can cause a misinterpretation of instructions, misinformation to the home office, and poor productivity in the region of the facility.
Lack of loyalty to firm	Host country nationals may be more loyal to their country than to the firm that employs them. This can be very disruptive when doing business in a global context. For example, if a host country national is forced to do business with or in countries where there is a history of animosity with the host country, the host country national might not do what is expected in terms of operational performance to customers.
Costly training	The host national may require substantial training to understand and operate facilities in acceptable ways to those performed by the home country managers.

Source: Adapted from Schniederjans (1998), p. 41.

Table 3.6 Advantages and Disadvantages of a Third-Country National Regiocentric Hiring Philosophy

Advantage	Description
Less costly	The third-country national employee is usually less expensive than a home country national who is relocated to a host country.
Easier to recruit	Because the third-country national can come from any third country, this opens a very large world labor market as a potential source of employee candidates.
Less need of training and adjustment	Third-country nationals are usually located in the same region as the host country for the operation. This would make them more familiar with culture and ways of business in that region than home nationals. They may even have unique knowledge of local regional markets that will make regional trading easier.
Minimizes politics	A third-country manager's decisions concerning host country operations will be under less suspicion of being politically motivated than a host country manager or a home country manager because of their lack of association with the home company country.

Disadvantage	Description
Lack of experience with foreign operations	Like the home national, third-country nationals cannot possibly be as knowledgeable in a foreign location as host nationals but may possess more knowledge than home country nationals. This disadvantage can also require costly training programs to get the third-country national up-to-speed in the foreign country that is hosting the production facility.
Communication problems	Because there is a high likelihood they may not share the same language as the host country, there might not be adequate communication capabilities between the home nationals giving the orders and the third-country nationals receiving them.
Repatriation problems	If third-country nationals or expatriates are unable to adapt to a foreign operation or its culture, they might have to be brought back to their own home country. This would require expensive costs (that is, direct and indirect) of repatriating the employees.
Cost of sending and retrieving personnel	Most expatriate programs require costly incentives to motivate third-country personnel to go to foreign countries. When they return to their country of origin, they can require extensive and expensive retraining of their own home country operations due to changes over the time while living abroad.
Psychological impact on host nationals	Bringing a third-country national into a foreign operation can be viewed as insulting to host national personnel.
Lack of the understanding of operations	The host country national may not be familiar with the organization culture of the home country organization. This can mean poor productivity in the short term.
Lack of loyalty to firm	Third-country nationals may be more loyal to their own country than the firm that employs them or the host country where they find employment.

Source: Adapted from Schniederjans (1998), p. 42.

Table 3.7 Advantages and Disadvantages of a Global-Oriented Geocentric Hiring Philosophy

Advantage	Description
Loyalty	For a global organization, loyalty will be to the firm, not to the country. Global-oriented individuals may find themselves periodically changing from one country location to another, making loyalties to one country less meaningful since employment will be worldwide. The only constant for global-oriented individuals will be the global organization, which by nature will be the most likely candidate for the employee's loyalty.

Advantage	Description
Improved communication	A global organization will employ personnel from all over the world. Global-oriented individuals tend to want to learn new languages or possess them since they are globally oriented. They have the best chances to have a collection of diversity of language skills on hand when necessary to do any job without the need of finding interpreters.
Ease of staffing	Recruiting in a global operation allows a global market pool of personnel to choose from. This increases the number and quality of personnel available for any employee-selection assignment. Global-oriented individuals support this ease of assignment because they are willing to go anywhere in the world.
Familiarity with host country	Because of the breath of personnel located in various countries, the global-oriented employee will stand a better chance of being familiar with any country or culture in foreign countries.
Positive motivator for other global-oriented individuals	Hiring some global-oriented individuals and treating them as equals will result in the perception that the home country operation values contributions to the firm from any culture. It will also act as a potential motivational aspect of promoting the ethical value of equality (that is, everyone in the world is equal to everyone else). Only a truly global operation can provide this equalitarian *esprit de corps*.
Possible reduced cost of personnel	A global-oriented philosophy permits an environment where ideal personnel cost compromises can be achieved. For example, a global organization that is growing toward decentralized operations might want a greater proportion of their home country nationals in some foreign operations, particularly startup operations where change and control of management practices are critical. This preference toward home country nationals can be implemented without negative impact to other host country nationals by rotating the global-oriented employees away shortly after the startup period is over. They make the shifts of personnel much easier than any other category of employee.
Less costly	The global-oriented organization will tend to use as much of the local foreign talent as is necessary. This will usually mean that an operation will be less expensive than an only home country national or only third-country national operation because less-expensive host country nationals can be used. Global-oriented employees take advantage of the talents from many nations, which can result in improved productivity in personnel and processes that any of the other more monoculture philosophies would not permit.
Less need for training and adjustment	The global-oriented philosophy permits the use of personnel from the host country that can help the non-host-country personnel to more quickly adjust to the local culture and the ways of business.

Advantage	Description
Minimizes politics	A truly global-oriented manager's decisions concerning host country operations will be under less suspicion of being politically motivated than either a host country manager (who might have a local hidden agenda) or a home country manager (who might have a home country hidden agenda).

Disadvantage	Description
Lack of experience with foreign operations	Although some personnel will not have host country experience, others will in a global-oriented organization. Many global organizations use a team approach of combining host country nationals with non-host-country personnel to provide a personal and more intensive learning experience. The team approach also helps to overcome communication problems because personal tutoring by peers on specific organizational subjects is the most efficient means of learning. Also, the team approach on production processes benefits the host country national that can learn new processes from the home country operations while teaching local host country processes to non-host-country personnel.
Repatriation problems	Global-oriented firms hire globally and relocate globally. With the worldwide choice of opportunities that exist in for a global organization, the need to repatriate is minimized under this philosophy because global-oriented employees can choose other international locations if an assignment in one country does not work out.
Costliness of sending and retrieving personnel	While most expatriate programs require costly incentives to motivate home country personnel to go to foreign countries, global-oriented organizations seek to keep their employees mobile, because global activities are expected. Global-oriented personnel do not usually go home; they move on to the next assignment in the next country.
Psychological impact on host country nationals	Bringing non-host-country personnel into a foreign operation can be viewed as insulting to host national personnel. This perception is minimized by the fact that global-oriented organizations will be bringing in personnel from all over the world and treating them and the host country nationals as equals.

Source: Adapted from Schniederjans (1998), pp. 43–44.

The balancing of the advantages and disadvantages listed for differing hiring philosophies in Tables 3.4 to 3.7 is a difficult task. Fortunately, it can be made easier by choosing the global-oriented philosophy for recruitment and selection. The global-oriented philosophy tends to have all the advantages of other recruitment and selection philosophies with little of the disadvantages. It is also a philosophy characteristic of current top supply chain talent (Slone et al., 2010, pp. 63–68).

3.3.2 Employee Selection

Obtaining the right global-oriented employee, developing them, and retaining them are all important factors in staffing global supply chains. Selection of global-oriented employees should start with an organization-specific set of criteria that can act to guide the selection process. Although the uniqueness of an organization makes the subject too voluminous to cover here, general guidelines can be suggested (see Table 3.8). While skills and abilities are important, being able to handle the stress in a supply chain management position in a foreign country is clearly a CSF for any global-oriented employee. The stress capacity of an employee, as well as the skills and abilities, should be measured, documented, and weighed in the analysis as critical inputs to the selection decision.

Table 3.8 Global-Oriented Selection Criteria

Types of Selection Criteria	Description
Handle stressful situations	Must be able to work in and accept assignments in strange environments; able to adapt to unfamiliar conditions; able to travel and be located in many foreign countries for long periods of time; psychologically able to handle unique stressful situations
Managerial skills	Must have extensive group and team orientations; able to work with home country personnel; able to work independently
Physical abilities	Must have good health and ability to adapt to climatic conditions in various possible locations; able to adjust to different time zones
Social skills	Must be able to understand and maintain good relations with personnel in home country operations and with foreign nationals; be able to understand and appreciate foreign customs and cultures; have good diplomatic skills in negotiation; conduct themselves ethically within the culture they are located in
Technical skills	Must be knowledgeable of relevant facility systems and processes, company technology, and communication systems; work within limitations on technology in foreign countries; willing to undergo extensive training

Source: Adapted from Table 3.3 in Schniederjans (1998), p. 46.

3.3.3 Employee Training

For important hires or individuals who are transferred from other countries and may lack a particular set of skills, training is an important part of the employee development program. Training can be used to determine and confirm whether a person has the ability to run global operations. Also, supply chain executives should be aware that a global operation using expatriates or home country nationals can expect to have substantially larger budgets for training than a typical domestic organization. Some firms try to keep training costs down by using specialized firms that focus on training specific skill sets. For example, language alone is a most important skill for expatriates to possess to be successful in jobs and adapt to the host country. Some global firms utilize private tutoring, such as Berlitz training classes (www.berlitz.us/). Another strategy is to use older employees and retirees to help educate and orient foreign employees in host country languages and share cultural experiences.

One of the most important types of training for anyone working in a global operation is intercultural training. *Intercultural training* is an educational program that can help impart knowledge to employees to prepare them to be sensitive to differing cultures. Intercultural training provides useful culture, customs, and role expectations for employees and their relationships in business settings. As a form of sensitivity training, the training begins with a self-awareness step where global managers learn to recognize their own personal assumptions and values and how they might impact or alter their understanding of differing cultures. Once self-awareness is established, training usually focuses on developing an appreciation of multiple perspectives, allowing employees to understand points of view from other cultures. Table 3.9 describes some other components of intercultural training. The implementation of this training often requires an investment in specialists, consultants, and educators with experience in foreign cultures.

Table 3.9 Intercultural Training Program Elements

Skill Set	Description
Cultural flexibility	To develop the ability to change or be flexible in the norms expected by the host country nationals
Cultural norming	To develop the ability to identify, understand, and appreciate different cultural norms and society expectations
Cultural robustness	To develop abilities to recover from cultural shocks or setbacks
Intercultural communication	To develop the ability to recognize and understand verbal and nonverbal communications accurately in host countries
Intercultural relationship	To develop the ability to identify, nurture, develop, and maintain interpersonal relationships with host country nationals

Source: Adapted from Table 3.4 in Schniederjans (1998), p. 47.

3.3.4 Employee Compensation

Global compensation requires consideration of pay-related factors impacting what employees receive in remuneration. Compensation can include the consideration of factors related to an employee's base salary, taxation, benefits and allowances, and pension.

The amount of base salary necessary to pay a global employee should be based at least in part on the following guidelines: (1) a rate consistent and fair in treatment of all employees regardless of position in the organization structure, (2) a rate that will attract and retain employees regardless of the global location of employment or the nature of the jobs, (3) a rate that will motivate employees to excel, and (4) one that establishes a system of pay facilitating movement within the global network. Table 3.10 describes additional guidelines.

Table 3.10 Global Compensation Guidelines

Compensation Guideline	Description
Home country pay scale plus some additional differential	This guideline offers a fairness advantage of being directly connected to the home country scale while still making some adjustments for living abroad. The differential additions can include education expenses for children, periodic trips home, cost-of-living adjustments, inflation and currency adjustments, membership fees in professional organizations, and work-related legal fees. Unfortunately, this approach can have a negative effect on personnel who come from countries where the standard of living (and its costs) are higher than the home country pay scale from which they are being paid.
Country of origin pay scale plus some additional differential	This guideline is designed to consider the national origin pay scale of the employee. Basically, the employee is paid a salary based on living or wage/salary standards of the country where the employee originated. So a person from the United States working in Japan will be paid a U.S. salary plus any additional differential deemed appropriate to adjust for the cost factors in Japan. Although this approach can be viewed as having a very ethical bias since the pay is country specific, it might have a negative effect on personnel who work at the same job but because they come from different countries are paid at a different rate.
Global pay scale plus some additional differential	This guideline is designed to provide equal pay for equal jobs. A global salary is established for specific categories of global jobs. With the exception of minor host country differentials, the pay scale is the same for all employees performing the same job at the same facility regardless of the country location. This approach avoids problems with personnel who move around the world a lot, because their salaries would stay basically the same. The difficulty with this method is to establish and maintain global job descriptions and globally fair pay scales.

Source: Adapted from Schniederjans (1998), p. 48.

One problem with all these guidelines is the rate of exchange impact that salaries experience in a global context. Some employees work in one country while their families are located in another country. If the rate of exchange does not favor a particular family located in another country, the employee will view this as a reduction in pay (and the appropriate motivational discouragement that comes from this reduction). Adequate adjustments to compensate for any exchange-rate penalties should always be considered when setting up global compensation programs. This adjustment is particularly important when country currencies are experiencing rapid valuation fluctuations.

Taxation is also an important consideration of any compensation program. Many expatriate employees are doubly taxed (that is, taxed by their home country and the host country). While in the United States, Section 911 of the U.S. Federal Government Internal Revenue Service Code allows a substantial deduction to mitigate the impact of double taxation. Most other nations tax part or all of their foreign-employed nationals' income. To help compensate for this double taxation where it is enforced, additional base salary or nontaxable benefits can be included in a compensation program.

3.3.5 Benefits and Allowances

Benefits and allowances (financial and nonfinancial) are important considerations in employee compensation programs. Benefits can include such items as medical and dental insurance, social security payments, pension plans, time off, membership fees in professional organizations, sabbaticals, vacation, sick leave, life insurance, and so on. Allowances can be financial equivalents to the benefits, as well, and they can be unique, such as a cost-of-living allowance or relocation allowance for shipping, moving, storage, or temporary living expenses for transferring employees. When establishing global benefits and allowances, supply chain managers should consider many factors, including the following:

- The benefits and allowances that should be included in a global benefits program
- Whether the home country employees and global employees should receive the same benefits and allowances
- Whether the host country, third-country, or global-oriented employees should receive the same social security payments as in the home country
- Whether there should be differentials in the benefits and allowances for employees in the global operations that are made up by salary increases

- What considerations should be made to address benefits and allowance limitations and requirements placed on the firm by non-home-country governments

Given the size and complexity of pension programs, which are sometimes mandated by governments, great care should be given to the management of any global pension plan. An explicit policy statement should be established documenting how pensions are managed and who is responsible for them. When developing a policy, an organization must address the following issues:

- Calculating the costs of global pension obligations and how they are financed
- Controls, reports, and approval procedures relating to pension planning implemented by the home country office or host country office managers
- What the home company's responsibility should be with regard to investing pension assets, and which executives from the finance department of a regional organization or national office control such decisions
- Guidelines for the organization's investment philosophy regarding pension funds and who must approve them
- Local, regional, state, and federal government law compliance
- Who is responsible for monitoring and reporting the performance of the pension fund investments in a timely manner

Creative employment benefit arrangements can be used to recruit host country national employees by offering them opportunities to work in their country of origin for a period and then return to a foreign country of choice. For example, Jennings (2011) reports that recruiting Chinese host country national employees can be difficult when they have been educated in the United States. Some Chinese nationals would like to get a job in the United States, but prospective companies need host country national employees for the advantages they offer in dealing with issues regarding operations facilities in China. One strategy is to offer these employees an attractive expatriate financial plan, which includes a future opportunity to return to the United States. Jennings suggests this is a key factor for having a permanent Chinese native working for U.S. firms in their offshore U.S. operations in China.

3.4 Other Staffing Topics

3.4.1 Staffing Retention Sabbaticals

When factoring in required travel, psychological pressure of constantly meeting deadlines, global competition, and many other typical tasks and considerations, few jobs are as stressful and demanding as those in supply chain management. For organizations, the best employees are ones who work the hardest (and smartest). As a result, many supply chain executives can become burned out mentally and physically well before they retire. For organizations that want to keep these talented staffers, they need to consider developing a sabbatical program. A *sabbatical program* allows employees a leave of absence from their jobs (Allen, 2011). It can be paid or unpaid time off from what they do on a regular basis.

Like an added vacation (whether paid or not), the sabbatical is a way of disengaging the employee from the job and the accompanying stress for a period of time. Unlike a regular vacation that a family may fill with work or one where the supply chain manager is still on call, a sabbatical is a means for really getting away from the work environment.

Some companies are not well suited for sabbatical programs because of the continuous nature of demands on executives whose roles are so significant that they cannot be spared for sabbaticals of any kind. Those who might be interested in implementing a sabbatical program might consider the steps in Table 3.11.

Table 3.11 A Procedure for Implementing a Sabbatical Program

Steps	Description
1. Research the industry.	For the firm seeking the sabbatical program, determine what their industry is doing to attract and retain employees. Even if other firms are not utilizing this type of program, it may offer a human resource competitive advantage for the firms that do offer it.
2. Research existing programs.	Where possible, learn from what other companies in other industries are doing in terms of a sabbatical program. Those that are offering sabbaticals may provide useful information on how to structure a program and their results.

Steps	Description
3. Research opinions of internal employees.	Research using surveys or focus groups to determine what is important to employees relative to a sabbatical program. Pinpoint and learn the differences in terms of gender and age that factor into such a program. From the more successful employees, learn what motivates them and would attract them to such a program. It might turn out that this latter information could be useful in recruiting additional successful employees. This information can help structure sabbatical programs internally in the organization.
4. Research opinions of external supply chain partners.	Research suppliers' opinions and ideas on how to work together to cooperatively develop employees in both organizations using a sabbatical approach. Spending time together in touring facilities and making a mini-vacation out of the adventure by taking an extra day or so might be a way of having a mini-sabbatical program that can build trust and foster retention with supply chain partners.

Source: Adapted from Allen (2011), p. 44.

3.4.2 Lateral Staffing Moves

Due to downturns in the economies of world, high-performing supply chain executives have found moving laterally to another internal functional area in an organization or laterally externally to a competitor's organization is a means to grow in experience and knowledge. Tuel (2011) suggests the best supply executives are those who have broad experience and knowledge in multiple functions of an organization and in multiple organizations. For example, an executive who has worked in both marketing and operations is likely to be more efficient in integrating those two functional areas than a less-experienced manager who only has marketing or operations experience.

Tuel suggests several beneficial ways to make the best of a lateral move, which also serves the organization. One way is to develop relationships and network with leaders of other internal supply chain functions to communicate a desire to learn. This will enhance organizational learning and knowledge sharing for both the employees who move laterally and those who are working with the new employee.

Lateral moves should be encouraged in organizations where upward mobility is limited or where highly successful employees might be restless and look to move elsewhere. Lateral moves help to cross-train executives and other staffers, making them better able to understand the organization and integrating their job with others for the benefit of the organization

3.4.3 Human Resource Succession Program

Its not enough to attract talented supply chain leaders. They must be retained. High-performing supply chain managers are assets to the organizations in which they work. Like talented sports figures, top-performing supply chain managers are highly mobile and represent a scarce resource that can easily be lost to competitive supply chain organizations that offer greater opportunities for advancement.

A successful strategy for retaining supply chain personnel involves establishing a succession program. A *succession program* uses a variety of methods for identifying and developing talented supply chain managers (Fulmer and Bleak, 2011). By identifying talents and career preferences of supply chain managers, a succession plan allows the firm to match them to future jobs within the organization. This best practices program helps firms track their employees own successes. It also helps the firm identify developmental opportunities, placing the right people in those positions, and identifying future shortages of talent.

Successful succession programs usually involve quantitative and qualitative measures that seek to determine talent dimensions of a manager's ability to lead an organization. Data for these measures can come from a broad range of raters, who are well trained in communicating such data. The raters might include administration staff, internal and external customers, support staff, superiors, and subordinates. A suggested method, *360-degree input* (that is, input provided by a variety of sources throughout an organization, including personnel who deal regularly with the employee and not just the immediate superior, but staff, subordinates, peers, and so on) provides a comprehensive collection of information that better characterizes the employee's abilities. Quantitative measures might include how well the manager meets goals important to the organization (for example, ethnic or gender diversity goals), retention and attrition rates, and job-performance evaluations. Qualitative measures might be based on a participant's transition experience in a new role, how well he or she was prepared, and reasons for attrition.

Long-term success in succession programs requires continual organizational commitment and continuous improvement according to Fulmer and Bleak (2011). Table 3.12 describes several characteristics of successful succession programs.

Table 3.12 Successful Succession Characteristics

Characteristic	Description
Everyday event	Succession planning should be integrated into everyday activities. Move from a formal annual or quarterly event to a set of daily activities that help to collect and communicate succession information.
Reliance on technology	Where possible, automate the information assessments to make it easy for participants to provide up-to-date information and for monitoring manager performance.
Functional sharing	Sometimes for the organizational good, it is necessary to lose a top supply chain manager to another functional area, which can be called *cross-functional succession.*
Objective appraisals and feedback	Objective assessments by competently trained superiors or subordinates as well as timely feedback to personnel is a critical success factor in any human resource program, including succession programs where the goal is to advance based on performance.
Equable selection criteria	Succession depends on making clear the competencies for any job, including skills, values, behaviors, and attitudes to succeed.
Diversity of choice	Successful succession programs should provide more than one qualified candidate for positions that become available.

3.4.4 Developing Supply Chain Procurement Teams

Creating, developing, and nurturing teams for projects and programs are important staffing functions for any organization. Building a supply chain procurement team, for example, can be a challenge for supply chain executives. Trowbridge (2011) reports there are fundamental CSFs that can lead to extraordinary results (see Table 3.13). The continuous application of the CSFs in Table 3.13 can result in outstanding procurement teams better trained, motivated, and empowered to do their jobs.

Table 3.13 Team-Building CSF

Team-Building CSF	Description
Provide adequate and appropriate training.	Determine skill capabilities to identify weaknesses using testing or other methods. Compare skills with current best practices to identify gaps in knowledge and help determine training needs. Develop an educational program that is formatted to best impart knowledge in a practical and not theoretical context.
Recruit the appropriate team members.	Recruit for the team employees with the right certifications (such as from ISM, CPSM, APICS, and *Certified Supply Chain Professional* [CSCP]) and educational training from supply chain organizations (such as CSCMP).
Create a performance-based environment.	A team must align to meet its stakeholders' needs, positioning them in an environment that both is supportive of their role and allows team managers to lead, coach, or mentor team development.
Select appropriate leadership.	Leaders or managers who run teams or work within them must be able to structure team conduct with formal written objectives that are achievable but offer some challenge to permit growth in learning for the team members. In addition, leaders should provide regular feedback to team members to help mentor performance toward stated goals.
Plan career succession.	Supply chain team members need to know where they are going in their careers. Two planning aids are recommended: a succession plan and a *career-path mapping* (that is, a logical progression plan for each job category). Both methods are helpful in matching employees with a career path plan.

One final aspect of team building should be suggested. Some employees may be productive individually but are not team oriented. Some specialized team training might be able to move them toward more of a team work ethic. However, it might be better to remove such employees from team projects. Effective supply chain management leadership requires a willingness to add and delete personnel to maximize the organization's outcomes.

3.5 What's Next?

The daunting task of training supply chain and manufacturing personnel does not appear to be getting easier. In fact, the future trends suggest a major effort is needed to bring prospective employees "up-to-speed" (Gold, 2012). The Manufacturing Institute (www.themanufacturinginstitute.org/) survey on skills gaps shows more than 80% of manufacturers say they are experiencing a moderate to severe shortage of skilled production workers. These shortages are present in the supply chain area as well. In a study by KPMG International ("Global Manufacturing...," 2011), the availability of skilled workers now tops the list of human resource concerns in emerging markets.

To help fill the gap between the desire to staff supply chains with capable people and the reality of shortages, many firms have chosen to enhance personnel capabilities they have and to develop strong training programs for new hires. The *Manufacturers Alliance for Productivity and Innovation* (MAPI) (www.mapi.net/) surveyed top human resource executives in manufacturing (Gold, 2012). The survey results revealed firms were planning to offer substantial in-house training. Many are expanding and diversifying their educational offerings. Some of the observed and recommended educational strategies to deal with shortages are as follows:

- Training entry-level and intermediate/advanced employees with in-person classes taught by internal and outside instructors
- Training programs giving more emphasis to enhancing team-building skills and the capacity to think through the logic of a process
- Training and development programs offered to engineers so that they can understand the needs of customers
- Financial support for employees to obtain multiple course certificates and certifications at technical schools or community colleges
- Financial support for Bachelor's degree programs for production employees

4

Managing Supply Chains

Novelette

4.1 Prerequisite Material

4.2 Managerial Topics in Planning/Organizing Supply Chains

4.2.1 Leading with an Entrepreneurial Spirit

4.2.2 Managing Complexity

4.2.3 Developing a Procurement Plan

4.3 Managerial Topics in Staffing Supply Chains

4.3.1 Building Teams

4.3.2 Mentoring Programs

4.4 Managerial Topics in Leading/Directing Supply Chains

4.4.1 Leadership Styles and Obstacles

4.4.2 Leading Evolutionary Change in Supply Chain Departments

4.5 Managerial Topics in Monitoring/Controlling Supply Chains

4.5.1 Setting Up an Internal Monitoring and Control System

4.5.2 Monitoring External Demand with Market Intelligence

4.6 What's Next?

Terms

Cause-and-effect diagrams or fishbone diagram

Committee of sponsoring organizations (COSO)

Continuous improvement (CI)

Controlling

Exercise price

Factor complexity

Failure mode and effect analysis (FMEA)

Groupthink

Leadership

Leadership styles

Market intelligence (MI)

Mentoring

Mentoring program

Monitoring

Opportunity flow chart

Options contract

Pareto charts

Portfolio contracts

Procurement management plan

Reservation price or premium

Self-managed teams (SMTs)

Should-cost modeling

Social loafing

Source complexity

Spot market purchasing

Novelette

While I am now responsible for the entire operations of my organization, the years I spent working as a supply chain manager were filled with a lot of problems that turned into opportunities for growth in relationships and knowledge. For example, inventory shortages are a fact of life that exist somewhere in every supply chain. Movements in the stages of product life cycles from Introduction to Growth can strip away the accuracy of any demand forecast, and yet supply chains must find some way to deal with these supply chain disrupting shortages.

After a luncheon at our corporate headquarters, my VP of the Medium-Sized Engine Division pulled me aside and posed a problem he was having with a major supplier of engine parts. "Bill, I am having a problem that is starting to impact my operation. The one and only supplier we have for the combustion chamber elements in all of our automobile engines is stonewalling me on delivery. I have a very good working relationship with the supplier's organization, everybody from the CEO down through most of their department heads, but parts are just not being delivered. I investigated through some of my contacts, and it's not like they have a quality problem. Their product is always excellent. I know they would like to ship us what we need, but they just don't have it on their shelves. As you know, we are their biggest customer, and yet we cannot for some reason get the product from them. Although I have pleaded with everyone I know there, the amount of inventory we are receiving from them is continuing to decrease, and I can see down the line that things will get critical. Do you have any suggestions?"

"Barack, as we both know, this is a key supplier, and I know you have managed the relationship well. I don't think they mean to stonewall us. I do know their CEO, and one of their board members is on our board of directors. I will get back to you on this shortly," I said.

In this Division, every day of shortage can cost thousands of dollars, so as a high-priority issue it took only a day to contact several of the players at the supplier's organization and our board member to find out what was causing the shortage. "Barack, it turns out that the supplier's brand name products have entered a Growth Stage in their product life cycle, and the excess capacity they have been using to serve our needs has dried up. At the same time, our board member mentioned that EPA regulations have been changing and increasing the complexity of their products. The added complexity has periodically caused them to struggle to meet the requirements, further sapping their capacity capabilities," I explained.

"Bill, this is our only single-source supplier for our products. I have explored alternative suppliers, and no feasible options exist short of closing our medium engine plants for a year to allow for retooling and having us produce the supplies we need. I know that is not acceptable, and I have tried everything I know to squeeze out additional inventory from those friends I have in that organization. I have enough inventory in the pipeline to keep going for now, but looking down the line for next year, I will be in big trouble unless something is done to correct this situation," explained Barack.

"Barack, because of the closeness of the relationship you have built with the supplier, I was able to reach down into their organization and talk with their operations and engineering people. The problems they are having are in terms of production capacity. The growth and regulation issues they have recently experienced have impacted their normal production efforts, destabilizing their operations enough to waste capacity in and of itself. What I propose is that you offer them the aid of our engineers to see whether they could help the supplier increase production capacity. If they agree, we can send a team of our black belt engineers into their facilities to see if they can identify capacity constraints and help the supplier overcome them. In the meanwhile, do what you can through any back channels to get whatever inventory there is in the supply chain pipeline and allocate it to critical shortages," I suggested.

The supplier agreed to use of the black belts, who use continuous improvement methods such as fishbone analysis and root-cause analysis. They identified areas that needed processes in place to improve their production output. What turned out to be a project of improvement for our supplier ended up developing into a long-term relationship-building exercise that benefited both firms. The improvements started allowing us to dig out from the shortages by the end of the year.

4.1 Prerequisite Material

In a general sense, managing a supply chain is an act of working and bringing people together to accomplish a desired set of supply chain goals and objectives using available resources efficiently and effectively. The basic functions of supply chain management involve the same functions all managers perform, which includes planning/organizing (that is, deciding what needs to be done to accomplish goals and generating plans to enact them), staffing (that is, recruitment and hiring personnel for jobs), leading/directing (that is, motivating and guiding people to do their jobs), and monitoring/controlling (that is, checking progress against plans and ensuring compliance) to achieve a common purpose (http://en.wikipedia.org/wiki/Management). To carry out these basic functions, managers are expected to perform a variety of roles, including interpersonal coordination and interaction with subordinates, peers, and superiors to communicate, motivate, mentor, and delegate work activities. Besides decision making, managers are also expected to provide an informational role of sharing and analyzing information.

The three management functions of planning/organizing, staffing, and leading/directing were introduced in the presentation on organizational design and strategic planning in Chapter 1, "Developing Supply Chain Strategies," and Chapter 2, "Designing Supply Chains." The staffing function was topically introduced in Chapter 3, "Staffing Supply Chains." The focus of this chapter is to build on these foundations with additional topics.

4.2 Managerial Topics in Planning/ Organizing Supply Chains

Some managers wait until a problem occurs to manage it. Better managers develop contingency plans just in case a problem comes up. Great managers establish a contingency roadmap for problem resolution that builds from the organization's mission statement through policy development and everyday events. Because of the diversity of problems and management issues that surface in any supply chain, only a cursory treatment of select planning topics can be presented here. The topics discussed include leading with an entrepreneurial spirit, managing complexity, and developing a procurement plan. Other related topics are presented in subsequent chapters.

4.2.1 Leading with an Entrepreneurial Spirit

In any stage of a product life cycle, but more so for the Introduction Stage, leaders should encourage employees to think like entrepreneurs. Entrepreneurs start up companies in the Introduction Stage of the product life cycle. They have to be adaptive, creative, innovative, and enthusiastic. Such spirit will unlock avenues of productivity and motivate employees to make substantial contributions.

To encourage supply chain personnel to think like entrepreneurs, Anderson (2011) suggests three managerial tactics: encourage experimentation, encourage what-if thinking, and appreciate the value of influencers. Experimentation can be encouraged by undertaking small projects that experiment with new ideas. What-if thinking can be encouraged by running though scenario problem solving exercises such as disaster planning, rapid customer growth modeling, or geopolitical disturbances. A manager needs to be able to influence employees and subordinates. While some managers rely on positional power, those who can genuinely influence others have real power to motivate and cause an organization to advance toward goals. A tactic to make everyone an influencer is for the manager to project a positive attitude. Other tactics might include proposing a continual set of new ideas to solve problems or to reexamine and modify ways for staff to do their jobs.

In summary, the key to an entrepreneurial spirit is for managers to encourage communication and change ideas. They should encourage development of new ideas as if the employees were starting up a new business operation. By doing so, new contributions and innovations will be an inevitable outcome.

4.2.2 Managing Complexity

Every component within the supply chain can add complexity and problems for management. There are many types of complexity in supply chains. Examples of a *source complexity* can include product complexity caused by an overly complex product design. Such a design might lead to an increased size of a supply chain globally to support the product. The processes used to produce a product can be highly complex, requiring substantial assembly work, thus adding distribution complexity of planning efforts to link the global assembly facilities. Network complexity can be created when the number of hubs in a network increases, requiring more effort to communicate and control it. Customer complexity can occur as customers demand more service options or when the customer base expands downstream or upstream as the supplier base increases to meet increased customer demand. The need for greater interaction with more numerous suppliers adds complexity in planning roles.

Regardless of the source of complexity, it needs to be planned for and managed. One conceptual modeling approach to aid in planning the management of sources of supply chain complexity is presented in Figure 4.1. The conceptual model in Figure 4.1 suggests that a source of complexity in a supply chain (and there are many) should first be identified and then studied to identify complexity factors or *factor complexity*. A customer may be a complexity source, but it is complexity factors such as the way the customer communicates with the firm to place orders or return merchandise that may be the complexity factor causing the problem. To aid in this planning task, several quality management methodologies can be used to break down complexity sources into complexity factors (see Table 4.1).

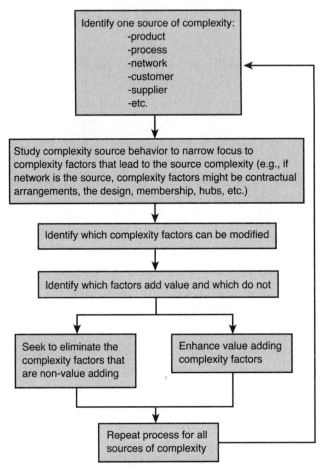

Figure 4.1 Conceptual model for managing complexity

Table 4.1 Quality Management Methodology Useful in Complexity Management

Quality Management Methodology	Description
Cause-and-effect diagrams or fishbone diagram	A visual aid diagram that permits a user to hypothesize relationships between potential causes of a problem. This diagram could help mangers conceptualize potential complexity factors from potential complexity sources in terms of human, technology, policy, and process resources. The diagram can be used to trace the complexity source back to possible causation complexity factors to allow the user to better picture potential causes.

Quality Management Methodology	Description
Pareto charts	A visual aid chart used to break down types of problems into several categories by frequency of occurrence and then prioritize the ordering of the revision. It is based on the logic here that the largest proportion of supply chain problems are usually small in number but occur frequently. For complexity purposes, application of Pareto chart helps to establish a ranking of these complexity sources or factors based on frequency of occurrence or costliness, helping managers plan how they should devote the most resources to solving the highest-ranked source of complexity first, second-highest-ranked problem next, and so forth.
Opportunity flow chart	Flow charts are graphic aids that are used to identify the tasks that make up a process. Opportunity flow charts are an application of flow charts in this case that helps to specifically identify complexity factors that waste resources or have non-value-added worth. Then the chart can be used as an opportunity to remove or reduce those factors.
Failure mode and effect analysis (FMEA)	FMEA is a structured means to identify, estimate, prioritize, and evaluate risk at each stage in a production process or in this case the collection of complexity factors that lead to a particular complexity source. The analysis can help to identify and assess the probability that the factor is contributing to complexity (occurrence) and the potential costliness caused by the factor (severity). FMEA analysis could also include suggestions for means by which to eliminate the complexity factor through redesign of the process associated with it.

Source: Adapted from Table 7 in Schniederjans (2010), pp. 21–22.

After the complexity factors have been identified, a determination of those that can be modified as opposed to those that cannot must be made. Assuming contractual and other constraints permit some modification, the next step in the conceptual model requires identification of those complexity factors that are value-added from those that are not. It should be understood that some complexity is actually a good thing. Customers may value a complex set of product offerings, making the diversity of those products within a distribution system a complexity challenge. The complexity factors that contribute value should be encouraged (or at least allowed), while those that are non-value-adding should be minimized or eliminated. Finally, the process of managing complexity as presented in Figure 4.1 needs to be repeated for each possible source of complexity. This repeating process, like the quality management methods in Table 4.1, needs to be viewed in the context of continuous improvement (CI) (that is, a never-ending sequence of quality activities ideally leading to perfection). Indeed, in the case of supply chain management, the need for repetition of the complexity modeling process is particularly urgent and critical because of the nature of dynamic changes undertaken in supply chains.

4.2.3 Developing a Procurement Plan

There are many dimensions to planning an organization's procurement operations. The *Institute for Supply Management* (ISM) (www.ism.ws/) suggests a formal statement be used: *procurement management plan* (that is, defines how supply management will oversee the procurement process). This plan covers such issues as contracts to be used, personnel assignments and responsibilities, documents, coordination activities for supply chain partners, and internal production/reporting requirements. The plan also designates the management of lead times and risk, processes to identify qualified suppliers, and performance metrics that will be used for monitoring and control. To develop the procurement management plan requires an understanding of *critical success factors* (CSFs) in establishing such a plan. Table 4.2 describes commonly considered procurement CSFs.

Table 4.2 Procurement Plan Critical Success Factors

Procurement Plan CSF	Description
Accurate forecasting	The accuracy of product or service forecasting is the foundation on which procurement is based. The more accurate the forecast, the less waste that will exist in a supply chain (for example, less inventory surplus or shortages, less costly overtime production effort to make up for customer shortages) By knowing accurately the items needed and sharing this information throughout the supply chain, needless effort is saved by all supply chain partners, leading ideally to reduced costs and greater efficiency for everyone. When demand volatility prevents accurate forecasts, delaying orders until customer orders are known can be a useful planning tactic.
Low financial supply risk	Financial risk is a measure of the effect on revenue if supply of a component or inventory item is disrupted. It can be computed as the component cost percentage of the cost of the finished product or percentage of total purchased costs. The higher the financial risk of a disruption in supply, the more planning is needed to minimize or avoid the risk.
Low network risk	Measured by the speed of delivery through a supply chain network, it is desirable to plan improvements that lead to further reductions in network delivery timing. Improving integration between suppliers, reducing distance components and other materials travel, and possessing adequate logistic support can minimize this risk.
Low operations risk	Unless the supply chain is delivering commodities, the components to finished products have to be produced by someone the upstream supply chain set of suppliers. Operations risk is the timing risk that any product runs when failing to meet with a planned production time schedule. The greater the variability in scheduling production in manufacturing operations, the greater the risk. The greater the risk, the more likely delays throughout the supply chain, causing costly inefficiencies. It is desirable to lower this risk by identifying sources of variation in the production process and removing them.
Low price risk	The greater the price volatility, the greater the price risk and the associated costs (that is, devaluing of inventory with price reduction representing a cost to the firm, increased pricing and the unexpected cost associated with the increase). The higher the price risk, the more difficult it is to budget material costs. An increase in costs can negatively impact profitability and run the risk of a product being discontinued due to excess costs to customers.

| **Procurement Plan** | |
CSF	Description
Low innovation risk	If an industry has rapid component technology innovations, there is an elevated risk of obsolescence of purchased inventory. Lowering innovation risks (for example, standardization of component parts is one tactic to avoid obsolescence) and their associated costs is desired in procurement planning.
Low supplier risk	Is measured in terms of the number of suppliers in a network, the suppliers' financial stability, product quality, probability of a supply stock-out, and product-substitution opportunities. Selecting a small number of reliable suppliers who provide high-quality products reliably will lower the probability of network suppliers stocking-out (and thus reduce the risk of the costs that any shortage may cause to the downstream customers).

Table 4.2 also illustrates a variety of risk taking required in planning procurement. Among other things, managing a procurement department involves managing risks. Many possible tactics can be implemented to manage procurement risk. One tactic to reduce risks with uncertain demand is through options contracts. An *options contract* is one where a buyer prepays a small faction of the product price in return for a commitment from the supplier to reserve the use of the supplier capacity up to a defined level. Like a reservation (it is actually referred to as a *reservation price* or *premium*) for a future order of goods from a supplier, the buyer has the option of purchasing goods up to the capacity limit for a given period of time. If the buyer chooses not to exercise the option, the reservation price payment is lost. Some options contracts can set a fixed price for the future purchase of items or allow the supplier to set a flexible price, where the supplier can charge an additional amount or price per unit (referred to as the *exercise price*) once the buyer exercises an option to purchase items. Although this approach removes some sourcing risk from the buyer, it can increase price risk if suppliers are given the flexibility to set any exercise pricing they desire.

Another risk minimizing tactic is though the use of portfolio contracts. In a *portfolio contract,* a buyer enters into multiple contracts with different suppliers. They have different prices and levels of flexibility, which allow the buyer to hedge against inventory shortages from any one supplier. By having a mixture of suppliers that offer low-price/no-flexibility/fixed-quantity contracts, average-price-with some-option-flexibility contracts, and *spot market purchasing* (that is, open market with no contractual arrangements for price or quantity), a buyer can hedge against shortages and price increases.

Although it might seem consistent with Japanese methods of supplier relations to establish long-term contracts, these tend to invite all the risks and difficulties presented in Table 4.2. Binding a firm to a long-term commitment is risky. It could lead to greater uncertainty for financial risk by wasting money on inventory that might not be needed because of declines in customer demand, network risks in shipping goods not demanded, operations risks in producing goods not demanded, greater price risks because of inevitable pricing changes over a longer period of time, higher innovation risks of obsolescence for inventory no longer demanded, and greater supplier risks in situations where long-term low prices during inflationary periods creates unfairly low prices that weaken and hurt the profitability of suppliers. However, if flexibility can be built in to a long-term supplier relationship, the mutual supply chain partners working together to help one another can eliminate many of the risk factors. Chapter 11, "Risk Management," discusses this collaboration.

4.3 Managerial Topics in Staffing Supply Chains

Chapter 3 introduced the topic of staffing, and now this section builds on that foundation by covering topics such as building teams and mentoring programs.

4.3.1 Building Teams

Many teams serve the planning and managing needs in supply chain management departments (see Table 4.3). However, team effort does not always lead to success. Teams that are poorly run have resulted in negative outcomes, such as increased costs, stress, and lower group cohesion (Lussier and Achua, 2004, pp. 263–265). In general, effective teams can be described in the context of four characteristics presented in Table 4.4 (Dunphy and Bryant, 1996; Cohen and Bailey, 1997).

Table 4.3 Types of Supply Chain Teams

Type of Team	Description
Advisory councils	Teams used to design and manage supply chain committees. Focusing on internal executive-level steering committees, customer advisory boards, and other supplier councils.
Cost management	Teams focused on supply chain cost reduction.
Customer relations management	Teams focused on building relationship with customers. They also help provide responses to customer inquiries and help solve customer problems.
Cycle-time management	Teams focused on reducing time in key supply chain processes to provide better customer service and better internal scheduling capabilities.
Information systems management	Teams focused on determining the information needs of the supply chain. They also contribute to information system design.
Inventory management	Teams focused on reducing inventory levels while ensuring an uninterrupted flow of materials. They typically include sourcing, operations, and marketing members to develop improved inventory procedures and processes.
Negotiation	Teams focused on procurement and other operations contract negotiations. They typically included cross-trained members from many departments and functional areas to ensure inclusion of those who will be impacted by the negotiation outcomes.
Product development	Teams focused on reducing the time needed to bring a product from concept to market. They usually included cross-trained members from many departments and functional areas, as well as customers.
Supplier management	Teams focused on helping suppliers upgrade their processes in engineering and manufacturing. They typically included members from production, sourcing, and engineering.

Source: Adapted from Table 14.3 in Fawcett et al. (2005), p. 445; Carter and Choi (2008), p. 166.

Table 4.4 Characteristics of Effective Teams

Characteristic of Effective Team	Description
Innovation/adaptation	Teams capable of rapidly responding to environmental needs and changes with creative solutions. They can define courses of action that are innovative and that will help adapt an organization's resources to meet the changes they are exploring.
Efficiency	Teams that enable organizations to attain goals with creative solutions, reducing resources and reducing costs to improve overall organizational profitability.
Effectiveness	Teams that can achieve superior results and can exceed customer expectations.
Employee satisfaction	Teams that can maintain employee commitment and enthusiasm for team efforts by meeting both customer goals and individual team member goals.

Source: Adapted from Table 5 in Schniederjans et al. (2010), p. 112.

How can teams become more effective? It starts with staffing the right leadership and participants and defining their roles. Leadership can guide teams and help them evolve toward achieving their objectives. Lussier and Achua (2004, p. 267) have suggested guidelines that can be used to aid teams to become more effective:

- Seek to develop trust and norm expectations.
- Seek to identify team strengths and build on them.
- Seek to place emphasis on team recognition and team rewards.
- Seek to recognize individual needs and try to satisfy them in a timely manner.
- Seek to recognize team needs and try to satisfy them in a timely manner.
- Seek to support team decisions.
- Seek to empower teams to accomplish their work.
- Seek to provide teams with work that will motivate and challenge them.
- Seek to develop team capabilities and flexibilities to deal with change.

To staff and build a team requires a basic understanding of the elements used in their creation. Table 4.5 lists a number of basic team-building elements. Team building also requires a balancing of advantages that teams bring to a firm with the disadvantages (see Table 4.6).

Table 4.5 Team-Building Elements

Team Element	Description
Goals	Teams must possess a common goal that motivates team members to focus their efforts to achieve something that is purposeful.
Leadership	Teams must be led by someone who understand team dynamics. Someone who has a vested interest in the goals being sought.
Talented members	Not everyone is a team-oriented individual. Care must be taken to select team participants who can understand the importance of the goals and can work together as a team.
Resources	Adequate information, financial backing, and time-related resources are needed to ensure team effort success.
Responsibilities	Roles and responsibilities of the team leader and members need to defined. Each member needs to be held accountable for his or her individual and team performance. Effective teams must be willing to cooperate and compromise to facilitate team success. Teams are responsible for establishing a process of identifying problems and opportunities and establishing plans to implement them.
Communication	Cross-functional communication is essential inside the team and externally with the functional areas or departments.
Measurement	Performance measurements must be established with time lines to motivate and facilitate team success. This would also include reward systems for participants.

Table 4.6 Advantages and Disadvantages of Teams

Advantage	Description
Strategy to introduce cross-collaboration	Teams can be used to bring different functional or departmental individuals together to not only deal with an issue but also to aid in helping participants learn of the advantages, knowledge sharing, and mutual issues that can be examined through collaboration.

Advantage	Description
Gains support for final solution	Teams become vested in their solution to problems or issue resolution. That builds ownership in the team participants, which can also filter down to others in the organization.
Enhances diversity	Teams can allow different people from different organizational levels to work together, offering unique and diverse perspectives not usually possible in hierarchical-oriented organizations.
Efficient task completion	A problem-solving-empowered smaller number of people representing a team and a clearer focus on a single issue can be much more efficient in dealing with a problem or issue than typical organizational structures.
Aids organizational understanding	Team members will gain a perspective of different individuals who bring their own perspectives on problem solving. This allows team members to span across departments and functional areas and see how the organization as a whole is integrated.

Disadvantage	Description
Groupthink	There is a need to be able to confront bad or weak solutions that surface in team discussion. Sometimes team members just go along with one person's idea (that is, *groupthink*) so that they don't appear to be resistant to the will of the group or argumentative. Groupthink can result is poor decision making.
Needless debate	A dominant team member can delay meaningful team progress by debating every little thing. As a result, decisions are not made in a timely manner.
Social loafing	Sometimes team members use the occasion of the team meeting to just chat with other members or do nothing but kick back and listen to other members' suggestions (that is, *social loafing*). This robs the team of the social loafer's input and can lead to less-inclusive decision making.
Social pressure	Team members sometimes view themselves as representatives of their functional area or departments. The social pressure from superiors or peers in those functional areas or departments can harden the team member's orientation to favor the social-pressure point of view. This counter acts the value of a team and leads to divisive and confrontational team behavior.
Missing link	A team might not have all the relevant members to deal with a problem or issue. For example, if a procurement problem was being solved without an essential supplier needed to provide an inventory item, the "solution" might be inappropriate, infeasible, or just wasted effort.

Source: Adapted from Table 14.5 in Fawcett et al. (2005), p. 447; Flynn (2008), pp. 101–103.

Some firms have extended their use of teams by allowing them greater autonomy through self-management. In *self-managed teams* (SMTs), the role of the leader is to facilitate processes and support team members, rather than focusing on traditional command and control functions. In SMTs, leaders set the general direction and goals, and team members make decisions on their own (and develop implementation plans). Characteristics of SMTs include the following:

- Having the authority to manage their work, set goals, plan, staff, schedule, monitor quality and implement decisions
- Members having a broad base of experience to avoid outside management but when needed expert support is included
- Coordination and cooperation to be independent of other teams and to handle their own coordination efforts
- Internal and flexible leadership where members often rotate as leaders within the team

The benefits of SMTs reported in the literature include the following:

- Employees are involved in controlling tasks whereby they are free to make original contributions and advancements.
- The leader has time for new or other planning activities.
- Employees have opportunities to learn and develop.
- Employee motivation and job satisfaction are increased.

4.3.2 Mentoring Programs

Today's lower-level manager may become a mid-level manager or even an upper-level supply chain executive. One of the best strategies to ensure adequately trained and experienced personnel exist to staff mid-level and upper-level management positions is to use a mentoring program. A *mentoring program* involves upper-level managers mentoring subordinates. *Mentoring* is a process for informal education or knowledge exposure as well as for providing psychosocial support to the recipient (that is, protégé) on topics relevant to work, career, or professional development. Mentoring involves informal communication transmitted by phone, Internet, video conferencing, or other technologies, as well as face-to-face communications over a sustained period of time, between a person who has greater knowledge or experience (the mentor) and a person who may have less (the protégé).

Roach (2011) believes that mentors act as guides to help protégés navigate workplace challenges. They provide insight to ensure mistakes are not repeated and common pitfalls are avoided. Mentors can provide opportunities for protégés to discuss ideas in a safe and trusted environment. Roach suggests that successful mentoring programs can be characterized by the following organizational factors:

- Programs should be open to all employees.
- Expectations of mentoring relationships should be understood by all participants.
- Mentor training or knowledge is needed for mentors.
- Flexibility in mentor assignments is needed.
- Confidentiality and integrity of participant interactions are maintained.
- Measurable targets are set and monitored frequently.
- Technologies are used to ensure consistency, timeliness, and frequency of interactions.

Mentoring programs not only help to provide adequately trained staff are available when needed but also increase retention rates, lessening the need for staffing in the first place (Roach, 2011).

4.4 Managerial Topics in Leading/ Directing Supply Chains

Providing leadership and directing the activities of a supply chain permits managers to set a course and guide employees along that course. The topics discussed in this section include leadership styles and obstacles and leading evolutionary change in supply chain departments.

4.4.1 Leadership Styles and Obstacles

Leadership is an integral part of the group phenomenon. There can be no leadership without followers in a group. Leadership is an influencing mechanism for guiding members of a group with a course of action to achieve specific goals. Leadership involves initiating a social structure (that is, a formal hierarchy with a leader on top). Some managers utilize a style of leadership to express their approach to leading an organization. There is considerable research on *leadership styles* (that is, a collection of leadership models and approaches used to implement leadership in an organization), and Table 4.7 describes some of the most common types. These styles can be used (and have often been used) as a model for implementing leadership in an organization.

Table 4.7 Leadership Styles

Leadership Styles	Description
Role modeling	Leaders whose image is used as a model for followers to emulate
Passion and self-sacrifice	Leaders who display passion for leading and demonstrate a willingness to make extraordinary self-sacrifices to achieve their objectives
Selective motive arousal	Leaders who are able to select specific follower motives and motivate them to be successful
Inspirational communication	Leaders who communicate messages using inspirational communications or interactions
External representation	Leaders who act as spokespersons for the organization to external organizations and supply chain partners
Image building	Leaders who are self-conscious about their image, such that their competence, credibility, and trustworthiness are perceived by followers in terms of image
Frame alignment	Leaders who can link and bring into congruence the interests, values, and beliefs of both the leader and the followers
Vision	Leaders who articulate an ideological vision based on personal values deeply held by the leaders

Source: Adapted from House and Podsakoff (1994, pp. 58–64).

Implementing a style of leadership is not without difficulties. There are always obstacles that prevent supply chain managers from managing areas of responsibility. In addition to the external reasons (for example, organizational resource constraints), some obstacles to leadership are self-inflicted by leaders themselves. Table 4.8 describes a number of these self-inflicted obstacles to leadership. They should be viewed as behaviors that can and should be avoided.

Table 4.8 Obstacles to Leadership

Leadership Obstacle	Description
Insisting on quick results	Seeking and relying on quick responses to solutions is not leadership and usually does not allow for learning or actual problem solving. In many cases, it is a band-aid approach that leads to failure in the longer term. Leaders should not expect quick results, plan for those kinds of results, or seek to force compliance with quick-result expectations.
Relying on simple solutions	Using old or simple solutions that no longer fit contemporary problems because they are more complex is a failed approach to leading an organization. Supply chains are complex, interrelated, and highly integrated. Leaders should expect to look at a supply chain as a complex system requiring complex solutions. Moreover, they should understand the application of even fairly simple solutions may have ramifications that will ripple through the supply chain. It is impossible to anticipate all of the impacts; good leaders understand this.
Inflexibility	Leaders who lack the capacity to be flexible will not be able to handle change when it is required. Using SOPs to handle new and differing supply chain problems that are not adequately covered by older polices or procedures will not optimize problem resolution. Indeed, it can result in confusion, distrust, and a loss of perceived leadership authority.
Ignorance of research	Leaders who fail to find and understand available leadership research will not be as competitively efficient as those who do. Firms often cannot solve problems because they fail to start the solution process by exploring professional organization research findings or academic research. The literature on almost any problem or leadership issue is available in substantial quantity and quality and easily available via the Internet. Many leaders fail to learn new concepts and tools that could resolve leadership problems because they do not utilize existing literature.

Leadership Obstacle	Description
Lack of leadership support	To have leadership in an organization, all managers have to support its development and application. This support has to come from executive management, mid-level corporate management, plant managers, general managers, plant production managers, plant production supervisors, or plant line supervisors.

Source: Adapted from Table 6 in Schniederjans et al. (2010), pp. 114–115.

4.4.2 Leading Evolutionary Change in Supply Chain Departments

The stable environments that supply chains historically operated in did not demand the rapid adaptation required today. The supply chain leaders who actively pursue organizational strategies that encourage developments needed to make overnight changes in supply chains will position their firms to evolve or reorganize based on up-to-the-minute world-market changes.

Supply chains and their departments need to change and evolve to meet the rapid demand shifts. Evolutionary leadership is the means to implement that change. Arnseth (2011a) suggests successful evolutionary leadership will include an orientation toward innovation, performance outcomes, a customer focus, and diplomacy. *Innovation orientation* refers to a constant reexamination of corporate activities as they relate to a firm's business model, both inside and outside. Suppliers will increasingly be asked to find applications of innovation in the performance of their missions. *Performance outcomes orientation* refers to a movement toward overall outcomes, rather than traditional contract cost outcomes. Supply management should look at the value side of things (for example, suppliers who work with a manufacturer to produce new cost-saving solutions through alternative materials or better quality) rather than just costs. The *customer-focus orientation* refers to moving supply chains into more customized networks to serve individual customers. For customers like Wal-Mart that primarily focus on a customer cost-reduction policy, the supply chain should be customized to focus primarily on just a cost-reduction objective. The *diplomacy orientation* refers to use of tact in negotiations to gain advantage or to find a mutually acceptable solution to a common problem or issue. Long-term suppliers may be needed for organizations. Being nonconfrontational and polite in negotiations is one way of being diplomatic. Although transactional partners who are meant to be short-term supply chain partners might not need the same treatment, in the longer term a firm might not know which firms will end up being long-term suppliers. It is a better policy to be diplomatic with all suppliers.

4.5 Managerial Topics in Monitoring/ Controlling Supply Chains

It is not enough to set and lead an organization's supply chain objectives. Managers must know the progress they are making toward those objectives and when corrective control is needed. The topics discussed in this section include setting up internal monitoring and control systems and monitoring external demand with market intelligence.

4.5.1 Setting Up an Internal Monitoring and Control System

The management function of *monitoring* usually refers to establishing appropriate supply chain metrics to track system performance for reporting to management. The management function of *controlling* refers to maintaining supply chain compliance based on designated metrics, which can be used to identify where a supply chain needs to be brought into compliance. Key to both functions are supply chain metrics.

Supply chain metrics literature is substantial and is organizationally specific in application. Supply chain metrics can be grouped by type of performance in various aspects and locations within a supply chain network. Some of the more typical performance areas include monitoring for control purposes of assets, cost, customer service, productivity, and quality. Table 4.9 describes some specific supply chain performance metrics.

Table 4.9 Supply Chain Performance Metrics

Type of Management Metric	Examples
Assets	Inventory turns, inventory levels, inventory number-of-days supply, obsolete inventory, return-on-net assets, return on investment
Cost	Total cost, cost per unit, cost as a percentage of sales, inbound/outbound freight cost, warehouse order picking/processing cost, cost of goods returned, cost of damaged goods, cost of service failures, cost of backorders, actual verses budgeted costs, administrative cost
Customer service	Delivery consistency, backorder cycle time, on-time delivery, shipping errors, customer complaints, completed orders, stock-outs, fill rate, overall satisfaction, overall reliability
Productivity	Units shipped per employee, units per labor dollar, order-entry productivity, warehouse labor productivity, transportation labor productivity, productivity index
Quality	Number of credit claims, number of customer returns, picking/packing accuracy, order-entry accuracy

Source: Adapted from Table 16.1 in Bowersox et al. (2007), p. 378.

To use metrics, monitoring and control systems need to be established. Unique to the supply chain they serve, these systems need to be customized to help each organization achieve its objectives. To help organizations plan monitoring and control systems, professional consultants are commonly utilized. Professional organizations are also devoted to developing monitoring and control systems. For example, the *committee of sponsoring organizations* (COSO) provides several comprehensive frameworks on guidance in enterprise risk management and internal control and fraud deterrence. The goal of this organization is to improve all organizational performance and governance while reducing the extent of fraud in organizations (www.coso.org/aboutus.htm).

Based on their frameworks, COSO suggests that effective and efficient monitoring is best achieved by

- Establishing a foundation for monitoring, including support for and by upper management, adjustments to organizational structure, and a baseline understanding of internal control effectiveness

- Designing and executing monitoring procedures that seek to evaluate control information used to address risks to organizational objectives
- Assessing results and reporting them to appropriate parties

COSO developed the framework in response to executive needs for effective ways to better control their firms and help ensure that organizational objectives related to operations, reporting, and compliance are achieved. This framework has become widely used as an internal control framework in the United States and has been adapted or adopted by numerous firms in countries around the world. COSO framework implies that five components are needed to establish an effective monitoring and control system applicable to supply chain management, as follows:

- Establishing a control environment foundation that guides the discipline and structure of the system
- Risk assessment, involving the identification and analysis of relevant risks to achieving predetermined objectives
- Monitoring control activities, including policies, procedures, and practices related to achieving objectives and any risk-mitigation strategies that are carried out
- Monitoring information and communication support for all control components at the individual employee level to ensure they can carry out their respective duties
- Monitoring external oversight of internal organization controls by management or by designated parties outside the process

Some have questioned the usefulness of the COSO system (Shaw, 2006) in light of recent U.S. government legislation, but few can deny the framework is an ideal place to begin the process of developing monitoring and control systems.

4.5.2 Monitoring External Demand with Market Intelligence

Monitoring the external supply chain partners upstream and downstream sometimes requires a more complex approach than just using metrics. This holds particularly true when examining future customer demand and how it may impact the entire supply chain.

Yet monitoring customer demand is essential to avoid waste and inefficiency in a supply chain.

In the Introduction Stage of a product life cycle (refer to Chapter 1) when demand gradually begins to increase, there are always risky situations where demand could drop off completely because a product turns out to be a market failure. Alternatively, demand could shift into the Growth Stage of the product life cycle. To manage either of these situations in the most efficient and effective manner requires market intelligence (Mullan, 2011). *Market intelligence* (MI) involves gathering and analyzing information about a firm's markets to determine opportunities and plan further strategies to deal with customer demand. Although MI is not a new approach in business, it has not been fully appreciated or fully utilized in the supply chain management field. Table 4.10 describes some of the areas where MI can be applied to support supply chain decision making and assessment.

Table 4.10 Supply Chain Market Information Analysis Applications

Market Information Analysis Application Area	Description
Supply market analysis	Gather product supply and demand information, including industry structure, profitability, and any expected trends for products or services. This would include information about all markets and market participants that might impact the supply chain. In addition, MI can be applied to all commodities in the supply chain to gather information about potential changes to products or services that are subject to market substitution risks and political risks.
Should-cost modeling	Should-cost modeling is a methodology that compares a firm's product/commodity costs with what they should be based on best industry/company information. MI for should-cost modeling is commodity specific, mainly relying on a variety of external data from private and public sources. In addition, key cost drivers such as basic raw materials and commodities (labor, metals, and so on) should be a part of the analysis. Understanding the relationship of the cost drivers with a firm's products and services can help find trigger points for supply chain management projects (for instance, projects that seek to lower purchase costs from suppliers).

Market Information Analysis Application Area	Description
Supplier assessment	By collecting information from a variety of sources (for example, public, contractually required from suppliers, new organizations, and government agencies), MI can assist in supplier assessments. This might include regular contacts with the suppliers for the purpose of collecting timely information. This information would be useful in determining ever-changing supplier capacities to serve a firm. Such information would also be collected from second- and third-tier suppliers as well.

Source: Adapted from Mullan (2011), p. 24.

Mullan (2011) suggests there are four areas where MI can be used to gain information applicable to managing a supply chain: supply market analysis, category/commodity intelligence, supplier health/performance, and financial risk management. In addition to proving product consumption and price-forecast planning information, the market analysis helps managers identify capacity changes that impact pricing and product availability to customers and trends in raw materials and currencies that could be useful for planning current and future supply chain scenarios.

The product category/commodity MI information helps identify category cost drivers, commodity should-cost models, and market inflation and deflation trends, all of which help operations decision making for product planning. One particularly important feature of this is the capacity of MI in helping identify the product life cycle, which in turn aids overall product and supply chain network planning.

Another informational dimension of MI in managing upstream suppliers is its ability to assess the financial stability and overall health of suppliers. MI helps identify how well suppliers have the capacity to deal with demand shocks and adapt to downstream supplier and manufacturing needs for growth or expansion. In this regard, it helps in managing risk that a manufacturer faces in dealing with upstream suppliers.

4.6 What's Next?

Control of supply chain operations has been tightening for the past couple of years because of the recessions in many countries. It appears that the trend is for further tightening for the foreseeable future ("Globalization and...", 2011). Factors such as the desire to cut costs have driven many firms to use tactics and strategies like outsourcing to achieve lower product costs. Supply chain departments have responded to such strategies by building longer and more diverse supply chain networks. As a result, the issue of controlling these supply chains has offered great challenges to managers. These challenges have not gone unnoticed in the literature. The Aberdeen Group ("Globalization and...", 2011) found in their survey of supply chain managers that most view the level of control and coordination with external supply chain partners has become a strategic critical success factor looking forward through the year 2015. To deal with the control issue, it is recommended that firms channel their customers' and other stakeholders' desire for visibility into a dual role. One role would be to provide information for the stakeholders and managers to use for monitoring and controlling their supply chains and other operations. Advances in mobile and other communication technologies permit monitoring of the flow of goods and services as far upstream as the first-, second-, and even third-tier suppliers through the operations transformation process to the customers. For example, customer order tracking systems, similar to those used by the U.S. Post Office or *United Parcel Service* (UPS), not only provide information to customers but can also be used to monitor *third-party logistics* (3PL) supply chain partner performance.

Other surveys suggest that an increase in control of various components of supply chains is essential going forward. KPMG International (www.kpmg.com/) has stated that with the growing number of design centers around the world and other dispersed R&D activities, there is a growing need for better governance and controls for the R&D function (Global manufacturing...," 2011). They caution that failure to do so can end up in tax disputes with various government authorities. To control costs, they predict a trend involving two cost-control actions: (1) collaborating more closely with suppliers, and (2) consolidating operations sites. Miller (2012) has forecast a similar trend in control consolidation. Some supply chain industry sectors, like warehousing, have found to be currently in fragile situations. This fragility is due to the inability to visualize what is happening across an entire supply chain network. They suggest to counter this lack of visibility firms need a centralized system of supply chain command and control.

5

Social, Ethical, and Legal Considerations

Terms

Adjudication

Alternative dispute resolution (ADR)

Arbitration

Bribery

Business in the community corporate responsibility index

Business law

California Transparency in Supply Chains Act

Commercial law

Common law

Novelette

Even when you try to comply with every governmental require-ment, it is easy to violate standards in one country while doing busi-ness in other countries. Suppliers in a foreign country might try to extort money in various difficult-to-identify (much less prevent) ways. Although governments try to prevent their businesses from acting unethically, the governments cannot be everywhere or stop industry practices that are entrenched so much so that they are the norm rather than the exception.

It's Friday afternoon on a beautiful day, and I am tired from a week full of exhausting adventures managing supply chain issues. At 3:30 p.m., I get a call from Choi, the Supply Chain Department Head who works under Pedro, the VP of Operations for the Large En-gine Division. Normally, Choi would deal directly with Pedro, but he was on vacation. Choi was very concerned about what he had discovered from a Chinese supplier and felt an urgency to report it to someone up the management chain. I was familiar with Choi and knew him well enough to be on a first-name basis.

"Bill, I am very sorry to bother you, but since Pedro is out of town and presently unreachable, I felt I should contact you about one of our Chinese 3PL supplier organizations. As you know, we work with one 3PL organization in China, using their supply chain to obtain parts we need for the large engines. It appeared for the last year to be a profitable arrangement for both of us, and particularly for supply chain efforts, since they took care of the Chinese end of the supply chain work for us. Even with the service fees we are pay-ing them, they have given us a 25% reduction in our cost of parts advantage over sources domestically, and we have been delighted with their logistics services as well," said Choi.

"Choi, that sounds pretty good. What's the problem?" I asked.

"I took a tour of their facilities recently and some of their supplier facilities to make sure that they had a handle on quality control and had the excess capacity we occasionally need to meet our cus-tomer demands. During the trip, I learned that even though our 3PL is giving us a 25% cost advantage, it turns out their suppliers are providing them with a kickback of 5% in cash. In other words, we really should be getting a 30% reduction in costs. We pay them well for their services, but they are making a sizable benefit from the kickback as well. Now I know that kickbacks are somewhat of a norm in some industries in China, but it looks unethical, and as our board of directors have launched an ethics response team to identify and weed out practices that look suspect, I wanted to make sure higher ups were aware of this behavior so that we could take an anticipatory course of action to decide what should be done, if anything," explained Choi.

"Choi, you did exactly right. Someone is always trying to line their pockets. This kind of unethical behavior is not unique to China, but happens all over, including in the United States and in Europe. We had a purchasing agent in our organization that we found was getting a kickback. We had to let him go," I said.

"Bill, what can we do about our situation now? It would not look good to have my department identified as being involved with an international kickback program," said Choi.

"Choi, you have done your job in reporting it, and now it's up to the rest of us to decide a course of action. For now, in your position I recommend you explore other 3PLs that we might be able to move our business over to in the short term. Of course, a new 3PL selection should be based with special attention to avoid another kickback situation. I will let Pedro know what I asked you to do so that he is in the loop and supporting the effort. If a change in supplier is warranted, Pedro will work with me and eventually with you to make that decision. In the longer term, we will create our own 3PL in China and staff our people over there. Of course, such an operation staffed by Caucasians are viewed by Chinese as "white ghosts," which will not be as welcomed as if we had locals working there; but perhaps if we remove the graft and other unethical practices of the operation, even if it is initially inefficient, we will be more profitable and less unethical in dealings with Chinese supply firms. As time goes on, our people will become better accepted by locals and will develop closer relationships, which in turn will permit us to command better prices," I surmised.

5.1 Prerequisite Material

This section is chiefly to acquaint less-experienced students of supply chain management with basic and elemental content and terminology. Experienced supply chain executives and managers might be tempted to skip this section in chapters where it is included, but they might instead want to use it as a review of basic concepts and terminology.

Corporate social responsibility (CSR) is defined by Svendsen et al. (2001) as "a company's positive impact on society and the environment, through its operations, products, or services and through its interaction with key stakeholders such as employees, customers, investors, communities, and suppliers." Many business organizations believe the government should regulate the environmental performance of organizations; others prefer to have the flexibility of voluntary standards. The increasing customer demand for companies to provide better environmental safeguards has pressured suppliers, manufacturers, and distributors to be responsible for environmental actions. In response, suppliers and manufacturers have attempted to produce more environmentally friendly products, establish recycling network systems, and minimize emissions to improve their reputations among customers and consumers.

What backs up CSR programs is a dual balancing of a firm's desire to behave ethically and what must be done because of legal dictates. The individuals who make up a business organization know that behaving ethically attracts customers and avoids legal problems related to issues like pollution and environmental waste. However, a CSR program can be very costly, and customers are not attracted to excessively high product prices, which a CSR program can cause. The balance between a firm's ethical conduct standards and a firm's desire not to incur substantial CSR costs is sometimes determined by government regulation. Unfortunately, government regulations often represent a low bar in constraining unethical business operations, but they are a factor and have become an increasingly powerful influence on a corporation's attitudinal change toward higher ethical conduct. The best firms exceed government regulations in order to not only avoid litigation but also to demonstrate to stakeholders that they do stand for high ethical values in the conduct of business operations.

Table 5.1 describes some of the laws and acts that have been passed that relate to supply chain management concerns. These constitute basic foundation law knowledge for all supply chain managers. On a more narrow focus, the *Institute of Supply Management* (ISM) suggests that the primary areas of legal concern that govern ethical issues applicable to supply chain management include the following (Carter and Choi, 2008, p. 266):

- *Defamation,* also called vilification, slander (for transitory statements), or libel (for written, broadcast, or published words), is the communication of a statement that makes a claim to be factual and that may give any person or thing (for example, products, brand name, company) a negative image (http://en.wikipedia.org/wiki/Defamation). For example, one supplier may falsely suggest to a buyer that a competitor supplier cannot be trusted to deliver products on time, when in fact there is no evidence to support that assertion.

- *Disparagement* is to falsely suggest a connection with persons, institutions, beliefs, or national symbols, bringing them into contempt or disrepute (http://en.wikipedia.org/wiki/Disparagement). For example, one supplier may make false statements about the brand quality of another supplier's product.

- *Bribery* is a form of corruption, an act implying money or gift giving to influence the recipient's conduct. Bribery constitutes a crime if the offering, giving, receiving, or soliciting of any item of value is offered to unduly influence the actions of an official or other person in charge of a legal duty (http://en.wikipedia.org/wiki/Bribery). For example, a manufacturer might offer a kickback to a procurement agent if the agent will do business exclusively with the firm to the exclusion of other competitors.

Table 5.1 General Legislative Laws and Acts That Can Impact Supply Chain Operations

Type of Legislative Law or Act	Description
Common law	Laws developed by judges through their decisions in courts or tribunals, rather than through legislative statutes or executive branch action. One part of common law relevant to supply chain management is the law of contracts, mainly applied to cases involving real estate or services in the United States. Common law provides the legal foundation for contracting, which is the backbone of procurement.
Commercial law	Also known as *business law* or *corporate law,* commercial law governs business and commercial transactions. It includes such laws as those governing the relationship between principal and agent; carriage by land and sea; merchant shipping; guarantees; marine, fire, life, and accident insurance; bills of exchange and partnerships; corporate contracts; hiring practices; and the manufacture and sales of customer goods.
Uniform Commercial Code (UCC) Act	One of a number of uniform acts seeking to harmonize the law of sales and other commercial transactions in all 50 states within the United States. The UCC focuses primarily on transactions involving personal property (movable property), not real property (immovable property). The UCC has achieved the goal of substantial uniformity in U.S. nationwide commercial laws but at the same time has allowed the individual states the flexibility to meet local circumstances by their modifications enacted in each state to the UCC text.
Sarbanes-Oxley Act	This act sets new or enhanced standards for all U.S. public company boards, management, and public accounting firms. The Sarbanes-Oxley Act was enacted in 2002 as a reaction to a number of major corporate and accounting scandals affecting U.S. corporations. The act does not apply to privately held companies and contains sections ranging from additional corporate board responsibilities to criminal penalties. It created a new quasi-public agency, the *Public Company Accounting Oversight Board* (PCAOB), charged with overseeing, regulating, inspecting, and disciplining accounting firms in their roles as auditors of public companies. The act also covers issues such as auditor independence, corporate governance, and internal control assessment, while requiring enhanced financial disclosure behavior.

Type of Legislative Law or Act	Description
Restraint-of-trade acts	This term refers to practices that help to ensure fair competition and in doing so uphold a free market philosophy. In the United States, four primary acts address restraint of trade: Federal Trade Commission Act (http://en.wikipedia.org/wiki/Federal_Trade_Commission_Act), Sherman Antitrust Act (http://en.wikipedia.org/wiki/Sherman_Antitrust_Act), Robinson-Patman Act (http://en.wikipedia.org/wiki/Robinson-Patman_Act), and the Clayton Act (http://en.wikipedia.org/wiki/Clayton_Act).

Source: Adapted from Carter and Choi (2008), pp. 278–282.

Suppliers act as agents for their respective buyer or supply chain customers. The *law of agency* in commercial law deals with relationships whereby a person (the agent) is authorized to act on behalf of another (the principal). The principal authorizes the agent to work on the principal's behalf, and the agent is required to negotiate on behalf of the principal (http://en.wikipedia.org/wiki/Law_of_agency). The law of agency is the legal basis for rulings concerning bribery in procurement.

5.2 Principles and Standards of Ethical Supply Management Conduct

"We operate with the highest standards of integrity and ethics."

—*Council of Supply Chain Management Professionals (CSCMP) statement of values, from the CSCMP Web site: http://cscmp.org/aboutcscmp/inside/mission-goals.asp*

Two ethics-oriented supply chain management professional organizations are the *Council of Supply Chain Management Professionals* (CSCMP) and the *Institute of Supply Management* (ISM). These organizations provide training on ethical concepts, principles, and conduct. Their certifications for supply chain managers also include a requirement of knowledge of social responsibility and ethical standards.

The ISM bases its ethical conduct behavior advocacy around three principles: integrity in decision making and actions, the need for supply chain employees to value employers, and loyalty to the supply chain profession (see www.ism.ws/tools/content.cfm?ItemN umber=4740&navItemNumber=15959). Based on these principles, ISM has established a set of standards for supply management conduct (see Table 5.2). These standards are excellent guidelines for supply chain organizations to adopt and use to develop an applicable set of standards. In addition, ISM offers training courses (www.ism-knowledgecenter.ws/KC/courses.cfm), research (www.ism.ws/files/SR/capsArticle_PurchasingsContribution.pdf), publications (www.ism.ws/pubs/journalscm/index.cfm?navItemNumber=5474) and educational materials (Carter and Choi, 2008), which are available to encourage and empower the development of an ethics program.

Table 5.2 Adapted ISM Standards for Supply Management Conduct

Standard	Description
Perceived impropriety	Avoid unethical or compromising conduct in relationships, actions and communications.
Conflicts of interest	Avoid any personal, business or other activity that conflicts with the lawful interests of the employer.
Influence	Avoid any behavior that may negatively (or appear to negatively) influence supply chain decision making.
Responsibility to employer	As an agent for the employer, seek to honestly uphold fiduciary and other responsibilities granted by the employer and do so by adding value where possible.
Supplier and customer relationship	Seek to develop and promote positive supplier and customer relationships.
Sustainability and social responsibility	Seek to encourage social responsibility and sustainability practices in supply management.
Proprietary information	Seek to protect confidential and proprietary organization information.
Reciprocity	Avoid improper reciprocal relationships or agreements.
Laws, regulations, and trade agreements	Seek to learn and obey laws, regulations and trade agreements in supply management.

Standard	Description
Professional competence	Seek to develop skills, expand knowledge, and conduct business that demonstrates competence and promotes supply chain management as a profession.

Source: Adapted from ISM website www.ism.ws/tools/content.cfm?ItemNumber=4740&navItemN umber=15959. Retrieved October 27, 2011.

5.3 Principles of Social Responsibility

ISM believes supply professionals are uniquely positioned to impact supply chains and encourage promotion of social responsibility through participation on supply chain committees, boards, and panels of governmental and nongovernmental organizations. In their management role, supply chain employees can help develop and implement social responsibility ideals and principles by inclusion and consideration of appropriate business strategies, policies and procedures.

ISM combines the principles of sustainability (see Chapter 6, "Sustainable Supply Chains") with those of social responsibility (www.ism.ws/SR/content.cfm?ItemNumber=18497&navItemNum ber=18499). Table 5.3 describes these principles of social responsibility. They can serve as a foundation for individual firms to map out their own unique set of social responsibility principles.

Table 5.3 ISM Principles of Social Responsibility

Social Responsibility Principle	Description
Business conduct	Seek an ethical philosophy in conducting supply chain business. Fundamentally, ethical behavior is expected and viewed as a critical element impacting personal, supplier, and governmental stakeholders.
Community activism	Seek to support community social responsibility initiatives.

Social Responsibility Principle	Description
Diversity and inclusiveness	For the supply based, seek greater diversity and inclusiveness in sourcing processes and in making decisions. For the workforce, seek diversity and inclusiveness to attract and retain a workforce that represents varied backgrounds, customers, and communities in which the firm operates.
Financial responsibility	Seek to use financial concepts to address allocations of funds, accurate reporting, and in the management of risk.
Health and safety	Seek to protect all stakeholders by developing procedures and methods of avoiding risk of injury, danger, failure, error, accident, harm, or loss.
Human rights	Seek to ensure human rights or status regardless of local jurisdiction issues.

Source: Adapted from the ISM Web site: www.ism.ws/SR/content.cfm?ItemNumber=18497&navItemNumber=18499. Retrieved October 27, 2011.

5.4 Measuring Social Responsibility Performance

It is one thing to establish a set of principles for social responsibility and quite another to ensure they are being implemented. Some companies use outside sources of information to determine whether social responsibility programs are working. For example, CRO Magazine (www.thecro.com/content/cr-announces-100-best-corporate-citizens-list) annually lists, in a Best Corporate Citizens list, companies that provide good corporate citizenship. It is viewed as an honor and recognition if a firm has achieved some social responsibility status in its industry and to be listed in this publication. The *Ethisphere Institute* (an organization dedicated to the advancement of best practices in ethics, corporate social responsibility, and anticorruption) is supported by more than 200 leading corporations. It also publishes a globally recognized publication that ranks contributions that firms make in the area of social responsibility and ethical behavior: *World's Most Ethical Company* (http://ethisphere.com/).

To aid in measuring social responsibility program progress, you can use a variety of performance metrics and indices (see Table 5.4). These can provide interesting information to guide results-oriented organizations to better levels of social responsibility performance.

Table 5.4 Social Responsibility Performance Metrics

Metric	Description (Web Site)
The Corporate Responsibility Index	Used to benchmark corporate responsibility performance. This index aids in integrating and improving social responsibility in operations by managing, measuring and reporting the impact of businesses on society and the environment (http://www.bitc.org.uk/cr_index/).
FTSE4Good	Used to identify Japanese companies within the FTSE Global Equity Index Series who are working toward standards of corporate social responsibility, developing positive relationships with stakeholders, and supporting and upholding universal human rights (www.ftse.com/Indices/FTSE4Good_Index_Series/index.jsp).
ECPI Ethical Index	Used to research environmental, social and governance with mainstream quantitative financial analysis. (www.ecpindices.com/Index.asp?IdSEZ=5).
Ethisphere Institute	Used to identify a ranking of organizations based on their ethical practices (http://ethisphere.com/).

Source: Adapted from ISM Web site: www.ism.ws/SR/content.cfm?ItemNumber=16738&navIt emNumber=16739; www.ism.ws/SR/content.cfm?ItemNumber=4755&navItemNumber=5511. Retrieved on October 27, 2011.

The metrics in Table 5.4 measure what a firm has done after an effort has been made, but to really manage a social responsibility program requires an ongoing measurement of progress to direct and redirect efforts as needed. One way to do this is to install an auditing process to provide feedback to managers and individuals on how well they are doing in specific areas of social responsibility. Table 5.5 describes some of the more popular auditing methods for social responsibility.

Table 5.5 Social Responsibility Auditing Methodologies

Auditing Method	Description (Web Site)
Sustainability and Social Responsibility for Supply Management: Assessment Elements and Criteria	A self-evaluative guide that surveys employees to determine their current status on social responsibility concepts and decision making throughout the supply network (www.ism.ws/Files/SR/Assessment.pdf).
Social Responsibility Maturity Matrix	A quantitative tool for assessing the current state of an organization's social responsibility efforts. Useful for auditing progressive steps toward social responsibility goals (www.ism.ws/files/SR/SRMatrix.xls).
The Fair Factories Clearinghouse (FFC) database	FFC is a nonprofit organization that seeks to support workplace compliance through the sharing of factory audit information. Its goal is to provide cost-effective Web-based information to facilitate the ability of buyers to make informed sourcing decisions. To help accomplish this goal, FFC provides a secure global database for maintaining factory compliance audit information that allows retailers and consumer brands to manage information about factory conditions. Under this system, information a company wants to share with another company can be shared, but at the same time a company's confidential information is protected. (www.fairfactories.org/).
The Global Environmental Management Initiative (GEMI)	A set of interactive tools and strategies to help businesses encourage global environmental, health, and safety excellence. Their Web site provides a forum for corporate leaders to work together, learn from each other through the activities, benchmark with peers, and create tools that can be used by others (www.gemi.org/).
The Information and Communications Technology (ICT) Supplier Self-Assessment Questionnaire	A self-assessment tool that companies can use to introduce their social and environmental expectations and engage with factory-level management in their supply chains. It consists of a multiple-choice questionnaire screening tool that can help identify labor, ethics, health, safety, or environmental issues that may require more in-depth assessments (www.gesi.org/Questionner.htm).

Auditing Method	Description (Web Site)
Social Accountability International (SAI) and the SA8 tool	SAI is a U.S.-based nonprofit organization dedicated to the development, implementation, and oversight of social accountability standards. They improve workplaces and combat sweatshops through the expansion and further development of the international workplace standard, SA8, and the associated SA8 verification system. SA8 is a tool to help apply these norms to practical work-life situations. SA8 contains eight core elements: health and safety, working hours, child labor, forced labor, discrimination, freedom of association and collective bargaining, wages, and discipline. It can also be used to audit the progress of third-party suppliers (www.sa-intl.org/index.cfm?&stopRedirect=1).

Source: Adapted from ISM Web site: www.ism.ws/SR/content.cfm?ItemNumber=4755&navItemNumber=5511. Retrieved on October 27, 2011.

5.5 Other Social, Ethical, and Legal Topics

5.5.1 Legislation: California Transparency in Supply Chains Act

The *California Transparency in Supply Chains Act* requires companies to disclose the extent of their efforts to evaluate and address the risks of forced labor and human trafficking in their supply chains. This act was passed in 2010 and implemented in 2012 to address human-rights concerns regarding human trafficking. This legislation is based on fundamental social responsibility expectations for companies to assess and respond to adverse human rights impacts associated with their activities. It is further supported by the principles espoused by the *United Nations* (UN) in *Guiding Principles on Business and Human Rights,* approved by the UN Human Rights Council in 2011.

The California Transparency in Supply Chains Act is limited to firms doing business in California and that have annual gross receipts of (U.S.) $100 million. This also includes any retailer, regardless of corporate locations, whose sales in California exceed the lesser of $500, or 25% of total sales.

The act requires a listing on corporate Web sites that details the following:

- Efforts in evaluating and addressing risks of human trafficking and forced labor throughout the supply chain
- A statement from direct suppliers certifying materials incorporated into products comply with the act and other laws in the countries where they do business
- Efforts in conducting audits of suppliers to evaluate compliance with the act
- Efforts to maintain accountability standards and procedures for employees and contractors
- Efforts in training employees and managers on the mitigation of human trafficking and forced labor risk

Similar federal legislation is being planned, so it behooves all socially responsible supply chain managers to take implementation steps now. Altschuller (2011) suggests the following steps for supply chain organizations be implemented to comply with this legislation:

- Review supply chain risks related to forced labor and human trafficking (for example, related to products consumed, services used, supplier activities) to identify possible problem areas that need correcting.
- Review internal organization polices and standards for prohibiting forced labor and human trafficking to ensure compliance.
- Review external organization supply chain partners' (upstream and downstream) organization polices and standards for prohibiting forced labor and human trafficking to ensure compliance.
- Review audit procedures to determine if independent social compliance audits are needed. This step should consider the nature and scope of the supply chain, risks of forced labor and human trafficking in partner operations, and whether existing auditing procedures are adequate to ensure compliance.

- Review accountability structures to ensure employees and partners are held accountable for compliance.
- Review training programs to ensure they are adequate to support compliance directives.

The requirements under this act for disclosure are specifically intended to provide consumers with the information they need to make purchase decisions related to these firms. For firms whose focus is on customer demand, exceptional efforts to comply with the act might lead to an exceptional customer competitive advantage.

5.5.2 Alternatives to Litigation

The undertaking of any contract involves risk taking. Most contracts and relationships between procurement staffers and suppliers run smoothly, but sometimes what takes place in those relationships creates legal issues that will involve legal remedies. Litigation is the most common method for resolving legal issues and is most suitable for multiparty disputes. Unfortunately, involving lawyers and courtroom time can be costly and may cause considerable damage to reputation and irreparable harm to business relationships. Making it worse, many contracts do not define dispute resolution procedures, complicating matters when problems do arise.

Suggested by Evans (2011) and others, *alternative dispute resolution* (ADR) processes such as mediation, arbitration, or adjudication provide effective alternatives to litigation (see Table 5.6). ADR processes are common in many countries, such as India, Australia, and the United States, which continue to provide leadership in their development and use.

Table 5.6 Alternative Dispute Resolution Methods

Alternative Dispute Resolution Method	Description	Key Points or Characteristics
Mediation	A third party, the mediator, acts as a facilitator. This method assists the parties to negotiate their own settlement. Some mediators may express a view on what might be a fair or reasonable settlement, but only if all the parties agree that the mediator may serve in an evaluative mode.	Mediation has a structure, timetable, and dynamics that ordinary negotiation lacks. The process is private and confidential. The presence of a mediator is the key distinguishing feature of the process. There may be no obligation to go to mediation. Settlement agreements signed by the all parties to a dispute may be binding on them. Mediators must be wholly impartial. Disputants may use mediation in a variety of disputes, such as commercial, legal, diplomatic, workplace, community, and family matters.
Arbitration	A proceeding in which a dispute is resolved by an impartial adjudicator whose decision dispute parties have agreed to, or legislation has decreed, will be final and binding.	Often used for the resolution of commercial disputes, particularly in the context of international commercial transactions. Frequently employed in consumer and employment matters, where arbitration may be mandated by the terms of employment or commercial contracts. Can be either voluntary or mandatory. Principal distinction from mediation is that a mediator will try to help the parties find a middle ground on which to compromise, the (non-binding) arbitrator remains totally removed from the settlement process and will only give a determination of liability (that is, in some situations an indication of the amount of damages payable).

Alternative Dispute Resolution Method	Description	Key Points or Characteristics
Adjudication	A legal process by which an arbiter or judge reviews evidence and argumentation, including legal reasoning, set forth by opposing parties or litigants to come to a decision that determines rights and obligations between the parties involved.	A quick solution process. Can be overturned by arbitration and litigation.

Source: Adapted from Evans (2011).

ADR enables both parties to preserve their commercial relationship while maintaining control during the process of dispute resolution. This keeps operations going despite these differences. Arbitration is particularly valuable with international contracts where parties are based in different countries, making legal judgments difficult to enforce. Arbitration is also conducted by someone with technical knowledge of the field and subject matter. For example, in international arbitration cases in London, arbitrators can be drawn from anywhere in the world and can be handpicked by the parties based on their experience and expertise. Also, arbitration can offer more flexibility than courts and in theory can be speedier, more efficient, and more cost-effective.

Mediation has grown tremendously in the past 15 to 20 years as a way of cutting through disputes. According to Evans (2011), it is a cheaper and quicker way of getting to a solution and has a greater than 80% settlement rate. This method also allows parties to reach an amicable agreement while maintaining ongoing relations. The focus of the process can be on the interests of the parties rather than on their legal rights alone so that other factors such as business pressures can be taken into account.

Adjudication, which is frequently used in the construction industry, is popular because it provides a quick answer. The resolver is likely to be a subject matter expert from the industry, such as an architect, surveyor, or engineer. The Construction Act of 1996 made the option of adjudication mandatory in construction contracts in the United States. Although it can be overturned by arbitration or litigation, it can also be a more economical solution because it minimizes disruption time to settlement in a long-term construction or project dispute, including supply chain project disputes.

The value of ADRs in supporting and building long-term relationships is an important critical success factor for procurement. By adding ADR to contracts, it sets up a framework that makes for more pleasant issue-resolution mechanism. Of course, for individual contracts, a dispute resolution clause has to fit in with the needs of the contract, which will differ greatly for different organizations.

Investment in dispute resolution does not have to be on a massive scale or expensive. For small contracts a focus on dispute-avoidance measures, as opposed to dispute resolution, can prove beneficial. These measures might include partnering or training staff in negotiation techniques. Partnering, for example, can be very formal and structured, forming part of an actual agreement that might include having a partnering coach and implementing team-building exercises. Alternatively, partnering can be merely agreeing to a positive early warning approach to managing the contract conflict. In summary, all of the ADR processes should be made available for the identification, investigation, and resolution of problems before they turn into disputes and before disputes turn into expensive litigation.

5.6 What's Next?

According to Monczka and Petersen (2011), a growth strategy that commits to sustainability and corporate responsibility is the trend for the near future. They believe that the major drivers found in the survey they undertook include (1) it is the right thing to do, and consistent with a history of responsible citizenship, while also (2) meeting the expectations of customers, consumers, and other supply chain partners.

One of the difficulties in implementing a corporate responsibility program in a global context is trying to make it transparent enough for management to keep track of what is going on in the program (Arns-eth, 2012a). The current trends appear to suggest that firms are presently and will increasingly step up in leadership roles to manage social responsibility programs, placing pressure on other firms to do the same. One example is IBM's Global Supply Social and Environmental Management System (www.ibm.com/ibm/responsibility/report/2010/supply-chain/index.html). Under this system, the first-tier firms that do business with IBM are now required to establish and follow IBM's management protocol system to address corporate and environmental responsibilities. IBM's suppliers are now required to

- Define, implement, and maintain a management system that addresses corporate responsibility, including supplier conduct and environmental protection.

- Measure performance and establish voluntary, quantifiable environmental goals

- Be transparent by publicly disclosing results associated with these voluntary environmental goals and other environmental aspects of their management systems

As a part of the program, IBM also expects its first-tier suppliers to communicate these same requirements to their own suppliers that perform work on products and services supplied to IBM in an effort to expand the program globally. This sets an example for the current trends in ethics and social responsibility in supply chain management.

6

Sustainable Supply Chains

Terms

ASPI Eurozone

Chief sustainability officers (CSO)

Dow Jones Sustainability Indexes

E-freight initiative

Emergy

Emergy sustainability index (ESI)

Energy Star

Green initiatives

Institute of Supply Management (ISM)

International Air Transport Association's (IATA)

International Standards Organization (ISO)

Production and Operations Management Society (POMS)

Reverse logistics

Supplier sustainability scorecard

Supply chain sustainability

Sustainability

U.S. Green Building Council

Novelette

Sustainability can mean many things. In my view, sustainable supply chains are those that maintain their supplier networks. Supply chains can survive and thrive, regardless of environmental or business changes they may experiences, if they are built to do so. The key to a sustainable supply chain is understanding and giving mutual value to both the supplier and the client firm.

Alan, the VP of the Small Engine Division, phoned me about a problem he was having. "Bill, I have had a lot of turnover in my Division suppliers during the last year. Many of them are just transactional suppliers, but we also have lost some of your key strategic suppliers as well. I have done some research on those that we have lost and found they are doing business with some of our competitors now. I discussed the matter with Takisha, our Supply Chain Department Head, and she also is concerned about the loss. It's not yet serious since we have a lot of alternative suppliers, but the number of suppliers we have lost is well above our expected value for a period of one year," explained Alan.

"Alan, have you done any exit interviews with these suppliers to find out anything about why they are leaving?" I asked.

"Yes, Bill, I have. But the responses are what you might expect. They claim it has to do with pricing and feel they are not getting a fair price for their products. Others to a lesser degree commented on a lack of communication, a lack of our participation with their organizations and several commented on the rudeness of our buyers," answered Alan.

"Stating a bad price is an easy out for them to use in ending their relationship with us. To the best of your knowledge, are they getting a fair price for their products, Alan?" inquired.

"Yes, they are. In fact, Bill, that's just it, I know they are not really getting a much better deal from the competition that they switched to," Alan said.

"Alan, the problem, then, is not pricing, but something else. How do you measure Takisha's supplier relationship management skills?" I asked.

"We use a number of criteria, but recently we have looked at the numbers of suppliers she brings onboard and how long they stay with us. Those numbers are what have been falling in the last year, which is not a good thing. I do know Takisha is concerned and wants to do what is needed to correct this problem," answered Alan.

After thinking about it for a minute or two, I commented, "There is a lot more to supplier relationship management than just the numbers you are using. You need to impart to her and her buyers that to sustain a supply chain network the effort requires a partnership where both parties can see mutual value in maintaining the relationship. There is more value from any supplier than what can be viewed from a commodity orientation. What I mean by that is that if we treat what we obtain from a supplier as just a commodity, then we can get it from anyone, and there is no additional value in the relationship other than price. If competition offers something more attractive in terms of pricing, personal contact or communication access, or when economic times get tough, they could drop us. That is not the way to build a sustainable supply chain, because there is no added value in the relationship. Mutual value is the cement that will ensure our supply chain sustainability. Building a close relationship with all suppliers should be the goal of our Supply Chain Department Heads because from that relationship added value can emerge. For example, back in 2008 when the economy tanked and our sources for steel (a commodity) dried up, several of our transactional suppliers, who were cutting back supplies from their client firms or jacking up the prices significantly, continued to supply us with what we needed at a fair and agreed-to price. Why? Not because we were a major customer, but because over a period of several years we had worked with them on joint communication and service problems. We helped them set up systems that helped us communicate with them, thus creating mutual value for all. They remembered the value enhancing work we did for them and returned the favor by continuing to sustain our production and supply chain needs in troubled times. If you want to create a sustainable supply chain, you need to create supply chain partner relationships that are lasting."

Alan replied, "Bill, I don't want to be seen like I am sending Takisha back to school to learn the basics of supplier relationship management partnering skills. Do you have any subtle suggestions on how I might broach this subject?" Alan inquired.

"Alan, I suggest you ask her if she has observed any of her buyers excelling in their respective treatment of our supply chain partners, as they should. If she doesn't have any to suggest, then that tells you how much help she needs. If she has some respectful buyers, suggest to her to use them as champions to promote respectful communication and interaction with her other buyers. The message will get through to the other buyers, who may have some problems in their treatment of the suppliers. Then, work with Takisha to develop a longer-term program that stresses the importance of all of our suppliers and how we might build value with them and for us through those interactions. Also, develop some survey measurement tools that can be sent to suppliers so that their feedback can provide some means of gauging your program's success," I suggested.

6.1 Prerequisite Material

A growing philosophy of business has emerged in the past couple of decades that suggests firms should undertake responsible steward-ship of capital, ecological, and human resources used in the produc-tion and delivery of goods to customers. The philosophy, referred to as *sustainability,* denotes that firms should meet humanity's needs without harming future generations (Christopher, 2011, p. 241). Sustainability is often referred to in a more colorful fashion as *green initiatives* or greening the organization. *Supply chain sustainability* means working with upstream suppliers and downstream distributors and customers to analyze internal operations and processes in order to identify opportunities to find alternative, environmentally friendly ways of producing and delivering products and services (Mollenkopf and Tate, 2011). It also means extending stewardship across prod-ucts' multiple life cycles to include all phases from development and introduction to final decline in demand and disposal. Krajewski et al. (2013, pp. 442–443) suggest that sustainability involves thee basic elements: financial responsibility, environmental responsibility, and social responsibility. As shown in Table 6.1, supply chain managers can make contributions in each of these three areas.

Table 6.1 Sustainability Elements

Type	Explanation	Application to Supply Chains
Financial re-sponsibility	Refers to the financial needs of the shareholders, employees, customer, business partners, financial institutions, and others who provide capital for production purposes.	Supply chains help to im-prove efficiency by improving processes, contribute to re-turn on assets, and therefore improve financial well-being of the firm.
Environmental responsibility	Refers to the ecological needs of the planet and the firm's stewardship of the natural resources used in the produc-tion and service of products. The goal is to conserve natures resources and thereby leave them for future generations to make use of.	The designs and integration of supply chains can reduce resource utilization. Recy-cling and remanufacturing programs extend available resources. Routing of delivery can reduce the use of fuel and improve efficiencies through-out the supply chain network.

		Application to Supply Chains
Type	**Explanation**	
Social responsibility	Refers to moral, ethical, and philanthropic expectations that society has of business firms.	Financial contributions to charities from supply chain partners and ethical conduct in purchasing goods can be important factors for supply chain participants.

Source: Adapted from Krajewski et al. (2013), pp. 442–443.

While some firms initiate greening their operations at an operational level (for example, reducing spoilage, remanufacturing old stock into new) many firms are recognizing and implementing sustainability as a strategic imperative. For a manufacturer or service organization, this may entail bringing many supply chain partners into a collaborative arrangement to work together to achieve sustainability throughout the entire supply chain. This collaboration alters more traditional supply chain product and information flows. Comparing the traditional supply chain Figure 1.1 in Chapter 1, "Developing Supply Chain Strategies," with the sustainability revised version in Figure 6.1, product and information flows now move forward and backward, up and down the supply chain. Customers, for example, may be asked to return products for disposal, particularly those that may pose an environmental hazard (for example, lead in batteries, products with poison components). As depicted in Figure 6.1, the ideal strategy to achieve sustainability includes all supply chain partners sharing information and products as needed.

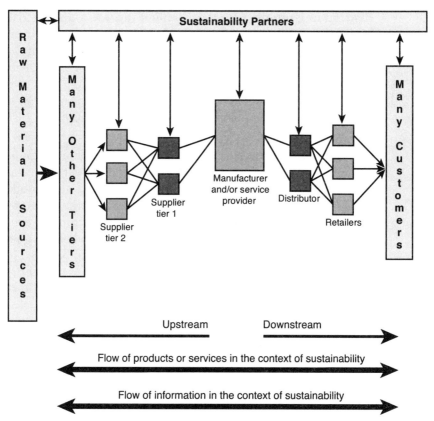

Figure 6.1 Supply chain network in the context of sustainability

Source: Adapted from Figure 5.1 in Schniederjans and Olson (1999), p. 70.

6.2 Managing Sustainable Supply Chains

6.2.1 Reasons for Sustainability

To manage programs well requires understanding and agreement with the reasons for their existence. What drives sustainability and green initiatives in organizations can actually benefit all supply chain partners. Mollenkopf and Tate (2011) suggest there are at least three reasons why firms embark on sustainability as a strategy, as follows:

- **Risk management:** Risk management involves reducing risk in all areas of a business. Such as identifying operations in business that may pose a later financial risk to a firm (for example, using toxic or hazardous materials in the production of products that may result in law suits against the company in the future) and reducing or eliminating those risks. (Risk management is an important subject that will be dealt with in Chapter 11, Risk Management.")

- **Government regulation:** Without U.S. federal regulations, automobiles would not have seatbelts to protect people, catalytic converters to reduce air pollution, increased automobile mileage to save the Earth's resources, and many other features that are commonplace today. By anticipating government regulation, many firms implement green initiates well ahead of government dictates and have found that resources can be saved in the long run, which more than compensates for the costs of the initial changes in operating systems. Indeed, recycling efforts can generate profits for organizations (Kuhn, 2012).

- **Supply chain influence:** Customers expect firms to have a friendly environmental record that provides environmental consideration in product requirements (for example, less packaging waste) and to make investments in sustainability in their facilities. Customers and other supply chain partners have a vested interest in both cost and environmental savings. Supply chain partners in one area of a supply chain can influence other partners to increase participation in sustainability programs. Most firms today embrace and comply with various *International Standards Organization* (ISO) guidelines to be competitive and in many cases as a requirement to do business. According to Mollenkopf and Tate (2011), customers seek suppliers who are environmentally responsible by using the ISO 14001 certification as a part of the selection criteria. In fact, there are four aspects of a sustainable relationship in the ISO 14001 guidelines: (1) awareness of a company's impact on the environment, (2) acceptance of responsibility for those impacts, (3) the expectation that harmful impacts will be reduced or eliminated, and (4) assignment of responsibility for environmental impacts (Haklik, 2012).

6.2.2 Implementing a Sustainability Program

There are as many different ways to launch a sustainability program as there are differing programs. To initiate one, a firm can simply identify where environmental and social-responsibility problems or opportunities exist internally within its manufacturing facilities and then expand to include the entire supply chain. In each case, an evaluation of alternative environmentally friendly ways to make improvements should be undertaken. This can be done by mapping the internal production/service processes and expanding to the external supply chain functions. Careful consideration of economic and social tradeoffs should be used to select the most desirable course of action. Once a course of action is selected and implemented, continual measurement of performance is needed to ensure that the program is achieving the right balance of environmental and social considerations.

A reverse-logistics program is an example of a sustainability program. *Reverse logistics* is a process of planning, implementing, and controlling the efficient, cost-effective flow of products, materials, and information from the point of consumption back to the point of manufacturing or origins for returns, repair, remanufacture, or recycling (Krajewski et al., 2012, p. 444). Krajewski et al. (2012, pp. 444–445) suggest that supply chains can be designed to be environmentally responsible if they plan for the entire life cycle of a product. This can be a closed-loop approach of planning that considers all processing possibilities from the product's creation to its final waste removal. An illustration of many of the features that can be used in a sustainable program are included in a combined forward and reverse logistics supply chain (see Figure 6.2). How many iterations a product or its parts may undertake in this closed-loop system will depend on a number of factors in addition to the product and participation of all the supply chain partners.

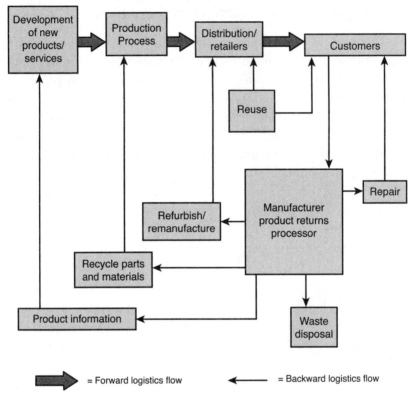

Figure 6.2 Sustainability closed-loop supply chain

Source: Adapted from Figure 13.2 in Krajewski et al. (2013), p. 445.

6.2.3 Barriers That Hinder Implementation of Sustainability

Mollenkopf and Tate (2011) have suggested several commonly occurring hindrances to sustainability programs, as follows:

- **Financial costs:** The upfront investments in waste reduction and reengineering products to be more ecologically friendly may in some industries be so substantial that firms might back away from any sustainability initiatives. This is a short-term view and often does not include consideration of longer-term benefits of such programs. Sustainability programs should be planned and analyzed in the context of the longer-term product's life cycle. Computer manufacturers have found that remanufacturing and recycling older computer components can generate substantial profits while saving the environment.

- **Corporate structure and culture:** As mentioned in previous chapters, functional silos can be an inhibiting factor to any kind of change such as programs of sustainability. It is recommended that coordinating a firm's internal structure, perhaps making it flatter and without the focus on functionality, should be a precursor to considering sustainability programs.

- **Supply chain influence:** If customers are unwilling to pay the extra costs for implementing a green initiative, resistance to sustainability can be substantial for the customer-focused supply chain. It is recommended that firms educate customers as to the benefits and tradeoffs of environmentally friendly products and services to overcome this hindrance.

- **Products and processes:** The nature of products, their design and contents, as well as the processes used to produce them can conflict with environmental goals in the areas of energy consumption and product durability. Products should be made so that they are more easily recyclable. Considering the entire life cycle of a product when it is being designed makes it easier to plan for both its use and reuse in a recycling environment.

- **Communication issues:** Inconsistent terminology and definitions of what *sustainability* means causes translation problems. Without clear definitions of effective measures and communications about environmental issues, it can be confusing. Without easy-to-measure and understandable performance information on the progress of a sustainability program, it is difficult to control and can lead to program failure. Developing a set of understandable terms and metrics of what *green* means to the firm will help participants throughout the supply chain be more effective in achieving sustainable goals.

6.3 A Model for Sustainability

In a review of multiple survey research studies, Nirenburg (2012) found a number of commonalities in supply chain practices that, when taken together, can constitute a model for sustainability. Based in part on a similar discussion presented in the preceding section, Nirenburg (2012) found a combination of three components (drivers, barriers, and enablers) forms a framework for a typical firm's sustainability supply management program. As presented in Figure 6.3, the combination of those three components will eventually lead to a variety of benefits described in the literature.

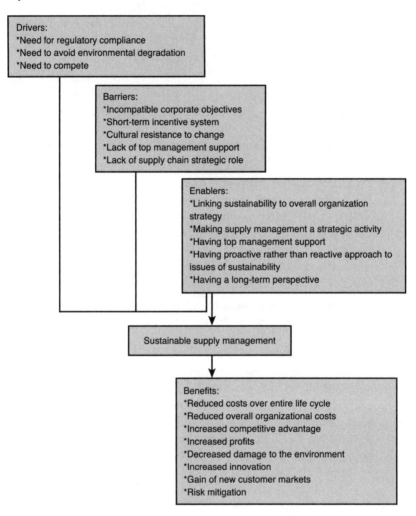

Figure 6.3 Model for sustainability

Source: Adapted from Figure in Nirenburg (2012), p. 30.

The review of research studies reveals other sustainability drivers beyond cost minimization, including pressure from employees, commitment of the founder, and championing from senior management. Barriers include cost of the program, a gap of employee skills and knowledge to implement and run a program, lack of measurement and reporting, as well as a lack of consistent standards and their implementation. Enablers are also identified in the literature that contribute to developing a successful sustainability program, including partnering with suppliers characterized as being close and cooperative, trusting, and ones that maintain transparent communications, establish effective supplier evaluation systems with rewards and penalties, use cross-functional teams, and collaborate in areas of innovation and process improvement.

To utilize this model to implement a sustainability program, Nirenburg (2012) suggests the following steps:

1. Identify sustainability champions:Regardless of who they are and in what level in the organization they reside, use them to motivate and move the program forward.

2. Conduct a self-audit of drivers:Particular issues that drive sustainability, are the best candidates to focus on and be strengthened in order to justify the program and support buying into it.

3. Find ways to mitigate barriers:Identify barriers and explore the organization for a means to counter or overcome any potential factors that act as barriers to a sustainable program.

4. Utilize other enablers:Identify any possible enabler to operationalize and maximize the outcome of a sustainable program.

The model presented in this section is a general framework for establishing criteria under which a sustainability program can be initiated. Other additional considerations have to be built in to it to ensure success now and in the longer term. Some of these topics are addressed in the following section.

6.4 Other Topics in Sustainability

6.4.1 Strategy for Achieving a Green Supply Chain

Logistics and green supply chain sustainability involve many elements, from packaging to processing time. For supply chains, time is money, and the fastest modes of distribution, particularly air transport and expedited ground freight delivery, often require the most energy-intensive efforts to serve customers. Manufacturing just-in-time modes of production are an additional requirement for speed often at the expense of energy consumption. How then does a logistics operation increase speed of delivery without a substantial cost of increased fuel usage? According to Kaye (2011), the best way to achieve a favorable balance in speed of delivery and fuel usage is by wringing out inefficient and wasteful logistics practices. Issues such as information snags, incomplete or missing data about the status of shipments, an inability to retrieve data when needed, an inability to adequately document shipment status, ill-prepared shipping documents, and inappropriate cargo routing can create huge and unnecessary waste of fuel, requiring expedited and energy-inefficient delivery to overcome delays. If you have ever seen a truck driver whose engine is running while waiting for a delivery paper to be signed, you know what wasted fuel can occur when a snag in paperwork happens.

To overcome these informational issues Kaye (2011) suggests that a supply chain founded on green principles must have comprehensive information on everything from fuel efficiency to aggregating and optimizing loads and routes that aid in the planning, which reduces the fuel consumption and carbon footprint of shippers. This information can facilitate up-to-the-minute route and load scheduling to take into account everything from weather conditions to just-in-time shipment adjustments. Taking these conditions into consideration can help avoid wasted logistic efforts when weather and other conditions cause costly delays. Starting with suppliers through the supply chain to the customer, products should be monitored using electronic tracking systems. This could involve creation of complete databases that show what is happening at every step in the supply chain. This necessitates electronic connectivity between producer, shipper, and forwarder to provide an ability to cross-check and validate progress and timings of shipments.

By using cutting-edge electronic tracking systems, manufacturers can ensure deliveries are on time and maintain proper quality. This improves both fuel efficiency and cost-effectiveness because it creates absolute shipment control at any given time. Other benefits of electronic tracking include elimination of inefficiency from physical keying or writing of routing and freight identification numbers and mistakes that force wasteful backtracking and searches.

Kaye (2011) reports that the *International Air Transport Association's* (IATA) e-freight initiative directly addresses the idea of minimizing documentation issues that waste fuel and other resources. The IATA e-freight project aims to replace 20 standard paper shipping documents with electronic documentation. The estimated result is a savings of up to $5 billion a year for the logistics industry in reduced paperwork and faster transit times, because sending shipment documentation electronically before the cargo itself arrives can reduce cycle time by an average of 24 hours (Kaye, 2011). If implemented by the industry, this initiative will eliminate the guesswork and backtracking to find misplaced shipments and affords maximum flexibility in route and load planning to minimize energy consumption and delivery problems. In turn, by saving fuel, energy, resources, and time, supply chain sustainability, based on the latest electronic technology, will give participants competitive advantages while minimizing the ecological footprint.

6.4.2 How to Begin Sustainability

According to Polansky (2012), sustainability initiatives should start by working with key suppliers to uncover ways to enhance supply chain operations and reduce the environmental footprint. These may include purchasing energy-efficient products or reducing packaging waste to increasing the percentage of purchased products made from recycled materials. Then, a list of key suppliers from major purchasing commodity groups who are willing to support sustainability initiatives should be developed. For example, at the plant level, plumbers may be able to suggest new plumbing fixtures that will save water, or local electric companies might suggest ways to reduce electricity usage. Internally, marketing and engineering departments might suggest ways to package products to avoid waste.

Once the sustainability ideas are suggested and converted into goals, supply partners should be selected that support these goals. This selection process should be based on a willingness to participate and offer suggestions to further support the organization's sustainability goals.

Polansky (2012), suggests that once well-defined goals are in place and the suppliers that will be included in the sustainability initiative are identified the firm should consider developing a *supplier sustainability scorecard* to measure performance based on sustainability criteria (see Kuhn, 2009). These scorecards can be assessed based on subject criteria (for example, sustainable idea innovations) or objective criteria (for example, reduction in cost of packaging). Creation of a scorecard gives both the purchasing group and the supplier a way to identify, track, and measure activities considered important for achieving a company's sustainability goals.

Invariably, the issue of price versus value comes up in any procurement program. Normally, price would weigh heavily on the supplier decision, but not so when considering a sustainability program. In a sustainable supply chain, this relationship is still important, but the weight is heavier toward longer-term considerations, such as energy saving offsets, tax incentives, life cycle and maintenance costs, reduced disposal costs, reduced waste, and productivity improvements.

As is the case with sustainability programs, higher upfront costs need to be understood by all partners. The best way to deal with the issues that will emerge from this cost fact of is to provide information to make defend green decisions. Polansky (2012) suggests procurement professionals should fully discuss any questions regarding cost-benefit analyses, life cycle costs, and recycling options with their key suppliers. Suppliers will need to know and be able to explain their products and life cycle costs. By probing suppliers for more cost and environmental options information, procurement managers will gain better insight into the bottom-line impact of sustainable purchasing, as well as potential better insight into impacts on product obsolescence, hazardous-material handling, and overall waste reduction. During these discussions, procurement professionals are more likely to identify suppliers that can work with them to genuinely implement green solutions. These suppliers can also help identify and prioritize green operational projects.

Supply professionals should also ask about internal green practices or programs that partners have undertaken. Working with suppliers who have implemented sustainable strategies helps ensure that suppliers have an understanding about the customers' needs. Finally, it will be beneficial to look for industry involvement, such as a firm being a member of the *U.S. Green Building Council,* a Washington, D.C.-based 501(c)(3) nonprofit organization committed to a prosperous and sustainable future through cost-efficient and energy-saving green buildings (www.usgbc.org/DisplayPage.aspx?CMSPageID=124) or having certification with *Energy Star,* a joint program of the U.S. Environmental Protection Agency and the U.S. Department of Energy helping to save money and protect the environment through energy efficient products and practices (www.energystar.gov/index. cfm?c=cbd_guidebook.cbd_guidebook_apply_3). Suppliers that have made investments in organizations like these validate their own sustainability position and tend to keep up with the latest industry information.

In summary, identifying appropriate partners and establishing key action items are helpful first steps in building an effective sustainable supply chain. What can result is a close collaboration that benefits all. Once procurement managers have a sense of how their suppliers can help, they can begin to create solutions that make sense for their business (Polansky, 2012).

6.4.3 Factors to Build on for Sustainability

Slaybaugh (2010), reporting on a larger study by the Boston-based Aberdeen Group "Sustainable Production: Good for the Plant, Good for the Planet," explored the status of sustainability intentions of more than 230 enterprise initiatives. Among the enterprises surveyed, clues as to the best-in-class that were making measurable steps toward sustainable production were identified. They found the best-in-class performers averaged over 80% with regard to equipment effectiveness (that is, a composite metric accounting for availability, performance, and quality), over 20% in energy-consumption reduction, at least 30% reduction in emissions versus the previous year (as measured by the year-over-year change in emissions controlled for year-over-year changes in production output normalized by energy intensity of the production processes), and almost 20% outperformance of corporate operating margin goals. In addition, best-in-class manufacturers were three times as likely to have appointed a chief sustainability officer.

The Aberdeen Group study also identified what firms could do to become best-in-class performers. They found four primary guiding principles contributed to the best-in-class performers:

- Seek visibility into energy and emissions data by investing in energy management and environmental management solutions. For example, establish a corporate supply chain management responsibility team as Del Monte did, consisting of vice president and director-level executives across functional teams. The company is also planning green plant teams made up of plant-floor employees.
- Seek to clearly outline the company's sustainability programs. The best-in-class companies are more likely to have standardized business processes in place across three major initiatives of sustainability: energy, environment, and safety.
- Seek to install a framework of data collection to support sustainability. The best-in-class performers are more likely to automatically collect energy data and store it in a central location. For example, Del Monte invested in a solution that collects information regarding sustainability programs every month and then compares it with the company's baseline year.
- Seek to establish an executive leadership framework. Successful sustainability initiatives require executive leadership support. Best-in-class organizations were found to be much more likely to have *chief sustainability officers* (CSOs) in place to execute, drive, and have responsibility for the success of initiatives.

6.4.4 Measuring Sustainability

A 2011 survey reported by ProPurchaser.com (www.propurchaser.com/green_supply-chain.html) examined the greening of production operations. They found a greener supply chain was definitely preferred, but it appeared measurement tools were lacking to aid these initiatives. Over 80% of the supply chain professionals in the survey responded by saying they would favor suppliers with green business practices, but only 25% had any type of carbon footprint evaluation process in place. To fill this gap, supply chain organizations like the *Institute of Supply Management* (ISM) have developed a variety of indices and metrics useful for measuring sustainability.

ISM incorporates corporate social responsibility with sustainability. The Institute of Supply Management's (2012) educational guidelines suggest the following indices might serve as useful measuring tools:

- *ASPI Eurozone* (Advanced Sustainable Performance Indices) is the European index of companies and investors wishing to commit themselves in favor of sustainable development and corporate social responsibility based on 120 best-rated companies in the Eurozone.
- *Dow Jones Sustainability Indexes* are the first global indexes to track the financial performance of leading sustainability-driven companies worldwide. They provide asset managers with reliable and objective benchmarks to manage sustainability portfolios.

The ISM also suggests practitioners consider impact, influence, and positioning when selecting and developing metrics. ISM developed a listi of areas for possible metric applications, including the following:

- Supplier qualification and certification decisions
- Product design, redesign, and statements of work
- Training to ensure understanding of decisions related to sourcing, recycling, and so forth
- Internal development, quantification, and basing decisions on financial and other risks related to nonconformance with or lack of support of sustainability initiatives
- Recordkeeping status on corporate sustainability reporting
- Measurement, tracking, and reporting mechanisms embedded at the worker level
- Implementation of end-of-life product management policies and procedures internally and with suppliers

In addition, ISM recommends senior management be engaged across the organization to ensure appropriate governance structures are in place; they also suggest making the CSO's contact information publicly available. It is also suggested that periodic reports on sustainability be released internally and in the marketplace to permit further transparency of sustainability activities.

Beyond guidelines for sustainability, there are a variety of quantitative ways to measure it. A theoretical approach has been offered by Brown and Ulgiati (1999), who published their formulation of a quantitative *sustainability index* (SI). This index is a ratio of the *emergy* (spelled with an *m*, that is *embodied energy*, not simply *energy*) *yield ratio* (EYR) to the *environmental loading ratio* (ELR):

$$\text{Emergy Sustainability Index (ESI)} = \frac{\text{Emergency yield ration (EYR)}}{\text{Environmental loading ratio (ELR)}}$$

Called the sustainability index, the *Emergy Sustainability Index* (ESI) accounts for yield, renewability, and environmental load. "It is the incremental emergy yield compared to the environmental load."

Many quantitative metrics for sustainability consist of very simple measures:

- Percent purchases from sustainable sources
- Percent of waste diverted from landfills
- Energy reduction caused by greening a building
- Recycling rates as a percent of total waste
- Percent of suppliers undertaking sustainable programs
- Percent of scape waste reduction
- Dollar investment in sustainability training, programs, initiatives, etc.

Many additional sources of information on sustainability and how to measure it are available:

- Green Office Guide:www.greenbiz.com/toolbox/reports_third. cfm/LinkAdvID=22121www.greenerchoices.org/eco-labels
- Responsible Purchasing Networkwww.responsiblepurchasing. orgwww.energystar.gov/
- US Green Building Councilwww.usgbc.org
- Center for a New American Dreamwww.newdream.org/ procure
- For specific chemicals and alternatives:Inform (www.informinc. org)Green Seal (www.greenseal.org)Scorecard (www.scorecard.org/chemical-profiles/index.tcl_)

6.5 What's Next?

Not all firms view sustainability as critical, but it appears they will in years ahead. According to a survey of more than 700 CEOs of major corporations, over 90% believe sustainability issues are critical to future success ("A New Era...," 2010). Almost 90% of the CEOs believe they should integrate sustainability throughout their supply chains, but only 50% believe they can achieve such integration. The gap between these percentages reflects the anticipated difficulty in selling sustainability to supply chain organizations. Regardless, the present trend for sustainability programs is one of growth. According to CAPS Research, whose findings are translated into guidance for senior supply chain managers, environmentally sustainability supply chains are necessary to deliver future value and performance improvements (Monczka and Petersen, 2011). A further institutionalization of sustainability is reflected in academic organizations such as *the Production and Operations Management Society* (POMS), which has created the *College of Sustainable Operations.* This college holds annual meetings on sustainability, developing curriculums and other educational support for this subject. Many other organizations are devoted to sustainability. Some of the more common Web sites for organizations devoted to sustainability in business includes the Business of a Better World (www.bsr.org/), Network for Business Innovation and Sustainability (http://nbis.org/about-nbis/profitable-sustainability/), and GreenBiz.com (www.greenbiz.com/section/business-operations).

7

Aligning Supply Chains to Meet Life Cycle Customer Demands

Terms

Affiliate joint ventures

Collaborative planning, forecasting, and replenishment (CPFR)

Consensus forecasting methods

Delphi method

Demand planning

Electronic point of sale (EPOS)

Equity strategic alliance

Joint equity swaps

Joint ventures

Market research

Mean average deviation (MAD)

Mean square error (MSE)

Nonequity strategic alliance

Qualitative forecasting methods

Quantitative forecasting methods

Regression forecast methods

Simulation forecast methods

Strategic alliance

Supplier alignment

Supplier integration

Supply chain synchronization

Synchronous manufacturing

Technology swaps

Time series methods

Voluntary Interindustry Commerce Standards Association

Work-share agreement

Novelette

Aligning supply chain capabilities to product life cycle demands is essential to supply chain success. Any mismatch between the customer demand stages of a product's life cycle and a supply chain's capacity to match it results in wasteful and costly effort. The key to matching the demand and supply chain capacity is found in an area of demand management called *sales and operations planning* (S&OP).

I received an email from Jessica, our VP of the Tools, Hardware, and Construction Materials Division. She mentioned that some of our franchised hardware stores, as well as external customers who retail our tools and hardware, had started reducing our shelf space and subsequently the size of their inventory orders for our retail products in those two areas. While the size in the reduction of orders was not significant, it was having an impact on our production and supply chain planning. As a result, I phoned Jessica to discuss the matter. "Hi, Jessica, given the economy right now is doing okay, I was wondering if the nature of the reduction was related to the life cycle of those products. When was the last time we revised some of the products whose sales are slipping?" I asked.

"Bill, I have been working here for over ten years, and none of the products have had even a packaging change. They have become staples of our product lines, and when you have something that works well, change is not always justified. Only recently did sales start slowing down. The marketing people have felt the products were doing fine and didn't need a facelift," commented Jessica.

"Jessica, have you ever gone into a house and it looked like it was 20 or 30 years old because of its furnishings or wallpaper?" I inquired.

"Yes, Bill, I have. In fact, I live in one of those types of homes. I just haven't had the time to upgrade my wallpaper or paint the house," Jessica replied.

"I understand, and I am sure you have been too busy doing a great job for our organization to update your home. My point in mentioning the impact of something looking older is that our customers don't want to fill their shelves with products that look old, even if they are great products. Sometimes changes, big changes to the product or small packaging changes might be a good strategy to reinvent and refresh our products, making them more noticeable again and hopefully, could generate more sales. The marketing people refer to this as moving the product back up its life cycle to a prior stage to make sales more vigorous. In addition, the refreshed products can be perceived as being newer and up-to-date by our retailing customers, motivating them to give us back our shelf space. Now all of this may sound great, but it may not be the solution we need. The fact is, unless we know where the products are positioned in their stages on their life cycles, it is not possible to really align our production and supply chains to support them. For example, we have on occasion not identified a decline stage trend fast enough and we got stuck with obsolete inventory that wasted labor and materials. In other situations, we predicted a Decline Stage for our product and didn't produce enough to satisfy the continual Maturing Stage demand that we didn't think was out there," I explained.

"Bill, we usually do the product life cycle planning during the monthly S&OP process, don't we?" inquired Jessica.

"Yes Jessica, and while each Division does things a little differently from the others, because of their product lines, it is important to have the right people working together during the S&OP process. I know you have sales and operations people together for your meetings, but you should also include your product design people, engineers, and marketing people. As you know, we also have the CEO participate in leading the process on occasion due to its importance in driving activities in the organization for the next month. Make your people come together and agree on what products they plan on launching that month, and which products are in the Growth, Maturity or Decline Stages of their product life cycles. The outcome should be forecast demand information that goes into your demand management system, which in turn drives all the operations for your Division. The more data, judgment, or marketing intelligence you can get in that meeting where members can debate, talk, and argue things through, the better will be the final plan that everyone can get behind for the next 30 days. Then, put that plan forward and the following month make adjustments as needed. Hopefully, those should not be major adjustments. Ultimately, the S&OP drives the supply chains, as well permits a close alignment with actual customer demand," I commented.

7.1 Prerequisite Material

Demand fluctuations that are not anticipated from forecast expectations are a constant challenge for supply chain executives. In the Introduction Stage of a product's life cycle, customer demand is at best a risky situation, particularly for new types of products that have no history from which to forecast accurately. In the Growth Stage of a product life cycle, there are also risks. Sometimes a rapid growth in demand can signal a positive event and a successful product. Unfortunately, too rapid growth can have negative impacts on a supply chain. When growth in demand exceeds the capacity of a supply chain to handle the needs of customers, it offers a great challenge to chase after the demand. Also, as a product enters its Maturity Stage, there is some stability in supply chain planning, but as demand levels off there are pressures to reduce costs in an effort to increase sales. If the product's sales suggest it is in a Decline Stage, other complications occur in planning the discontinuance of a product. Supply chain managers must be able to align and realign resources to meet the unique demand requirements of all stages of a product's life cycle. The more closely those resources are aligned with actual customer demand, the more efficient and effective the supply chain.

What causes unexpected variations in demand can include a variety of factors. Promotional actions (for example, reduced pricing, special product offers), competitor actions (for example, increase product prices) and newly introduced products that take off beyond what is expected (because there is no history on which to base a forecast) can all lead to unexpected variation in customer demand.

A prerequisite planning effort to anticipate and prepare for the possibility of variations from planned to actual demand is called demand planning. *Demand planning* is concerned with fulfillment of customer demand. From the perspective of supply chain management, this involves knowing the customer's product needs and when and where needed. This involves forecasting efforts to project customer requirements and installation of control measures to ensure the customer is in fact receiving the products and services they need. Basically, the demand planning can be divided into three functions: structures, processes, and control (see Table 7.1). The planning structures require understanding each product's demand time horizon so that each phase of demand (over the product's life cycle) can be matched with supply chain capacity capabilities. This includes consideration of demand in geographic areas where demand is distributed from supply chain partners (into and out of manufacturers, distributors and so on), as well as supply chain considerations for aggregating product lines for logistic reasons (for example, shipping full truck loads of multiple products from a single product line).

Table 7.1 Demand Planning Functions

Demand Planning Functions	Elements to Be Considered
Planning structures	• Timing dimension: The time horizon of forecast demand
	• Product dimension: The product types, supply chain capacities to produce and deliver product, and aggregation into groups and disaggregation into unit demand
	• Geographic dimension: Grouping demand by regions, by supply source (for example, distribution centers, manufacturing) and grouping by key customer accounts
Planning processes	Statistical forecasting
	Judgmental forecasting
Planning control	Forecast accuracy metrics
	Aligning resources to meet with forecast exceptions

Source: Adapted from Kilger and Wagner (2008), pp. 133–160.

Once the product and geographic distribution of demand are understood, a process to generate the forecasts must be selected. We can divide forecasting methods into two types: quantitative and qualitative. *Quantitative forecasting methods* are based on mathematical formulas. Commonly used quantitative forecasting methods include time series analysis, regression analysis, and simulation. Common *qualitative forecasting methods* are based on judgment, opinion, experience, consensus, and other subjective measures. They can include the Delphi method and market research. *Time series methods* are statistical forecasting techniques that use historical data to predict the future. There are many time series methods such as moving average, weighted moving average, exponential smoothing, regression analysis, and Box Jenkins technique, to name a few. *Regression forecast methods* attempt to develop a mathematical relationship between demand and the factors that cause it in an effort to explain why the relationship behaves the way it does (for example, competitor pricing, economy). *Simulation forecast methods* are used in decision making (for example, forecasting) under risk, where variables that impact customer demand follow a probability distribution (for example, likelihood of high demand during economic properous times versus low demand during downturns in the economy). Simulation forecast methods allow the forecaster to make assumptions about the condition of the enviroment that impact customer demand. *Market research* is a systematic forecast approach using field surveys or other research methodologies to determine what products or services customers want and will purchase and to identify new markets and sources of customers. The *Delphi method* involves obtaining insightful judgment and opinions from a panel of experts using a series of questionnaires to develop a consensus in forecasting.

Which methodological process can be used will depend on the environmental aspects of a decision situation and on the particular planning task. For example, different approaches may be appropriate for different stages of the product life cycle. At the preproduct development Introductory Stage, the Delphi method or market research forecasting techniques may be the more appropriate means of analyzing forecast demand trends. In the life cycle Growth Stage, where rapid demand growth is experienced, quantitative methods for short-term forecasting (for example, averaging or exponential smoothing averages) may be appropriate, whereas the market Maturity Stage of the life cycle might require the use of regression models to estimate trends and longer-term cyclical variation. Where customer demand forecasts are inputs to decisions about inventory in the supply chain, the forecasting horizon is often short term, and historical in-house data might be used. In contrast, when customer demand forecast is used as an input to a capital investment decision such as a plant or machinery, the forecasting horizon is longer term, and the forecast may be qualitative rather than quantitative. Supply chain managers often utilize a combination of qualitative and quantitative methods in these situations.

Once the forecasts are prepared and released to management for implementation, planning control activities should be undertaken. These include monitoring the forecast values against actual demand behavior on a continuous basis. These accuracy measures can be simple variance statistics that are integrated into management information systems or *enterprise resource planning* (ERP) systems. Commonly used variance statistics in forecasting accuracy metrics include the *mean average deviation* (MAD) (that is, the mean difference between actual and forecast demand) and *mean square error* (MSE) (that is, mean squared difference between actual and forecast demand). Many firms establish a simple unit difference threshold (that is, minimum unit demand needed to denote a problem or justify the continuance of a product) to bring attention for corrective action. Because of the number of products most supply chain managers handle, information systems use measures like these to trigger exception reports to the appropriate manager and even the appropriate outside supply chain partner. If exceptions like rapid growth are observed from the planned forecast, actions are taken to align supply chain capacity to meet the spurious demand requirements.

7.2 Demand Planning Procedure

Before supply chain managers can align their resources to serve customers, they must learn what customer demand will be. This demand information can be derived by the demand planning procedure suggested in Figure 7.1.

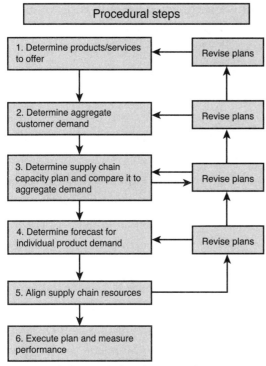

Figure 7.1 Demand planning procedure

The steps in this procedure can be characterized as follows:

1. **Determine products/services to offer:** Factors to consider include products or product lines that are new products in the Introduction stage of their product cycle and others in a Decline Stage that are being discontinued or eliminated. The same is true of services offered in supply chains to partners. This step seeks to determine the types of products/services to offer. Extending from strategic planning percentages in expansion or contraction of a firm, aggregate planning of customer demand can begin from a simple percentage increase or decrease in total product/service offerings. This step is heavily dependent on marketing intelligence and executive judgment to guide the selection of new products that will be winners and older products that will be losers.

2. **Determine aggregate customer demand:** Based initially on statistical forecasts, but modified by judgmental input, total expected demand is estimated. The idea is to come up with a general expectation of total product/service demand that can be used to guide longer-term decisions for the organization as a whole (for example, office and facility leasing requirements, total labor needs). This would be the aggregate demand plan for the entire organization.

3. **Determine aggregate supply chain capacity and compare it to aggregate demand:** This step requires an estimation of aggregate supply chain capacity capabilities. This is accomplished by auditing supply chain partners from historic behavior in contractual partnerships. This step is tied to the procedure discussed in Chapter 1, "Developing Supply Chain Strategies" (refer to Figure 1.7 from Chapter 1), on developing supply chain strategies. The components of this step are further delineated in Figure 7.2. This permits decision making at an aggregated level of planning. Planning decisions, like increasing total staff by some percentage for growth or the acquisition of new facilities, can be supported by the information gleaned at this step in the procedure. This may be necessary because of capacity limitations to revise the aggregate demand estimates down or even to reduce the number of products the firm is planning on offering. One of the methodologies that can be used to compare aggregate demand with aggregate capacity is rough-cut capacity planning (See Jacobs et al., 2011, pp. 244–253).

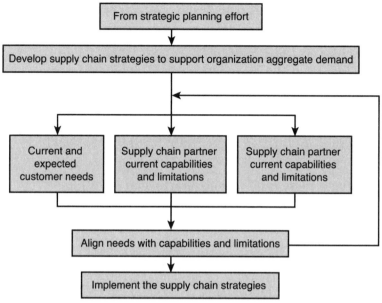

Figure 7.2 Determining the supply chain capacity plan

4. **Determine forecast for individual product demand:** To plan any product's future demand requires disaggregation down to a product line and to the individual product. This is because of the nature of a product's life cycle that impacts product demand. As explained in Chapter 1 (see Figure 1.5), aggregate product demand can be made up of many individual products in various stages of a life cycle. Adequate forecasting for purposes of aligning supply chain resources often requires individualization of product demand. Computer generated statistical estimations are commonly used here. In addition, subjective methods are often used to update and adjust statistical forecast values of customer demand. The greater the need for judgmental adjustments to forecast demand, the greater is the effort invested to ensure accuracy. In this step, it is not uncommon to use *consensus forecasting methods* (that is, a group of experts pool opinions on forecast demand values). The outcomes of all these estimations are the necessary forecast values of individual product and product-line customer demand.

5. **Align supply chain resources:** This step begins by disaggregating the aggregate supply chain capacity from step 3 and relating or allocating it to fulfill the individual product demand requirements from step 4. The alignment might require a revision in all of the prior steps depending on the ability of the supply chain planners to meet the individual customer demands. Suggestions on how to align supply chain resources will be discussed in the following sections of this chapter.

6. **Execute plan and measure performance:** After the supply chain resources have been aligned to achieve specific objectives, the plan to meet customer demand should be launched. In addition, short-term metrics should be established, data collected continuously, and results monitored to compare planned versus actual performance.

How often this demand planning procedure is repeated depends on the firm planning policies and the volatility of demand in the industry. It is advisable to have supply chain managers meet with sales and other operations managers frequently (for some firms weekly) to discuss market demand and capacity planning alignment issues.

7.3 Aligning Supply Chain Resources

Aligning supply chain resources can be viewed internally and externally. Alignment of a firm's internal supply chain resources refers to the alignment of the organization's own internal resources. It is expected supply chain managers will do so within the context of improving efficiency of their own operations. In most of the literature, the topic of alignment of supply chain resources is focused externally on the partners that make up the supply chain network that the organization uses. While both internal and external organization alignments are important, our discussion focuses mainly on the external supply chain partners and how their efforts help align the external supply chain, which consequently impacts the internal operations of supply chain organizations.

7.3.1 Alignment and Integration

According to Siegfried (2011), *supplier alignment* is defined as the alignment of the supply organization's and the supplier's vision, goals, and strategies to ensure consistency of direction and objectives. The definition for *supplier integration* is a management activity that combines resources and capabilities of supply management with those of key suppliers to achieve a competitive advantage. When you align and integrate at the same time, you can develop a powerful competitive advantage. This can be accomplished by suppliers who align their business strategies, visions, and goals with the firms to which they provide supplies. Under this scenario, as supply management firms grow, so too do their suppliers. Some of the tactics to implement this approach include building relations, roadmapping technology, and seeking a good fit with suppliers:

- **Building a relationship:** A *work-share agreement* (that is, suppliers agree to produce a product that is interchangeable with those manufactured by the supply management firm that employs them) can be a useful tool in developing an aligned and integrated strategy. By closely sharing production and engineering information, firms like Rolls-Royce are aligning their production capacity for longer-term business strategies and building a workable base for further collaboration (Siegfried, 2011). Rolls-Royce understands and works with some of suppliers to help them deal with the cyclical nature of their workload. This permits Rolls-Royce to help balance the suppliers workload during their up and down demand periods and thus strengthens them. This is important to Rolls-Royce because of the need for capacity over the longer term of products whose life cycle is substantially longer than most.

- **Roadmapping technology alignment:** If suppliers are to serve their customers, a commitment requiring close integration and alignment of technology is essential. For suppliers who want to align themselves with a supply management firm, the supplier should demonstrate commitment by investing in technology that enhances communication. This requires the supply management firm to ensure the supplier's business model and business strategy is aligned with them and that the supplier has the financial stability and capabilities to afford the investment and maintenance. Equally important is a commitment from the supplier to invest in growth to support the supply management customer. Siegfried (2011) reports that Rolls-Royce does all this by working closely with suppliers to get them to agree to an integration technology plan. The alignment with suppliers involves roadmapping the timing of technology investments for all partners to ensure information sharing and understanding of where each organization is going in terms of technology investments.

- **Seeking a good fit with the supplier's business model:** Some suppliers seek a quick turnaround on products they produce on a transactional basis; others have a business model where longer-term relationships are essential to reap the financial benefits needed to make a relationship worthwhile. Some suppliers invest in dies that are disposable and used for a single production run and are then discarded. Other suppliers invest in dies that are more costly and are engineered to last decades. The business model of a supply management firm should be aligned with the business model of the suppliers for the type of products and services they require. There has to be a good fit between the business models of the supply management firm and their suppliers.

Aligning and integrating the supply management firm with their suppliers can be time-consuming and costly, but also can have many benefits. Some of the benefits reported in the literature include improved delivery, elimination of waste, improved innovation, lower costs, improved supplier stability, quality improvement, and better risk management (Siegfried, 2011).

7.3.2 A Technology Approach to Aligning Supply Chain Resources

Software technology exists to support the communication that is vital to aligning supply chains in a timely manner. *Collaborative Planning, Forecasting, and Replenishment* (CPFR) (also mentioned in Chapter 2, "Designing Supply Chains") is software that seeks to integrate supply chain partners, including their customers (Jacobs et al., 2011, pp. 46–52). It was developed by *Voluntary Interindustry Commerce Standards Association* (www.vics.org/) to improve the competitiveness of retailers in fast-paced demand situations in terms of both cost and delivery performance. CPFR seeks to reduce the variation between supply and demand for individual products by making organization changes. The software seeks to change both customers and supplier partners to improve communication and collaboration by aiding in the development of new business processes for creating forecast information so that it can be shared on a daily basis. This software helps trading partners work together to reduce forecasting errors and increase product availability by improving the synchronization within a supply chain for inventory replenishment. In addition to building trust with supplier partners, this software is credited with reducing inventory and improving in-stock product availability (Sherer et al., 2011). To successfully implement this kind of system requires a commitment to cooperate with supply chain partners in planning, sharing information, and a coordinated fulfillment strategy. The software actually forces collaboration of partners. In doing so, it permits timely information to everyone to coordinate resources and align them to better serve customers throughout the supply chain.

By using CPFR, timely information allows supply chain partners to update inventory information for replenishment, saves sales, provides better delivery services, and allows partners to align inventory resources more efficiently. Also, the constant updates on forecasts and the ability for collaborative help to generate consensus forecasts are of benefit throughout the supply chain. This permits partners to align and realign production and supplier based decisions avoiding waste in production and unwanted inventory.

7.3.3 Synchronization of Supply with Demand

Goldratt and Cox (1984) espoused the notion of *synchronous manufacturing*, which refers to the production processes working in harmony to achieve a profit goal for the firm. The idea is that when an entire manufacturing facility and its processes are synchronized, the emphasis can be on total system performance and not on optimizing individual components, which might suboptimize the overall performance of the facility.

Supply chain synchronization means all elements that make up a supply chain are connected and move together to avoid waste and achieve timing requirements for all partners (Christopher, 2011, p. 141). In the same way that two people can dance beautifully together, so too must the partners in a supply chain move together to achieve service performance objectives. The way firms are connected in supply chains is through information sharing. The kind of information shared includes customer demand and supplier capacity information. To achieve the needed degree of information visibility and transparency requires substantial process alignment of communication technologies and a willingness of all partners to share necessary information upstream and downstream.

Several tactics can be used to help implement a synchronous supply chain strategy:

- Set early identification of shipping and replenishment requirements
- Ship smaller shipments, but more frequently
- Look for ways to consolidate inbound shipments
- Implement *quick response* (QR) logistics supported by technology (for example, bar coding, *electronic point of sale* [EPOS] systems with laser scanners) to speed information from customers to manufacturers and other suppliers

A synchronized supply chain is both responsive to the customer and to supply chain partners. While making the product available to the customer, this strategy minimizes the amount of inventory, providing immediate information and an ability to quickly identify where the supply chain needs alignment to better serve the customer.

7.3.4 Strategic Alliances and Alignment

A *strategic alliance* can be defined as a temporary agreement between two or more organizations that have a joint interest in accomplishing a specific task. They are willing to pool some resources to analyze the task. A strategic alliance is a generic phrase encompassing most forms of collaborative relationships. Although many relationships are not technically considered an alliance (for example, supplier-purchaser relationship), they can become an alliance when both parties incur some form of risk (for example, financial loss, quality image risk) connected to their strategically important interests. Strategic alliances are meant to be flexible agreements (almost relational rather than contractual) to permit both parties to work together on a particular problem or issue. They are a means by which differing types of businesses, governments, and even competitors can temporarily join financial, technological, process, and personnel resources to permit a common problem, issue or complication to be studied.

There are two types of strategic alliances: nonequity and equity. A *nonequity strategic alliance* involves little investment of financial equity. Examples include two firms entering into an R&D cooperative effort or consortium (for example, designing a new product for both firms), making *technology swaps* (for example, trading technology between firms that own patents and want to avoid paying royalties), entering into a joint product development agreement, or having informal alliances that bring staff together from differing firms to study supply chain problems.

An *equity strategic alliance* is a more formal agreement that involves a substantial commitment of equity (for example, financial, technology, property) from both parties. It is often more enduring and tends to be focused on results. These alliances are often structured with complex legal and contractual agreements. Examples of an equity strategic alliance might include joint ventures, joint equity swaps, and affiliates. *Joint ventures* are temporary partnerships in which the resources of two or more organizations are combined to form a separate new business entity. The legal form of the new business might be a new corporation or just a contracted entity of limited duration. *Joint equity swaps* are similar to joint ventures, but no new organization is created. Instead, the parties simply exchange or swap equity ownership. *Affiliate joint ventures* have even less formal equity transactions than the joint equity swap. Here one of the parties simply takes some form of equity position with regard to the other. An example is where Chrysler took a 25% stake in Mitsubishi Motors when Mitsubishi agreed to develop and produce an engine for the Chrysler's E-Car during the 1980s.

Alignment advantages for supply chain managers in using strategic alliances include the following:

- **Enhances organizational skills:** Alliances allow for a great deal of shared information and opportunities for organizational learning. Suppliers can learn from supply management firms and vice versa.
- **Improved operations:** Alliances can result in lowering system's costs and cycle times. Firms can join together to better utilize off-season capacity by forming an alliance of firms not in the same industry.
- **Improved financial strength:** Administrative costs can be shared between allied firms, reducing expenses and increasing profitability. This, in turn, can improve both firms' financial positions.
- **Enhanced strategy growth:** New partners can provide access to business opportunities that would otherwise have high entry barriers. Alliances allow firms to pool expertise and resources to overcome barriers and explore new opportunities.
- **Improved market access:** Partnerships can lead to increased access to new market channels, particularly when partners' markets do not complement each other.

7.3.5 Using a Supplier as an Alignment Partner to Meet Customer Demand

Suppliers can be used to change supply management firms by helping them align their current or new businesses to better meet customer demand. When a supply management firm needs to change its business model because it is introducing a new business channel or is having problems with an old one, suppliers can be engaged to help in the transition. An example of this type of collaborative arrangement is illustrated by the actions of Wehkamp.nl, the largest Dutch online retailer of home goods, technology, and apparel in the Netherlands. In recent years, according to Cooke (2011), Wehkamp.nl's combined model using both online sales and a more classic catalog business caused problems. Timing between weekly inventory ordering and replenishing (which worked fine for the catalog business) caused lost sales in the online business because customers were not willing to wait for orders. Wehkamp.nl needed to move from a weekly to a daily replenishment system and from a *push* model to a customer *pull* model.

To accomplish the transformation process, they turned to their best supplier, ETC, a wholesaler (Cooke, 2011). The two companies agreed to a pilot project where ETC would perform a *vendor-managed inventory* (VMI) role by assuming responsibility for keeping the right items in stock at Wehkamp.nl's warehouses. In addition, to make the daily replenishment possible, supply chain partners were required to acquire software that would determine appropriate levels of inventory needed. The software calculated stocking levels based on customer pull, as well as gave supply chain planners strategic, operational, and technical perspectives on inventory levels.

This project proved to be so successful that within three months Wehkamp.nl made this a permanent way of their doing business. The enhanced inventory replenishment systems fueled a rapid growth rate and provided the firm with excess capacity to deal with its growing online business. In addition, it enhanced sales by providing the right product at the right time to the customers, while minimizing total inventory and safety stocks. Reduced inventory freed up capital, which allowed Wehkamp.nl to expand its product lines.

7.3.6 Optimizing Life Cycle Production with Produce-to-Demand

In the ups and downs of a product's life cycle, product demand can change almost daily. As a result, the potential for products to linger in supply chains taking up valuable space and financial resources until demand meets up with them or they are written off as a loss is common. As lean experts advocate, any product that is not moving in a supply chain is generating a variety of waste (Myerson, 2012; Schonberger, 2010). The firms that are lucky enough to be able to use a product-to-demand strategy avoid much of this waste.

As illustrated in Figure 7.3, there are differences between the make-to-stock strategy most supply chain organizations utilize and the produce-to-demand strategy. Chiefly the difference is that the produce-to-demand adds information sharing between customers and distribution centers with the respective manufacturer. The result of these added interactions, according to Schutt and Moore (2011), is less inventory waste in the chain. To make this strategy happen requires some classic just-in-time changes to the way production is undertaken (Schniederjans, 1993; Schniederjans and Olson, 1999), examples of which include more timely scheduling (for example, a time frame from daily to hourly), smaller production quantities, and help from suppliers to manage inventory.

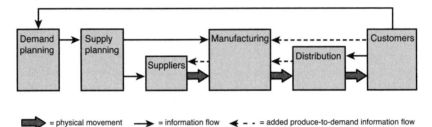

◼▶ = physical movement   ⟶ = information flow   ◀ - - = added produce-to-demand information flow

Figure 7.3 Comparison of make-to-stock and produce-to-demand systems

Source: Adapted from Schutt and Moore (2011) Figures 1 and 2, pp. 56–57.

Many firms that operate under the make-to-stock strategy may be able to change over to or at least move toward a produce-to-demand strategy. To determine whether a firm is a candidate for this approach, Schutt and Moore (2011) suggest four factors be in place:

- **Production technology:** Reliable production technology is needed as the firm moves to a short-cycle production of finished goods. Reliable information is needed to accurately fit demand requirements with production capacity. Flexibility in production capacity and the ability to reduce set up times are necessary requirements

- **Product characteristics:** Some products are more suitable for produce-to-demand than others. Products that have a short lapse from the time a decision is made to manufacture a product until the product is available to ship are best. Others include high-volume products (for example, manufacture of paper) and products that have few components. Products that have long-term processes (for example, fermentation) are not good candidates. Ideally, necessary raw materials and finishing elements (for example, packaging) must be readily available.

- **Supply chain organization:** Suppliers should take on most of the responsibility for maintaining component inventories. There is a need for quick response to demand needs, necessitating the formation of strategic and collaborative procurement relationships.

- **Information visibility:** Sharing customer information with distributors, the manufacturer and suppliers (see Figure 7.3) is essential to make customer demand and finished goods inventories visible for plant schedulers on a real-time basis.

Building on these prequalifying conditions, Schutt and Moore (2011) suggest candidates for produce-to-demand should face and be prepared to make changes in their manufacturing capacities, production reliability, changeover times and costs, component rationalization across products, supplier relationships, and technology that support near-real-time customer order and inventory information. In addition, potential candidates for produce-to-demand should consider four related issues.

- **Changing production planning and scheduling processes:** Changes in *master production scheduling* (MPS) efforts might include planning against lower finished goods inventory targets, planning more frequent production of smaller batch quantities, and reducing the number of planning horizon days. This moves the MPS from the status of an exact plan to basically a guide that permits greater flexibility under a produce-to-demand strategy. In addition, plant-level planners will have to watch daily customer order streams and redevelop short-term schedules to better match production with demand.
- **Rethinking inventory policies:** Reducing inventory is the main objective in using this strategy, and part of that effort involves recalculating safety stock, cycle-stock levels, *work-in-process* (WIP) levels, and materials inventory policies to take into account shorter lead times.
- **Improving supplier communications:** There is a need for frequent communication with suppliers. Inventory items that are needed for production in large quantities and those that are unique to each finished goods must be closely managed to flow through the production facility so that there is very little lead time. (Schutt and Moore suggest one day or less.) To achieve the intensity of monitoring these inventories require, there is a need for good software tools. Communications-oriented spreadsheets posted on shared Web sites that show daily or hourly delivery requirements and actual current materials status are suggested as a means to augment communication.

The same information can be shared via smartphones and other telecommunication devices to enhance the speed of delivery.

- **Aligning the organization:** To make the produce-to-demand strategy happen requires realignment of the manufacturing organization, moving it from a cost minimizing, department centered orientation to a supply chain orientation. In manufacturing-oriented firms, production cost per unit has been the major metric for evaluation. In a produce-to-demand organization, cost per unit is still going a major metric for evaluation, but a broader range of economic information reflecting the supply chain environment will be included. The cost metric will consist of inventory, warehousing, transportation costs, and disposal costs for excess and obsolete inventory. New metrics will also have to be employed to measure and track inventory materials at the suppliers, materials at plants, WIP, finished goods in plants, and finished goods in distribution centers.

In summary, it is not that a firm has to move completely to the theoretical just-in-time goal of production on demand, but rather the strategy should be to move a firm as close to this ideal as possible. The closer a firm is to one to one (that is, one unit demanded and one unit produced and delivered), the less waste in the supply chains. Some of the world's greatest researchers on goal setting have found the best organizational results are achieved by goals that have been spelled out exactly in terms of what needs to be accomplished and where the bar has been set for high achievement (Johnson, 2012).

7.3.7 An Academic Perspective on Alignment

Noted scholars have offered suggestions on supply chain resource alignment strategies. Lee (2011, pp. 1–19) has suggested that in situations where the supply chain has become unaligned with customer demand managers should not try to tweak the supply chain but instead rethink it from end to end. The newer core issues on which the realigned supply chain foundation will be constructed, like sustainability, needs to be incorporated into the foundation, rather than just added on.

Where do you begin with such a Herculean effort? Slone (2011, pp. 195–214) suggests an alignment or realignment strategy. Basically, begin with the customer and work backward through the supply chain. Start with the customers' current needs for the product, delivery, and price. Benchmark where it is possible to ensure competitive competence in the market place for the desired customers. Move backward through distribution channels to manufacturing and through the multiple tiers of suppliers, taking into consideration information technology, processes, management roles, and talents. Finally, make new partners as needed to meet the new customer demand.

Strategies like this sound simple, but are very challenging to implement. The lessons here are important guides in any alignment undertaking. Simply put, do not waste time making small changes to supply chains. Retool them completely and focus on the customer.

7.4 Other Alignment Topics

7.4.1 Strategy for Dealing with Explosive Growth During Introduction and Growth Stages of Product Life Cycle

Some firms are able to put an enormous amount of products before consumers during the Introduction and Growth Stages of the product life cycle. During these stages, a product is essentially alone in its market before other companies have a chance to introduce competitive products. Profit margins can be considerable during these life cycle stages, but once competitors enter the market, competition drives down prices and profit. One firm, Apple Computers, has found it could afford to spend more on manufacturing and distribution to get more product into the pipeline during these all-important early and exclusive high-margin stages (Turbide, 2011). One strategy is to build extra supply chain capacity in to the current system in anticipation of a spike of demand growth. For example, a firm can contract for a great deal of air cargo space in anticipation of a new product's initial release. While air transportation is more expensive, shipping time may be reduced to a day rather than take weeks for slower transportation modes (for example, shipping cargo) costing firms profit. Slower modes are simply untenable in fast-changing markets. Apple also buys manufacturing capacity and locks up supplies of certain components and materials that may have limited availability. This strategy has the added advantage of reducing supplies of these components for competitors, delaying competitors' efforts to bring competing products to market.

7.4.2 Dealing with a Logistics in Seasonal Growth Surge

Express freight carriers, who are major partners in many firms' supply chain, have to deal with seasonal or holiday growth surges from customers. How a firm like FedEx handles volatility in service demand can be applicable to any firm having to align its supply chain resources to deal with excessive growth in customer demand.

FedEx projected the company would have to ship more than 260 million packages between Thanksgiving and Christmas in 2011, which represents a 12% increase from 2010 (Strategic Sourceror, 2011). FedEx's worldwide shipping hub at the Los Angeles International Airport employs hundreds to handle and process packages on miles of conveyor belts. Moving the packages from the airport to a sorting warehouse, the latest in material handling technology is employed. To ensure packages are not misplaced, FedEx invests heavily in advanced technological monitoring devices. These systems help FedEx not only to track boxes but also to measure them. This enables the company to leave no space unused when loading packages on planes and trucks. Even with that capital investment, substantial growth surges can overwhelm the normal staff capacity. To deal with the growth in demand, FedEx augments its strategy of increasing staffing capacity by employing an additional 20, employees. To process the millions of boxes, FedEx separates these employees into groups tasked with individual duties. For example, some employees work specifically to investigate where packages containing no address labels should be directed, while others unload planes and trucks.

Utilizing specialization of labor, materials handling technology to improve efficiency in shipping, and a temporary increase in staffing are all useful approaches for dealing with rapid growth surges.

7.4.3 Contingency Planning as a Growth Strategy

Aligning physical facilities for future growth in products or for an entire supply chain is prudent contingency planning. Knowing that growth will eventually occur, it is prudent to be prepared with sufficient supply chain capacity. An example of a firm that undertook a major change in distribution centers in 2011 is illustrated by Skechers USA, a major footwear company.

The company started with five leased distribution centers in Southern California representing 1.7 million square feet of facilities. Each of those facilities had different equipment, and each handled a different piece of the order fulfillment process. Regardless, the facilities resulted in higher costs due to the additional handling required to move a product between facilities for order fulfillment processes. The product was received from the ports in one building, picked and packed in another, and potentially picked up in a third. A great deal of effort was spent constantly shipping products from one building to the next until they arrived at the appropriate locations. Skechers wanted to consolidate operations under one roof, but it also wanted to maintain a central point for North American distribution rather than develop a distribution network. Having regional distribution centers resulted in having inventory on the East Coast that was needed on the West Coast and vice versa.

With the idea of product growth in mind, they designed a single facility of 1.82 million square feet located about 80 miles west of the port in Long Beach, California, where Skechers imports all of its footwear and athletic gear. The facility seeks to meet two important strategic goals: consolidate operations, and set the stage for continued growth. The new distribution center is one that is highly automated and able to handle all the footwear company's North American distribution. The new distribution center consists of three distinct areas for work, each measuring about 600, square feet. Two areas are devoted to receiving with about 400, square feet of reserve storage in each; the space in the middle is dedicated to order fulfillment and shipping.

The new facility is one of the largest distribution centers in California and was designed to be one of the most efficient. The facility has an automated materials handling system that minimizes the number of times a pair of shoes is handled between receiving and shipping and is capable of managing an inventory of 70, *stock keeping units* (SKUs) and processing approximately 17, pairs of shoes per hour. The improvement in performance to meet growth goals is more than double the 7, pairs per hour handled in the former five leased distribution centers, and it is doing so with less than half the number of employees previously required. The facility and its automation systems are designed for flexibility. For example, both *automated storage/retrieval systems* (AS/RS) units are expandable. Thinking well ahead, Skechers also purchased an adjacent lot big enough for another facility should it outgrow this new one.

7.5 What's Next?

Social media (that is, Web-based or mobile technologies used to generate communications with interactive dialogue among organizations and individuals, allowing creation and exchange of user-generated content) has been used in businesses primarily in marketing and human resources. Examples of social media platforms include Social-Flow and Attensity (both used for social media measurement) and Central Desktop and Creately (used for collaboration).

Casemore (2012) suggests social media will become increasingly important in all business operations, including supply chain management, and offers four areas of potential future benefits:

- **Aid in creating knowledge networks:** Using social media venues like Facebook and Twitter, a firm can rapidly capture and respond to customer feedback. Social media can then be used to obtain real-time feedback from the supply chain, both internally (inventory, warehousing, and procurement departments) and externally (suppliers and contractors). For example, a client firm with a materials or equipment need could have a network of suppliers watching its supply chain Facebook page. It can post the specs on what it needs, including pictures and video of the materials or equipment, with due dates for bids, and other relevant information. The suppliers and client firms can then use mobile technology to respond back and forth, leaving a trail of communications that constitute a complete record of the request, the supplier selection and performance, and any related issues.

- **Speeding up the decision making process:** The speed with which many social-media platforms can provide video, audio, and written communications across a vast network of suppliers in real time, will support agility and flexibility goals in supply chain decision making.

- **Portable information:** The increase in demand for information portability availability over mobile devices requires the ability to instantaneously access information. Social media is well positioned to offer the necessary platforms.

- **Transforming collaboration with community:** The need for transparency in supply chain business requires ever-closer relationships with key suppliers. Building a network community of suppliers, where critical information, opportunities, and ideas for improvement can be shared and implemented in real time, provides a competitive advantage for organizations. Also, engaging suppliers through social media is a useful way to stimulate supply chain innovation. Social media platforms are an ideal foundation for such communities.

8

Negotiating

Terms

Advocacy approach

Artificial intelligence (AI)

Autonomous agents

Best alternative to a negotiated agreement (BATNA)

Genetic algorithm (GA)

Hardball strategy

Intelligent agents

Knowledge query manipulation language (KQML)

Least acceptable solution (LAS)

Maximum supportable solution (MSS)

Multi-agent systems

Negotiation

Negotiation strategy worksheet

Particle swarm optimization (PSO)

Stalling

Statement of work (SOW)

Third-party suppliers

Win-lose strategy

Win-win strategy

Zero-sum game

Novelette

Just about everything we do in supply chain management comes down to a negotiation. The knowledge, skills, and innate talent that supply chain managers bring to this area of expertise determine what their supply chains become. Negotiating with suppliers to achieve a contract that benefits both parties should be the goal of any negotiation.

During the course of our usual monthly phone conversation, my VP for our Medium-Sized Engine Division, Barack, shared a concern he was having about his chief buyer, who works directly for this Supply Chain Department Head, Todd. "Bill, you and I have enough years in the business to know that negotiating contracts with suppliers is critical and needs constant skill-development efforts. Our chief buyer, who works under Todd, our Supply Chain Department Head, appears to be slipping a bit. One of the contracts I had to sign off on seemed overly pricey to me. I asked Todd the specifics about how, where, and when it was negotiated only to find very little negotiation went into the process. The deal was done in one day. I don't have all the specifics on what the chief buyer process was, but between the inflated prices we are paying, relative to other suppliers I found to benchmark off of, I believe we can do a whole lot better in negotiating," Barack said.

"Barack, as you know from your own experience as a buyer, more than likely you don't get your contract on your first sit down with a supplier, and if you do, you probably haven't pressed as hard as you should have. The fact that your chief buyer was getting contracts negotiated in a day should have been a red flag to Todd to investigate what was happening. As a rule, the negotiation process is very iterative, going back and forth, gathering more information and taking considerable time and effort. Let me ask, how much prep work does your Division do before they enter into any supplier negotiations?" I asked.

"Basically, they take bids on what we need and factor in other services in addition to pricing with three suppliers. Beyond that, there is not a lot of prep work before entering into negotiations. The chief buyer feels his continual understanding of current market prices is adequate for the negotiation processes we use." explained Barack.

Bill was surprised to hear this and replied, "You were right to contact me on this issue. I started my career in supply chain management as a buyer and know what it takes to build a supply chain network with suppliers through negotiation. Barack, your chief buyer's approach is not an adequate process. We trust your Division to spend millions of dollars on our behalf with our suppliers. A much more careful and inclusive effort must be expended in future negotiations to ensure you are all doing the best job you can to support our supply chain activities."

"What do you suggest, Bill?" asked Barack.

"There are some basic concepts in the negotiation process that are needed to be put into place to ensure mutual benefit in contractual relations with our suppliers. In negotiations, which don't always lead to a contract, and we sometimes have to walk away from a deal. We should strive to have a win-win situation that benefits the supplier as well as us. We don't want to drive our suppliers out of business because they give us the lowest cost they cannot themselves afford. That will not result in a sustainable supply chain. In fact, we should look at suppliers in terms of other things they may bring to our operation, like world-class delivery service. Your people need to know that they are negotiating good terms and conditions, and that you're getting favorable treatment, but you are also managing your best total cost of what is important to you. Total cost includes more than just prices. Again, extra services that the supplier provides may have value that would otherwise cost you extra with other suppliers. It's important to lay out what is of interest to us and let the supplier lay out what is of interest to them in the negotiation process. Remember that negotiation doesn't mean you will always end up with a contract. Negotiation means you are just trying to identify terms and conditions by which you can interact with a supplier. Some of the time that leads to a contract. Now, your people should know that if we have to fall back on a contract to make suppliers do what they have agreed to do, it does not lead to a sustainable supply chain. Contracts are put into place by lawyers to give organizations some risk-avoidance protection, but to use it in a dependent relationship-intensive supply chain is very heavy-handed and will not foster the kind of partnership needed for a supply chain to grow. Ideally, we would like to have suppliers that help us in many of our areas of production like in the Design Stage to help us select materials and make the products as efficient as possible. These are the kinds of extras that some suppliers give and why just looking at prices is not the best policy in negotiating," I explained.

"Bill, the framework you have mentioned here is conceptually good, but I have to have my subordinates actually sit down with suppliers and negotiate contracts. What tactics can you share with me that I can share with them about the actual interaction that takes place during a negotiation?" asked Barack.

"Barack, negotiation is a dance where one side leads for a while and then the other side may try to take the lead. The dance is iterative, back and forth, filled with surprise, mystery, and game playing. When your negotiation team sits down across the table from you, don't let them assume the opposing team will be honest in everything they say or do. They may give you shades of truth to tease information out to use against you. Your team will have to do the same. International negotiations are sometimes unique. For example, I have observed that the more pressure you put on foreign negotiators whose language is something other than English, the faster they start losing their English skills and have trouble understanding English. Again, that is just a negotiation tactic. There will be a lot of posturing. For example, in some of the negotiation teams I brought 2 people while my opponent brought 20 people. When you go into a negotiation, you have to decide what it is you want from a supplier and what you are willing to accept at minimum. As you know, that is called the *best alternative to a negotiated agreement* (BATNA), or what we will do instead of doing the agreement with the supplier (our backup plan). Your chief buyer needs to gather data about industry pricing, and it should be based on more than just three suppliers. It should be industry-level information on all the commodities that make up the products we seek from this supplier and include what is going on in the industry, government, and any other markets for our products. In addition, your chief buyer should also collect information about the supplier's performance on delivery, production capacity, and technology capability to ensure that they have a good record and capacity sufficient for our needs. If you know the current or previous prices for a component part, and you have information on the pricing trends on the raw material commodities used to make that component, you can forecast at least if the price for the component should be going up or down. Then you should factor in the value added of the supplier by comparing the extras that other suppliers might be offering. Consistent with your current practice, you should be in negotiation with at least three different suppliers. Now, having done all that, you are ready to confront the suppliers. On very important contracts, you, your Supply Chain Department Head, and your chief purchasing manager should at least be on the negotiation team. Sometimes we have to play games, like "good cop, bad cop," to move the discussion along. In other situations, things may move too quickly, and in those situations we may want to slow things down by caucusing or just leaving the room to go elsewhere to discuss what is or maybe is going on in the negotiations (like people lying to you or playing games as well). Some of the supporting team members whom we can caucus with might include the negotiation team, product engineering personnel, and quality managers. Of course, you might just be exhausted and need a break from the negotiation efforts. When you come back, you need to put on your game face. Do not let the opponents know what you are thinking or that what they may have said bothers you. Fortunately, as you develop your relationship with this supplier over time, the negotiation process gets much easier and quicker," I commented.

"Thanks, Bill, all of this is helpful and I will bring it back to Todd and others in my Division," stated Barack.

"Barack, may I also suggest you utilize a negotiation training organization, like Karrass (www.karrass.com/), to build your team's negotiation skills. Two of our other Divisions use outside training organizations for their new and experienced buyers and management. Negotiation trainers are a great way of staying up-to-date in this critically important supply chain skill area," I suggested.

8.1 Prerequisite Material

The various stages in the product life cycle for any product alters demand and in turn can change the relationships with suppliers. At each stage in the product life cycle, new contracts/agreements have to be negotiated or renegotiated because product demand has altered. This necessitates negotiation skills for anyone who hopes to have a supply chain management future.

On an esoteric level, *negotiation* is a dialogue between people or parties who seek to reach an understanding, resolve a point of difference, or gain advantage in producing an agreement upon courses of action that both parties will follow. Negotiation is intended to achieve a compromise between two parties, with each party trying to gain an advantage at the end of the dialogue process.

Supply chain negotiations commonly follow an *advocacy approach,* where a skilled negotiator serves as advocate for one party (for example, a purchaser) in negotiation to attempt to obtain the most favorable outcomes possible from the other party (for example, a supplier). (We use the purchaser and supplier relationship paradigm throughout this chapter.) In this negotiation process, the negotiator (which could be a lawyer, contracts specialist, purchasing agent, a business executive, or in complex situations, a whole teams of individuals) attempts to determine the outcomes that the other party (for example, supplier) is willing to accept, and then adjusts the purchaser's demands accordingly. In this context, a successful negotiation occurs when the negotiator is able to obtain all or most of the outcomes his or her party desires. Negotiating is sometimes called *win-lose strategy* because of the assumption that one person's gain results in another person's loss. This is not true except in the most limited of negotiation situations, where participants are playing a *zero-sum game* (that is, what one gains, the other loses).

Table 8.1 describes a typical negotiation process as suggested by the *Institute of Supply Management* (ISM). As shown in Table 8.1, a great deal of analysis is needed for most any negotiation for the purchaser and the supplier to maximize their positions and to benefit their respective organizations. Like prepping for a debate, both parties must seek an outcome that achieves a winning compromise. Before the actual face-to-face negotiations take place, both parties should be positioned to know the needs of the other and what can be done to provide need satisfaction.

Table 8.1 ISM Overview of Negotiation Process

ISM Steps in the Negotiation Process	Description
1. Define objectives.	Define what it is that should be negotiated with a supplier. Factors to include at this step include product or service pricing (that is, the cost to the purchasing firm), timeliness of delivery performance, meeting essential organization needs (for example, a long-term arrangement), control over contract performance (for example, outlining cancellation procedures for nonconformance), and a desire to achieve a mutually beneficial agreement.

ISM Steps in the Negotiation Process	Description
2. Collect facts and analyze data.	Both parties have power to influence the negotiation process. Collect and analyze data to better understand the market forces and power of the purchasers and suppliers that will impact the negotiation process and the final contract. While the greater the substitutability of a product favors the purchaser, the fewer the suppliers in the market for the desired product, the greater the power of the supplier in the negotiation process. The importance to the supplier as being seen selling the product in a particular industry, the ability of the purchaser in producing a product in-house, and the offering of a large contract to the supplier all favor the purchaser in negotiations. Entry barriers to the purchaser for the desired product, the innovation capacity of the supplier in working through problems, and sole distributorship of the product by the supplier all favor the supplier in negotiations. Other facts and data include factors that affect market trends (for example, growth or decline in the industry), price indexes values (for example, wholesale prices as predictor of future retail market trends), and cultural dimensions (for example, expected social conduct and behavior during the negotiation process that does not negatively impact or insult either party).
3. Prepare plans and engage in preparatory groundwork.	Adopt a negotiation philosophy that will lead to both parties perceiving they have won the negotiations. This will require consideration of any past history of negotiations with the supplier (good or bad) or any historical data that can be gleaned from other companies who have done business with the supplier. Such a philosophy should embrace a desire to be collaborative and require an extensive interaction between both parties. It should avoid adversarial or confrontational positions. The ISM recommends that the negotiations be held at the supplier's location. (Note there will be a later exception to this recommendation in this chapter.) Other factors that can lay the groundwork for negotiations include establishing a team to undertake the negotiations, the development of win-win strategy, and tactics to anticipate what the suppliers might seek to achieve in a negotiation (that is, both parties should develop anticipatory strategies and tactics in anticipation of the other so both parties gain or win in the final contract).

ISM Steps in the Negotiation Process	Description
4. Analyze negotiation positions for both purchaser and supplier.	A comprehensive analysis to identify strengths and weaknesses in both parties on which to add to their power in the negotiations and avoid perceived weaknesses in power. Technical and purchasing information, market information, proposals related to services and products, as well as technology and pricing information should be included in the analysis at this stage in the process. Other factors such as the supplier's desire or need for the contract, the supplier's reputation standing in their industry, and the supplier's sources of financial strength are all factors that can and should be considered in this step of the process. For the purchaser, strengths and weaknesses originate in their skill and authority to negotiate. Factors such as persistence, insight, intelligence, tact, flexibility, verbal clarity, and the ability to listen can play a major role in the negotiation team's success or failure. Other factors include the amount of time allowed for negotiation, acceptability of cost and pricing, and the ability of the purchaser to accept alternative options as needed to make a deal.
5. Establish an anchor point for negotiations.	Negotiations have to begin at some point, some initial point (an *anchor point*) where the purchaser using the analysis collected can propose what it is they want and expect from the supplier. Usually a purchaser does not vary far from this anchor point in further negotiations. The anchor point originates after a careful analysis of what the purchaser needs and what they live with in terms of price, quality, and other factors. It also depends on what the supplier is willing to be able to do and willing to except in terms of an agreement. A common expression used in the development of an anchor point is the *best alternative to a negotiated agreement* or BATNA. The BATNA can be characterized in most organizations as an alternative that a purchaser can choose to do if they cannot obtain an agreement with a supplier. BATNA is a fallback plan. BATNA can serve as a low-end baseline to help the purchaser to seek a higher level of service or product outcome. It can be used to leverage their negotiations with suppliers.

ISM Steps in the Negotiation Process	Description
6. Engage in negotiations.	Engaging in negotiations evolves strategy and tactics. The development of the strategy depends on the power the purchaser has going in to negotiations. Negotiating with a sole supplier can be a weak power position, and a strategy that focuses on the supplier benefits of doing business with the purchaser (for example, long-term contracts and what that can mean to the supplier) might be a successful strategy going in to a negotiation in this situation. Alternatively, purchasers who represent a consortium or cooperative are usually in a stronger position because of the substantial size of the potential business they can give the supplier, and therefore can use more a hardball strategy. There are an unlimited number of possible tactics, each with its own benefits and risks. For example, a *hardball strategy* like a "take it or leave it" offer can get a quick acceptance or a complete rejection. The latter outcome being a complete failure at negotiation. Using a "target tactic" where the purchaser makes clear that everything else except price is in line with their needs and then a target price is suggested to pressure the supplier to make allowances on that one item is considered to be useful tactic in arriving at a successful negotiation.

Source: Adapted from Carter and Choi (2008), pp. 149–183.

8.2 Guiding Principles in Negotiating Agreements

There are only two things important to supply chain managers in the theory of negotiation: what they want, and how to get it the way they want it. What purchasers want is a winning agreement with a supplier that serves their supply chain needs to their best advantage. Likewise, suppliers want a winning agreement to serve their needs. How to obtain an agreement for both parties involves knowing how to undertake negotiation using the right negotiating strategies and tactics.

8.2.1 Winning Agreements

Winning agreements today are those that are transparent and detailed and provide a comprehensive statement of what both parties want and expect. There are many ways to achieve such agreements. The guidelines presented in Table 8.2 are a beginning framework to verse supply chain managers in the general content that should be included in the process of generating purchasing agreements.

Table 8.2 Principles in Guiding Content in Negotiating Purchasing Agreements

Negotiating Principle	Description
Clearly state strategic intent of the product or service.	The agreement should make clear to supplier what the strategic goals of the purchaser are in the use of the products or services so that the supplier can work to build and grow in the direction necessary for future success.
Clearly state goals, objectives, and expectations.	As detailed as possible, define the purchaser's expectations on time, place, who, what, where, and when for all goals and objectives. It is best if expectations can be quantified. Include detailed metrics that can later be used to monitor performance. The *statement of work* (SOW) is a common document that outlines the specific services a supplier or contractor is expected to perform. There are four SOW documents: design SOW, level-of-effort SOW, performance SOW, and functional SOW (see *ISM Glossary of Key Supply Management Terms, 4th Edition,* 2007; www.ism.ws/glossary/?navItemNumber=7800).
Establish clear time horizons.	In agreements where the purchasing agreement is for a fixed period of time, clearly state the beginning and end times for arrangements so that the supplier knows what is expected. In arrangements where the agreement have no end time, there should be fixed periods of review where parties can reevaluate the agreement and make changes without penalty.
Define scope of services or products from the supplier.	As detailed as possible, it is necessary for the purchaser to define what the supplier is expected to cover and what they should not cover. This can be defined in term of hours of service coverage or units of production. It can involve quality control issues and other subjective tasks.
Role of purchaser firm in aiding the supplier.	A clear statement of the financial, systems, human resource, and technology support from the purchaser should be defined in the agreement so that the supplier knows what they can expect from the purchaser. This should include time horizons and specific amounts and any efforts expected of the purchaser firm.

Negotiating Principle	Description
Define transition roles.	During the startup period, each party's responsibilities should be defined and clearly agreed upon over this period of time to avoid confusion on roles each must play. More effort needs to be utilized in the beginning to ensure everyone is on board with what is expected.
Define management and control activities.	A designated purchasing team or manager of some sort should be clearly defined to manage and control the purchasing process from beginning to end. This may be as shared task with the purchasing team leader and the supplier but clear roles must be assigned. As the design, implementation and follow-up activities are all crucial to the overall success of purchasing, each phase should have specifically assigned to managers who will oversee and control the entire process.
Define lines of communication and reporting requirements.	Reporting and working efforts between the purchaser firm and the supplier must be clearly defined so that everyone knows who to report to via lines of communication and to ensure control functions are clearly understood. Reporting on the progress of the purchasing agreement should also be defined in terms of what is being done, how it is meeting any benchmarks previously established, and to whom the information is to be communicated.
Make the agreement a win-win situation.	The agreement should not favor one party over the other. Both should see advantages to maintaining the agreement in the short term and long term. It must be mutually beneficial, with no hidden surprises rewarding one party at the expense of the other.
Set up provisions to reward benefits and penalties for noncompliance.	A reward system should be established that motivates the supplier to meet and possibly exceed goal expectations of the purchaser firm. Likewise, when a supplier fails to do the job, the costs to the purchaser should be paid (in part or in full) by the supplier. Clear statements on rewards and penalties must be established and communicated.
Establish metrics to assess supplier performance.	A clear statement on the measurement metrics used to define compliance and supplier success must be agreed on by both parties in writing. Even how these measurements are taken (by whom, when, where, and reported to whom) must all be established.

Negotiating Principle	Description
Establish pricing terms.	Clearly state the domains of pricing control and limitations. This includes not only what the supplier agreed to charge the purchaser firm for the basic service or product agreement but also any flexibility allowing for overtime or extra service charges. This may also include *third-party suppliers*, where the supplier purchases items for the purchaser firm from other subcontractors or suppliers.
Establish agreement termination provisions.	The terms under which either party can terminate the agreement should be clearly defined. These include definitions of what constitutes noncompliance for both parties and fair time frames for making adjustments to correct problems. They should be tied to the performance metrics and mutually agreed on by both parties.
Establish provisions for unexpected contributions.	During any partnership, a new idea, technology, process, or product can be developed or innovated by either or both parties. A clear statement as to how ownership is to be shared should be included in the agreement. This might also include new processes that highly benefit the purchaser firm, where the supplier is justifiably due additional compensation for the contribution.
Establish a provision for unexpected situations.	In any relationship, unexpected situations (for example, markets disappearing, financial problems, labor disputes, wars) can erupt and prevent the agreement from being fulfilled. No agreement can possibly cover all situations that may arise. There needs to be a system in place to handle these situations so that they do not result in lawsuits or termination of the agreement. A panel or council of executives or experts can be used to judge the situation and make fair recommendations to both parties to avoid legal problems.

Source: Adapted from Schniederjans et al. (2005), pp. 62–63.

8.2.2 Negotiating Strategies and Tactics

Currently, supply chain management is moving too rapidly to waste time making agreements that may have little impact on a firm's bottom line. That is not to say negotiation efforts of supply chain managers do not make major contributions to a firm's bottom line; but long, protracted "game playing" is becoming an obsolete practice.

However, some game playing might enable a purchaser to procure the best deal from a supplier. Old hardball practices (for example, "good guy, bad guy" or offering a "red herring") will not lead to successful negotiations.

So, where does a winning negotiation strategy come from? It has been observed that some negotiators possess and use a particular style of negotiation. There are many styles a negotiator can adopt, and each has its own advantages and disadvantages (see Table 8.3). Understanding the differences in styles can help a supply chain manager identify underlying behavior that impacts agreement negotiations. For example, if supplier's negotiating style is accommodating, the purchaser's negotiator might be able to take advantage of this sensitivity to weaken or disrupt the negotiation process to the purchaser's advantage.

Table 8.3 Negotiation Styles

Negotiating Style	Description	Possible Strategies for Dealing with Them
Accommodating	Negotiators who seek to be accommodating by solving the other party's problems and preserving personal relationships. Accommodators tend to be sensitive to the emotional states, body language, and verbal signals of the other parties.	They can be taken advantage of in situations when the other party places little emphasis on the relationship or where false body language can be used to manipulate the negotiator.
Avoiding	Negotiators who don't like to negotiate unless warranted. When negotiating, these individuals tend to defer and avoid the confrontational aspects of negotiating.	Pressing these individuals by being confrontational in negotiating can motivate them to give greater concessions just to avoid further negotiations.

Negotiating Style	Description	Possible Strategies for Dealing with Them
Collaborating	Negotiators who enjoy negotiations that involve solving tough problems in creative ways. Collaborators are good at using negotiations to understand the concerns and interests of the other parties.	Pressing for a quick resolution to negotiations can spoil the enjoyment for collaborators that might otherwise want to drag out negotiations time-wise. Indeed, if allowed to drag negotiations out, they can create problems by transforming simple situations into more complex ones.
Competing	Negotiators who enjoy negotiations because they present an opportunity to win something. Competitive negotiators have strong instincts for all aspects of negotiating and are often strategic gamers.	As game players, they can be easily led into needless and endless negotiations where delays and other repressing actions favor the purchaser. Also their style tends to dominate the bargaining process, neglecting the importance of relationships.
Compromising	Negotiators who are eager to close the deal by doing what is fair and equal for all parties involved in the negotiation. Compromisers can be useful when there is limited time to complete the deal.	A strategy of delay can disrupt this type of negotiator, beating them down to a better deal for the purchaser. Compromisers often unnecessarily rush the negotiation process and make concessions too quickly, which can be taken advantage of by purchasers.

Source: Adapted from Shell (2006), pp.112–145.

No one formula or single strategy can fit every situation in a negotiation process. The best advice for developing a winning strategy is to develop one that contains elements of criteria characteristic of winning strategies for negotiation. Table 8.4 describes a number of winning strategy criteria. As a check list, the suggestions in Table 8.4 can help supply chain managers avoid oversights in negotiation strategy development.

Table 8.4 Criteria for the Development of a Negotiating Strategy

Winning Negotiating Strategy Criteria	Description
Develop business intelligence on all salient factors.	To know what is possible in dealing with a supplier, a purchaser has to know the supplier very well. Negotiation does not take place in a vacuum of information but should be based on a complete and thorough analysis of any factors relevant to the negotiation. For the purchaser, the supplier's capabilities to provide the service or products should be known as well as they are to the supplier. The risks, reputation, and short/long-term abilities of the supplier should be researched and clearly understood by both parties.
Use positive statements.	Understanding the supplier's point of view and letting the supplier know that you understand it with a positive statement can help communicate a preemptive willingness for continued and further collaboration.
Use questions effectively.	The right question at the right time can help to avoid an unacceptable agreement by undermining an unacceptable position or deflect criticism.
Security.	If unethical behavior is a possibility in the negotiations, the negotiations should be undertaken at the purchaser's location. This has the added benefit of reducing travel costs and places the purchaser's team in their normal working environment (that is, the home-team advantage).
Listen effectively.	Listen not just to the words but also to the tone of the voice and any other body language information that can be gleaned during negotiations to gain insight into the supplier's position and objectives.
Honesty and trust.	"Honesty" is the best policy because it is the foundation for trust, and without trust a successful long-term partnership or even a short-term agreement is unlikely to occur.

Winning Negotiating Strategy Criteria	Description
Transparency and openness.	Transparency and openness here mean sharing general directions the negotiation will take, but does not mean sharing every goal and objective parties might be considering. Transparency in negotiations is where all members of both parties are kept in the loop on the various moves each party makes. Transparency might be accomplished by recording the daily negotiation efforts and sharing them with all the negotiation participants. Openness in negotiations means sharing information but not surrendering the strategy or tactics that are to be used in the negotiation process.
Just say no.	Regardless of the investment of time or effort, an unacceptable agreement should be turned down. This is particularly true when suppliers give deadlines that might rush a decision on an agreement that is risky to the purchaser.
Be considerate.	Treating suppliers with respect and dignity builds goodwill and helps to lessen the normal antagonisms associated with negotiations.
Reply to questions fully.	Proper and truthful answers from the purchaser can help to delineate the supplier objectives and quicken the responses to reduce time and game playing in the negotiation process.
Analyze every offer.	Every offer from the supplier, regardless of how exceptional it is, should be analyzed in terms of the motivation for the offer and the capabilities of the supplier in delivering the offer. In addition, short-term and long-term opportunities/threats should be considered in the analysis.
Exhibit patience and tolerance.	Some agreements require a long-term protracted negotiation process. A strategy based on waiting patiently for the supplier to reveal their objectives and being tolerant and overreacting each time a supplier makes an unreasonable request is a more successful approach.
Appreciate cultural and gender differences.	Negotiation in a global context makes understanding cultural differences, including perception of gender, race, and ethnicity, critically important to any negotiation strategy.

Source: Adapted from Fawcett et al. (2007), pp. 361–368; Carter and Choi (2008), pp.178–181.

Once a general strategy is planned, tactics to help implement it are needed. Many different tactics can be used in a negotiation process. Table 8.5 describes some of the more commonly used tactics. Which ones you use depend on the preferences of the members on the negotiation team, the nature of the strategy selected, and the primary goals for the purchaser in the negotiation process.

Table 8.5 Common Negotiating Tactics

Negotiating Tactics	Description
Fact based	Arguing based on facts avoids possible damage to credibility if falsity is revealed later. It also adds power to the purchaser's point of view, and in some situations it places the supplier on the defensive in the negotiation process (if, for instance, the facts reveals the presence of a supplier weakness).
Best and final offer	This is a take-it-or-leave-it tactic. It may serve the need for a quick conclusion but risks credibility if the negotiator is not willing to walk away from a negotiation to enforce the finality of the offer.
Best initial offer	Making a strong initial offer helps to let the supplier know the purchaser is serious about doing business and can set a climate for subsequent serious and effective negotiations.
High-ball	Begin the negotiation with an extremely preferential offer, knowing that concessions will be made.
Maintain the initiative	Establish the initiative early and maintain it by probing the other party's position and asking for justifications and supporting documents to justify any movement away from the initiative.
Missing team member	Deliberate absence of a negotiating team member with the authority to make a final decision gives that party an opportunity to escape negotiations if they are not proceeding as expected.
High-priority issues	Deliberately lead off with a discussion of the highest-priority issues to resolve them quickly. This gets to the heart of important issues that are needing resolution and lets the supplier know what they might be expected to achieve quickly in the negotiations.
Low-priority issues	Deliberately lead off with a discussion of low-priority issues. This is a useful tactic in situations where there is a need to feel out how the supplier might be dealing later with higher-priority issues.

Negotiating Tactics	Description
Scheduled breaks	Scheduling breaks during the negotiation allows both parties an opportunity to evaluate how the negotiations are going, gather information, and reassess any needs to revise strategies and tactics.
Limited-time offer	Make an offer with the threat that unless it is accepted it may not be available later. Typical of win-lose negotiations, frequent use of this tactic reduces credibility. Alternatively, it can push a supplier to make a quick decision, saving time and effort.
Diversions	For problematic issues that a purchaser might not want to draw attention to, diversions like timeouts can help avoid revealing or discussing a weak issue that could be used against the purchaser.
Silence	Silence can be effectively used to make a supplier nervous, seek concessions without specifically asking for them, and redirect the discussion away from problematic issues.
Use caucuses	Taking a break where a purchasing team can regroup and discuss the status of negotiations can interrupt the supplier's momentum and help to reposition the purchaser for renewed negotiations.
Narrowing differences	During the negotiation process, differences between the purchaser and supplier will occur. Brainstorming ideas can be a useful tactic used to lessen the differences for both parties and move the discussion toward a compromise.

Source: Adapted from Fawcett et al. (2007), p.366; Carter and Choi (2008), pp.178-181.

8.2.3 Select Best Practices

In general, supply chain managers have found solace in a variety of best practices recommended by colleagues in industry. These best practices change over time. Robinson and Harkness (2011) suggest some best practices should be part of every negotiation strategy, no matter who is on the negotiating team or whether the team is negotiating for a product or a service:

- **Silence is golden:** Do not engage in outside communications with a supplier during ongoing negotiations. This does not violate the principle of transparency and openness. Some suppliers try to gain competitive information in outside communications that could be leveraged against the purchaser during contract negotiations.

- **Maintain secrecy in approved budgets:** Do not disclose information about approved budgets, nor about the internal vision for investing dollars in specific projects or whether a project is part of a key initiative or imperative for the purchasing organization. Information on any of these topics could indicate to a supplier that they have the upper hand and in turn could disadvantage the purchaser during negotiation discussions.

- **Provide adequate timing:** Allow the purchasing organization enough time to work through the negotiating process and communicate this is all parties. Business deadlines should not dictate negotiation strategy and execution.

Another important best practice concerns getting started in the negotiation process. In the beginning of any negotiating process, supply chain managers should maintain tight control over individuals taking part. Every participant should have a clear role and an intended purpose. All business organization staffers with a stake as internal customers should be included during strategy sessions as candidates for the negotiating team. Once the trusted potential members of a negotiating team are identified, supply chain mangers can then decide on the approach most beneficial for the assembled team. It is critical that all internal participants are in lock step with their roles. They should understand the ultimate strategy of the supply chain leaders in the negotiation process.

The outcome of the negotiation efforts is a final agreement that both parties agree on and that should benefit both. The amount of time and effort spent on negotiation of purchasing agreements is usually in direct proportion to the importance of the agreement to both parties. The suggestions offered in this chapter are a starting place and provide general guidelines for a negotiation process. Unfortunately, many issues can occur during the negotiation process and must be dealt with to have a successful agreement. Some of these issues are discussed in the next section.

8.3 Other Negotiation Topics

8.3.1 Overcoming Negotiation Roadblocks

Robinson and Harkness (2011) have suggested that when a planned negotiating strategy is not successful in reaching the desired result, bringing in executive leadership may be appropriate. Timing their entrance and understanding their roles are critical success factors in the use of this strategy.

Experienced or not, negotiators can usually tell when suppliers are stalling or when progress on issues is slowed or halted on purchasing agreement negotiations. Moving things along sometimes requires that negotiations move to the next level, in which the purchasing organization makes a declarative statement to show how serious it is about negotiation efforts. The strategy to break the stalemated process involves bringing in executive oversight. When a high-ranking executive is brought into the process, a clear message is sent to the supplier that the negotiation is strategic to the purchasing business. It can be an effective message communicating the purchasing organization's desire for alignment and achieving an equitable solution for all parties. Negotiations usually take on increased attention when a high-ranking supply chain professional is engaged.

Once the high-ranking executive has decided to enter into the negotiation process, it is important that the strategic role of the executive be clearly defined, as is the case for the entire negotiating team. The executive's role, according to Robinson and Harkness (2011), should be confined to when an agreement is nearly complete or when there is a stalemate that can be broken only by discussing or changing internal policy. For example, in an agreement close to completion there may be a few final high-level items that must be incorporated as part of the contract. Robinson and Harkness suggest that is when it is appropriate for an executive to step in. If the executive decides the proposed conditions are met, the negotiated agreement can be finalized.

Robinson and Harkness also suggest that it is critically important that once the supply chain executive is engaged, he or she should not disengage, because the negotiation team will appear weaker if the leader leaves the proceedings for any reason. An executive disengaging or stepping back from negotiations may be interpreted by the supplier that that particular executive is the decision maker who will need to be consulted prior to negotiations being finalized. This may be perceived by the supplier as reduced roles for the rest of the purchaser's team, and in turn, may diminish the team's ability to conclude the negotiation.

Bringing an executive into the negotiation process should always be accomplished in a precise manner to achieve a very specific goal. Because the negotiating process changes when a supply chain executive steps into the proceedings, executives should follow two key guidelines to direct negotiating tactics:

- **Focus on problem solving in negotiating:** This requires an executive to focus on the larger issues, such as long-term strategic vision, research and design initiatives, and collaborative long-term strategic partnerships. Avoid smaller issues that tend to only diminish the executive's standing in the eyes of the opposing party.
- **Learn from the supply management team:** Before stepping into the negotiating arena, the supply chain executive should gain a full understanding of key challenges and the competitive landscape of the negotiation.

Executive-level support in the negotiating process can help supply chain organizations navigate the difficult negotiations and execute a successful agreement for all parties. A high-ranking executive, when engaged at the right moment with a clear and defined role, can be a catalyst to help negotiators arrive at a successful purchasing agreement.

8.3.2 Delaying Tactics

Stalling, according to Jensen (2011), is usually employed as a tactic to inspire uneasiness and doubt in an opponent. Stalling can also be used more ethically to buy time in situations where additional research or internal discussion is needed and also if the negotiator is worried about emotions bleeding into the work (that is, gives them time to cool off).

Like any delaying approach, there are risks in using this negotiation tactic. A supplier, for example, might read a sudden absence of communication or a delaying change in discussion as being combative. The effects of a delay may end up placing the purchasing team under even more pressure instead of buying more time. Indeed, a supplier feeling neglected might simply decide to withdraw the offer.

How can we know whether a supplier is stalling? There are several ways. For example, being asked to look at further documentation when all the necessary information to begin negotiation is already present may be a stalling tactic. Similarly, if a supplier's negotiation team suddenly decides they are not qualified to negotiate, that may be a stalling tactic. In addition, always be on the lookout for the same questions or ideas being recycled.

The best practical way to deal with this is to use the same tactic. Jensen (2012) suggests taking the time the supplier negotiator provides by his or her absence and using it to the purchaser's advantage. The extra time may be spent on analysis of the supplier to be better prepared when the supplier finally decides to return to negotiate again. The ideal option is to circumvent the situation altogether by setting timetables and deadlines at the outset. If the purchasing team expects stalling tactics from the supplier, they should make sure the supplier understands right off what is expected as far as scheduling is concerned.

Finally, purchasers should be aware that some supplier negotiators stall not as a ploy, but as a defense mechanism. If a negotiator does not appear to want to make up his or her mind, or uses overly formal language or obscure procedural issues, it might be to simply scale things back or take things slower.

8.3.3 Preparing for Supply Chain Negotiations

It is essential for purchasing teams to craft a clear strategy for the negotiation. This strategy should formalize the objectives to be addressed with the supplier negotiating team. It should also help to identify acceptable ranges of solutions for each negotiable element such as the *maximum supportable solution* (MSS) and *least acceptable solution* (LAS), as well as to clearly identify the best alternative to a negotiated agreement (BATNA) or fallback plan in the event that the negotiation is not successful. Developing the strategy is essential to the preparation work needed to enter purchaser/supplier negotiations. Negotiation experts recommend 75% of the total time spent in the negotiation process should be spent in preparation activities. These preparation activities should include data collection and analysis of suppliers and strategy development and education of the purchaser's negotiation team. Unfortunately, the levels of preparation of the typical supplier negotiating team is substantially greater compared to their purchasing opponents.

According to Trowbridge (2012), a number of proven steps can be followed to prepare negotiators for even the most complex negotiations with suppliers, as described in Table 8.6.

Table 8.6 Winning Negotiation Preparation Steps

Prep Technique Steps	Description
1. Purchaser team should be familiar with supplier organization.	The purchasing team should spend time studying the supplier's organization by any means necessary, including visiting the supplier's Web site to learn everything possible. Knowing the supplier history or that they are expanding their operations can give the purchaser information useful about the supplier. Web sites can also list major customers of the supplier that might share information and be useful in gleaning information about the supplier's performance. Information about the supplier's sales and profitability is also useful in negotiations where the purchaser's agreement might profit the supplier's operations and add to their financial strength. In addition to the Web site information, purchasing stock for information-access reasons or using online services like Charles Schwab or TD Ameritrade can also result in useful financial information about the supplier's financial strength and business stability. All of this can prove useful in negotiating mutually beneficial contracts.

Prep Technique Steps	Description
2. Determine the supplier's agenda.	The purchasing negotiation team should seek to gather information about the supplier's team and its strategies even before the negotiation begins. Requesting a list of supplier participants and topics in advance of the beginning of negotiations is a way to know whether important players (for example, lawyers or executives) are going to participate right off. This provides a useful heads up on possible topics so that the purchasing team is not surprised during the negotiations. Such a list is not unrealistic to request.
3. Learn about the supplier's negotiation team.	Given the list of supplier participants from step 2, collect information on individual participants. If possible, develop profiles on each participant with the idea of learning their trustworthiness, education, ages, and any other background information (for example, hobbies) that might be useful in understanding how they think. Social networks like LinkedIn or Facebook are good starting places for this information.
4. Review performance history of supplier.	Obtain information about past relationships between buyers and suppliers. Supplier selection scorecards can provide useful criteria in rating past performance behavior. Learning about performance failures with other purchasing firms or willful misrepresentations of a supplier's supposed performance can be important in leveraging benefits for the purchasing organization. In areas of weakness, penalties against the supplier might be negotiated ahead of time to balance out risk in pricing or potential quality problems.
5. Select and prepare purchaser negotiation team.	The purchaser's team should be chosen based on their leadership and negotiation abilities. They should be decision makers who have the ability to cover the scope of negotiable elements and should be on a cross-functional sourcing team preparing for the negotiations. In addition, they should have a common understanding of the history leading up to the negotiation and the goals for it. If obliged to include a team member who is ill suited for the job for political or positional reasons, having a larger team and breaking it into subteams where this team member will have a limited role in the negotiations is a useful tactic to ensure best team performance.
	Once the team is assembled, each member should be assigned their responsibilities. Beyond the organizational responsibilities for which they were selected for the team, each member should be assigned additional responsibilities that facilitate the smooth functioning of the team. One person should be assigned to take notes to document progress at the meetings, and others might be assigned to perform financial calculations using spreadsheet technology. Still others might be tasked with observing and reporting on the body language of the supplier team members.

Prep Technique Steps	Description
6. Learn and prepare non-verbal signals.	Nonverbal signals from the supplier team can provide substantial information on the way they view how the negotiations are going. The purchasing team should use nonverbal signals to know when to stop talking or change directions in discussion. What is important here is that the purchasing team should know their own signals to share the nonverbal information. These signals should be rehearsed and prearranged. Texting with mobile phones can be used to communicate the purchasing team information during the negotiations as needed.
7. Communicate strategy.	A purchasing negotiation team needs to set forth its strategy in writing to ensure full understanding and buy-in from the team members. The purchasing negotiating team should go through a structured strategy development process in advance of the meeting with the suppliers. This may involve review of the internal analysis where the purchasers lay out their targets, describing the negotiable elements, stating the need level (for example, must have or like to have), ideas for solutions that are needed, and any other factors that are relevant to the negotiations (for example, fallback BATNA plan). While this information should be used preemptively before a meeting, it is recommended a *negotiation strategy worksheet* be prepared and used to help the team to review its objectives before entering the negotiation rooms. Purchasers should under no circumstances ever let the suppliers see the negotiation strategy worksheet or planning materials. During negotiations, electronic tools like an iPad can be used to display strategy information in a safe and secure manner.

Source: Adapted from Trowbridge (2012), pp. 46–51.

8.4 What's Next?

Many advances in negotiation theory are continuously appearing in the academic literature. Many of these advances are behaviorally theoretical and do not have much application for many years to come because of their unproven, theoretical nature. One area of development in the trend of negotiation practice is the use of automated technologies to augment and conduct negotiations.

As Ito et al. (2012) illustrate, technology can be used for active negotiations by permitting (or not permitting) revelation of information for decision making. An important and emerging area in the field of negotiation is the use of *autonomous agents* (that is, software that is at least partially autonomous) and *multi-agent systems* (that is, MAS composed of *intelligent agents* that are software applications with algorithmic and other procedural programming). MAS actually has the ability to share information using *knowledge query manipulation language* (KQML) (a software programming language to search for answers to queries). Autonomous agents and MAS can self-organize and self-steer efforts to control negotiation paradigms operating without human intervention. Autonomous agents can support automation or simulation of complex negotiations and can provide efficient bargaining strategies. To achieve such complex, automated negotiation, advances in *artificial intelligence* (AI) technologies (that is, logic and mathematical algorithms), *genetic algorithm* (GA) (that is, a search heuristic that mimics the process of natural evolution), and a *particle swarm optimization* (PSO) (that is, a computational method that optimizes a given solution through iterative steps) can be used.

9

Building an Agile and Flexible Supply Chain

Terms

Agile supply chains

Agility

Automated guided vehicles (AVG)

Available-to-promise (ATP)

Business analytics

Cellular manufacturing

Change management

Composite business service

Demand management

Executive dashboard

Flexibility manufacturing systems (FMS)

Flexible manufacturing systems (FMS)

Flexible supply chains

Interactive freight systems (IFS)

Knowledge management

Knowledge management technologies

Management by exception

Milestones

Project life cycle

Project management

Proof of delivery (POD)

Quick-response manufacturing (QRM)

Sales and operations planning (S&OP)

Service-oriented architecture (SOA)

Novelette

Seeking to achieve agility and flexibility in a supply chain means being able to adapt to change quickly. Supply chains, more than any other area in business, require the ability to provide rapid changes to meet customer and industry demands. The best way to build an agile and flexible supply chain is to anticipate ahead of time the need for agility and flexibility and then to design systems to achieve it.

In a conversation with Alan, our VP of the Small Engine Division, the topic of a disaster impacting supply chains, as it did during the disruptions caused in Japan with the earthquake and subsequent nuclear reactor problems in 2011, came up. Many of the small electrical modules we incorporate into our small engines are produced in Japan, and that disaster cut off many of the must-have items needed to complete our engines. The delays cost us millions of dollars in penalties, and it was a hard lesson to learn.

After reviewing the totality of impact to his Division of the 2011 Japanese earthquake and subsequent nuclear disaster, Alan asked what I had learned from the situation and what steps we, as an organization, were taking and planned on taking to avoid the risks of such disasters in the future. "Alan, our supply chain agility and flexibility are important, regardless of what causes the need for them. Our experience with the Japanese disruption of our supply chain gave us a good chance to take another look at our agility and flexibility program," I said.

"Bill, in the meetings on planning for greater agility and flexibility in our supply chains during disasters in general, we outlined some important preparative plans, but what about the cost of agility?" asked Alan.

"Yes, Alan, there can be costs, hefty costs to build agility in to a system, but I have found that planning to enhance our supply chain's agility can have many benefits that not only pay for the investment but also help us to advance other supply chain goals. If you try to install agility to deal with rare disasters that only happen every 10 or 20 years, the investment may not pay off or be warranted in the first place. Building agility into supply chains to meet more frequent short-term disruptions helps lessen the impact of full-blown disasters when they happen," I said.

"Bill, do you have a recent example you can share with me on agility and flexibility building and the benefits you experienced that I can share with our Division?" asked Alan.

"Yes! We had a recent problem with a supplier. In the Medium-Sized Engine Division, our carburetors have always been single sourced to one supplier. The building season for new car models was coming up in early 2012, and 90% of what we planned on producing was to be determined. As we began planning our demand requirements, the single source supplier plant burned to the ground. There presently were no other sources for the carburetors we needed, since they required special tooling. It was a disaster that we had to respond to quickly. As a response, we threw all the corporation's engineers into a think tank to start figuring out how we might be able to secure new sources. The engineers defined the types of special tooling needed to produce the carburetors. From there, we used our supply chain connections to locate suppliers who had equipment that could serve in the tooling process. In the meantime, we had some inventory and materials in the pipeline. We went into a scrabbled allocation mode to redistribute what we had various locations to these suppliers. We parceled the resources out a little here and little there, giving just enough to meet minimum demand requirements in each location. Within a matter of weeks, we were back online with sources for our carburetors. Now all of that was just response to a crisis situation, agility after the fact, but it gave the entire supply chain an opportunity to test just how agile we were. In some places, we found we needed to shore it up with new logistical methods and transportation modes to get the job done more quickly and efficiently. To build agility and flexibility, we have to install a means to be able to handle problems quickly, not just respond to crisis situations. Out of this supplier disaster, we ended up developing three new suppliers who could handle our future demand needs for this critical engine part. The benefits include the fact that we added agility and flexibility by creating a more global supply chain network, because our suppliers were on different continents, which provided some risk-avoidance protection against regional material shortages and labor stoppages. This global dispersion of suppliers also benefited us by being more logistically agile in meeting the timely customer demand requirement in different locations, since we had suppliers who were located geographically closer to our international markets, thus supporting our corporate growth goal," I explained.

"Bill, I am not trying to be argumentative here, but doesn't spreading out the suppliers sometimes result in differing quality, and that could also be a cost of agility?" Alan inquired.

"You are right, Alan, it can be, but to avoid that risk and to further our agility program, we ensure that products are produced using the same quality standards, same raw material specifications, same tooling, same manufacturing equipment, and the same training for people on the procedures for using the equipment. We standardized all of that, and also had dual sourcing plants in each location as backup in case problems developed in one or the other plant. This provides us with a consistent level of quality and a highly agile and flexible production system to reliably respond to customer needs. As an additional preparative step, we have been disaster planning by looking at possible contingencies based on disaster scenarios just in case we have a bad day with suppliers or earthquakes," I added.

9.1 Prerequisite Material

9.1.1 Agile and Flexible Supply Chains

Agility can be defined as a business-wide capability that integrates organizational structures, information systems, logistics processes, and a philosophical orientation (Amir, 2011). Agility as a concept in planning evolved as a response to ever-increasing levels of volatility in customer demand markets. It is viewed as a market-response strategy. In situations where demand levels are unstable and the customer requirements for variety increases, a much higher level of agility is required to meet those needs. An important characteristic of an agile organization is flexibility and adaptability. To meet the challenge of demand volatility, organizations need to focus efforts on achieving greater agility such that they can respond in shorter periods both in terms of volume change and variety change. According to Amir (2011), the origins of agility as a business concept relates to *flexible manufacturing systems* (FMS) (for example, automated systems like the *automated guided vehicles* [AVG] used for quick production-line changeovers). Originally, manufacturing flexibility and adaptability were achieved through automation to smooth the progress of swift changeovers and reduced setup times. This in turn enabled a greater responsiveness to changes in product mix and production quantities.

Flexible supply chains are those that can adapt quickly to market needs and deliver products and services to customers in a timely manner. Nagel and Dove (1991) extended the idea of manufacturing flexibility to other areas of business, and from this, the concept of agility as an organizational orientation originated. One definition of *agility* by Yusuf et al. (1999) encompasses the notion that firms successfully explore their own competitive base on characteristics of speed, flexibility, innovation, quality, and profitability through the integration of reconfigurable resources and knowledge to provide customer driven products and services in a fast changing market environment.

Agile supply chains are the alliances of legally separated organizations (for example, suppliers, designers, producers, logistics) distinguished by flexibility, adaptability, and quick, as well as effective, responses to changing markets (Rimiene, 2011). Agile supply chains are those that utilize strategies aimed at being responsive and flexible to customer needs. While agility focuses on increased responsiveness (for example, speed of delivery) and flexibility in what is delivered, there is a costly downside to this strategy. For example, the cost of speedy delivery, like express mail, is greater than regular first-class mail. These costs are assumed to be supported by the customer who values the responsiveness. In a competitive environment, the costs are often absorbed by the seller who must look internally to reduce overall costs of the supply chain. Agile supply chains often look upsteam in their production efforts or from their suppliers to find cost reductions to support the agile response initiative downstream nearest the customers. One of the strategies often used to reduce the cost in agile supply chains is the implementation of principles of lean management (Borgstrom and Hertz, 2011). (The topic of lean management in supply chains is presented in Chapter 12, "Lean and Other Cost Reduction Strategies in Supply Chain Management.") Lean management is often connected to supply chain agility, where tradeoffs between reducing costs (via lean management) is balanced with improved responsiveness (via agility and flexibility).

The only way to have agile and flexible supply chains is to undertake ongoing programs that move an organization toward agility and flexibility. Each step is usually undertaken as a project that needs to be managed. The systematic process of managing projects is known as project management.

9.1.2 Project Management

Chapter 8, "Negotiating," examined the subject of negotiation. The act of undertaking a negotiation constitutes a project. Selecting suppliers, planning new products, and setting up budgets are all examples of projects typical to supply chain management. To manage such projects, an entire field of study has emerged: project management. *Project management* involves the planning, controlling, directing, and scheduling of temporary activities that are undertaken to achieve a particular set of goals (for example, establish a new policy on transportation modes) or objectives (for example, reduce production costs). Like products, there is a *project life cycle* that involves a number of steps over a period of time that defines what is done in a project. Table 9.1 describes an example of a supply chain project life cycle, which is the embodiment of project management.

Table 9.1 Steps in Supply Chain Project Life Cycle

Stages in the Project Life Cycle	Description
1. Define the project.	Define the project, its goals, and objectives. Review current supply chain strategy and understand the new project's relationship to that strategy. This would also include an analysis of the potential time-phased benefits to the supply chain and its costs. Establish project team and management structure (that is, team leaders, coordinators). Determine and allocate needed resources to accomplish proposed project. This would include a feasibility study to determine the likelihood of the project's success and concept development to make sure the project was initially a sound idea.
2. Develop the solutions.	Define, document, and communicate the scope of project to limit expectations to the feasible. Conceptualize possible solutions or ideas to achieve project goals and objectives. This will include designing possible solutions to the problems being studied. It also details the supply chain processes, organization, and systems impacted by the solution. Plan a business release and rollout period for implementation. This step can also involve some prototyping to test the feasibility of developed solutions.

Stages in the Project Life Cycle	Description
3. Refine the solution details.	Add detail to step 2, such as specific dates, costs, personnel needed, and so on. Define the implementation team members and organization. This is an exercise in change management (that is, a process where changes to a project are formally introduced and approved, consisting of an approach of shifting or transitioning individuals, teams, and organizations while helping change stakeholders to accept and embrace changes in their business environment. This step also involves training efforts to condition everyone to new processes or behaviors needed to implement the planned changes. This step may also involve building and testing of proposed policies, procedures, processes, or products.
4. Deploy the solution.	Establish and monitor project performance during the project by establishing *milestones* (points over time where specific actions or tasks are required to be completed). Develop and implement the proposed solution based on the previous steps. Obtain necessary approvals from stakeholders, establish a schedule for deployment, and budget needed resources. This will usually require a resource requirements planning effort to know what will be required as well as determining the risks involved in the project in an effort to minimize them. The milestones can also be used as the basis for metrics on project performance.
5. Follow up and end the project.	Evaluate the project (that is, beginning expectations verses final outcomes is undertaken). Depending on the length of time for the project, follow-up may end once the project solution is deployed. In other projects, monitoring the progress or lack of progress is a part of the project effort. In either case, the project will have an end time, and once that is reached, it is formally ended.

Source: Adapted from Wetterauer and Meyr (2008), pp. 325–346; Matthews and Stanley (2008), pp. 24–69.

The diversity of projects that supply chain managers deal with is almost infinite, and even the general step-wise framework presented in Table 9.1 is only a simple review of basic elements that are considered in any project management undertaking. Most all projects require the services of a project manager and a project team. The project manager has the following roles (Krajewski et al., 2013, p. 52):

- **Facilitator:** The ability to resolve conflict between individuals and departments, to also appropriate the resources necessary to complete the project
- **Communicator:** The ability to communicate new resource needs and project progress to stakeholders
- **Organizer and decision maker:** The ability to organize team meetings, establish decision-making rules for the team, and determine the nature and timing of reports to senior management

As to the selection of project management teams, the criteria should include the following:

- **Technical competence:** Members need to have the ability to understand the technology required for the project.
- **Sensitivity:** Members need to have sensitivity to interpersonal issues that can arise in group decision making, such as the influence of senior management on junior members of the team.
- **Dedication:** Members should be dedicated to completing the project and be able to handle issues that might impact multiple departments.

9.2 Agile Supply Chains

Over more than 20 years, the concept of agile supply chains has evolved into a much wider range of topics as opposed to just being responsive to the market (Rimiene, 2011). Agility characteristics today include responsiveness to customer demand, responsiveness in general to any organizational need, flexibility as to what products and services are delivered, speed/time of delivery, efficiency in terms of costs, quality of product or service, cooperation with customers (both internal and external to the organization), the ability to allow and make changes in relationships of all kinds, the ability to move quickly to seize new market opportunities, and the use of *knowledge management* (that is, strategies and practices used in combination with computer technology in an organization to identify, create, represent, distribute, and enable adoption of acquired insights and experiences) to guide decision making (Rimiene, 2011).

How can an organization know whether it has an agile supply chain? Based on criteria established in the supply chain literature, managers should look to have or enhance the following components recognized as characteristics of agile supply chains (Harrison and Van Hoek, 2008):

- **Agility in customer responsiveness:** The ability to respond to the market according to customer demand and not company forecasts
- **Agile network of partners:** Partners who have a common goal to collaborate in order to respond to customer needs
- **Business process:** A view that the network is a system of business processes and not a stand-alone process, which may create penalties in terms of time, cost, and quality for the whole network
- **Agile information technology:** Information technology that is shared between buyers and suppliers creating a virtual supply chain that is information based rather than inventory based

Another set of criteria useful in determining whether a firm has an agile supply chain was suggested by Christopher (2). The philosophy that drives Christopher's (2) criteria is based on the assumption that supply chains compete against one another, not their companies. Successful supply chains will be those companies can better structure, coordinate, and manage relationships with partners in the supply chain network to support better and agile communications with the customers. Christopher (2) distinguished four characteristics or criteria that an agile supply chain must possess:

- **Market sensitivity:** A supply chain is able to understand and respond to real demand. Many organizations continue to use forecasts, assessing the sales and supply volumes of previous years and then turning this information into stock, rather than real needs. Today, by using advanced technology, actual customer requirements are identified from data derived from fixed sales points almost as soon as the customer consumes it. An example of this is the new Coca-Cola Freestyle machines, which provide daily, per-customer actual demand usage of beverage product information that enables Coca-Cola to plan for their customer needs.

- **Virtual supply chain:** There is electronic transference of information between buyers and suppliers rather than inventory.

- **Process integration:** This involves constantly increasing cooperation between buyers and suppliers, joint production, joint systems, and information sharing to join and integrate systems with all supply chain partners.

- **Network structure:** This comprises a supply chain network of associated partners structured with alliances to achieve needed functions.

What justifies the need for an agile strategy? According to Goldman et al. (1995), four classic and key principles are sought in agility programs:

- Desire to increase the number of customers
- Desire to control of changes and uncertainty in the supply chain environment
- Desire to possess cooperation enhancing the competitiveness of the firm
- Desire to control supply chain participants, their information, and technology

Lin et al. (2006) found that agile companies can achieve lower production costs, increase market share, meet customer demands, facilitate the rapid launch of new products on the market, and eliminate the activities having no value added, all while increasing the company's competitiveness. In addition, empirical research has consistently confirmed agile supply chains usually lead to successful business performance (Vickery et al., 2010).

There is a need to differentiate between an agile response to customer demand and an efficient response to demand that can be exhibited as it is related to the different stages of a product's life cycle. As shown in Figure 9.1, an almost inverse relationship exists between the need for an agile response to customer demand and an efficient response (that is, cost minimizing). Illustrative of the need to consider product life cycles in supply chain planning over a product's life, the agile approach is not always the best strategy to follow in every case and for every product when you look at the product life cycle. The use of agility should be matched to the needs of the product and its life cycle to maximize business performance.

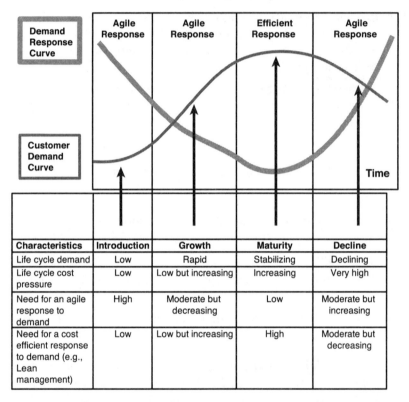

Characteristics	Introduction	Growth	Maturity	Decline
Life cycle demand	Low	Rapid	Stabilizing	Declining
Life cycle cost pressure	Low	Low but increasing	Increasing	Very high
Need for an agile response to demand	High	Moderate but decreasing	Low	Moderate but increasing
Need for a cost efficient response to demand (e.g., Lean management)	Low	Low but increasing	High	Moderate but decreasing

Figure 9.1 Product life cycle stages and agility/efficiency implementation

Source: Adapted from Davis (2011).

What specific strategies are used to affect an agile supply chain? Many general strategies can be incorporated into a supply chain to make it more agile, depending on the type of organization and where they can be applied. Embodying some of the criteria already mentioned in this chapter can help achieve agility, but specific strategies can be followed as they relate to specific elements. Table 9.2 describes some of those.

Table 9.2 Strategic Positions for Agile Supply Chains

Strategic Element	Suggested Agile Position
Product	Seek to have a wide variety of products to meet varied demand and a supply chain network that can service the breath of the product lines.
Price	Seek a moderate price level that does not have to be minimized. Because agile supply chains provide quick response capabilities, the value of that service level adds to the value of the product and so pricing is not as important in the competitive mix as the service. Also being able to deliver a product in the Introduction Stage of their product life cycle quicker than competitors can afford a firm a more profitable and higher price in the market place.
Promotion	Seek to have higher levels of investment in promotional efforts to gain new customers. Develop plans to build up supply chain capacity to anticipate volatility of demand and service the higher-demand peak-time rates.
Customization	Seek to provide substantial capability to meet varied type of product demand. This also allows firms to explore new product ideas based on customer demand suggestions. Develop a supply chain network that can quickly adapt and change to differing suppliers that offer unique customization services.
Market awareness	Seek to use business analytics to define market trends and be guided in new directions for products and services. Use the business analytic metrics and trend information to guide supply chain investment decisions.
Innovation	Seek to invest heavily to support and explore new products that evolve from research and development as well as customer ideas. Adopt a strategy where supply chain personnel are included in innovation planning to allow for their contributions (for example, cost reduction, quick response) to add value to new products or services.
Risk	Seek to accept higher risk in contracts and other arrangements with suppliers to support innovation efforts and new product developments. Develop risk-mitigation strategies to minimize total potential risk (as discussed in Chapter 11, "Risk Management").
Procurement	Seek to select supply chain suppliers based on their capacity to be flexible and responsive, not necessarily on their ability to minimize their prices.
Customer service	Seek adequate supply chain service capacity to provide timely service to customers.

Strategic Element	Suggested Agile Position
Customer fulfillment	Seek to provide supply chain quick response to customer demands. Where necessary, add buffer inventory in the supply chain to ensure timely delivery of product.
Supply chain capacity	Seek to have adequate excess supply chain capacity (that is, backup supplier, inventory buffers, production capacity, information support, and so on) to deal with the customer-demand fluctuations.

Source: Adapted from Gattorna (2010), pp. 234–235; Gunasekaran et al. (2008); Krajewski et al. (2010), pp. 342–343.

What strategies are suggested for increasing supply chain agility? Identifying agile variables under the control of supply chain managers that could lead to increased agility is a good starting place to know where agility can be increased. According to Agarwal et al. (2007), managers can alter or change the following 15 variables or areas of responsibility to increase supply chain agility: recognizing market sensitivity, delivery speed, data accuracy, new product introduction, centralized and collaborative planning, process integration, use of IT tools, lead-time reduction, service-level improvement, cost minimization, customer satisfaction, quality improvement, minimizing uncertainty, trust development, and minimizing resistance to change.

Some researchers have proposed strategies for increasing agility (Gunasekaran, 1998; Rimiene, 2011; Yang and Li, 2002), including the following:

- **Virtual manufacturing:** Eliminating the physical structure of the manufacturing operations through, for example, outsourcing is a the strategy that enables core competency integration to achieve a more efficient operation of the company in an agile environment.

- **Agile product design:** Building flexibility in the product design is a strategy that allows companies to adapt to changed consumer requirements (for example, using modular product design solutions).

- **Use of knowledge management:** Utilizing knowledge management technologies (that is, document management systems, expert systems, semantic networks for search and retrieval, relational and object-oriented databases, simulation tools, and artificial intelligence) for innovative solutions and implementation in design and production processes.

- **Mass customization:** This focuses on offering customers personally tailored products and services with new technological innovations.

9.3 Flexible Supply Chain

There are differences between *agility* and *flexibility*. Gunasekaran et al. (2008) compared agile supply chains with responsive (that is, flexible) supply chains. They found responsive or flexible supply chains are more interested in supply management and minimizing costs than they are interested in agile supply chains. Flexibility in supply chains is often related to other flexibility and agility programs. For example, *quick-response manufacturing* (QRM) is a flexibility program that emphasizes time-reduction efforts throughout the supply chain both internally (that is, distribution and manufacturing) and externally (that is, suppliers and other business partners). With shorter lead times, a supply chain can reduce cost and eliminate non-value-added waste, while simultaneously increasing the organization's competitiveness and market share by serving customers better and faster. Under QRM, suppliers seek to negotiate reduced supplier lead times, because long lead times can negatively impact costs such as those relating to extensive inventory, freight costs for rush shipments, engineering changes, and obsolete inventory. There is also reduced flexibility to respond to demand changes. The time-based framework of QRM accommodates the flexibility strategy, even in custom-oriented organizations. Short lead times allow a firm to respond more quickly to customer demand requirements, particularly in highly fluctuating demand markets.

What drives the development of flexible supply chains is the desire to quickly serve the customer. A number of tools can be used to implement flexible supply chains. One of the tools used to manage flexibility involves *demand management* (that is, various tools and procedures that enable firms to balance demand and supply in such a way as to better understand and manage demand volatility). One software solution used to accomplish this balancing is *Collaborative Planning, Forecasting, and Replenishment* (CPFR) (see Chapter 2, "Designing Supply Chains"). Another important flexibility and agility tool is *sales and operations planning* (S&OP). This business process continuously balances supply and demand. According to Simchi-Levi (2010, p. 144), S&OP is cross-functional in nature integrating sales, marketing, new product introductions, manufacturing, and distribution into a single plan. Another business process tool that can aid in matching demand with supply is known as available-to-promise. *Available-to-promise* (ATP) is a process that provides a response to customer order inquiries based on resource availability. Basically, it generates available quantities of a requested product and delivery due dates so that customers are aware of these ahead of time (and has the firms to supply products to meet customer demand). ATP processes consist of computer technology and usually are integrated in *enterprise resource planning* (ERP) management software packages (see Chapter 2).

Unfortunately, even with the best demand management systems in place, customer demand can vary substantially, resulting in costly impacts. The variations in the product life cycle alone make demand planning very difficult. One strategy to deal with unexpected demand volatility is for firms to build in to their supply chains some flexibility. Where to begin to implement or improve flexibility is unique to every supply chain, but several areas can serve as starting places, including examination of three components: product, process, and system. Table 9.3 describes some suggestions for building flexibility in these areas. How much flexibility a firm should implement, suggested in the comments in Table 9.3, should be determined by perceived benefits and their respective costs.

Table 9.3 Areas for Building Flexibility in Supply Chains

Area in Which to Build Flexibility	Description	Supply Chain Planning Considerations
Product	Consider in the design of a product the supply chain functionality capabilities. During the development phase, explore availability of materials for product and supply chain potential advantages in the acquisition process. During the manufacturing phase, build in modular features and standardized parts where possible to ease inventory and supply chain requirements	Factors to consider include the following: • Assessing the demand uncertainty and variability • Economics of scale in production, distribution and transportation • Lead times, both domestic and globally
Process	Consider in the workforce the needed skills and processes to make the supply chain flexible. The workforce should be cross-trained to allow for greater flexibility in the production area as well as positions in the supply chain area. The use of lean management principles (see Chapter 12) to avoid waste and improve workforce abilities to deal with variability should be incorporated. Advanced production technology should be purchased and installed to maximize flexibility. This would include processes such as *cellular manufacturing* (that is, the grouping of people, processes and technology into production cells) and *flexibility manufacturing systems* (FMS) technology (for example, automated guided vehicles for flexible production lines).	Factors to consider include the following: • Reducing variability in machines, human resources, and job processes in supply chain equipment and staff • Maximizing production throughput by equalizing workforce skill levels through cross-training • Identifying sources of variability in all supply chain processes and reducing them

Area in Which to Build Flexibility	Description	Supply Chain Planning Considerations
System	Consider in the design of supply chain systems how best to incorporate flexibility. Supply chain delivery efforts to time materials and product delivery to exactly meet demand requirements is one area of application. Redesign production and distribution facilities to support supply chain functions of delivery, loading, and unloading. Move away from forecasting-driven production systems to more customer-driven systems. Utilize advanced customer contact and interaction communication systems to feel the pulse of customer demands rather than produce to forecast (for example, *customer relations management* [CRM] software).	Factors to consider include the following: • Cost of benefits to the supply chain • The degree of flexibility desired to serve the customers • The ability and benefits in volatile demand environments

Source: Adapted from Simchi-Levi (2010, pp. 133–171); Schniederjans et al. (2010, p. 51); Bowersox et al. (2007, p. 160).

9.4 Other Topics Related to Agile and Flexible Supply Chains

9.4.1 Agility and Global Business

Global supply chains can be overwhelming to operate and challenging as to an end-to-end view. Butner (2011) suggests that creating an agile supply chain can be a part of a strategy that will help managers in running global supply chains, making them more manageable. Butner recommends building agile supply chain operations with the capability to respond not just to customer demands but also to demand shocks, shifts and variability, and to problems in supply production and logistics activities. Demand shocks and shifts can happen because of promotion activities. Variability in demand can cause rapid upward and downward spikes as result of many factors, including poor logistics to markets or an overly successful advertising program. Regardless of the cause, an agile supply chain needs to quickly respond to serve the needs of a global market.

To achieve a supply chain that is agile enough to deal with demand-variation issues in a global context, Butner suggests the following features be incorporated into global supply chains:

- Bundle visibility and control of supply chains into a synchronized portal like an *executive dashboard* (that is, a computer technology that gathers, analyzes, displays, and disseminates planning and operational data).

- Consolidate supply chain events across the entire global value chain, whether related to customers, distribution, manufacturing, or multitiered suppliers.

- Use *management by exception* (that is, a style of management that is focused on limiting of efforts to rule breaking exceptions, rather than routine monitoring and control procedures) to notify and recommend corrective actions.

- Use the Internet to establish collaboration with supply chain partners.

- Use service-oriented architecture and a composite business service for rapid integration of data from multiple sources. *Service-oriented architecture* (SOA) is an information technology architectural style that supports the transformation of a business into a set of linked services that can be broken down and accessed when needed to examine performance over an entire global network. A *composite business service* is a collection of business services that integrates with a client's existing computer applications to provide a specific business solution.

- Use *business analytics* (that is, a combination of mathematical and statistical models and computer software systems like data mining) to guide decision making.

- Use the latest computing and communication technology to monitor and aid in controlling global components of the supply chain.

9.4.2 Achieving Agility with Supply Chain Synchronicity

According to the *Journal of Commerce* (2012), six core business processes must be closely synchronized to enable organizational agility. Failure to synchronize them will keep global supply chains from achieving their highest potential:

- **Sales and operations planning (S&OP):** S&OP should be a continuous process where executives seek to have visibility and input to reconcile short-term demand predictions with long-term organizational goals. The S&OP must occur at both the operational and executive levels, bringing views together in a closed-loop planning process that focuses on achieving consensus. The S&OP process should provide a discipline across every part of the organization, including the supply chain, establishing cadence for monitoring, and synchronizing demand, production, supply, inventory, and financial plans.

- **Demand planning:** Business analytics should be applied to ensure sourcing, production, inventory, transportation, and distribution functions are optimized based on a shared forecast. Business analytic solutions provide a single set of forecasts and other decision-making solutions that can be used for 24 months or longer, with each element of the plan translated into specific actions, goals, and implications for every part of the supply chain. The analytics should also account for the impact of promotional and external events that may have repercussions across any global supply chain.

- **Inventory planning:** Use advanced tools to create highly customized designer inventory strategies based on consumption patterns, criticality, velocity, and other key product attributes. Products are segmented on product life cycles based on other critical characteristics listed earlier. Inventory levels are managed by exception to maximize time and cost-efficiency, and wherever possible, decisions are postponed to minimize financial risk. Advanced technology solutions should be employed to consider existing, multi-echelon network complexity, lead times, costs and constraints, as well as demand and supply variability to ensure inventory plans are aligned with the rest of the global supply chain. For example, *interactive freight systems* (IFS) are software applications that can be used to find the least-cost routing for trucks, real-time freight tracking, including *proof of delivery* (POD), and freight-invoice reconciliation (Supply Chain 2020, 2012).

- **Master planning:** Review, analyze, and update supply plans daily to maximize customer satisfaction while protecting profits. Through a problem-oriented approach, planners should monitor performance issues and exceptions wherever they occur in the global supply network. A layered planning approach for planners to rank their business objectives and make informed tradeoffs should be used. Utilizing clear visibility into the root causes or constraints creating problems, planners should interactively adjust constraints and business rules that result in continuous performance improvements for the business overall. Despite the complexity of global supply chains, advanced technology solutions can provide sophisticated modeled capabilities to study and resolve issues of supply chain networks.

- **Factory planning and scheduling:** Detailed and optimized production plans based on the business analytics should be defined for plants, departments, work cells, and production lines by scheduling backward from the requirement date, while considering material and capacity constraints to create feasible and executable plans. Advanced computer software solutions should be used to streamline and align the activities of production control, manufacturing, and procurement planning teams by automating mundane tasks. The software-guided solutions should also provide time-phased reporting on key factory performance metrics, enabling planners to take corrective measures for short-term and long-term planning. Use of a management-by-exception approach can eliminate unnecessary work, minimize planning fatigue, and be useful in assessing a variety of scenarios when the unexpected occurs.

- **Collaborative supply planning:** Utilize advanced computer information systems for the purchase of parts and assemblies from a range of diverse and geographically scattered suppliers in a typical global supply chain. These parts undoubtedly have different lead times, demand profiles, and inventory strategies, but can be managed through customized business rules and policies that track performance exceptions based on a unique set of part characteristics. Technologies such as executive dashboards, exception-based reporting, and early warning systems can allow supply issues to be identified and resolved before they impact the global network. Today these technologies can track the entire life cycle of procured parts, enabling organizations to adjust forecasts, production schedules, transportation plans, and other supply chain activities when late deliveries or other events impact the overall manufacturing flow.

9.4.3 Agility and S&OP

In a recent survey by Supply Chain Insights LLC (www.supplychaininsights.com/) of 100 supply chain executives, *supply chain agility* was defined as the ability to recalculate plans in the face of market demand and supply volatility and deliver at the same or comparable cost, quality, and customer service (Cecere, 2012a). The survey identified agility as one of the three key attributes expected in any supply chain. The other attributes were flexibility and strength (that is, the ability of the supply chain to make changes). The survey went on to suggest that S&OP has in the past focused on building strength into the supply chain while ignoring the impact of flexibility and agility. It was noted that companies with the most experience with S&OP processes have been successful in adding agility to their supply chains. While the respondents in the survey overwhelmingly viewed agility as important, they rated agility-generated performance as being very low (that is, agility is important, but results from it, so far, are not). Because the firms that have been successful in using S&OP appear to have gained more from an agility strategy, the results of the survey have led to a set of five recommendations that can aid in increasing the performance of agility within corporate supply chains based on S&OP usage:

- Design agility into the supply chain based on future levels of supply and demand variability.
- Utilize S&OP to plan for unexpected demand events, and understand inherent tradeoffs as a means to explore and simulate alternative decisions based on market demand.
- Utilize employee participation in simulations to understand how to increase supply chain reliability.
- Anticipate and simulate potential supply chain disruptions for scenario explorations.
- Execute the S&OP plan, instead of making it a mere academic exercise.

9.5 What's Next?

In 2012, thanks largely to a worldwide economic slump, corporate growth has flattened, and supply chain costs have increased. According to Cecere (2012b), 90% of businesses are grappling with skyrocketing costs, rising supply volatility, and longer supply chains that add greater risk. Factors such as commodity volatility being at its highest level in 100 years, materials scarcity, rising standards for social-responsibility programs, shorter product life cycles, and customers having higher expectations and a need for greater customization in products and services all add to a challenging supply chain environment going forward in the next five years. Also, as companies become more global, they face ever-rising supply chain complexity, demand volatility, and supply uncertainty.

Agility and flexibility are viewed as opportune strategies to deal with current and near-future supply chain challenges. In a survey by Cecere (2012b), 89% of 117 supply chain executives rated agility as being important in supply chain success, even though only about a third of the executives had the prerequisite agility to compete. The desire to catch up and narrow the gap between the recognized need and the capacity to deliver agility clearly shows that substantial interest in agility will be a future trend.

Increased interest and expansion of flexible supply chains is viewed as a major trend going forward, as well. According to Miller (2012), when time to market is more important than costs, having flexible processes and systems will be an important strategy to achieve competitive advantages.

10

Developing Partnerships in Supply Chains

Terms

Basic alliance

Business alliance

Business analytics

Collaborative growth model

Competence trust

Contractual trust

Cross-enterprise problem solving teams

Cross-organizational team

Customer of choice

Developing partnerships

Experienced competency

Goodwill trust

Key account management (KAM)

Key performance indicators (KPIs)

Operational alliance

Partnership

Purchaser and supplier development (PSD)

Relationship management (RM)

Request for information (RFI)

Request for proposal (RFP)

Strategic alliance

Supplier performance management

Supplier collaboration

Supplier management (SM)

Supplier performance measurement (SPM)

Supplier relationship management (SRM)

Supplier relationship management intensity continuum

Supply base rationalization (SBR)

Supply scorecards

Transactional

Trust

Vendor-managed inventory (VMI)

Novelette

Supply chain success is dependent on the relationship client firms have with their suppliers. Developing partnerships to advance and build strong relationships is a primary role for supply chain managers. The payback for investing in the development of partnerships with suppliers can be incredibly beneficial to both the client firm and suppliers. Like a trusting friendship, the relationship can be a safety net when trouble disrupts supply chain activity.

As the VP of Operations for a major manufacturing organization, I am responsible for many things, including holding an annual meeting where I bring the four Division VPs and their management staff together for internal relations-building purposes. I selected a theme for this meeting of developing partnerships in supply chains. To get things started, I thought I should give everyone an example as to how supply chain partnership development has had a positive impact on our organization's operations, and in doing so, sell the idea of partnership development in all four Divisions.

Addressing the audience of about 50 people, I began by saying, "Hi, everybody, before we begin the usual meeting activities, I want to share something about our organization and our efforts in developing partnerships with our suppliers. I have found from personal experience that two important terms are essential in developing supplier partnerships: *collaboration* and *performance measurement.* Collaboration works both ways when you do it right. Most of you know one of our major suppliers to our Large Engine and Medium-Sized Engine Divisions does business in our industry, but fortunately, we are not competitors for the products we each sell. As we have gotten to know them and have shared information about our needs, we also have learned about their needs. We have worked with them to establish a unique relationship of sharing more than just transactional needs. For example, they partnered with our product design teams to help bring cost reduction and improved efficiency to products we wanted to introduce. Sure, they benefit from increased sales of products and services to us, but we also benefit through the collaboration. Our exchanges with their engineers allowed our supply chain people to observe how they operated their supply chain and inventory planning. Given their extensive size, we were able to learn new best practices, which we could bring back to our operations to improve our efficiency. In return, we helped them more fully implement their lean management program, since we were more experienced in that area of operations. Then, combining the supply chain best practices with lean, we were able to extend our own lean practices up and down our supply chain to achieve fuller compliance with our suppliers, distribution, and retail partners. In addition, like a good partner, when we experienced commodity shortages a few years back, they helped us locate new sources globally for those commodities. All of this collaboration has helped us create a long-lasting partnership that is mutually beneficial and handy when problems surface."

From the audience, Pedro, the VP of Large Engines, blurts out, "Hey, Bill, not all of our suppliers are as helpful and beneficial as the firm you are talking about."

"You are right, Pedro, and that is why collaboration must be combined with performance measurement efforts. Even our best partners, who we have little problems dealing with, expect us to monitor their performance in serving our needs, and we expect them to do the same. We collect the information about suppliers from our people. The kinds of criteria we seek depends on the Division needs; but clearly, criteria like on-time delivery, pricing, and joint problem-solving efforts are important performance measures we need to keep track of. Most of the suppliers have their own performance measures of what they think is important, such as warranted returns to us from our customers. They track what they think is their own on-time deliveries to us, their own e-connections, service quality, and pricing increases that they have given us. In addition, they track costs and pricing in the industry, all of which is creating a negotiation opportunity. This jointly collected information is valuable, so when we get together with them, we have something to talk about to improve what we both do to serve our customers. To help implement the performance measurement efforts for our organization, we will be using supplier scorecards that list the criteria each Division decides is important in monitoring their suppliers, which allows us to rate supplier performance. The respective Division VPs will work with their supply chain departments to draft the scorecards. The purchasing manager and purchasing team, which should include the specific buyer or commodity manager who manages the relationship and an associate for daily clerical tasks, will collect the information for the supplier scorecards. We will also be adding some tech support by offering each Division a supply quality engineer to help develop the scorecards. What you will find is that these scorecards will help create a better dialogue to develop an honest and trusting relationship with our suppliers," I explained.

10.1 Prerequisite Material

10.1.1 Introduction to Supplier Relationship Management

A firm as large as Wal-Mart depends on suppliers to have the capacity to supply the large quantities needed in its global retail operations. Other firms, such as Home Depot, need suppliers who help them differentiate by carrying distinctive brands of products. Supply chain purchasing organizations have to build the right relationships/partnerships with the right suppliers to enable them to compete with other world-class supply chains.

Developing partnerships in supply chains involves more than just the process of purchasing goods from a supplier. It involves rationalizing the supplier network that is created to serve the purchaser, manage the suppliers and the relationship that develops between the purchaser and supplier, enhance and developing that relationship, and measure supplier performance (Banfield, 1999, pp. 223–252; Carter and Choi, 2008; Monczka et al., 2011). Depending on the needs required and the level of intensity in the relationship, the entire process could be done in a few days or many years of interaction between a purchaser and a supplier. A *partnership* that aligns both partners to achieve a desired set of goals and that builds from a simple transactional relationship to a true partnership in business involves considerable time and effort. Ideally, the interactions lead to a trusting relationship, a partnership that helps both firms become profitable and successful in their respective industries. This is what building and *developing partnerships* in supply chains is all about and is the subject of this chapter.

10.1.2 Types of Supplier Relationships

Part of developing a supplier partnership is initially deciding the type of relationship a purchasing firm might need. The supply chain literature identifies at least five different types of relationships a purchasing firm can have with a supplier. The relationships are placed on a *supplier relationship management continuum of intensity*. Not all relationships fit neatly into a particular relationship category (see Figure 10.1).

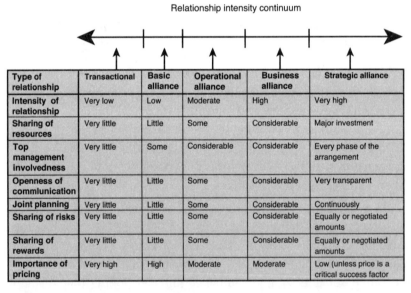

Relationship intensity continuum

Type of relationship	Transactional	Basic alliance	Operational alliance	Business alliance	Strategic alliance
Intensity of relationship	Very low	Low	Moderate	High	Very high
Sharing of resources	Very little	Little	Some	Considerable	Major investment
Top management involvedness	Very little	Some	Considerable	Considerable	Every phase of the arrangement
Openness of commlunication	Very little	Little	Some	Considerable	Very transparent
Joint planning	Very little	Little	Some	Considerable	Continuously
Sharing of risks	Very little	Little	Some	Considerable	Equally or negotiated amounts
Sharing of rewards	Very little	Little	Some	Considerable	Equally or negotiated amounts
Importance of pricing	Very high	High	Moderate	Moderate	Low (unless price is a critical success factor

Figure 10.1 Characteristics of differing types of supplier relationships and the SRM intensity continuum

Source: Adapted from Carter and Choi (2008, pp.238–241); Fawcett et al. (2008, p.347); Ellran (2).

Some types of relationships may be a hybrid and fall between two categories or may be some combination. The types of relationships typically fall into one or more of those defined here:

- **Transactional:** This is a short-term, temporary alliance or contract to provide a product or service. The supplier is sometime characterized as being at "arm's length," implying that a relational distance from the purchasing firm exists. Transactional suppliers simply provide an economic exchange with the purchaser. This category of relationship is usually used by a purchaser as a test to see whether a supplier can provide a least cost product or service reliably, and in doing so, determine if the firm is worthy of a more intense role as a supplier to the purchaser.

- **Basic alliance:** An agreement between a purchaser and supplier that does more than just provide a transaction of moving goods from the supplier to the purchaser for a fixed price, but includes participation by the supplier to undertake additional tasks or services needed by the purchasing firm (for example, *vendor-managed inventory,* or VMI, where monitoring of inventory levels would be undertaken by the supplier). Many competitive sources of basic suppliers undertake this type of alliance, so it is low risk and has limited impact on the purchasing organization's overall value proposition. Purchasers and suppliers at this level share information as needed, but do not allow suppliers great access to the purchaser's information network. Both parties know where they stand with the other. This type of relationship can be used with any supplier, and it is a prerequisite for moving toward other relationships on the supplier relationship management continuum.

- **Operational alliance:** This includes all the elements of a basic alliance, but there is a closer working relationship one- to three-year contract. It is one in which the supplier performs value-added services or provides additional products as part of its business. There may be some joint problem solving, but no ongoing *cross-organizational team* (that is, a group of individuals from different departments and organizational functional areas to bring unique perspectives to decision-making efforts). Information sharing becomes more critical because day-to-day operations must be shared for the alliance to operate successfully.

- **Business alliance:** Different from the previous alliances, the purchasing organization wants the supplier to provide unique or specialized products or services. Characterized by an increased recognition of mutual dependence, it is to be expected that the supplier will invest additional assets, specialized personnel, or technology to carry out the alliance. However, the purchaser will significantly reduce the supply base to commit a higher volume of business to the supplier for an extended period of time. The benefit to the purchasing organization is added value, but not strategic or core values to the organization's business success. Some joint engineering or technology development may occur. In addition, ad hoc cross-organizational teams may be formed for joint development or problem solving.

- **Strategic alliance:** This alliance involves goods or services that are of strategic importance to the success of the purchasing organization and a sharing or alignment of long-term strategies for both parties. This usually involves early supplier involvement in new product/service/process idea conception and mutual recognition of a long-term ongoing relationship between the purchasing and supplier organizations. Other resources that are typically shared under this agreement include products, distribution channels, manufacturing capabilities, project funding, technology transfers, capital equipment, knowledge, expertise, or intellectual property. It is also characterized by agreements that articulate the risks and rewards and how these will be shared. Ongoing joint cross-organizational teams and top management involvement are required for strategic alliances.

As Figure 10.1 shows, the five types of relationships follow a supply chain management intensity continuum based on the intensity of the desired relationship. The differing characteristics given in Figure 10.1 are simply tendencies that have been observed in the supply chain literature. Although all supplier relationships are important, some require very close and integrated support for the client purchasing firm (that is, strategic alliance). On the other end of the continuum, transactional suppliers are firms that merely provide a fixed product or service at a fixed rate for a fixed period of time. Perhaps, if the supplier's performance were exceptional, the firm might be considered as a candidate to move along the continuum to a higher level of usage by the purchasing firm.

Clearly, there is a spectrum of types of supplier relationships available from which to choose. It is not necessarily a goal to move every supplier from a transactional level to a more intense alliance unless there is strong mutual benefit for doing so. Also, as markets change, the appropriate alliance for a given supplier may change. Strategic alliances require active top-management participation, support, and visibility on a regular basis. However, developing partnerships with suppliers might only involve a purchasing firm helping its suppliers travel along the continuum to achieve strategic importance. All of these considerations are vital for developing supply chain partnerships.

10.2 Supplier Relationship Management Implementation Model

To undertake a supplier relationship management program requires several programs that are holistically integrated to provide a continuing basis for a successful program of partnership development. These elements are listed in Figure 10.2. The implementation model suggested in Figure 10.2 is based on the literature in this field (Monczka et al., 2011; Carter and Choi, 2008, pp. 191–199; Matthews and Stanley, 2008, pp. 295–315; Fawcett et al., 2007, pp. 345–361). Let's examine each of these five elements.

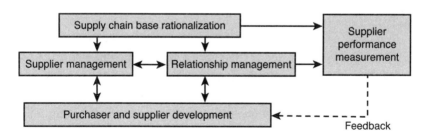

Figure 10.2 Supplier relationships management implementation model

Source: Adapted from Monczka et al. (2011), Figure 2.2, p.19.

10.2.1 Supply Chain Base Rationalization

A purchasing firm starts with an idea for a product or service and seeks to find a supplier that will help fill the need. In some situations, a supplier may be brought in just to help develop the idea in hopes of providing a continued service or product. These suppliers might have been identified when they responded to a *request for information* (RFI) (that is, a request for suppliers to provide information about how they might qualify to become a supplier for the purchasing firm). In other situations, a *request for proposal* (RFP) (that is, a document stating the desired requirements of a supplier to fulfill a particular set of product or service needs in terms of pricing or timing) might be used to find eligible candidate suppliers to join the purchaser's supply chain team of suppliers or subsequent supply chain network.

Supply base rationalization (SBR) seeks to identify suppliers that could create significant value and contribute to a purchasing organization's business performance. SBR is also defined as a means of determining and maintaining the appropriate number of suppliers in a supply chain network, segmented by item, category, strategic/ transactional, and so on, depending on the risk and value of each segment (Carter and Choi, 2008, p. 249). SBR is a rationalization process that can involve judgmental or other quantitative means to evaluate and determine the worthiness of suppliers in terms of supplier capabilities (that is, supplier technology, quality, cost, capacity, manufacturing operations, financial strength, flexibility, and responsiveness), past performance (that is, technology contributions, price or cost improvements, quality performance, and responsiveness and flexibility to volume and scheduling needs), core competencies and match with purchasing firm's needs, their organizational culture, and communications fit with the purchasing firm (that is, supplier's ability and willingness to work closely with the purchaser, be culturally aligned in decision making, and the degree of risk inherent in the working relationship). In a survey by Monczka et al. (2011) leading supply chain managers viewed SBR as a foundational step in reducing the number of suppliers in a given network. The criteria on which this rationalization process is typically based includes the following:

- Seeking suppliers (both present and perspective) that are able to achieve performance improvement in terms of costs, quality or delivery in response to purchaser needs
- Seeking suppliers who can reduce administrative costs, including the reduction of the number of suppliers in the network
- Seeking suppliers who want to build a good working relationship that will create value through revenue enhancements, flexibility, responsiveness, and innovation with new products

SBR uses criteria such as these to determine which suppliers to retain, which should be added, and how many are really needed to achieve supply chain business goals. Carter and Choi (2008, pp. 188–253) suggest, and Monczka et al. (2011) observed, that during implementation of the SBR process a series of steps should be followed. They are presented here. (Note that the ordering of these steps might differ for every purchasing organization, but they are commonly used in this phase of developing supply chain partners.)

1. Evaluate supply chain base capability, performance, and effectiveness. Compare them against those of competitor purchasing firms.

2. Establish a targeted number of suppliers required in each market segment purchase category by volume, location, competitive requirements, and so on.

3. Conduct detailed supplier assessments based on criteria previously suggested and listed earlier. Analyze candidate suppliers both internally and externally through supplier self-assessments of global market possibilities.

4. Determine current and future purchasing organizations' business situations and needs. Match those needs with the candidate suppliers in terms of volume, remaining contract commitments, and investment in specialized equipment and tooling.

5. Try to determine how suppliers will or do perceive the purchasing firm as a customer.

6. Develop goals for each purchasing segment category (from step 2) regarding economic considerations (for example, price, cost, quality) and size of the supply base. Determine suppliers to target for each segment.

7. Select and finalize the suppliers to be included in the supply chain base or network.

8. Establish a transition plan to align the suppliers in a network and implement it.

10.2.2 Supplier Management

Supplier management (SM) involves the development and implementation of ongoing supplier strategies, including short-term and long-term purchase commodity and other product category contracts (Monczka et al., 2011). For SM to be effective in improving the working relationship between the supplier and purchaser requires (1) a strategic sourcing process with commodity and supplier plans and (2) supplier performance measurements and review. The strategic sourcing process is similar to the strategic planning process presented in Chapter 1, "Developing Supply Chain Strategies." Figure 10.3 lists the general steps involved in a typical strategic sourcing process.

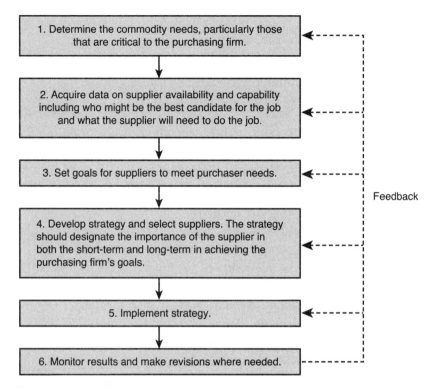

Figure 10.3 Typical strategic sourcing process

Source: Adapted from Monczka et al. (2011), Figure 3.2. p. 28.

The supplier performance measurement and review requires supplier performance and capabilities to be regularly assessed and reviewed for performance deficiencies, as well as for exceeding expectations. To oversee this review process, Monczka et al. (2011), Carter and Choi (2008, pp. 191–199), and Matthews and Stanley (2008, pp. 295–315) suggest using a *supplier performance management* process that involves the following tasks:

- Supplier-purchaser agreement on which metrics are to be used for supplier relationship performance measurement
- Comparative analysis of progress toward strategic goals
- Consideration of problems that require addressing
- Continuous analysis of resource requirements
- Analysis of competition changes that impact the supplier-purchaser relationship and expectations

- A review of the status of the relationship and suggestions on alterations or discontinuance
- Communication on any future goals
- An analysis of overall performance of the supplier

All of these elements in the supplier performance management program should be integrated and managed holistically for maximum benefit in developing supplier relationships.

10.2.3 Relationship Management

Relationship management (RM) is the process of maintaining and developing a closer relationship between the purchaser and suppliers. When applied to the supplier side of the relationship, as it is here, the *Institute of Supply Management* (ISM) suggests a more appropriate term, *supplier relationship management* (SRM) or *supplier collaboration,* both of which are defined by ISM as a process in which purchasing organizations work with suppliers to accomplish common goals and objectives. According to Monczka et al. (2011), relationship management (by any other name) is based on the three fundamental elements described in Table 10.1.

Table 10.1 Relationship Management Elements

Relationship Management Element	Description
Information transparency	All supply chain partners need to be able to share information, making their efforts and needs as transparent as possible without giving away any competitive advantages. Making goals and objectives of the purchasing firm clear to suppliers aids in their efforts to help the purchasing firm achieve them.
Building trust	A critical element in any long-term relationship is the need to build trust between partners. Trust can be built on *experienced competency* (that is, consistency in performance excellence creates known promise keeping), honesty in transactions and behavior, and establishing goodwill where partners share benefits from the working relationship and no one is seen as benefiting at the other partner's expense.

Relationship Management Element	Description
Equitability	Equitable commitment to sharing resources, results, risks and rewards equally is needed to build relationships.

Trust is a particularly important variable in developing supply chain relationships and long-term partnerships. Ring and Van de Ven (1994) define *trust* as "an individual's confidence in the good will of others in a given group and belief that others will make efforts consistent with the group's goal." Research on trust has shown it to be an important factor in business success, having a significant effect on many organizational activities, such as cooperation (Axelrod, 1984), communication (Roberts and O'Reilly, 1974), information sharing (Fox and Huang, 2005), reputation (Sampath et al., 2006), and performance (Earley, 1986). Depending on the nature of the supply chain relationship, different types of trust may exist. *Contractual trust* refers to a situation where there is an expectation that promises are kept; *competence trust* is the level of confidence that the partner will accomplish tasks; *goodwill trust* refers to the level of commitment of the partner to maintain the relationship (Sako, 1992). Araujo et al. (1999) and Choi and Krause (2005) have found that it is the existence of goodwill trust that enables supply chain managers to fully integrate processes and develop cooperative learning mechanisms and governance structures.

10.2.4 Purchaser and Supplier Development

Purchaser and supplier development (PSD) is focused on identifying and correcting the approaches, practices, and beliefs that limit supplier effectiveness and competitive performance on behalf of the purchaser. Fawcett et al. (2007) suggested and Monczka et al. (2011) confirmed through research that to develop relationships between the client purchasing organization and suppliers, supplier capabilities must meet the purchasing firm's market needs. The PSD program of SRM helps to identify and overcome both performance capability limitations and the obstacles both parties may have in working together. The research by Monczka et al. (2011) that explored what firms are doing in PSD programs revealed they utilized *business analytics* (that is, results and analysis of surveys from both purchaser and supplier) to determine problems areas and opportunities for improvement in working relationships. The firms were also observed to have made resource commitments to PSD. In addition, PSD programs were marked by substantial joint efforts toward improving purchaser and supplier capabilities, products, processes, and working relationships. To implement these joint efforts, improvement workshops were developed and used to focus on cost-effectiveness related to value analysis, value engineering, innovation, manufacturing excellence, design specifications, policy improvements, and purchaser and supplier processes.

10.2.5 Supplier Performance Measurement

Supplier performance measurement (SPM) involves measuring supplier performance as it relates to SRM. The instruments used to measure supplier performance include surveys of opinions on supplier performance and interviews with internal client purchasing firm managers. In addition, supplier and *supply scorecards* (that is, a rating system on specific criteria important to a supplier's performance) used in the evaluation process were also found to be useful for measuring ongoing performance. Metrics found beneficial for measuring supplier performance reported in the literature include financial, operations, internal and external customer orientation, and innovation measures. Other metrics commonly used in this element of SPM typical to supply chain management include cost and price improvement, quality, delivery, flexibility, responsiveness, and the use of technology.

Of critical importance is whether the SRM efforts have had a positive impact as measured in an SPM program. In the study by Monczka et al. (2011) several recommendations for SPM were suggested as means to enhance SRM, including the following

- Establish *key performance indicators* (KPIs) using metrics such as cost reduction, technology improvement, innovation, on-time delivery, responsiveness, and flexibility. Then evaluate performance on collaboration projects with targeted return-on-investment goals.

- Encourage both purchasing and supplier firms to utilize cross-functional teams on joint *cross-enterprise problem-solving teams* (that is, problem-solving teams composed of individuals from differing organizations, like external suppliers and the purchasing firm's executives). Establish metrics to ensure an equitable amount of resources are committed to joint projects by both parties.

- Ensure risks and rewards are equitably shared by purchaser and suppliers. Make clear in communications how both parties will benefit from efforts to improve efficiency.

The use of SPM plays a pivotal role in SRM in that it provides feedback to the purchaser and supplier development program (see Figure 10.2) as to where they can impact and change the SM and RM programs. Also, the RM program feedback to the SPM allows for a closed-loop process of monitoring change and advancement in the supplier relations management program.

10.3 Other Topics Related to Developing Partnership in Supply Chains

10.3.1 Sharing Resources to Strengthen the Supply Base: Collaborative Growth Models

Suppliers can go out of business and thus cause difficulties for purchasing firms. Sometimes just a little financial or other expertise might be able to help keep the company from going under. Arnseth (2012b) suggests that during economic downturns it is good business for purchasing firms to undertake support for troubled key suppliers with funds or expertise. Such practices are observed in industry today. Referred to as a *collaborative growth model* (that is, purchaser supports needy supplier with shared resources), purchasing organizations reach out to key suppliers that may be having difficulties (for example, cost related, operational related, financial) and share resources of personnel, equipment, and finances to strengthen and build up their suppliers. These are not just acts of kindness to the supplier by the purchasing firm, but are viewed as a mutually self-serving source of benefits for the supplier and purchaser as well.

Going back to the 1970s and 1980s in the United States, it was not uncommon for purchasing firms and suppliers to work closely together to implement programs for mutual benefit, such as the principles of just-in-time management (Schniederjans, 1993, pp. 33–38; Schonberger, 1982, pp. 157–180). According to Arnseth (2012b), collaborative growth models are focused on building both purchaser and supplier. For example, a supplier that needs greater financial strength might be given the opportunity to enter into a revenue sharing model with the purchasing organization to strengthen the financial situation. Such a model might be perceived by banks and other financial institutions funding the supplier as a stronger revenue position than just selling goods to a purchaser. Ways purchasing organizations currently add resources back into their supplier organizations to build, strengthen, and add value to them include the following:

- R&D support
- Quality-improvement support
- Purchaser-paid tuition and educational expenses for supplier personnel to attend conferences to learn current trends and technology
- Financial support for supplier loans
- Purchaser cash payment policies to help guarantee a supplier's payment
- Use of purchaser's supply chain to help build the supplier's supply chain infrastructure and explore new markets for further growth
- Accelerated payment program to suppliers to help those who are undercapitalized continue in business
- Purchaser provided teams of experts to suppliers to improve their efficiency (and reduce or hold costs down for both parties)
- Joint research in technology developments with both first- and second-tier suppliers

10.3.2 Being Perceived as a Customer of Choice

In times of crises, there is great value in being considered the top-priority customer of a supplier. According to Day (2011), the importance of price does not ensure a supplier will automatically guarantee the purchaser as *customer of choice* (that is, a term used to describe the highest ranking by suppliers of the desirability to do business with a purchaser). As previously discussed in this chapter, SRM activities begin with the segmentation of a supply base into categories such through tiers, strategies, products, and so forth. A similar approach is taken on the sales side when looking at a customer base using *key account management* (KAM) (that is, candidate customers of choice). Suppliers the three main elements to select key accounts:

- **Financial benefits:** Past, present, and potential for superior revenue income streams.

- **Customer requirements:** The alignment of the purchasing organization's goals and objectives with the supplier's vision and objectives, including factors such as the length of time in the relationship, perceived trustworthiness. and the number of competing suppliers.

- **Customer attributes:** The factors and behavior that a purchasing organization signals to the supplier as to whether the firm is viewed as a trusted partner. These include transparency in information sharing, openness to ideas, a willingness to collaborate and reward the supplier for value, access to purchasing executives, brand and market share, and efficient decision making.

The survey of 400 suppliers reported by Day (2011) identified what suppliers view as important and what is of less importance in their relationships with purchasers (that is, identifying purchaser as a candidate customer of choice):

- What key suppliers value the most: Profitability, alignment of supplier business strategy, revenue (that is, actual and potential), alignment of technology and innovation, and long-term perspective

- What key suppliers value the least: Length of relationship, purchaser's speed of decision on purchases, and purchaser's ability to execute orders

Notice that although profitability and revenue are important, other, less-tangible factors are also important and represent opportunities for relationship development. Strengthening the perception of what suppliers view as important is one way to move an organization from being one of many to a customer of choice.

10.3.3 Ending Supplier Relationships

Terminating a supplier relationship can happen for many reasons. A purchasing organization may have a change in strategic direction and may no longer need a particular supplier. More commonly, the product life cycle may be nearing its decline stage, necessitating a product's discontinuance. Other reasons might include a supplier that no longer is able to have access to a particular material or product, which a purchasing organization needs, or that the working relationship simply no longer works.

Mitchell (2012) suggests that a number of important issues need to be considered in the decision-making process before ending a purchaser and supplier relationship. Some of these issues are presented in Table 10.2. As Mitchell (2012) suggests, purchasing organizations should try to end strategic supplier relationships on a positive note, because a supplier ending a relationship today might be a supplier for the same firm in the future.

Table 10.2 Issues to Consider When Ending Supplier Relationships

Issue	Description	Suggestion
Shared investment	Consider the funds invested in the supplier.	Compare the lost benefits with the cancellation loss of the investment.
Time and resources	Consider the investment of the time and resources to maintain a relationship with a supplier.	Compare the loss of those resources with the expected costs of starting up a new relationship with a new supplier. Include also consideration of the loss of knowledge of the old supplier and ramp-up time for a new supplier.

Issue	Description	Suggestion
Workflow	Consider the transition of workflow and problems related to a cancellation of a supplier's contract. Also consider the discontinuance of services interface of the current supplier and the potential impact on all operational departments.	Compare the tradeoffs with a new supplier in terms of how the change will impact report generation, billing, order placement, invoice generation, funds transfer, inventory availability, technical help, and warranty work.
Beginning the ending process	Although the time has come to consider ending the contract or discontinue the relationship with the supplier, a last chance can and should be offered.	A meeting should be undertaken to discuss the area of concern with high-level representatives from both purchaser and supplier firms. During the meeting, review pertinent up-to-date performance data about the supplier, recommend a joint action plan that defines the concerns, outline specific steps for all parties to take to correct any problems, and mutually agree to dates when goals should be met. This places the burden for correction on the supplier, and even if there is no chance for the supplier to correct the issues, this approach provides the kind of transparency needed to stage an end process with understanding on why a discontinuation is needed.

Issue	Description	Suggestion
Completing the ending process	Time has come to end the contract or discontinue the relationship with the supplier.	Whether the purchaser or supplier chooses to end the relationship, a plan must be developed that allows a seamless transition from ending the current supplier's relationship. To ensure this kind of transition, current agreements need to be reviewed in terms of the conditions that could disrupt the termination of the agreement, financial consequences must be determined, upper-management's support must be secured, and a backup plan must be in place. Other issues to consider include synchronizing the timing of the ending of the supplier relationship to match up with any new supplier relationships that may be coming online, enforcing with contractual agreements any nondisclosure or information-exchange requirements to protect the parties involved, and ensuring any intellectual property by contractual agreement.

Source: Adapted from Mitchell (2012).

10.4 What's Next?

What's next involves what a purchasing firm is willing to do to move its SRM efforts toward a true partnership. Recent research has reviewed what firms with SRM programs are doing either to begin SRM programs that will build supply chain partnerships or to move a firm's SRM program to the next level (Arnseth, 2012a; Carter and Choi, 2008, pp. 189–200; Monczka et al. 2011, pp. 38–39; Smith 2011). Using the criteria listed on Table 10.3 as a quality checklist, it is possible to move suppliers along the SRM continuum in Figure 10.1 to achieve a closer partnership. The listing in Table 10.3 should be viewed as a qualification process to know whether a purchasing firm is ready to achieve organizational excellence in SRM. Not all firms can or even want to do everything on the list, but the closer the firm exhibits the checklist suggestions in Table 10.3, the closer it will move toward excellence in SRM.

Table 10.3 Checklist for Excellence in SRM

SRM Programs	Checklist Suggestions to Qualify for Excellence in SRM
Strategy and organization philosophy	A philosophy of treatment by functional purchasing personnel recognizing the importance of key suppliers and treating them fairly and equitably in working relationships.
	A philosophy that supports joint problem solving with suppliers that is long term and strategic.
	A philosophy that values key suppliers and views them as essential to the purchaser's success.
	A philosophy of treatment of suppliers with dignity and respect.
	Purchasing managers know key suppliers and establish effective communication systems for a working relationship.
Supply chain base rationalization process	Identify the supplier category as approved, preferred, partnered, or certified.
	Utilize supplier-assessment tools.
	Segment purchasing to fit and determine strategic suppliers.
	Select strategic suppliers from those who a partnership is desired.
Supplier management program	Establish a clear program of supplier certification and ensure compliance with all categories of suppliers.
	Specify asset improvements, cost reductions, and other less-tangible goals sought of suppliers in enhancing value to the purchaser.
	Specify supplier rewards for creating value. Examples of rewards can be shared savings, increased business for the supplier, and no-interest or low-interest loans for the supplier.
	Establish regular collaborative workshops with suppliers that focus on directing the supplier toward purchaser goals and objectives.
	Specify short-term and long-term written purchase categories to help define supplier roles.
	Specify supplier strategies to target enhanced value goals, such as cost reductions, product and service design values, and overall business process and improvements.

SRM Programs	Checklist Suggestions to Qualify for Excellence in SRM
Relationship management program	A philosophy that builds trust between the purchaser and suppliers.
	A philosophy that encourages the purchaser to support key suppliers when financial, operations, or other problems may impact agreement deliveries.
	A philosophy of transparency in communication between supply chain partners and with internal organization partners as well.
	A philosophy of supplier evaluation where multiple criteria, not single criteria, is used to determine a revision or continuous of an alliance relationship with a supplier. Price importance chiefly used at the transactional level of the supplier relationship continuum.
	Ensure that both purchaser and supplier have capacity to achieved desired goals.
Purchaser and supplier development program	Focus supplier development efforts on supplier performance goals and expectations.
	Establish a program for purchaser to provide resources to key suppliers based on a fair expected return on investment.
	Establish supplier performance based on improvements in working relationships, as well as on the cost and desired other product/service characteristics. Results are what are important here.
	Develop and deployment plan that a purchasing firm can dispatch human resources to fix supplier problems in supply chain management areas.
	Establish a procedure to obtain information from suppliers on company policies, practices, and processes that may serve to improve both parties' abilities to work together.
Supplier performance measurement program	Establish core sets of supplier measurement metrics to measure working relationship process and initiatives.
	Establish a system to measure holistic contributions of supplier to purchaser performance
	Identify both short-term and long-term supplier results.
	Establish metrics on ongoing programs, including such programs as design-to-cost, value analysis, and innovation.

Source: Adapted from Arnseth (2012a); Carter and Choi (2008, pp. 189–200); Monczka et al. (2011, pp. 38–39); Smith (2011).

11

Risk Management

Terms

Black swans

Business-continuity planning (BCP)

Commodity manager

Data-mining software

Disrupter analysis stress test

Disruption risk

Heuristics

Operational risk

Preparedness strategy

Product resiliency

Real-time risk assessments

Resilience

Resilient supply chain

Risk management

Risk management process

Risk management team

Risk mitigation

Risk profile

Risk scorecard

Supplier risk

Supply chain incident management

Traceability

Novelette

Sometimes, a contract can contain highly risky provisions that scare even the most experienced managers. Accepting risk is an important part of any supply chain manager's job, and so too is managing that risk to avoid negative consequences. The first step in risk management is recognizing you have risk.

"Bill, did you see the multi-million-dollar penalty clause in the purchase order for our largest scale electrical generator to their government in Singapore? I have never worked under these kinds of liability risks before," said Pedro.

"Yes, Pedro, I did see the contract and understand the risks. The penalty was very high due to the contractor's penalty for not finishing the building on time. They wanted protection from us to ensure we would deliver our 50-pound generator in place by their production schedule so they could finish the building on time as well," I explained.

"How nice for them! We have done things like this in the U.S., Canada, and Mexico markets, but we are now talking about delivering this generator on top of a 40-story governmental building in downtown Singapore by a very specific date. Usually we build in some timing flexibility, like a range of weeks or months for delivery. The permits for the logistics efforts of transporting to the coast, shipping it to Singapore, unloading it there, transporting it to the building, obtaining the crane to raise it and other building permits are going to be incredible to obtain in the time we have. I am concerned and just wanted to let you know there are some risks here that we usually don't have to face in domestic or nearshore purchases," Pedro added.

"Pedro, the CEO and I both feel the payoff is so substantial that the risks are worth the gamble. We understand the liability risks and believe they are acceptable. We have confidence you can pull it off. Please keep me informed of your progress as you achieve your milestones in the delivery, and if any problems occur, contact me for help. A job like this will have problems, and I will help you through them," I assured.

As the VP of Operations for the Large Engine Division, Pedro set up a project team to handle the delivery of this customer order. The team consisted of the Supply Chain Department Head, two lawyers (one specializing in U.S. domestic issues and one specializing in international business), the Production Department Head, and several engineers from production familiar with the specifics of the product who could test the system when in place. Each was asked to identify the risks of what it takes to deliver the product. The lawyers took care of the permits needed to truck transport the product through each of the U.S. states to California for shipping to Singapore. Due to the size and weight of the generator, permits to transport for seven different states had to be obtained along with shipping documents for port authorities. Likewise, permits in Singapore had to be obtained to unload and ship the product to the building site. Other permits to block off the streets during the craning process, so that the product could be raised to the top of the building, were obtained. Because of the weight and size of the generator, it was shipped in pieces to be assembled on site.

The Production Department Head selected a Production Manager along with a team of technicians to travel to the building site where they could reassemble the generator and test it. All of these actions constituted risk situations where anyone failure could have brought the delivery of the generator to an end. Pedro minimized the risk by delegating as much of it as possible. For example, the work to obtain a crane, the permits, and permissions to raise the generator onsite were given to the building contractor's staff, because they were knowledgeable of many of the weight factors critical in raising the generator and could work with the engineers and the VP included on the project team. The team selected to reassemble the generator were the same employees who built the generator, and the production manager was the supervisor over those employees. But despite great planning efforts on Pedro's part, there was one small hitch: A labor strike stopped the loading on the docks in the United States. The generator was stuck in California, and the clock was ticking.

"Hi, Bill, well I have a problem with the Singapore order. The only loading docks to ship our generator to Singapore are on strike. We can risk waiting to see if the strike will end in time to get our generator to Singapore, or we can ship it by air in pieces. The latter approach will be more expensive, but not more than the penalty for failing to get it to Singapore on time. What do you recommend?" Pedro asked.

"Pedro, there are cargo planes available at LAX airport that you can hire to airship the generator. I will have my staff call ahead and secure their rental. Re-route the trucks shipping the generator to LAX. Also, I will let your lawyer know to draft any documents you now need to air ship the generator," I instructed.

The generator parts were delivered to Singapore, where they were subsequently transported to the building site, raised to the roof with cranes, and reassembled by the production team. After a brief systems test by the engineers, the building contractor authorized the acceptance of the generator, and so the contract was fulfilled.

Happy to share the good news, Pedro called his boss and said, "Bill, I am happy to report to you that the delivery of the Singapore

electric generator was ahead of schedule and a success. It is functioning well, and the contractors have signed off on its delivery.
The air delivery actually put us well ahead of schedule, and it was
much appreciated by the building contractor. We actually are going to receive an early shipment bonus that will help pay some of
the difference in cost of shipping the generator overseas versus fly-
ing it in as we did."

"Pedro, that is good news. Congratulations!" I said proudly.

"Bill, I would like to ask you a question. Suppose the delivery would
have been late. What would we have done to deal with a failed contract other than pay the millions in penalties?" Pedro asked.

"It comes down to a negotiation. First, you contact the customer
and see what you can work out. Sometimes in this situation the
contractor might be late, so a delay won't matter. If that is not possible, you try discounting the price. Of course, I would have to work
with the CEO to make sure the discounts were acceptable to her.
If that doesn't work, because the customer is very upset by our failure, you try to get an arbitrator to come in and work to resolve the
issue. It is not uncommon for the CEO to be involved in obtaining
a resolution with the customer. Sometimes a customer just wants
to take a legal action against you to make an example out of you.
When that happens, we turn the matter over to our lawyers, and
more often than not, a settlement is reached that is not as costly as
the contract in this situation would have us believe. Let's hope we
don't have the latter happen too often, but it is a risk," I explained.

11.1 Prerequisite Material

11.1.1 What Is Risk Management?

Risk management is a process of identifying potential negative
events, assessing their probability of occurrence, reducing the probability of their occurrence, or seeking to avoid them completely, and
preparing contingency plans to mitigate the consequences if they

happen (Blanchard, 2007, pp. 241–245). In every stage of the product life cycle, risks are taken as customer demand changes. Risk needs to be managed, reduced, or eliminated to prevent the product life cycle from being shortened. *Risk mitigation* means lessening or eliminating risk or its impact. In general, there are two types of risk: operational risk and disruption risk (Knemeyer et al., 2009; Wakolbinger and Cruz, 2011). *Operational risk* involves a supply-demand lack of coordination resulting from inadequate or failed processes, people, or systems (Bhattacharyya et al., 2010). Examples of operational risk include the possibilities of poor quality or unsuccessful delivery. *Disruption risk* can be caused by human or natural disasters such as terrorist attacks, strikes, earthquakes, and floods. Leach (2011) reports that 51% of the 559 companies in a global survey said the most common disruptions in their supply chains were caused by adverse weather conditions, while 41% reported information technology outages were the next major source of disruptions. Christopher (2011, p. 194) and Flynn (2008, pp. 112–120) suggest there are several sources of disruption risk (see Table 11.1).

Table 11.1 Sources of Potential Supply Chain Disruption Risk

Source of Risk	Description
Demand	This is the potential deviations from forecasted demand to actual demand (Kumar et al., 2010). Caused by the volatility of customer demand. Example of risk: bullwhip effect.
Control	Caused by internal control systems that inhibit performance or can cause damage to operations. Examples of risk: distortion of order quantities, production batch sizes, and safety stock policies.
Environmental	Caused by weather and other external factors (for example, war). Example of risk: bridges being flooded, causing disruption of delivery and transportation routing.
Market	Caused by changes in customer needs in product available in marketplace. Example of risk: discontinuation of product lines.
Process	This is the potential deviations from producing the desired quality and quantity at the right time (Kumar et al., 2010). Caused by a lack of resilience in supply chain systems. Example of risk: unneeded deadheading of trucking due to labor contractual requirements.

Source of Risk	Description
Supply	Caused by fluctuations in the availability of product in terms of inbound supply in terms of time, quality and quantity (Kumar et al. 2010). Example of risk: loss of customers due to lead time delays caused by long supply chains.

Risks can be categorized into three levels: controllable, somewhat controllable, and uncontrollable (Byrne, 2007). Using this framework, disruption risk is more likely to be uncontrollable, whereas operational risk is relatively controllable. A survey by Byrne (2007) reported that supply chain managers believed the predominant and most daunting risks to supply chains were controllable risks associated with performance of supply chain partners. Figure 11.1 lists a selection of supply chain risks and provides a related continuum of controllability.

Controllable risks

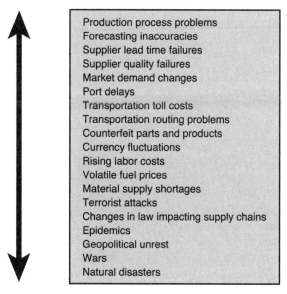

Uncontrollable risks

Figure 11.1 Types and controllability of supply chain risks

Source: Adapted from Simchi-Levi (2010), Figure 5.1, p. 74.

11.1.2 Types of Supply Chain Risk

One type of supply chain risk is *supplier risk,* which focuses on event outcomes that are detrimental to the sourcing plans in a supply chain for a purchasing organization (Carter and Giunipero, 2010). These events usually fall into either operational or disruption risk suggested earlier, except if the event relates more narrowly to suppliers: (1) supplier financial distress, and (2) supplier operational failure. Other supplier operational risks that impact the purchasing organization can include factors like those listed in Table 11.2. There are as many types of supply chain risks as there are things that could go wrong in a business. In formalizing a risk management program Fawcett et al. (2007, pp. 105–108) suggests a *commodity manager* (that is, someone responsible for a particular commodity or grouping of products) should take ownership for the risk management process and oversee risk assessment. One risk assessment method is the *risk scorecard* (that is, a survey listing risk criteria that can be scored to determine an overall risk rating). Results are later reported to appropriate managers to develop risk mitigation plans.

Table 11.2 Types of Supplier Operational Risk Factors Impacting Purchasing Organization

Risk Factor	Description
Supplier lead time	Variation or fluctuations in lead times, causing disruptions in purchasing organization's ability to deliver product to their customers
Technology capacity	Limited or dated technology inhibiting supply chain capabilities, causing an inability to provide state-of-the-art product or services to purchaser's customers
Volume capacity	Limited production or service capacity, causing an inability to provide adequate supplies of product or services to purchaser's customers
Source process capacity	Limited process capabilities, including human resources, technology, and information, causing an inability to provide quality product or services to purchaser's customers as well as generating costly inefficiencies to the purchaser
Incoming materials	Inability of supplier to obtain or deliver needed materials, causing an inability to provide product or services to purchaser's customers

Risk Factor	Description
Reputation	Losing reputation due to supplier misdeed or behavior, negatively impacting the purchaser's reputation
Financial	Loss of key supplier for financial reasons that impacts sales and revenue of purchaser firm
Legal	Legal or governmental regulations that negatively impact the operations of supplier limiting their capacity to serve the purchasing firm

11.2 A Risk Management Process

The *risk management process* that is presented here is viewed as a project, but in reality, it should be seen as an ongoing program. Risk creeps into every task that a business undertakes, so supply chain managers should have in place a supply chain system or group to continually scan for risks in their operations or environment. In addition, supply chain managers should have in place multiple means of risk detection within the organizational structure. These multiple means should include automated technology systems, processes, policies, procedures, and personnel within and external to the organization to ensure potential risk is identified and reported quickly.

Many steps can be incorporated into a risk management process. The type of organization, industry, and products can all alter the steps needed during the risk management process. Christopher (2011, pp. 198–206) and Flynn (2008, pp. 112–127) suggested the ordered steps listed here as a framework for a risk management process (see Figure 11.2):

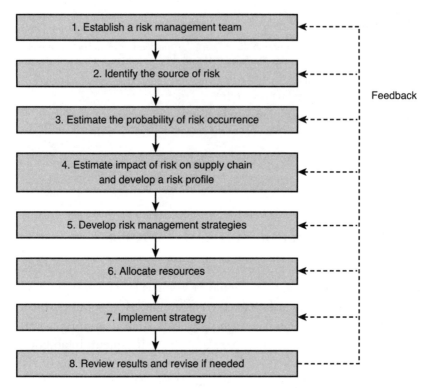

Figure 11.2 Steps in the risk management process

Source: Adapted from Flynn (2008, pp. 112–127).

1. **Establish a risk management team:** A *risk management team* is an internal and formal cross-functional team made up of individuals who are connected to the domain of interest and are assembled to undertake and manage the risk management process. In highly supplier dependent or strategic supplier situations, a cross-organizational team that includes members from the key supplier should also be included. While engineers and supply chain managers related to the risk domain of concern will be members of the team, other specialists can be included, particularly those that bring quantitative skills useful for assessing or estimating risk probabilities. Team members must be skilled in identifying potential risk elements, estimating impacts on the organization, developing strategies of mitigation, and suggesting strategy implementation steps. Members may

later be added or released when dealing with new or differing issues of risk that are uncovered or become obvious during the latter steps of the risk management process. Also, executive management must decide how much control over the risk situation the team will have. Risks that come from external sources may not be eligible for consideration by a team that is chiefly comprised of internal organization members. Therefore, executive management might reserve the right to control aspects of the team's decision-making process.

2. **Identify the source of risk:** The risk management team must identify the sources of risk. The sources of risk can be general in nature like those listed in Table 11.1 that impact broad areas of disruption in supply chain operations. Alternatively, the sources of risk may be focused narrowly on a single area in supply chain management like risks connected with one supplier (see Table 11.2). Using similar reasoning to that of the fishbone diagram (see Chapter 4, "Managing Supply Chains"), which seeks to trace sources of undesirable quality variations, identifying the sources of risk may involve starting with an observed disruption or change in the environment, then tracing it back to the factors that contribute to the cause of the disruption or changes.

3. **Estimate the probability of risk occurrence:** Assessing the exact probability in any risk situation is almost impossible, but generating a likelihood of a particular event happening (for example, a key supplier going out of business) is what this step concerns. Rating systems that rank or reflect the riskiness of a particular event are common in the literature. Rating the occurrence of an event as (1) very high, (2) high, (3) moderate, (4) low, (5) very low, or (6) unlikely is the subjective-judgment evaluation that is expected. The internal organizational experience of supply chain managers, executives, engineers, knowledgeable staffers and external industry experts, consultants, and lawyers may all be a source, for this estimation process.

4. **Estimate impact of risk on supply chain and develop a risk profile:** This step requires a judgmentally determined estimation of how risk tolerant an organization is to any likely risk event occurring. A *risk profile* defines an organization's risk-aversion level. At this step of the risk management process, the analysis may be complete if a firm is highly risk tolerant and not averse to accepting a particular risk situation. If the risk event is judged to exceed a firm's tolerance and it is averse to accepting the risk situation, however, the potential impact of the risk event must be determined. This can involve investigating best and worst case scenarios regarding the impact of the risk to the organization. This would also involve looking at the potential impact in terms of various stakeholders (for example, supply chain, other departments and personnel) and estimating the impact on each. This assessment may also lead to the end of the risk management process if the amount of risk is so great that management deems the project too risky an undertaking. A useful scale for measuring impact might be a rating scale (for example, (1) marginal impact, (2) significant impact, (3) critically damaging impact, and (4) catastrophic impact). These assessments are also judgmentally estimated based on executive experience, and in some cases, external expert opinion. The outcome of this step for organizational avoidance of risks is a clearly assessed impact of risks that the firm may be facing and a rating, ranking, or prioritization to delineate an ordering of the importance of each so that they can be dealt with efficiently.

5. **Develop risk management strategies:** Given that in the previous steps risks were identified, impacts assessed, and risks prioritized according to importance, management strategies can now be developed to deal with each. According to Flynn (2008, pp. 123–124), risk management strategies typically fall into the four categories listed in Table 11.3. Which strategy to accept

depends largely on the tolerance of the firm for taking risks. (The next section deals with strategy and tactics in risk mitigation.)

Table 11.3 Types of Risk Management Strategies

Risk Management Strategies	Description
Acceptance	When a firm's risk tolerance is high, this strategy is simply one of accepting the risky event may happen and accepting the consequences of the impact. No action is needed other than to recognize the potential of the assessed risk changing and making the event intolerable. For example, a purchasing firm might be temporarily hurt by the loss of a key supplier but feels the lost in sales due to the supply shortage is not going to have a major impact because of the purchasing firms significant cash reserve.
Mitigation	Risk mitigation means looking for and finding ways to deal with reducing the risk and its impact to the organization. Knowing what causes the risk (that is, in step 2) and the likelihood and impact of occurrence (that is, steps 3 and 4) permit actions to lessen them and, in doing so, mitigate the risk situation. For example, a purchasing firm fearing a potential loss of a key supplier builds up inventory in anticipation of the shortage to avoid complete stock-outs and significantly damaging their customer base.
Transference	Under this strategy, a firm seeks to transfer some or all their risk to another party. For example, a purchasing firm taking out an insurance policy to insure the potential losses caused by a shortage from a supplier will partially recouped their losses by transferring the risk and event outcome impact to an insurance company.
Avoidance	If during the risk management process the amount of risk is viewed as too great, the risk situation can be avoided by simply not undertaking the project. For example, if a strategically important core competitive advantage might be threatened by taking a particular risky course of action, a firm may just decide that the project is too risky and cancel it.

6. **Allocate resources:** In this step, the allocation of adequate personnel, technology, and capital resources must be determined and affixed to each strategy. It also involves estimating the cost of implementing risk management strategies and allocating resources to implement them. One way to rationalize investment in these strategies is to reexamine the assessed impact to the organization of the risk and to measure those costs relative to the costs of the strategies. Although it is difficult to accurately estimate potential cost savings of mitigating a risk versus the actual cost of the strategy, it is often true that the cost of accepting a risky situation far exceeds that of lessening it.

7. **Implement strategy:** In this step, tactics for the implementation of the risk management strategies are developed and put into place. The implementation of any strategy should begin with alignment to the organization-wide strategies. Once done, the implementation of multiple strategies to deal with risk situations can proceed. This step also involves the execution of allocated resources (from step 6).

8. **Feedback results and revise if needed:** The risk management team is usually held responsible for ensuring strategies and resource allocations are effectively implemented and desired results are achieved. Sufficient time after the implementation of the strategies should be allocated to the team to assess the success (or lack thereof) of the risk management project. If less-than-desirable results are observed during this evaluation period, changes might be made to correct or realign the strategies to achieve better results. Regardless, the end report of the risk management team is expected to be available to areas in the organization that are impacted by the risk management efforts.

11.3 Strategies and Tactics for Mitigating Risk

Risk taking is inherent in supply chain management. Given the complexity of most supply chains, it is difficult to conceive any supply chain not having risk. Supply chain management and risk taking are synonymous terms for most managers, but that does not mean risk should be excused or ignored. The best defense to reducing risk is a good offense of risk mitigation. Risks should be reduced or eliminated wherever they exist, consistent with the cost viability of reduction or elimination. To that end, a variety of risk mitigation strategies and tactics are evident in the literature.

11.3.1 Preparedness and Resilience Strategies and Tactics

The best strategy for mitigating risk is to build preparedness and resilience into supply chains. A *preparedness strategy* involves anticipating and preparing for worst case scenarios in supply chain operational disruptions or environmental catastrophes to mitigate risks. Global companies with clear visibility of supplier activities are better able to leverage that visibility and act quickly when a detrimental event occurs. With information, they can make an informed decision to divert to qualified alternative suppliers if necessary, ensuring correct commodity pricing and assessing the effects of currency changes on buying decisions. Companies can strategically utilize information technology to optimize supplier activities and avoid disasters. According to Correll (2011), one preparative tactic to avoid pricing disasters is to use Internet access to track negotiated commodity pricing, commodity index, and final delivery rates to avoid overpayments. Purchasing organizations can use this tactic to avoid supplier-based billing errors and ensure that competitive suppliers in different locations are price reliable in the event a purchasing organization needs to make a last-minute supplier change. Another preparative tactic based on the use of communication technology is to disperse out vendors over a large geographic area to avoid the impact of a natural disaster that might adversely affect production or disrupt a transportation network of a supply chain at any given time. Having a set of preapproved alternative suppliers in multiple geographic locations creates a solid foundation of preparedness in dealing with natural supply chain disruptions. Currency fluctuations can also be costly and potentially might negate expected cost savings of going global. Although no company can accurately predict the risk in a foreign exchange rate that changes over the long term, a purchasing firm can prepare and insulate itself against major impacts by ensuring up-to-date information on the latest currency valuations are available to decision makers regarding supplier pricing.

Sirkin (2011) also suggests a strategy of preparedness to deal with supply chain disruptions that includes the following tactics:

- **Diversify supply bases:** Identify and recruit suppliers in different locations, including some close to home to avoid regional problems (like war) from risking a loss of key suppliers.
- **Secure supplies:** When a disaster happens, lock up needed supplies with contracts to avoid shortage risks.
- **Flexible supply chains:** Create supply chain networks that have the flexibility (see Chapter 9, "Building an Agile and Flexible Supply Chain") to adjust to sudden changes in demand and supply chain needs, in order to avoid risks associated with meeting market or environmental changes.
- **Produce locally:** Utilize local suppliers to augment existing distant suppliers to avoid the risk of not meeting shifts in demand and avoid price increases.
- **Alter costs:** Purchasing firms should lower fixed costs and seek to exchange them for variable ones that fluctuate with the market to avoid the risk of overcapitalization and the associated financial risks. One tactic is to outsource (see Chapter 13, "Strategic Planning in Outsourcing") to exchange fixed costs, through surrender of capital investments to an outsource provider, for variable costs of an outsourcing contract.

Risk management is not static but dynamic and needs continual consideration of new and varied situations. There is so much change in the types and situations of risk that viewing internal capabilities to resist and deal with future risk has become an important part of risk management. *Resilience* implies a capacity to return to a normal state quickly after being disturbed. A *resilient supply chain* is one that can handle negative impacts from risky situations without having its life cycle come to an end. Knemeyer et al. (2009) and Siegfried (2012) suggest firms become proactively resilient by embedding supply chains end to end with resiliency in products, supply chain, planning, and managing incidents. A tactic for a resilient supply chain strategy is product resiliency. *Product resiliency* involves working with product development staff during the introduction of new products to identify areas of risk in the early product development sourcing phases. Knowing the product risk weaknesses allows for risk reduction efforts prior to the product's introduction and mitigates risk factors. Another tactic is supply chain resiliency. It involves the identification and mitigation of risk areas in the supply chain that might prevent quick recovery from major disruptions within a specific time period. Working with supply chain organizations and consultants to perform this risk analysis and mitigation is suggested by Siegfried (2012).

Another tactic is through use of Web-based *business-continuity planning* (BCP). BCP is an information tool that compiles dozens of resiliency data metrics for all critical supply chain partners and keeps those metrics up-to-date. The information, which includes emergency contacts, alternative power providers, and estimated time to recover from a disaster, can be used for a supply chain incident management process. *Supply chain incident management* takes the information from a BCP and uses an alert service to help monitor worldwide environmental events (for example, disruptions of transportation lanes) that might have disruptive impact on a purchasing organization's supply chain. Siegfried (2012) reported that firms like Cisco Systems utilize an executive dashboard to provide visibility of the supply chain incident management process to report incidents, as well as to develop a crisis playbook detailing processes for reacting to disasters and mitigating different types of risk. Cisco actually developed a resiliency scorecard that includes four categories of resiliency for manufacturing, suppliers, components, and test equipment (O'Connor, 2008). Still, another resiliency tactic is building redundancy in to supply chain systems (Sheffi, 2005, pp. 270–278). While opportunities to reduce resources and capacity in supply chains are important for cost reduction goals, there should be a balance to avoid distressing the entire supply chain, which could cause disruptions. The amount of excess should be in direct proportion to the variability in the supply chain in much the same way safety stocks are computed to determine a desired service level.

11.3.2 Supplier-Related Strategies and Tactics

Risks related to suppliers can lead to a critical or even catastrophic situation impacting the purchasing firm. Some of the strategies used by purchasing firms that have singularly focused on cost reduction have also led to an increase in risk, according to Carter and Giunipero (2010, p. 11). Strategies that should be reconsidered in light of the desire to reduce supply chain risks include the following:

- Reducing the number of suppliers or having single-source suppliers, risking costly dependency
- Reducing inventory, risking shortages
- A high concentration of business with a few suppliers or customers, risking dependency on those partners
- Dependancy on a specific type of infrastructure, risking bottlenecks in transportation systems or facility loading needs
- Increasing the use of outsourcing, risking dependency on suppliers
- Use of low-cost suppliers in developing countries, risking dependency on sources located in countries that may be politically unstable
- Long lead times, risking timely deliveries and stockouts

Risk mitigation tactics suggested by Carter and Giunipero (2010, p. 11) to deal with a suppliers who may have financial or operational distress include the following:

- Investing or buying the supplier outright
- Giving the purchaser's business to another supplier
- Paying early to help the supplier with cash flow
- Accepting early delivery to advance payments to the supplier more quickly
- Visiting the supplier to see if long-term help can be provided
- Seeking collaboration from other suppliers to help the disstressed supplier
- Making direct loans with low interest to financially weak suppliers
- Increasing business with the supplier in the short-term to improve cash flow

11.3.3 Managing Global Risks

Experienced supply chain managers know that the impact of a global supply chain adds an additional layer of risk complexity to an already risky environment. The result is an exponential increase in risk that is required in today's supply chain and yet should require reexamination of the amount of global involvement that a firm should undertake. The literature suggests a variety of different strategies to deal with global risk taking, including the following (Kogut, 1985; Colicchia et al., 2011):

- **Hedging:** Under this strategy, a supply chain is designed that any loss in one part is offset by gains in another. In global operations, where production facilities are located in different countries, the individual currencies of each country can hedge against currency fluctuations. Where one country's currency is lowered, another in the supply chain network is increased. This is the same strategy used to reduce risks by diversifying investments in a variety of financial instruments.

- **Speculation:** Under this strategy, a supply chain is focused chiefly on one goal that provides substantial benefit to the firm. In the past, the primary reason why most firms went global was to seek lower product or operational costs. Speculating on a single unique opportunity, a global organization may have lower production costs in low-wage countries, resulting in a significant competitive advantage through lowering prices to the customers. This strategy can work well, but as time goes on, conditions can change to minimize the primary cost reduction reason. As wage levels increase or inflation impacts an economy, the desire to maintain a goal such as low labor costs might require a continuous process of moving from one country to another to chase lower wage levels globally.

- **Flexibility:** Building a supply chain based on this strategy would seek to have flexibility in partner quantity, quality, and capabilities. One of the virtues of global operations is the ability to have a much larger supply chain base from which to select partners. Having more suppliers, manufacturers, and distribution operations allow for greater flexibility in dealing with supply chain disruptions in any area of the world. Having redundant production resources and alternative supply chains permits a hedge against many risk factors that keep supply chains from performing well.

This strategy allows for quick changes and rerouting when risky environmental changes (for example, wars, weather) take place in one particular region.

Global strategies to overcome risk are almost infinite. Most firms use a combination of the strategies mentioned here to accomplish global goals.

Christopher (2011, p. 194) has hypothesized a function that defines supply chain risk as follows:

Supply chain risk = Probability of a disruption x Impact

Some of the strategies and tactics of risk mitigation in this section can reduce the probability of a disruption of supply chain operations or reduce the impact of the risk event on the purchasing organization. In doing so, the risk to a supply chain can be reduced. That is the purpose of risk management.

11.4 Other Topics in Risk Management

11.4.1 Innovating Risk Management

According to Leong (2012), much of traditional risk management is a backward-looking process at past risk situations, but should be made forward looking to anticipate risks. Leong (2012) reported that four components are needed to innovate risk management programs to a forward looking mode:

- **Develop a supplier-based database system:** Risk situations are constantly occurring. Under this system, supply chain professionals, working for or in a purchasing organization, continuously feed information about potential or real risk factors they observe in their job situation environment. These observations form a database of real-time information on risk situations that may be developing and that therefore need more attention and focus. This information may be gleaned from public sources such as news releases, annual reports (for example, supplier financial reports), and analyst reports (for example, *Harvard*

Business Review blogs). Observations might include changes in economic conditions, organization leadership, industry, and technology. They may also include initiatives and new strategies from competitors, as well as legal or government action against supply partners.

- **Apply business analytics:** Taking raw data from the database, *heuristics* (that is, logic based rules to guide searches), and other search methodologies, *artificial intelligence* (AI) and *data-mining software* (that is, a software driven process that seeks discovery of patterns or trends in databases and transforms them into human understandable structures for further use) can be applied to find trends or behavior revealing risk leading situations that are yet to be formally recognized ("Intelligence Agent," 2012). Combined knowledge of competitors and industry behavior, executive experience, and intuitive judgment can also be applied to analyze data. For example, the loss of several suppliers in a purchasing organization's network may reveal a competitive risk factor such as a competitor's moving into markets, which the purchaser previously dominated, and recruiting former suppliers. Although this situation might indicate some other cause and effect, identifying risk possibilities such as competitive actions is worthy of further consideration because it may reveal actual risk-related factors leading to supplier loss.

- **Frequent risk assessments:** To stay current and have what Leong (2012) refers to as *real-time risk assessments* requires updates to the database of every significant transaction (for example, a supplier bid transaction). This could require daily or even more frequent reporting efforts. This allows the purchasing organization to keep timely track of risk ideas, risky behavior, and risk assessments and to note changes that might indicate an alteration of risk trends.

- **Simplifying the process:** The variety of information inputs from a wide and varied set of sources throughout a supply chain network is channeled into useful and timely decision-making information. Under this system, it becomes easier to identify the variety of risks that actually impact a purchasing firm and its supply chain network. Therefore, the opportunity to reduce and simplify risk data collection makes the process easier and more efficient. In turn, the amount of time available to focus on key risk factors is increased and better controlled.

The goal of this risk assessment system is to increase knowledge of risk for a particular purchasing firm and to locate where disruptions may occur using a broad and diverse set of inputs. By increasing awareness, this system allows firms to respond more quickly to risk situations and minimize disruptive impacts on the supply chain network.

11.4.2 Risk Management Tool: Traceability

Sometimes, a product problem (for example, a defective product that may cause a safety issue) surfaces and the firm responsible has to undertake corrective action. The longer a firm allows a known product problem to continue, the greater the risks for impact costs (for example, legal action against the firm). Just finding the source of a problem for a large organization with a global supply chain network is a challenge. The longer a problem remains hidden and is not remedied, the greater the associated costs and other risks to the supply chain organization. Given the complexity of products, their sources of manufacturing, and the length of their supply chains, it can be very difficult to determine where a problem originates. Conversely, the faster a problem's origin is identified, the less risk and related costs will be incurred.

Siegfried (2011) suggests that *traceability* (that is, the ability to trace down a problem or issue) is an ideal risk management tool. Being able to trace a product back from its origin can improve supply chain management by facilitating the identification of safety and quality issues. How much traceability is required depends on what an organization wants to achieve and how much it is willing to pay. A product, the component parts, and the location of the materials used for the component parts are all traceable if the firm is willing to expend the effort.

Siegfried (2011) suggests three characteristics are mandatory in the design of traceability systems: (1) breadth (that is, the amount of information that is to be kept on each product or component), (2) depth (that is, the depth of information that traces backward or forward in time for the product or component, which can be updated as the item moves through the supply chain), and (3) precision (that is, the degree of assurance that the tracing system has the ability to pin-point a particular item's movement or characteristics).

Technologies like bar codes that are read by scanners and connect to the storage of information on mainframe computer systems can help locate and detail product characteristics. *Global positioning systems* (GPS) can be used to determine location in transit when timely physical location information is needed. *Radio frequency identification* (RFID) technologies that permit electronic and distant inventory monitoring can also support a traceability program. Such technologies can make the program easier and more affordable.

Traceability as a strategy for supply chain operational success is becoming a reality. Governmental requirements for product safety and the desire by consumers to trace products as they are logistically moved through a supply chain, are some of the competitive reasons for adopting/enhancing this supply chain capability.

11.4.3 Disrupter Stress Test to Estimate Risk of Future Catastrophic Events

Large firms can handle risk management efforts by allocating one whole department to risk. Referred to as *enterprise risk management* (ERM) departments (Le Merle, 2011), their purpose is to identify potential business disruptions, determine the most likely effects, and develop risk mitigation plans, while also taking preventive actions to reduce risk exposure. ERM departments focus on more frequently impacting risk issues (for example, failure to comply with government regulations). They tend not to focus on *black swans* (that is, an infrequent, but extremely impacting disaster that can be related to an environmental, economic, political, societal, or technological cause). A black swan can occur anytime, anywhere and is highly impossible to predict, which explains why most ERM departments are not necessarily prepared to handle these kinds of risk events.

To deal with a black swan event, Le Merle (2011) suggests the use of a *disrupter analysis stress test*. These stress tests should be administered periodically by a risk management team that would work with the ERM department. While the stress test is not meant to be a continuous effort (that is, they should be considered a project activity), it should be considered as an occasional tune-up effort to anticipate and suggest strategies for dealing with the supply chain ramifications of a major disaster. While ERM departments or a special risk management team would seemingly undertake this task, some organizations may select to have an external third-party conduct the analysis for a host of reasons including external objectivity.

A disrupter analysis stress test can consist of the following four steps (Le Merle, 2011):

1. **Map the enterprise to define locations of potential catastrophic risk:** This step involves determining a firm's geographic footprint in terms of operations and supply chain partners. This mapping includes multiple-tiered operations: first-, second-, and third-tier suppliers. This also includes the external industry structure and competitive dynamics in the market the firm faces. Given such information, a map of sources and concentrations of revenue, profit, and capital of the firm is also needed to understand other areas of potential risk and how everything is interrelated.

2. **Create a list of black swan events:** A list of potential disrupting events should include any that may be related to the organization in the context of environmental, economic, political, societal, or technological impacts. This is expected to be a long list that may be categorized in different ways, such as by type of risk. The categorization helps reduce the number of types of risks, making it more manageable.

3. **Explore "what if" scenarios:** Determine the relative impact and consequences to the organization of a given catastrophe as it relates to each of the listed black swan events (from step 2) and its relationship to the organization's mapped concentrations of potential risk (from step 1). The idea is to expand and look for as many possible risk factors and relationships, while also assessing the potential magnitude of what the catastrophes might cause. Matching up concentrations of risk with the

potential impact of the catastrophe helps identify how the current structure of the firm (that is, from the mapping effort in step 1) may be a factor contributing to the potential magnitude of the impact.

4. **Implement contingency plans:** Develop risk mitigation options for each risk situation from step 3. Develop options that address multiple risks and prioritize them by magnitude of risk exposure, expense, and ease of implementation. Coming up with these contingency plans can be a brainstorming activity for the risk management team, the ERM department, or for consultants could utilize with unique experience in risk contingency planning, which an organization hires to augment internal staff knowledge.

The idea in using this disrupter analysis stress test is to prepare an organization in advance with standby emergency plans that could be quickly implemented to minimize future risks and their consequences during black swan events.

11.5 What's Next?

Based on the World Economic Forum (www.weforum.org) research report, the trend for watchfulness regarding the topic of risk in global supply chains tops the list of major concerns of supply chain managers ("Outlook on...," 2012). Both businesses and government agree there is a strong need for supply chain security that mitigates risk. Despite the desire for less-risky supply chains, the forecast for the near future appears to be risk endowed. As shown in Table 11.4, there are not only a great many risk factors (this list is incomplete from those originally surveyed by the World Economic Forum ["Global Risks...," 2011] and other sources) (Simchi-Levi, 2010), but each has a likely to high probability of occurrence. Unfortunately, most of these risks are estimated to be high and will negatively impact global supply chains.

Table 11.4 Global Risk Categories, Examples, and Estimated Probable Occurrences in 2012

Categories of Risk	Examples	Estimated Probability of Occurrence°	Estimated Impact°
Economic	Asset valuation collapse	Likely	High
	Extreme commodity price volatility	High	High
		High	High
	Extreme customer price volatility	High	High
	Extreme energy price volatility	High	High
	Extreme inflation	High	High
	Regulation failures		
Environmental	Air pollution	High	High
	Climate change	High	High
	Earthquakes	High	High
	Flooding	High	High
	Storms	High	High
Geopolitical	Corruption	High	High
	Fragile governments	High	High
	Geopolitical conflict	High	High
	Illicit trade	High	High
	Terrorism	High	High
Societal	Pandemics	High	High
	Economic disparity	High	High
	Migration disparity	High	High
Technological	Infrastructure breakdown	Unlikely	Moderate
	Online security leaks	High	High
	Threats from new technologies	Low	Low

*Most based on World Economic Forum estimates (Global Risks 2011, 2011).
Source: Adapted from Global Risks 2011(2011); Outlook on Logistics & Supply Chain Industry 2012 (2012); Simchi-Levi (2010, pp. 73–77).

What can be done to mitigate the global risks that are looming is to take proactive measures that anticipate and strengthen the resilience of supply chains to handle eventual impacts. Similar to previous strategies offered in this chapter, the World Economic Forum research suggests supply chain managers maintain an oversight to capture risk information, synthesize, and analyze it to the point where useful action-oriented information can be shared rapidly to formulate anticipatory decision responses ("Outlook on...," 2012). Moreover, this research recommends building agility, flexibility, and adaptability in to the supply chain (see Chapter 9) to make it more resilient and better able to handle risky situations and their impacts.

12

Lean and Other Cost-Reduction Strategies in Supply Chain Management

Terms

Bottlenecks

Centralized buying strategy

Commoditization

Computerized maintenance management system (CMMS)

Cost driver analysis

Cost management

Cost management program

Cost-reduction team

e-auction

e-sourcing

Horizontal collaboration

Key initiative (KI)

Leagile

Lean management

Lean supply chain

Lean supply chain management

Lean supply chain productivity cycling process

Mixed model scheduling

Pool buying

Price analysis

Reverse auction

Standardization

Supply chain flow constraint

Target costing

Total cost of ownership (TOC)

Value management (VM)

White boards

Novelette

Controlling costs in manufacturing determines the successfulness of the product in the marketplace. Operations managers have for decades used lean cost-reduction strategies to develop a mindset or philosophy to guide an organization to think in terms of eliminating waste and subsequent costs.

Jessica, the VP of the Tools, Hardware, and Construction Materials Division, called me one afternoon with a problem and said, "Bill, the average manufacturing and supply chain costs I have to add to our new products end up in excess of the expected market prices. My expected costs are just too high. This has killed a few of the new product proposals given to me by the marketing people. I started worrying about this and thought maybe our Division should be doing a better job on cost management. I looked at what Alan in our Small Engine Division was doing in his cost management program. Interestingly enough, I found similar lean management principles being applied, but in different ways. Some of the ideas there can be transplanted to my Division, but I welcome any additional ideas you might have that will help me reduce costs and make our new product proposals more price-wise feasible."

"As you know, Jessica, the use of lean principles has become so fundamental in industry that most firms automatically think lean without even being taught the principles. Their use is second nature for all of us. Some of the principles are applicable to manufacturing, and some can be applied to supply chain management. I am going to be traveling to your Texas tools machinery plant next week on other matters. I will get a review of what your people there are doing, lean-wise, and see if anything can be added to help out costs," I said.

"Bill, the Texas plant is a good example of our use of lean principles. There we have a cost management team well trained in lean leading our cost efforts. Bill, anything you can suggest to augment and change our processes to make them more cost effective will be greatly appreciated," added Jessica.

After the Texas plant visit and discussions with the Plant Manager and the Division's Supply Chain Department Head, Bill contacted Jessica to discuss what might be improved in the supply chain area. "Jessica, your application of cost controls and lean principles in your manufacturing areas are as good or better than in our other Divisions. Transferring those lean principles to a service area like supply chain management in your particular Division is not always as easy to see or understand. One area that is commonly overlooked is information flow. Just like inventory that can choke a production floor, making it inefficient, too much information can overload managers and waste their time in considering nonimportant statistics. For purposes of cost information, keep the information brief and clearly directed toward the specific items that are essential. There is just too much nonsensical information that is put into cost management reports that does not add value and wastes managers' time. Use the cost management information reports as a tool to focus on the most pressing cost-reduction areas by including information as hot points to be focused on. To implement this revision of reports, have your staff identify what they feel are non-needed content in reports and, where possible, edit it out. You and your Supply Chain Department Head should also develop a Pareto listing of hot points to help the staff focus attention on what in your opinion requires weekly or monthly critical attention. Typical areas that add impact costs in supply chains include poor product quality causing returns, expediting or de-expediting to achieve on-time delivery, safety issues that can be costly if injuries occur, and of course, the cost of the product from our suppliers. Use supplier scorecards to help you in this effort. Also, you need to focus not only on costs in your operation but also throughout your entire supply chain network. Specifically, ensure your suppliers track and monitor their own quality, on-time deliveries, safety issues, and costs. Helping them to see and control their costs will reduce your costs in the longer-term," I explained.

"Bill, what if we learn of a way for the supplier to cut costs, but in doing so, if will increase ours. Do we really want to share that information with the supplier?" Jessica asked.

"Yes, Jessica, because that sharing of information will positively impact our bottom line if the supplier eventually shares the cost reduction with us, and in many cases they will. In addition, the supplier will recognize our commitment to helping them. This will help develop a stronger relationship and endear them to us. When times are tough, they will be there for us, saving more than just a little money, maybe our entire business. In fact, this leads to another area of cost collaboration with our suppliers that you may consider undertaking with every new product. Use suppliers' right up front in design of new product proposals. Challenge them to help you cut costs. It has been my experience that 90% of all the costs that end up in the supply chain eventually become legacy costs that could have been designed out of the process day one, using quality function deployment, FEMAs, and other statistical data to avoid waste. Consider the fact that some of those wastes are in the standards you are designing! This is caused by stating specifications that require customization efforts, rather than using standardized materials or parts. Anything that requires customization is going to increase the cost of the item. Using a supplier's standardized product or component parts in a new product whenever you can will substantially reduce the total costs of the product. Designing for manufacturability internally and externally is important to cut costs (by designing within your suppliers' capabilities to save costs). Adding customization that a customer does not need adds costs, not value," I commented.

12.1 Prerequisite Material

12.1.1 Cost Management

Cost minimization is one the primary functions of supply chain managers and operation managers in general. To aid in accomplishing this task, firms often establish a cost management program. *Cost management* is an ongoing process of managing the uses of an organization's funds to minimize the cost of operations. A *cost management program* involves an ongoing planning and cost estimating process for projects and programs, budgeting costs for the firm as a whole, and controlling costs. This is a broad topic that impacts planning in all functional areas within a firm. A detailed discussion of this subject is beyond the scope of this book and is not the focus of this chapter (which is, instead, on cost strategies). For a detailed discussion on cost management, see Carter and Choi (2008, pp. 44–79).

While cost management is a continuous program, many applications of cost management projects are undertaken in supply chain departments. Typically for supply chain organizations, cost management is used to support a larger cost-reduction strategy. To accomplish this, a *cost-reduction team* is established whose role is to seek out and find areas in the supply chain department cost structure that can be reduced (Fawcett et al., 2007, p. 445). The composition of this team is similar to as a cross-functional team (see Chapter 10, "Developing Partnerships in Supply Chains"). The focus here is on identifying cost-reduction areas and tactics on projects, processes, policies, and practices. To accomplish cost-reduction goals, a cost driver analysis is often undertaken.

12.1.2 Cost Driver Analysis

To reduce costs in a firm, a cost-reduction team needs to identify what drives costs. A *cost driver analysis* determines the processes, activities, and decisions that actually result in supply chains costs (Fawcett et al., 2007, p. 251). Cost drivers can be unique to a product or practice. For example, a cost driver might be the amount of inventory a firm is willing to permit. An excess of finished inventory increases or drives up the costs of insurance, taxes, handling, and so on, but it provides a quick response to customer demand surges in highly volatile markets. Also, excess logistics equipment such as trucks can drive up capital expenditure costs, maintenance costs, obsolescence costs, and so on, but excess transportation equipment might be beneficial in volatile transportation situations where a firm might possibly have to outsource their trucking needs. In such situations, shortage of availability might be very expensive.

Cost analysis can include the following elements (Carter and Choi, 2008, p. 37):

- Determine the competitive structure of the industry (for example, highly competitive market situation with lower costs for services or higher costs in a monopolistic economic environment).
- Determine the market structure (for example, international or domestic).
- Determine cost drivers and supplier pricing trends.
- Determine the cost impact of other trends (for example, changes in technology, new processes.).

Ideally, cost analysis will indicate what reasonable costs (or prices paid to a supplier) should be in terms of the market, industry, supplier's cost structure, and the client organization's needs.

12.1.3 Other Cost Management Tools

To support cost analysis efforts in cost management, a number of analyses are available. Other tools useful in cost management include the following (Fawcett et al., 2007, p. 254, Carter and Choi, 2008, pp. 60–62; Wincel, 2004, pp. 162–178):

- **Price analysis:** *Price analysis* is a comparative study of item prices in the market. It is used to help understand price availability in a competitive marketplace.
- **Total cost of ownership:** *Total cost of ownership* (TOC) seeks to determine the total cost of acquisition, use, maintenance, and environmental disposal of products, processes, and equipment. It is used to determine the true total costs of an item (see Carter and Choi, 2008, pp. 54–58).

- **Target costing:** *Target costing* is a methodology that seeks to establish a fair price for a product by starting with the product's estimated costs and what a firm expects in terms of profit. It figures existing market prices for supplier provided goods and services, then works backward, determining what a purchasing firm can afford to produce, while still making a profit. The steps in a target costing process are presented in Figure 12.1.

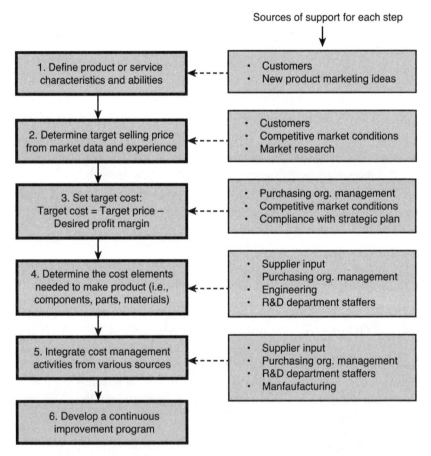

Figure 12.1 Steps in a target costing process

Source: Adapted from Ellram (1999); Matthews and Stanley (2008, Figure 3-8, p. 94).

- **Cost control and improvement:** This specifically identifies the annual price improvement and cost-reduction tasks consistent with industry and commodity conditions. It employs short- and long-term efforts to find opportunities that can be benchmarked against industry practices and uses collaboration with suppliers to improve agreements.

- **Value management:** *Value management* (VM) can be defined as a collection of various efforts to capture and retain improvements at each step in the value chain of a supply chain. It determines the entire supply chain value stream cost elements to identify cost opportunities. It provides valued added workshops to facilitate the identification of design-based savings and institutionalize VM data collection methods to aid in supplier/purchaser cost-reduction strategies.

- **Supply chain process improvement:** This introduces process improvement techniques to the supply network and creates an institutionalized process improvement focus. It includes cost control methods and utilizes modeling of the supplier network to explore and implement cost-reduction strategies.

To guide any of the cost management program and analyses mentioned here, a firm must determine an overall cost strategy. There are many different cost strategies. Some are focused on limited areas in a supply chain, and others are global, covering an organization's overall approach or guiding philosophy of operations. One global strategy that has developed into a field of management is lean management.

12.1.4 Lean Management

Lean management involves the use of a set of principles, approaches, and methodologies that can be applied individually or collectively to guide organizations toward world-class performance. Lean can be implemented as a process, project, program, principle, approach, methodology, or philosophy. It can be applied to individual processes, individual departments or entire organizations as a project for short-term efficiency improvements or extended, longer-term programs, where projects are undertaken to permanently install lean for continuous process improvement.

Lean management applies a series principles used to eliminate waste of all kinds that rob efficiency and add needless cost to operations. By eliminating waste, the respective operating costs are reduced. Some of the lean management principles are presented in Table 12.1. These and other lean management principles were originally developed by the Toyota Corporation as a program to improve efficiency by eliminating waste in its production system. The principles have evolved through contributions from scholars and practitioners to be the most commonly known cost management strategy. The principles have also been adapted for use in supply chain management (Wincel, 2004; Kerber and Dreckshage; 2011, Schniederjans et al., 2010; Zylstra, 2006).

Table 12.1 Lean Management Principles

Operations Area in Which the Principle Is Applied	Principles
Inventory	Seek reliable suppliers.
	Seek reduced lot sizes and increased frequency of orders.
	Seek zero inventories and reduce buffer and work-in-process inventory.
	Seek improved inventory handling.
	Seek to continuously identify and correct all inventory problems.
Production	Seek a synchronized pull system.
	Seek improved flexibility in providing product changeovers and in scheduling production.
	Seek uniform daily production scheduling.
	Seek improved communication.
	Seek reduced production lot sizes and reduce production setup costs.
	Allow employees to determine production flow and schedule work at less than full capacity.
	Increase standardization of product processing.
	Seek improved visualization.
	Seek to continuously identify and correct all production management problems.

Operations Area in Which the Principle Is Applied	Principles
Human resources	Seek to establish a family atmosphere to build trust, empowerment, and pride in workmanship.
	Seek long-term commitment to employ all employees.
	Seek to maintain a substantial part-time workforce.
	Establish compensation plans that reward individual and team efforts.
	Encourage employee team approach to problem solving
	Provide continuous and extensive training.
	Seek to continuously identify and correct all human resource problems.
Quality	Seek long-term commitment to quality control efforts.
	Use fail safe methods to help ensure quality conformity.
	Utilize statistical quality control methods to monitor and motivate product quality.
	Maintain 100% quality inspection of products through *work-in-process* (WIP) efforts.
	Seek to make quality everybody's responsibility.
	Seek to empower workers by sharing authority in the control of product quality.
	Seek to continuously identify and correct all quality related problems.
Facility design	Seek a focused factory. Identify and eliminate production bottlenecks.
	Seek to maximize flow through layout.
	Use automation (that is, robots) where practical.
	Use group technology cells (that is, U-line or C-cells) in production layouts.
	Seek continuous redesign efforts to improve facility layout and facility structure.
Supplier relationships	Seek certification in quality of items purchased.
	Seek timely communications and responsiveness.
	Seek single-source suppliers.
	Seek long-term relationships with suppliers.
	Seek to continuously identify and correct all supplier relation problems.

Topics in lean management have been a dominant cost-reduction strategy for decades (Schonberger, 1982). Their subsequent use in supply chains (Wincel, 2004) as a best practice (Blanchard, 2007, pp. 95–97) has become second nature for most supply chain managers. Therefore, its coverage as a cost-reduction strategy can be viewed as mandatory in any supply chain book exploring cost-reduction strategies.

12.2 Lean Supply Chain Management Principles

A *lean supply chain* is one where there exists no waste and no inefficiencies. Few supply chains ever fully implement all the principles of lean management to actually eliminate all waste and inefficiencies. Seeking a lean supply chain should simply be viewed as a strategic cost-reduction goal that is continuously sought under a *lean supply chain management* program. To operationalize a lean supply chain management program requires the application of lean management principles within the context of a firm's supply chain.

Lean supply chain management principles are derived from a larger set of lean management principles dealing with broader operations management areas of responsibility (for example, inventory, production, human resources, quality, and facility design). As such, the applicability of these principles to supply chain management includes a broader management perspective that impacts all areas of operations management.

The following subsections cover a number of select lean supply chain management principles that can be used collectively as a cost-reduction strategy.

12.2.1 Seek Leadership and Growth Strategy

A lean supply chain project or program requires a driving force of effort from a leader for implementation (Dolcemascolo, 2006). For firms that focus on their supply chain as a strategy for competitive advantage, the creation of an upper-level organizational position such as vice president of supply chain management should be a requirement. In addition, supply chain executive training sessions on lean supply chain ideas should be undertaken to help managers develop into lean leaders who champion, promote, and motivate the implementation of lean principles within a firm's supply chain (Martin, 2007). Reflecting the support of upper management for a lean supply chain, a champion might also use lean training, problem solving, and other groupings to help champion the use of lean principles within the firm's supply chain. Successful leaders avoid waste in organizational change by giving direction and improving the efficiency of change by coordinating the steps toward a lean supply chain.

12.2.2 Seek a Strategic Customer Value Focus

Focusing on customer needs is a driving force in all supply chains (Christopher, 2011, pp. 6–7). Communication and Internet technologies have empowered customers to use global markets to acquire products and services; so in turn, firms must compete in those global markets. One of the main ways to be successful in such a competitive environment is to offer customers greater need satisfaction opportunities than other firms. This is achieved in a lean supply chain by having lean principles directly impact the value given by the product (for example, enhanced product or service quality, reduced costs) and having the supply chain provide exceptional (for example, quick response) delivery. Lean supply chain management can generate value and become a competitive advantage for firms that utilize its synergy (see value proposition in Chapter 1, Section 1.6).

12.2.3 Seek Single-Source and Reliable Suppliers

Having fewer but reliable supply chain suppliers reduces administrative costs (as compared to having a larger numbers of suppliers). Moreover, a smaller number of suppliers should be able to provide quicker responses, because both partners are more familiar with each other due to increased frequency of contact (that is, a greater amount of ordering per supplier will occur because there are fewer suppliers in the network) (Mangan et al., 2008). When a firm has only one or a small number of suppliers, the purchasing organization is more dependent on them, resulting in a greater need for supplier reliability. That dependency should be a shared concern of the suppliers because they realize failure to deliver a product or service can be disastrous for the client firm. In some situations, this puts psychological pressure on the supplier to do the job right every time. Supplier reliability might also include timely communications and responsiveness of the supplier to solve problems and meet customer demand issues. Reliability also works both ways in lean supply chain management. Purchasing firms should seek to establish long-term contractual relationships with suppliers to assure them of continual support and future business (Martin, 2008).

12.2.4 Seek to Build Trust Based Alliances with Ethical Supply Chain Partners

One of the most common approaches for developing trust in supply chain partners is for all partners to maintain high ethical standards in all business activities and behaviors. If the suppliers observe the purchasing firm in a supply chain seeks to maintain ethical values of fair play, they may come to understand and habitually act in a similarly ethical manner toward the client firm. Even in fairly short-term transactional or supply chain alliances with suppliers, the notion that a client firm conducts business in an ethical way helps to establish an implied standard operating procedure of ethical conduct.

Ethical conduct can help avoid waste and save time and money. For example, the unethical conduct of suppliers sending knowingly poor quality goods will waste time and result in wasteful costs of scrapping goods, reprocessing them, or returning the items. One of the lessons of lean management principles is that establishing an atmosphere in supply chains that seeks to build trust and empowers members will aid trust building and foster pride throughout the supply chain. To implement this kind of environment, the lean supply chain principle suggests that the contracts should include compensation plans that reward supply chain partners for ethical conduct efforts. Part of those efforts should be to work toward building trust by bringing suppliers together to work in teams on problem solving. Working together while displaying ethical conduct and seeing how each can help the supply chain as a whole will build trust among members.

Another lean supply chain tactic for building trust is to offer long-term contracts to supply chain partners. All contracts have time limits, but the longer contracted time of a supplier's service will signal a more trusting relationship in business.

12.2.5 Seek a Demand Pull, Synchronized Supply Chain

In a demand pull system (see Chapter 1), customers place orders before the products are produced or services are delivered. Synchronizing the supply chain with demand pull simply means each supply chain partner is viewed as a customer. When the final downstream customer places an order, it triggers a sequential and systematic chain of customer demand requests back upstream from the final customer all the way through the entire supply chain (Arnseth, 2012d). The key is to manage the demand pull transactions for each supply chain partner in such a way that minimum time and effort are needed to process the demand request, thus reducing wasted time. As lean principles in supply chains are applied in addition to the demand pull synchronized supply chain network, efficiency caused by waste removal is inevitable. Why? Because what is produced and delivered in the supply chain and all the effort to generate the product occurs without waste (for example, overproduction, inventory piling up).

What do many firms that are dependent on forecasts of customer demand do if they cannot wait for customers to place orders ahead of time and pull demand through the production and supply chain systems? One tactic is to segment forecast demand into two categories: certain demand and volatile demand. The certain demand category has to be estimated, but might be only half of the forecast demand that a firm with a high degree of certainty knows will be experienced during a particular time period. The other half can be designated as volatile demand and is considered at risk for the same time period. The certain demand can be produced reliably without wasteful overtime costs or layoffs. Also, the supply chain contracted logistics costs can be bid out in competitive transportation markets, because of the certainty and known demand requirements. This helps reduce supply chain costs on the known demand and permits more to be spent on volatile demand planning efforts. The risk inherent in volatile demand can be outsourced to avoid potentially costly fluctuations (for example, the bullwhip effect).

12.2.6 Seek to Maximize Flow and Eliminate Supply Chain Flow Constraints

Under lean principles, we seek a level and stable production schedule and therefore, a level and stable set of requirements regarding the use of supply chains. This lean supply chain principle suggests stability from stable production scheduling needs to be integrated over the entire supply chain (Nicholas, 2011, p. 393; Kerber and Dreckshage, 2001, pp. 41–51). This principle further advocates that all product flows be in small and frequent amounts, continuously pulled by customers with little variation in production, inventory levels, labor levels, and so on. When variation of any kind is present in any area of the supply chain, it can create congestion, retard flow, and cause wasted time and effort. To maximize flow, we seek an entire supply chain guided by the firm's level and stable production schedule. Ideally, it will be one that has a fixed number of goods seamlessly scheduled for shipping, production, and distribution that does not require a quick shift up or down over the planning horizon. This means all processes or supply chain activities that contribute variation in production should be investigated for improvement, modification, or even elimination.

Production scheduling variation is not the only limiting factor maximizing product flow through a supply chain. Supply chain flow constraints surface from time to time, which also need to be managed. A *supply chain flow constraint* might be a supplier that takes too long to deliver goods or a local ordinance or regulation that slows the speed limit to such an extent that it inhibits timely deliveries. Some constraints can be dealt with quickly (for example, replacing a supplier), but other constraints might be impossible to avoid or change (for example, changing laws). Any flow constraints that can be identified should be restructured or eliminated in supply chains where possible. Where it is not possible to eliminate supply chain constraints, other means should be found to compensate and enhance flow. For example, if a speed limit law increases transit time (thus, increasing delivery time), then perhaps new equipment can be used in truck loading and unloading to reduce the time for those tasks (that is, making up for the increased transit time).

The goal of this principle is to maximize flow throughout the entire supply chain (Kerber and Dreckshage, 2011, pp. 67–69). Identifying *bottlenecks* that create flow congestion, reduce system efficiencies, and reduce performance in the supply chain is essential for eliminating them. Bottlenecks in the production area can be caused by poor equipment that breaks down and delays production, ill-trained employees who cannot complete work on time, or technology that cannot make products fast enough to meet customer demand. Bottlenecks in supply chains can be caused by unaligned capacity in a network, supplier failures of delivery and support, geographic distances that hinder transportation systems, distribution centers whose procedures are outdated or inefficient, or information systems that provide misinformation.

Implementing a lean supply chain management principle of a demand pull system, the synchronization process will often reveal bottlenecks within and between supply chain partners. Bottlenecks in supply chain suppliers can also be caused by supplier service variability (some partners moving faster than others, for example). The slower supply chain partners represent a potential supply chain flow constraint. The imbalance in flow creates congestion, which can in turn lead to bottlenecks. Table 12.2 describes a process to identify supply chain flow constraints.

Table 12.2 Finding Supply Chain Flow Constraints within Lean Philosophy

Step	Description
1. Compartmentalize supply chain variation.	Treat the supply chain as a single system with components each capable of creating a constraint to flow.
2. Smooth customer demand volatility.	Focus on customer demand pull as a fundamental source for volatility. Synchronizing to customer demand establish a rhythm of demand that determines the supply chain flow (that is, both its speed and volume). Implement approaches to smooth demand, including batching of orders, delaying order processing, and even turning down business when necessary. Given these implemented system smoothing efforts, customer demand may still possess some demand volatility that can prove disruptive (for example, the bullwhip effect).

Step	Description
3. Identify and measure remaining volatility.	Efforts to respond to that demand volatility will help identify potential supply chain flow constraints (for example, examining slower partner performance). This might require an internal investigation into order processing delays or external supply chain transportation and distribution systems disruptions. The objective in this step is to lower the volatility down to a point in the system where its boundaries are defined and behavior can be measured.
4. Determine acceptable volatility standards and compare those with identified actual behavior.	Determine ideal performance standards for the constrained partners, partner systems, and partner subsystems. Performance standards might be identified from researching industry standards, and benchmarks. Actual performance determined in step 3 can then be compared with desired or expected performance. One additional tool to identify troubled performance areas is the use of gap analysis. Gap analysis (see Chapter 3, "Staffing Supply Chains") can be used to show differences between expected and actual results. Pareto analysis (see Chapter 4, "Managing Supply Chains") can be used to rank more serious supply chain flow constraints for immediate correction.
5. Redesign sources of variation to better serve supply chain needs.	Where it is possible and economical, redesign products and processes to mitigate variation in supply chain flow. Designing the size and shape of products to better fit in trucks or material handling equipment can greatly improve flow within and between supply chain facilities without necessarily impacting marketability of the products. Identifying and eliminating processes (for example, shipping product by rail rather than by truck) that vary in delivery times can also reduce supply chain flow problems.
6. Monitor and control flow to customers.	Coordinate and manage the flow throughout the supply chain to the customer. Managing flow of products through an entire supply chain is a coordination task that requires continuous monitoring of product flow and resolving of flow issues as they develop. Computer technology (for example, GPS systems) should be intensively used and augmented by management follow up where needed. As a part of the monitoring effort, establish a monitoring system based upon supply chain performance metrics. This means a continuously tracking of the changes in supply chain performance metrics.

Source: Adapted from Schniederjans et al. (2010, pp. 87–89).

Under this principle, lean supply chain information systems are key elements for controlling and enhancing supply chain flow. With highly integrated information systems, supply chain partners can quickly communicate shifts in demand that can avoid costly bullwhip impacts, which add supply chain flow congestion and contribute to other product-flow problems.

12.2.7 Seek Supply Chain Agility

In a customer-focused demand pull environment, lean supply chain operations must be responsive to market changes (Nicholas, 2011, p. 85). They need to be agile (see Chapter 9, "Building an Agile and Flexible Supply Chain") and able to quickly alter products, processes, and even the supply chain network as changes emerge from customers, both internal and external. While a firm's production operation can become agile in meeting customer demand changes by lean methods such as *mixed-model scheduling* (that is, multiple products can be produced without major changeovers in production cells), supply chains, in contrast, permit agility in redesigning network configuration (that is, altering supply chain partners) and flexibility in their capacity to serve customers. One tactic to enhance lean supply chain agility is to redesign and acquire transportation and material handling equipment that possesses a wide range of performance capabilities. Flexibility in equipment capacity permits easy modification to meet shifts in customer demand requirements as needed. In addition, highly flexible information technology may also be critically important to implementing this principle. For example, some *radio frequency identification* (RFID) tags (see Chapter 2, "Designing Supply Chains") can be easily reprogrammed to provide additional information as changes in product identification numbers or other product features are altered. Another lean supply chain tactic that can be used to implement this principle is to have highly cross-trained personnel to handle a variety of jobs. These added skills in supply chain staffers allow rotation of personnel from purchasing functions (for example, a purchasing agent moved to a supplier evaluation task). Cross-training can also prevent a breakdown in a supply chain during employee absences (for example, fill in for other supply chain employees absent due to heath or vacation reasons).

According to Amir (2011), the combination of agility and lean supply chain management is a principle referred to as *leagile* and is a suitable way to exploit both approaches, lean and agile. Basically, it requires selection and setting up of a material flow decoupling point. The positioning of the decoupling point depends on the longest lead time and, at the same time, customer willingness to tolerate a time lag in the decoupling effort. It also depends on the point at which variability in product demand dominates. Downstream from the decoupling point, all products are pulled by customer demand consistent with the lean supply chain management principle. In this way, part of supply chain is market driven, as it should be, by demand. Upstream from the decoupling point, the supply chain is essentially forecast driven. This combined approach enables a level schedule and opens up an opportunity to drive down costs upstream, while simultaneously ensuring that downstream at the decoupling point there is an agile response capability for delivering to an unpredictable demand in the marketplace.

12.2.8 Seek Continuous Improvement

Continuous improvement (CI) must be implemented throughout the entire supply chain and by all supply chain partners (see Chapter 4, "Managing Supply Chains"). For the purchasing firm and its partners, CI may involve advancing visual management in facilities (for example, the use of white boards to post activities where everyone can see them), education, and personnel training to build cross-training skills, education in quality control statistical control methods (for example, to provide continuous monitoring of quality progress), transportation law education, and redesigning physical facilities to improve material handling and product flow. Supply chain partners need to continuously look for ways to add value. Parts suppliers might seek less-expensive, more durable, more aesthetically valued parts for use in supply chains. For example, a supplier component that reduces the weight of a product can create a ripple effect across a supply chain by reducing transportation costs and handling. Teaming supply chain and production personnel might help supply chain managers develop shipping schedules to reduce costs (for example, shipping at low-volume times of the day that might permit a shipping discount). Teaming quality management personnel with supply chain managers can prove beneficial. High quality can benefit the entire supply chain, and low quality can hurt it. High-quality products reduce customer returns. Returns cause wasteful transportation because goods have to be replaced or might even cost the firm valued customers. Inventory managers can be teamed with supply chain managers to help balance small, frequent, lot-sized orders from suppliers to downstream retail customers to minimize costs across the entire supply chain, yet still act to serve the market demand.

12.2.9 Seek Reduced Cost Through Waste Elimination

All the lean supply chain principles previously mentioned can contribute either directly or indirectly to eliminating waste in supply chains. Waste within a supply chain partner's operations and waste between partners are related to one or all three primary resources of labor, materials, and technology. Lean supply chain management principles seek opportunities for the avoidance of waste within a supply chain partner's operations. For example, under lean, more frequent shipments to a fewer number of facilities is the norm. A supply chain network to support this type of shipping arrangement can help in negotiating lower-cost contracts with transportation partners. Suppliers also do not have to manage large transportation systems, but focus instead on a fewer number because of the reduction in facilities, which saves time and money. In addition, the same arrangement under lean provides an opportunity to reduce administrative efforts and achieve economies to scale in contracts downstream with distribution and warehousing, because these organizations will be doing business with a fewer number of supply chain partners.

Sourcing supply chain goods is a critical decision in supply chain management. Selecting materials, parts, component supplies, and suppliers can have a substantial impact on the firm's ability to control waste. Planning decisions on sourcing are usually determined at the strategic level of supply chain planning. Whether to make products or deliver services within the business firm or allow external supply chain partners to handle these tasks can be strategically important in helping avoid waste. For example, suppose a customer demand surge is anticipated in a supply chain that is greater than the supply chain's capacity to handle it. *Third-party logistics* (3PL) partners can be contracted for supply chain services in the same way that actual production activities can be contractually outsourced. This tactic can help avoid bullwhip effect wastes that can occur if the firm moves from a stable system to a highly volatile demand situation. Such a strategy helps avoid wasted resources and minimizes rushed and costly decisions that focus on short-term flow problems with potentially wasteful long-term investments in supply chain resources.

The justification for the application of lean supply chain principles is to improve the value of the supply chain to the organization by reducing waste and becoming more cost efficient, helping the firm increase profitability and market share. The impact of the lean supply chain management strategy is illustrated in *lean supply chain productivity cycling process* listed in Figure 12.2. Making the lean supply chain management productivity cycling process work well requires reduction of waste. Reducing wasted resources reduces costs, and the cost reduction lowers customer prices, helping make products and services more competitive and consequently increasing market share and profitability.

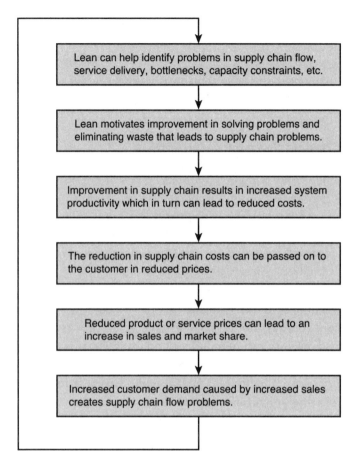

Figure 12.2 Lean supply chain productivity cycling process

Source: Adapted from Schniederjans et al. (2010, Figure 2, p. 14).

The lean supply chain principles presented in this section illustrate how the principles are interrelated. Lean supply chain principles are actually intertwined; that is, they relate to one another and require integration, one with the other, to maximize potential benefits.

12.3 Other Cost-Reduction Strategies

Lean-based strategies are invasive and can completely encompass a firm's cost-reduction strategy. Other strategies are more focused on limited domains (for example, procurement) within organizations.

Cost strategies available to reduce or control costs for organizations are as numerous as there are costs to be controlled. Some listed here afford users opportunities that, when combined with lean supply chain management principles or other cost strategies, can create a comprehensive cost management program.

12.3.1 Procurement Partner Competition

In most supply chains, procurement represents the largest long-term cost item. To help ensure the best price for supplies, a firm should seek a pure competition environment that is highly competitive with large numbers of suppliers helping to create market pressure that will force prices down, helping to contain costs. In some situations, the purchasing firm should adopt a strategy to help build those competitive markets. A proactive role in fostering competition on bidding prices by suppliers is a part of this strategy. A tactic for this strategy is a reverse auction. A *reverse auction* is a process where a supplier offers a fixed duration bid in a purchasing event hosted by a purchasing firm (Blanchard, 2007, p. 82). While potential bidding suppliers have to be prequalified to meet the purchasing firms other needs, the purchasing organization's hosted event collects and shares bid prices with other suppliers offering bids. The reverse auction is usually accomplished over the Internet (giving rise to the terms *e-auction* or *e-sourcing*). Suppliers are then allowed to revise bids during the fixed time period of the auction in hopes of getting the contract. Bidding helps to reduce the prices charged, which reduces the cost to the client firm.

12.3.2 Standardization and Commoditization

Under the *standardization* and *commoditization* strategy, and wherever possible, products and services should be transformed into standardized products that use standardized components ("Global Manufacturing...," 2011). Standardization reduces customization of products and components, thus reducing the need for larger inventories and associated costs. In addition, as products and components end their life cycles and become obsolete, fewer inventory items are needed, and that means fewer will become obsolete. In fact, the component parts may actually have their life cycles extended (for example, a standardized screw that can be used in hundreds of products will last as long as the oldest product in the set of hundreds).

Standardization of services reduces the number of service skills and tasks needed to perform jobs. That can help reduce service costs and training. In addition, standardized services provide opportunities to use the same sets of service related supplies (a form a standardizations of supplies), reducing those costs.

The downside of this strategy is that it can increase competition. Transforming a product or service into a commodity (that is, an undifferentiated product or service) means other competitors can offer a similar product or service. Some balancing of customization with the standardization of the product is called for in using this strategy.

12.3.3 Combined Organization and Opportunity Analyses for a Cost Strategy

This cost strategy is similar to the basic organizational strategic planning process (see Chapter 1). It has two parts represented by two types of analyses: (1) an organization analysis and (2) an opportunity analysis (Carter and Choi, 2008, pp. 60–62). The organization analysis looks internally at the supply chain organization, seeking to determine how the supply chain functions can be streamlined and reorganized to cut costs and improve effectiveness and productivity. A reorganization and realignment of supply chain functions takes place to reduce costs in the short term. This is followed by the opportunity analysis, which looks externally to determine any best-in-class practices in various industries of cost management practices that can be applied to the firm's supply chain department.

12.3.4 Centralized Buying

Under a *centralized buying strategy*, an organization-wide buying agreement can be used for cost management purposes, whereby one department or specific supply chain professional is given total authority and responsibility of purchasing for an entire organization (Carter and Choi, 2008, p. 64). Consolidating purchases for entire departments or divisions gives the person in control greater clout to obtain a better purchasing price and therefore can reduce organizational costs. This strategy also reduces administrative costs by reducing the need for multiple decision makers and purchasing personnel. One tactic useful in the implementation of this strategy is *pool buying* (that is, the consolidation of purchasing requirements from multiple departments or divisions of a purchasing firm into a single order). This helps lower the price because of the volume of business with the suppliers is attractive, so it is worth lowering prices to obtain the contract. It helps reduce the supplier's costs, because the firm can run larger production runs and experience economies-to-scale cost reductions.

The downside is that there are fewer decision makers to glean information from the purchasing firm's internal customers. Also, it can slow the procurement process down if there are not sufficient numbers of procurement staffers to process requests from distant divisions in the firm.

12.3.5 Outsourcing

Outsourcing (see Chapter 13, "Strategic Planning in Outsourcing") supply chain activities to reduce costs is a common strategy in a cost management program (Schniederjans et al., 2005, pp. 10–11). The act of engaging suppliers to provide goods to a purchasing organization is an act of outsourcing production and procurement tasks needed to produce and deliver the supplier's goods. The cost advantages of outsourcing are rooted in the use of others to do the work for the client firm. This strategy reduces costs when used by a client firm to perform a supply chain task where an outsourcer can provide a service cheaper than the client firm. Supply chain firms all have core competencies (see Chapter 1) allowing them to perform some activities better than other firms. They also have noncore activities that outside firms excel in (and perhaps with less expense to the client firm). Those noncore activities are the candidates for outsourcing. If a price can be negotiated for less expense, costs can be reduced by outsourcing those tasks.

12.4 Other Topics in Lean and Other Cost-Reduction Strategies in Supply Chain Management

12.4.1 Transforming Lean Procurement Principles in Service Organizations

Organizations have transformed lean management principles from manufacturing to service organizations in supply chain functions like procurement. Arnseth (2012d) found such a transformation for a global procurement organization, Capital One Financial Corporation. Utilizing the following lean principles, Capital One was able to transform administrative and service activities connected to their financial transactions into a lean supply chain management environment. Lean procurement changes reported include the use of the following principles:

- **Use of operational visibility:** Use of massive *white boards* (that is, marking boards on which notes and other messages were written) allowed them to keep track of the steps involved in complex procurement projects. The white boards allow management to keep up-to-date on progress (and lack thereof) and to identify problems to reposition efforts quickly in order to correct and improve service flow on slow progress projects.

- **Use of work segmentation:** Segmentation of tasks required for procurement projects so each task could be tracked to help identify and avoid wasted time updating personnel on the current status of progress, as well as helping to locate wasted efforts and remove them. The firm identified processes that needed to be changed to avoid disruptive and wasted efforts. For example, some internal customers brought in disorganized and incomplete procurement contact information that would delay the procurement process. Internal customers were encouraged to improve the completeness of their procurement documentation or would face delays in processing.

- **Use of cross-functional teams:** Applying Pareto analysis, the firm employed teams to figure out ways to fast-track low-complexity projects, improving flow. Learning what worked best, the same principles were eventually applied to high-complexity projects.

- **Empowering employees:** Building transparency in job opportunities, the firm allowed employees to select the types of job assignments they believed would be of most interest, rather than having the firm select and assign staff to jobs, which increased motivation and improved efficiency for the firm.

- **Use of education to transform the organization:** Creating a program called *key initiative* (KI), forums were initiated that allowed team members to quickly share information on lean implementation tactics and new ideas that emerged over time. Staffers were able to think "out loud" and learn in public.

- **Use of continuous improvement:** As a part of the KI, weekly meetings were also used to integrate members from other departments to see the status of projects and share ideas for continual improvement.

The reported impact resulted in eventual acceptance of lean supply chain management principles. The benefits included a faster flow of procurement documents in less time and greater consistency in delivery and contract outputs. Contracting cycle time was reported to have dropped by 80%. In addition, the lean principles were, after some anxiety, quickly accepted, altering the culture in procurement practices in record time.

12.4.2 Mistakes in Lean Implementation

Supply chain activities are often highly connected to successful use of equipment (for example, trucks, material handling, technology). Unless the equipment is well maintained, it may result in costly repairs, product failures, and unsafe conditions. Poor maintenance results in costly waste that runs counter to lean supply chain management principles. Fitzgerald (2011) has suggested several practices in the implementation of lean supply chain management programs that should be avoided as they relate to equipment maintenance, including the following

- **Inadequate measurement of lean maintenance implementation:** Failure to measure the maintenance function before and after a lean maintenance program has been implemented should be avoided. Using a *computerized maintenance management system* (CMMS) (that is, computer software that can compile maintenance records, review work orders, track spare-parts inventory) can help supply chain managers make informed decisions about buying versus repairing and utilizing preventative maintenance. It is important to invest time to create work processes and train supply chain personnel in order for the CMMS to correctly report operational performance metrics needed to monitor maintenance performance and avoid wasted effort.

- **Lack of lean educators:** Most lean supply chain management programs are lacking instruction, which leads to less than desirable outcomes. The implementation of lean needs to become a culture within a supply chain organization and the greater organization as a whole. To accomplish cultural change requires the use of corporation coaches and mentors backed by upper-level management.

- **Failure by overreaching on an implementation project:** Selecting an initial project that is too big or too complex dooms the program and future initiatives to failure, discouraging future use and damaging the motivation needed to implement the project quickly and successfully. Selecting a smaller and less-complex initial lean supply chain project will likely result in immediate success and provide momentum for future lean initiatives. The firm should plan to obtain a series of initial successes whereby lean projects help to quickly move an organization's cultural acceptance of the principles.

- **Failure to build organizational support and promote the idea of lean supply chain management:** Without constant reminders by upper management and maintenance managers of what lean supply chain management means, how it is implemented, and what value it contributes to the organization, staffers may not feel it is worth the effort to implement. Consistency and reinforcement of the lean directive from top management down through supervisors to operators and maintenance personnel must be visible to all. As employees start to associate the implementation of lean with the successes it brings, the culture will change to better support lean principles.

- **Avoid shortfalls of needed resources:** To make lean happen requires education, training, skill development, and time. It necessitates resources. In addition, to aid in making lean happen requires a willingness to listen to employee lean suggestions and, where possible, to implement them, even if it involves some risk to operations. The real potential of lean supply chain management principles will always be realized through the employees who implement them. They are closest to the implementation, so who better to know what might work?

12.4.3 Collaboration as a Cost-Reduction Strategy

Competitors tend to own the same technology and equipment use the same processes and understand the same business needs and wants as any firm in a particular industry or marketplace. Sometimes, a firm may have excess capacity that it would like to transform into an alternative source of funds, whereas others might need the extra capacity. Indeed, in many industries, as one firm increases sales, another competitive firm might have a decrease. Sharing warehousing, distribution, and manufacturing resources may be a cost strategy that can provide unique and beneficial improvements for both firms. According to Siegfried (2012), competitors collaborating to share resources can be a useful cost-reduction strategy. Referred to as a *horizontal collaboration*, working with a peer competitor to share resources must be in accordance with U.S. antitrust laws. Siegfried (2012) suggests that to enter into a horizontal collaboration for mutual cost-reduction benefit will require several prerequisites considerations:

- **A trusting relationship:** A solid working relationship that will build trust based on openness is needed. An initial outsourcing arrangement between two competitors might be a useful tactic. This would include sharing financial information relative to the alliance as well.
- **Identify areas where performance can be enhanced:** While collaboration is exploratory, there may be known areas where competitors excel and can bring resources to the table as an enticement for horizontal collaboration. The supply chain area of joint collaboration can and should be comprehensive, including procurement, manufacturing, and distribution.
- **Establish joint planning committees:** Both companies need to enhance transparency and cooperative planning by have

meetings of a joint steering committee to regularly examine and address process improvements, service levels, inventory issues, and other operational areas of concern related to the alliance. The committee should include vice president-level members and executives from manufacturing, finance, logistics and planning. The meetings should be held face to face (to build trust) at corporate headquarters, at least on a quarterly schedule.

- **Establish a willingness to work together attitude:** Problems may develop with this type of alliance, and both parties must be mentally conditioned to work together, regardless of how challenging the problems that surface may become.

The results of this cost-reduction strategy reported by Siegfried (2012) include significant cost savings in fixed costs and capital investments, exceeding the firms' expectations. Other benefits include the opportunity to afford resources that the firms individually could not invest in, but benefit by sharing.

12.5 What's Next?

Cost volatility trends appear to be the major concern now and into the future. Cost management is predicted to be at the top of the list of concerns for supply chain managers. Several studies suggest cost management is now more than ever a critical success factor for supply chains going forward. According to a survey by the Aberdeen Group ("Globalization and...," 2011), cost management concerns were the top two pressures for global supply chain managers looking forward in 2011. According to IDC Manufacturing Insights ("Reducing Overall...," 2012) a survey of 350 supply chain managers found 80% of the respondents thought reducing overall supply chain costs was the number one supply chain priority for 2013. Miller (2012), looking at critical success factors for the year 2012, echoed the cost management concern theme, suggesting that efforts to reduce costs are what is needed. One tactic that can be used to deal with increasing cost trends is to use purchasing contracts. The present volatility in prices (costs) and their trend upward could be reduced in the short term by offering a longer-term purchasing contract that takes into consideration future reduced prices (similar to long-term loan rates offered by banks in fund construction of homes and buildings). Another tactic to support a cost management program is suggested by the World Economic Forum ("Outlook on...," 2012). They propose unpacking the sources of potential supply chain costs into different components, to separate policy drivers from other factors (for example, infrastructure weaknesses) as a means to focus corrective cost-reduction efforts more efficiently and to eliminate waste.

13

Strategic Planning in Outsourcing

Terms

Backsourcing

Business process outsourcing (BPO)

Business transformation outsourcing (BTO)

Cloud computing

Continual renewal outsourcing agreement

Co-sourcing

Crowdsourcing

Culture

Fixed-term outsourcing agreement

Global outsourcing

Governmental ideology

Implementation provider-selection criteria

Insourcing

International outsourcing

Multisourcing outsourcing

Nearshore outsourcing

Netsourcing

Obligatory selection criteria

Offshore outsourcing

Outsourcing

Oversight council

Qualitative provider-selection criteria

Quantitative provider-selection criteria

Reshoring

Shared outsourcing

Spin-off outsourcing

Transitional outsourcing

Value-added outsourcing

Novelette

One of the common strategic plans used by firms to improve non-core capabilities is outsourcing. In supply chain procurement activity, outsourcing is chiefly a matter of looking anywhere in the world for the most savings you can get and the greatest opportunities where they are found in terms of dollars times volumes. Once a firm decides they will outsource some of its operations, it is usually up to the VP of Operations to make it happen. For several decades, outsourcing has been based on minimizing labor and supply chain costs by finding low-cost labor in foreign countries, but times are changing.

Signing off on $100 million contracts is always scary, and it appears I will be facing just such an outsourcing deal in the near future. We have for several years worked with a Chinese firm to acquire parts for our large and medium-sized engines. The relationship can be described at best as transactional. In fact, the original contract was extorted on the basis of either allowing this firm to produce our parts exclusively or not at all. The contract end time is shortly arriving, and I need to confer with the VPs in the Large and Small Engine Divisions to see whether we should continue with this supplier or find someone else.

"Pedro and Barack, thanks for setting up this video conference call. It is nice to see you both and talk with you as if you were in my office," I said.

Pedro, the VP of the Large-Sized Engine Division, jumping in quickly, said, "Bill, it's always a pleasure, and I know we can't waste time on this expensive video technology communication, so let's get to it. I don't want to continue doing business with our current Chinese firm."

I was a bit shocked by the directness of Pedro, but then Barack, the VP of the Medium-Sized Engine Division, adds, "Bill, I completely agree with Pedro. We have had delivery issues and quality issues since day one with this supplier. When I try to call them, I get the cold-shoulder routine, and that doesn't cut it anymore. Those delays from that supplier have cost my Division in terms of us failing to deliver to our customers."

I, again reeling from the directness and determination of the VPs, reply, "Okay, guys, message received. Now, so that we are all on the same page on this, we presently don't have the necessary capacity to insource this work. Is that right?"

Pedro and Barack said in unison, "Yes!"

"Okay, the board of directors have actually moved the outsourcing decision down the organization to us, or where the problems exist. This means you each can find the suppliers you need to procure these parts. While this decision authority level has been lowered to us, I will still have to explain to the CEO why we need to change our outsource partners and reallocate hundreds of millions of dollars to other suppliers. To help me do this, I will ask you to draft proposals based on the prior contract with explanations of deviations from current price, product, or quality factors. Also, you can call on the resources of the original executive outsourcing team that drafted our present contract. This team includes corporate procurement personnel, the VP of Marketing, the VP of New Product Development, and myself. Of course, make sure your Supply Chain Department Heads, Purchasing Managers, and important sourcing Buyers are considered in the proposals, as well. If you plan to source the parts internally as we have it now, we need to bring in the director of international operations. Please remember in your proposals that on procurement we want to reduce costs to improve overall total cost, improve throughput, improve the value stream, and improve customer response time by reducing lead times, all of which should be directed at adding to our bottom line. One last thing that you should be aware of is the location of outsourcing is changing. We are doing a lot more nearshore planning or finding local suppliers, rather than outsourcing to firms in foreign countries. In the past, any product that required 30% or more labor we automatically outsourced to China or India because of their low wage levels and inexpensive currency. Now that currency rates are changing and the cost of logistics in long supply chains is increasing, there are advantages to going locally with our outsourcing needs. At the same time, the hourly labor costs in the United States have decreased as recession and other economic factors have impacted the economy and increased unemployment.

We are finding that by having local suppliers we have shorter supply chains and that they are more agile and able to respond to our and our customers' needs. We are also finding it's a better way to control inventories. Ramping up new products and ramping down old products are quicker with a local outsourcing strategy. So, look to North America for suppliers in your proposal research, and you might find it enhances many of our supply chain goals," I instructed.

13.1 Prerequisite Material

13.1.1 What Is Outsourcing?

As organizations mature and grow, many find themselves with limitations on labor resources, services availability, materials, or other economic resource shortages in a particular geographic location. To compensate for these shortages, firms subcontract what they need from external sources or businesses. Sometimes these are geographically distant sources outside the contracting firm's own country. Contracting for or procuring to meet these shortages represents the act of *outsourcing* if what is needed is acquired from a source external to the organization (that is, not owned by the client firm) (Krajewski et al., 2013, p. 369). *International outsourcing* involves activities between nations or the boundaries of two or more countries. When sources come from all over the world, they represent *global outsourcing* (Schniederjans et al., 2005, p. 5). Conversely, some firms keep all their production needs internal or use an internal strategy of *insourcing*. Insourcing is an allocation or reallocation of resources internally within the same organization, even if the allocation is from different geographic locations. In an outsourcing arrangement, a *client* firm seeks to outsource its internal business activities, and an *outsource provider* firm provides the outsourcing services or resources to the client.

13.1.2 The Role of Management in Outsourcing

The fundamental role of managers in undertaking an outsourcing project involves a balancing of allocating insourcing and outsourcing needs to serve the client firm. As shown in Figure 13.1, the balancing process is a function of the costs and benefits to the client firm. How much or how little outsourcing to use depends on balancing the organization's perception of benefits in using this strategy and the risks associated with it.

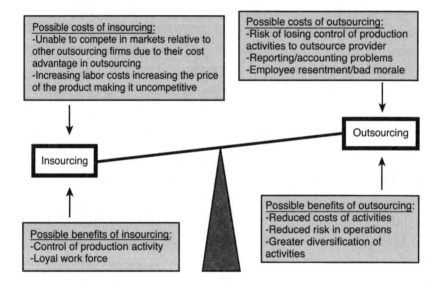

Figure 13.1 Balancing outsourcing and insourcing benefits and costs

Source: Adapted from Schniederjans et al. (2005, Figure 1.1, p. 4).

Outsourcing can be viewed as a strategy and can be used to achieve many organizational objectives (for example, cost reduction, risk reduction) in any area of business activity. All or part of any of the unique functional areas (for example, accounting, supply chain, information systems) that have been historically insourced can be outsourced. Outsourcing origins can be found in the historic use of subcontracting, which makes outsourcing not revolutionary but an evolution of business organizations (Schniederjans et al., 2005, p. 5).

13.1.3 What Are the Common Types of Outsourcing?

Some common types of outsourcing projects found in the literature are listed in Table 13.1. Strategically, outsourcing can be used as a change agent or a means of altering business organizations to better fit the needs of the client firm and its customers. For example, a *business transformation outsourcing* (BTO) project might entail a small educational change such as an in-house training session provided by an outsourced educational trainer to educate a client firm's executives on supply chain legislation (outsourcing used as a change agent). However, *business process outsourcing* (BPO) might involve the complete outsourcing of all supply chain tasks to a *third-party logistics* (3PL) provider (a complete alteration of a client firm's operations).

Table 13.1 Common Types of Outsourcing Projects

Type of Outsourcing	Description
Backsourcing or reshoring	*Backsourcing* or *reshoring* is another term for returning to insourcing, where a client firm, having experienced less-than-desirable outsourcing, moves the business activities back internally to be performed within the firm.
Business process outsourcing	*Business process outsourcing* (BPO) is outsourcing of an entire process or department within a firm (for example, outsourcing all information systems services or finance or accounting departments).
Business transformation outsourcing	*Business transformation outsourcing* (BTO) typically focuses on helping the client firms create a new infrastructure or business model.
Co-sourcing	*Co-sourcing* is where the provider's payment is based on achieving a particular goal or improving the client's business performance.
Crowdsourcing	*Crowdsourcing* is where a task or a problem is outsourced to an undefined group of public employees to resolve.
Multisourcing outsourcing	*Multisourcing outsourcing* is where multiple outsource providers are used simultaneously to ensure, for example, competitive bidding in the outsourcing arrangements.
Nearshore outsourcing	*Nearshore outsourcing* is the same as international outsourcing, but in this case the countries are neighbors (for example, a U.S. firm outsourcing to a firm in Canada).
Netsourcing	*Netsourcing* is where a firm rents computer applications, services, and infrastructure over Web networks.

Type of Outsourcing	Description
Offshore out-sourcing	*Offshore outsourcing* is between a provider located in a different country than the client firm. A variant of this is where a client firm offshores their operations in another country by starting up a business owned by them in the foreign country. This latter type of offshoring operation is not considered outsourcing, but is a form of insourcing.
Shared out-sourcing	*Shared outsourcing* is where one outsource provider works for more than one organization at the same time (for example, a software outsourcing provider working on the same computer software code for several banks requiring the same type of software for their customers).
Spin-off out-sourcing	*Spin-off outsourcing* is a form of outsourcing where business activities of one company are being brought together into a completely new and separate firm (for example, an outsourced accounting department becoming a separate accounting services firm). This is more of a result of outsourcing than a form of outsourcing.
Transitional outsourcing	*Transitional outsourcing* is where an older business system is run by an outsourcing firm so the client firm can concentrate on making a new system work (for example, letting an outsourcer run an older computer-based ordering system for current customers while the client firm installs and makes a new system operational).
Value-added outsourcing	*Value-added outsourcing* is where the client and provider strengths are combined to market products or services.

Source: Adapted from Schniederjans et al. (2005, Figure 1.2, p. 8); Moser (2012).

13.2 Strategic Planning and the Outsourcing Process

13.2.1 Relationship of Organizational Strategic Planning and Outsourcing

The strategic planning process introduced in Chapter 1, "Designing Supply Chains," begins with an organization's mission statement, and then continues with general strategies at the organization-level that are segmented and given to individual departments as a basis to establish their own strategic departmental goals (see Figure 13.2). An organization-wide strategy of reducing costs to be more competitive in the market can be translated into an outsourcing strategy in a supply chain department as a desire to reduce costly inefficiency. This would be implemented by finding inefficient noncore competencies in the supply chain process, practices, policies, or tasks that might be better handled by outside outsource providers. The decision to use outsourcing to achieve goals is usually decided at the board of directors level in most organizations, based on finding the core and, more important, the noncore competencies from the external environmental analysis and internal organization analysis. Once the decision to use an outsourcing strategy is approved and accepted, the question of how much outsourcing is needed has to be determined. In situations where whole departments are outsourced (that is, business process outsourcing, BPO), the process would be handled by the CEO or vice presidents as needed. In less-invasive outsourcing efforts, the decision process is directed to the appropriate department. Experts from within and outside the organization are often employed to aid in making these assessments. Experts might be brought in to help in the analysis, including lawyers with international law backgrounds, international economics experts, and cultural experts from universities (Cavusgil et al., 2002, p. 83). During the analysis, board members may find the risks in some aspects of international outsourcing are too great. (We discuss international risks later.) They could change their minds on the outsourcing strategy or on some component of it (for example, a preference for going local, not global to find an outsource provider) and select a new strategy to achieve their goals. This new strategy may still involve international or global outsourcing, just not those aspects that are viewed as potentially too risky.

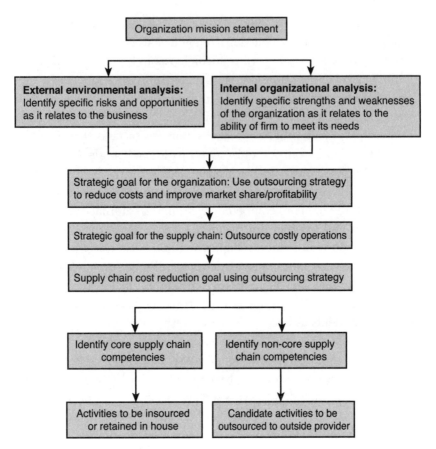

Figure 13.2 Relationship of strategic planning and outsourcing

Source: Adapted from Schniederjans (1998, Figure 2.2, p.22); Schniederjans et al. (2005, Figure 1.3, p. 10).

13.2.2 Outsourcing Process

The process by which an outsourcing project is undertaken is much the same for either a *fixed-term outsourcing agreement* (that is, where there is a fixed, end-time period for the project), or a *continual renewal outsourcing agreement* (that is, the outsourcing provider expects to be doing the project indefinitely, resulting in an outsourcing program). The general steps in an outsourcing process used to implement an outsourcing project are presented in Figure 13.3 and described here:

1. **Select candidate activities to outsource:** Not every noncore competency identified will automatically be a candidate for outsourcing. Many of the noncore competencies, once recognized, can be dealt with by improving organizational weaknesses and insourcing them. Those that cannot be handled by insourcing means become ideal candidates for outsourcing.

2. **Establish goals and draft outsourcing agreement specifications:** Once the noncore competency candidates are selected, goals are established in the context of the strategic objectives. For example, if a client firm had a strategic goal of achieving a market growth in sales of 25% per year over the next three years, that figure could be broken down into yearly targets. From that point on, existing client firm capabilities are determined on an aggregate yearly basis. What remains can be used to finally determine what needs to be stated in the outsource agreement. So the client firm would be in a position to start drafting it. Some of the typical outsourcing agreement specifications are presented in Table 13.2.

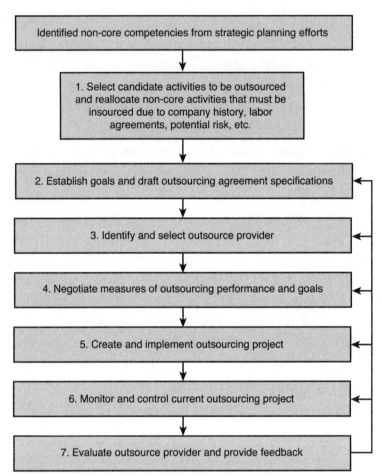

Figure 13.3 Steps in the outsourcing process

Source: Adapted from Schniederjans et al. (2005, Figure 1.7, p. 14).

Table 13.2 Typical Outsourcing Agreement Specifications

Features	Description
Define scope of outsourcing project	Define what work (1) is to be outsourced to the provider and (2) other work to be performed by the client firm. Organizations have operational boundaries and corporation borders that a outsource provider may intrude upon them.

Features	Description
Define objectives and goals	Define the exact set of objectives and related goals to be achieved. Quantification in units of production or service hours provided per specific objective and goal must be well defined. These should include all critical success factors the client firm believes is necessary to achieve organizational goals. Success factor criteria such as quality, delivery, timeliness, compliance, flexibility, responsiveness, and cost reduction should be established as a guide to encourage the provider to better understand the needs of the client and develop a closer partnership.
Define contribution of resources	Define what resources are expected from both the client and provider firms to implement the outsourcing agreement work. Be as specific in terms of human resources, technology, and system resource requirements as they relate to the defined unit/hour service objectives. This would also include issues of transitioning resources that are transferred to an outsource provider during the startup period of the agreement.
Define duties	Define where the areas of individual and joint management responsibilities are to be assumed in all phases of the project over the life of the agreement. This will include all issues of governance including roles, responsibilities, meetings, reviews, evaluations, communications, and any management procedures required. This would also include the transition planning efforts including such factors as training and retaining of staff that transfer from client to provider.
Establish timeline on goals and objectives	Define the specific dates for goal and objective accomplishment along with the means of measuring, evaluating, and reporting requirements. This would cover the entire outsourcing project planning horizon from start to finish.
Establish flexibility procedures	Define opportunities for both the client firm and the provider to initiate some forms of change in the outsourcing agreement. Specify which changes might come with penalties for noncompliance or rewards when deadlines or goals are exceeded. Define any bonus systems for the provider to help achieve client-desired outcomes in the longer term.
Risk management	Identify and specify as much as possible any possible risks the client firm may face with this agreement. Some assessment of how these risks will be managed (by whom) and how they should be minimized is necessary should be included in the agreement. Risks factors such as shifts in costs, information security, and developing dependence by the client firm on the provider are just a few of the tactical issues that should be addressed here.

Features	Description
Procedure on terminating agreement	Define the circumstances where either the client or the provider may terminate the outsourcing agreement. This may be at a planned end time for the outsourcing agreement or specific circumstances that justify either party ending the agreement without risk of legal recourse or penalty.

Source: Adapted from Cullen and Willcocks (2003, pp. 67–111); Milgate (2001, p. 60); Schniederjans et al. (2005, Figure 4.2, p. 57).

3. **Identify and select an outsource provider:** Once a draft of the proposed outsourcing assignments is prepared, the next step is to find and select an outsource provider to do the work. Traditionally, a list of known possible providers can be prepared from industry association directories and outsourcing directories (*FS Outsourcing Company,* www.fsoutsourcing. com). From this list, referrals from experts or other experienced managers can be used in a systematic check-sheet needs and wants selection process to choose possible candidates. Another approach to identifying potential outsource providers is to establish a set of provider qualifications and use them to identify worthy candidates. Qualification criteria might be suited to support the particular needs of the client organization (for example, transportation connections and approved transportation permits in a targeted foreign market). The qualifications might include such criteria as excellence in service delivery, security, trust, flexibility, agility, and value. Pint and Baldwin (1997) suggest evaluating the outsource provider in terms of current capabilities to meet client needs; consideration of costs and risks jointly; knowledge; skills; breadth and depth of experience (including past performance); financial strength; and commitment to technological innovation, quality improvement, and customer satisfaction. Using these criteria, client firms can then make a *request for information* (RFI) proposal to individual outsource providers to conduct a preliminary evaluation to gauge the market for prevailing prices/rates or any criteria that is viewed as

critical. A *request for proposal* (RFP) can also be used like an advertisement in outsourcing media stating the outsourcing requirements, including who is making the request, project scope, location of business activity, reasons for outsourcing, time horizons, and general pricing information. Both the RFI and RFP help to reduce the selection of an outsource provider, but additional effort is always needed to sort the best from the best and to make an optimal selection of a provider. Provider-selection criteria can be divided into four categories: obligatory, quantitative, qualitative, and implementation. *Obligatory selection criteria* (that is, must-have requirements to be considered eligible) include risk avoidance factors, English-speaking country, and so on. *Quantitative provider-selection criteria* and *qualitative provider-selection criteria* items found in the literature are used to judge the ability to satisfy (at least at some risk-rated level) the additional "niceties," which a client firm might appreciate. Quantitative provider-selection criteria include such items as financial strength, high-quality service standards, adequate numbers of personnel to do the job, and so forth. Qualitative provider-selection criteria include such items as trustworthiness, outsourcing experience level, proven customer satisfaction, and so on. *Implementation provider-selection criteria* are focused on three phases of implementation related risk in the design, transition, and follow-up of outsourcing projects.

4. **Negotiate measures of outsourcing performance and goals:** The client firm is now in a position to begin negotiations for the actual outsource agreement that will clearly list specific goals and how goal accomplishment will be measured in using some form of performance indicator. For guiding principles in negotiating agreements, see Chapter 8, "Negotiating."

5. **Create and implement an outsourcing project:** Once the agreement is negotiated, it can be put down on paper as a roadmap to implementation. The transition details for the

implementation of the outsourcing project should be included in the agreement so that both parties know and agree to their responsibilities. Although most problems can be anticipated and planned for, many cannot. Therefore, provisions in the agreement must anticipate unexpected events and problems and provide a means for dealing with them during the implementation phase of the process. While the transition phase of implementation may be outlined in the outsourcing agreement, detailed human resource or staff assignments for both client and provider will need to be made at this planning step. The transition planning at the operational level should be very detailed and must cover human resources, facilities, equipment, software, third-party agreements, and all functions, processes, and business activities related to the outsourcing agreement. In addition, management responsibilities and functions of day-to-day planning, coordinating, staffing, organizing, and leading must be defined at this stage of the outsourcing process.

6. **Monitor and control the current outsourcing project:** After the transition from the client firm is made handing off the supply chain or other tasks to the outsource provider, the day-to-day efforts of implementing an outsourcing agreement are usually performed by middle-level and lower-level managers in both the client and the outsource provider firms. During this step in the outsourcing process, it is important to share information with those people who work in the areas where outsourcing is being implemented. Sharing the planning and implementation efforts is the best way to head off fear, suspicion, anger, or even disruptive behavior. As Elmuti and Kathawala (2) found in their study on international outsourcing, the number one reason for a negative impact on an outsourcing project was employees' fear of the loss of their jobs. Other international factors such as cultural differences in work attitudes and differences in social norms might surface and reveal the

need for education and desensitizing. Also, measures for monitoring ongoing goal achievement must be installed. Both the client firm and outsource provider must agree to measures that are to be taken: who collects information, where and to whom it is reported, and at what times both parties review the measures. These measures should be viewed as a quality-assurance system, which ensures the provider is doing the job it was hired to do for the client firm. Actually, a good monitoring system works for both parties. While the client firm uses the system to monitor goal achievement, the provider uses it to determine whether it qualifies for extra benefits for doing an exceptional job.

7. **Evaluate the outsource provider and provide feedback:** Based on the monitoring measurements and their comparison to the agreed levels of business performance, monitoring can become a routine process. This should be viewed as a continuous effort of the evaluation phase of the outsourcing process. The goal is to provide a timely system of checks on the outsource provider to the client firm to ensure compliance with the outsource agreement and the expectations of the client firm. Sharing information on the progress of the outsourcing project and providing feedback for corrective control and further improvements is essential for a successful outsourcing project. The evaluations of the outsource provider might also take the form of periodic audits performed by client firm's staff or outside auditing firms. Greaver (1999, pp. 272–273) suggests an *oversight council* (that is, internal and external supply chain members who monitor and counsel a firm regarding issues that arise from the evaluation of suppliers) be appointed to review annual supplier performance. In addition, the oversight council could act as a forum for discussing major issues, making recommendations for corrective adjustments based on results and to act as an arbiter if problems arise.

13.2.3 Risks in the Outsourcing Process

The outsourcing process presented in Figure 13.3 has limitations. Most are related to the potential of risks entering each step in the process. Some examples of risks associated with the steps in the outsourcing process are listed in Table 13.3.

Table 13.3 Examples of Risks Associated with the Steps in the Outsourcing Process

Outsourcing Process Steps	Examples of Possible Risks
Identify noncore competencies	Incorrectly identified as a core and not as a noncore competency.
	Incorrectly identified as a noncore and not as a core competency.
Select candidate activities to be outsourced	Lists of candidates may be incomplete, suboptimizing the choice.
	Activities may not be improved by outsourcing.
Establish goals and draft outsourcing agreement specifications	Impossible goals can be set so high failure is certain.
	Language in agreement may not be clear enough for successful understanding and compliance by outsource provider.
	Unable to align outsourcing efforts with organization goals.
Identify and select outsource provider	Can incorrectly identify those who should be excluded as candidates.
	Can select the wrong outsource provider.
	Incomplete analysis of selected outsourcer provider capabilities resulting in less than acceptable performance.
Negotiate measures of outsourcing performance and goals	Misinterpretation of measures and goals, how they are measured, and what they mean.
	Cost of negotiations might be greater than cost advantages of outsourcing.

Outsourcing Process Steps	Examples of Possible Risks
Create and implement outsourcing project	Senior management not supporting project.
	Employees react negatively.
	Necessary cost and performance information unavailable.
	Poorly written agreement or contract.
	Technical problems delay handoff of activities.
	Outsource provider experiences startup problems.
	Management of client firm does not willingly participate in handoff of activities to outsource provider.
	Employees resent and resist transfer of their work.
Monitor and control current outsourcing project	Unable to provide timely monitoring of daily operations.
	Unable to control project activities.
	Performance measures are not reported or misreported to client firm.
Evaluate outsource provider and provide feedback	Unable to accurately evaluate outsource provider performance.
	Unable to provide timely information to outsource provider on results.
	A nonresponsive outsource provider (that is, ignores feedback).
	Outsourcing agreement defaulted.
	Outsourcing agreement penalties end up being paid by both parties.

Source: Adapted from Schniederjans et al. (2005, Table 1.2, p. 15).

Risks abound in outsourcing projects, as surveys of supply chain executives attest to (see "Global Risks...," 2011; Global Manufacturing...," 2011; Carter and Giunipero, 2010; Leach, 2011). Yet outsourcing risk can be viewed as a strategy for eliminating risk. In Figure 13.4, the Da Rold model for risk transference is presented (Gouge, 2003). As illustrated, the more a firm outsources its business activities, the less operational risks (like the risks in managing a supply chain) the firm will have to worry about. However, firms run outsourcing risks just by undertaking a project.

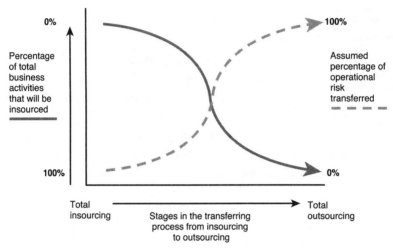

Figure 13.4 Da Rold outsourcing transfer of risk model

Source: Adapted from Gouge (2003, pp. 150–152).

Several outsourcing risks that can lead to project failure are listed in Table 13.4. To deal with some of the risks, firms have embraced outsourcing strategies utilizing one or more types of outsourcing. For example, Badasha (2012) reports that large numbers of European manufacturers are focusing on their supply chain risk challenges by turning to nearshoring as a potential mitigation method (reduces geographic distances in supply chains). Moreover, supply chain risk management programs are viewed as a key issue for manufacturing companies going forward. Risks are particularly prevalent in supply chains that operate internationally or on a global basis.

Table 13.4 Outsourcing Risks and Project Failure

Type of Risk Issue	Examples
Client-provider relationship issues	Not building relationships, taking a passive role managing the outsourcing project, poor understanding of the requirements of the agreement (Verner and Abdullah, 2012).
Cost issues	Cutting the costs on the outsource provider results in provider reducing service to the client (Digman, 2003).
Customer complaint issues	Client firm customers' complaints are elevated by move to outsource provider (Smith, 2004).
Employee issues	Communication failure of outsource provider to listen to own employees ("Employees Ignored...," 2002).
Government issues	Government laws and regulation are changing and can reduce cost advantages of outsourcing ("Accounting Rule Wipes...," 2003).
Security issues	Sending individual and corporate records to foreign countries may open the firm to substantial security and confidentiality issues (Nassimbeni et al., 2012).
Structural issues	Experiments in different types of outsourcing (for example, multisourcing outsourcing) experiences failure in the longer-term ("Multisourcing Just...," 2003).

Source: Adapted from Schniederjans et al. (2005, Table 2.7, p. 32).

In the final analysis, managing risk is a balancing act between acceptance and avoidance. Ideally, the balance is reflected in the number of business activities a firm insources versus outsources, but to accomplish this, supply chain managers must understand the risks faced in international/global outsourcing.

13.2.4 Risks in International/Global Outsourcing

Whether it is recognized or not, outsourcing today, although it can be local, is usually international or even global in scope, dealing with supply chain topics such as procurement, distribution, logistics, inventory, manufacturing, almost anything a supply chain organization can do. Even when a firm believes it is outsourcing to local supply firms, one or two tiers later those suppliers are probably outsourcing to international suppliers. Therefore, grasping the risks that are being undertaken is essential to running a successful long-term outsourcing project. To aid in this task, there is a need to recognize risks that a firm takes when it knowingly goes international with its supply chains. Potential international/global risk taking can be divided into four categories: economic, political, cultural, and demographic risks. Examples of related supply chain international/global outsourcing risk categories are presented in Table 13.5. There are numerous related risks within each of the four categories in Table 13.5. To help conceptualize some of the various risks that exist within the four categories, a framework in Figure 13.5 is presented listing 12 types of risk. Questions related to these 12 types of risk raise are described in Table 13.6. Table 13.6 is not intended to be a definitive listing, but seeks to offer typical questions that may stimulate further consideration of the risk of doing supply chain business with international outsource providers.

Table 13.5 Examples of Related International/Global Risk Factor Categories and Outsourcing Risk in Supply Chain Management

Risk Factor Categories	Example of International or Global Business Risk Factor	Related Outsourcing Risk Factor in Supply Chain Management
Economic	Does the country where the outsourcing firm is located have sufficient road infrastructure?	What is the likelihood the infrastructure will allow trucking firms of the outsource provider to move fast enough to permit an agile or quick response capability?
Political	Is the country politically stable?	Will the transit permits granted the outsource provider by the current government allowing goods to be distributed still be useful if the current government collapses?
Cultural	Is there a difference in language such that it might inhibit successful business operations?	Will the use of our outsource provider's truck drivers from one country lack the communication capabilities needed to communicate with other partners in the client firm's supply chain network?
Demographic	Is there sufficient growth in the population of this country to meet labor growth needs?	Can the outsource provider firm find the employees they need to handle logistics and distribution goals in their outsourcing agreement if the population has no growth and labor markets dry up?

Source: Adapted from Schniederjans et al. (2005, Table 3.2, p. 40).

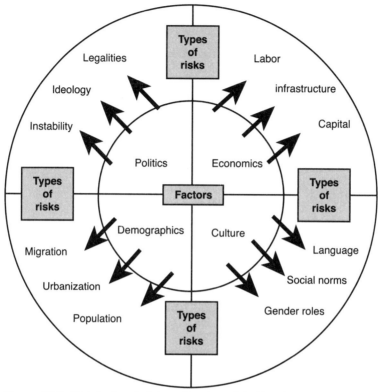

Figure 13.5 Risk factors in international or global business

Source: Adapted from Schniederjans et al. (2005, Figure 3.4, p. 41).

Table 13.6 Types of International/Global Risk Factors

Risk Factor Categories	Types of Risk Factors	Risk Factor Issues
Economic	Labor	Does the outsource provider have the necessary skilled or unskilled labor to do the job they are contracted to perform, and does the country in which the provider is located have the necessary labor pool? Without the right quantity and quality in mixture of labor skills, an outsource provider will not be able to complete the work and risks contract noncompliance.

Risk Factor Categories	Types of Risk Factors	Risk Factor Issues
Economic	Capital	Does the outsourcing provider have the necessary capital to finance the operations in fulfillment of a contract, and does the country in which the provider is located have the necessary capital markets (that is, both domestic and foreign) to support the firm's needs? Without adequate funding to the outsource provider, they may not be able to finance operations. Even the transference of funds into and out of the outsource provider's country to assist the provider may pose risks for the client firm.
Economic	Infrastructure	Does the outsource provider possess the necessary physical assets (for example, transportation equipment) and technological/informational systems (for example, computers) to support contracted business activities, and does the country in which the provider firm's operations are located possess the necessary infrastructure (for example, transportation system, roads, electrical power systems) and technological/informational (for example, Internet system, telephone system) to support contracted business activities? Without an adequate infrastructure for transporting physical products or delivering informational services, an outsource provider and their subcontractors risk not being able to carry out supply chain delivery requirements.
Political	Instability	Is the government in the country where the outsource provider operates unstable and likely to collapse during the time period of the outsourcing agreement? Without a stable government, outsourcing firms may not be able to provide security to employees or uphold legal agreements (that is, the outsourcing contract) as well as the risk of having technology or financial assets that have been loaned to the provider confiscated by the outsource provider's government.

Risk Factor Categories	Types of Risk Factors	Risk Factor Issues
Political	Ideology	Does the country in which the outsource provider operates have high or low coherence in *governmental ideology* (that is, a government's views, beliefs, and assumptions concerning its role in controlling the private sector). This would include the type of political system (for example, capitalism, socialism) and its role in the economy. Some countries have very clear the roles for everyone and their business institutions. Because of clarity in the role of government, the business operations for both outsource providers and the client firms have less uncertainty in doing business and therefore less risk. Other countries where there is lower ideological coherence involve greater risk in doing business because roles are unclear and can be interpreted in many ways and at the government's whim.
Political	Legalities	Are the legal systems in the country in which the outsource firm operates understandable or overly complex and are they well structured with formal procedures for adjudication or are they informal with preferential treatment, bias, and bribery possible? Without an understandable and well-structured legal system, both the outsource provider and the client firm may not be able to defend themselves if legal action is undertaken against them.
Cultural	Language	In businesses with verbal interaction is essential, is the spoken and written language of the country in which the outsource provider is located fully understandable to the client firm's employees, customers, and so on? If not, the client firm runs risks (in every communication) misinterpretation of communications and therefore contractual agreement violations.

Risk Factor Categories	Types of Risk Factors	Risk Factor Issues
Cultural	Social norms	*Culture* (that is, a set of shared values, behaviors, and attitudes of a group of people, including gender roles, religious influence, diversity in language, values in governance, societal divisions, and the idea of trust) can be very important in some outsourcing agreements. Is it possible that business activities asked of the outsource provider violate social norms in the country in which it is located? If the business activities that an outsource provider has agreed to contractually perform in some ways violate social norms of the country, there are substantial risks of property and legal torts both involving the outsource provider and the client firm.
Cultural	Gender roles	In situations where communications are necessary for the success of an outsourcing agreement between different-gendered employees, might both the outsource provider and the client firm be culturally upsetting to the parties involved? The roles of women and gay people in businesses worldwide have been changing, and so have attitudes toward their contributions. Although advancements in many countries have taken place concerning the rights of these two groups, role expectations differ substantially between nations. There are gender role risks if firms are not sensitive to cultural differences between countries.
Demographic	Migration	*Migration* (that is, the movement of people into, out of, or around a country) can be an important risk factor in labor-intensive agreements. Does the country in which the outsource provider operates have high or low population-migration rate? If a country has a high migration rate, it may be difficult to employ the necessary skilled or unskilled workers needed to run the outsource provider's operation because labor is moving around so quickly and because migration might add to political instability risks.

Risk Factor Categories	Types of Risk Factors	Risk Factor Issues
Demographic	Urbanization	Does the country in which the labor-intensive outsource provider operates have highly urbanized or concentrated population centers? Highly concentrated populations in dense metropolitan areas permit an easing of access to labor markets and are more efficient in reaching customers for marketing purposes. The more evenly dispersed the population, the less efficient it is to reach segments of markets, labor or customers. In addition, other factors, such as the concentration of transportation and information systems, often follow populations, making higher-density urbanization a desirable demographic. Without some degree of urbanization, the client firm and the provider run risks of not reaching labor or consumer markets.
Demographic	Population	How does the population growth rate, age, and health status of the country in which the outsource provider operates impact risk? Growth in population, lower-then-average age levels, and good health are all important factors that create an environment in which an outsource provider can find highly productive employees. Conversely, having a declining or older population may make finding adequate employees more difficult and costly for the outsource provider.

Source: Adapted from Schniederjans et al. (2005, pp. 41–43).

13.2.5 Combining Outsourcing with Lean Strategy in Supply Chain Management

Given the risks and complexity of outsourcing projects, the use of outsourcing has to be driven by the benefits this strategy provides to a client firm. It is clear there exists a substantial body of literature that supports the use of outsourcing as a strategy for many reasons, including the mitigation of risk (Banfield, 1999, p. 228; Slone et al., 2010, p. 136; Schniederjans et al., 2010, pp. 283–302; Zylstra, 2006, pp. 34–35). Few organizations and their supply chain departments use only one strategy to achieve goals. One of the more popular supply chain strategy combinations is a mixture of lean and outsourcing strategies. As previously mentioned, supply chain strategic planning can be greatly enhanced when combinations of supply chain strategies are used to move a firm to world-class performance levels. Table 13.7 provides a list of possible advantages of combining outsourcing with a lean supply chain management strategy. This table can be used to help justify an outsourcing/lean project and provide ideas on areas of possible advantage that an outsourcing project can bring to a client firm.

Table 13.7 Potential Benefits of Outsourcing for Lean Supply Chains

Area of Outsourcing Advantage	Lean Principles and Potential Advantages
Reduce cost and increase profit	Waste-elimination principle: The cost of business activities outsourced to a provider can be less than in-house costs, reducing total costs.
	Synchronized efficiency: When a client firm outsources business activity, they can be left with assets (for example, technology) that can be converted to cash to deal with short-term cash problems (that is, saving interest costs on loans) by contractually requiring the outsource provider to purchase the client assets.
	Synchronized efficiency: Cost savings results as fixed costs (for example, trucks, material handling equipment) are turned into variable costs (leasing agreements) by having the outsource provider buy and lease them back to the client firm.
	Waste-elimination principle: When the client firm becomes part of the outsource provider's network or supply chain, this helps to reduce costs for both parties.
	Waste-elimination principle: When external financing is too costly to invest in a capital expansion, outsourcing can save investment costs by using the provider's investments in capital equipment.
	Flow-constraint removal: Greater profits because the cost of business activities outsourced to a foreign provider operating under less-restrictive laws (for example, environmental protection laws, labor laws) can be considerably less than insourced client firm costs.

Area of Outsourcing Advantage	Lean Principles and Potential Advantages
Gain outside expertise	Build alliances: A firm can gain access to a broad base of supply chain expertise and skills.
	Strategic focus and waste elimination: Outsourcers can be a source of original ideas for improvements in core and noncore competency services and products. This is particularly true in hot subject areas like green supply chain management.
Improve service capabilities	Demand pull, flow constraints, and agility: Improvement in operation flexibility and agility to more easily increase production or service distribution during high customer demand is achieved by adding outsource provider supply chain capacity; just as quickly, capacity can be decreased during decline periods by ending outsourcing agreements.
	Continuous improvement: With outsourcing, there is flexibility to transform the supply chain networks to become more efficient.
	Customer value and waste elimination: By reducing costs, which can be passed on to the customers, customer value and satisfaction can be increased.
	Customer value: Improved delivery performance through superior supply chain outsourcing can result in better delivery service quality and greater customer satisfaction.
	Leadership of change: Outsourcing can be used as a rapid introduction strategy for change in new products and services to meet shifting customer demand and be used to introduce new technologies or systems in the client organization.
	Flow constraints: New products can achieve a faster time to market with specialized skills of outsourcing firm.
	Growth strategy: Outsourcing can help the organization develop and gain access to new distribution channels and supply chain networks quickly for purposes of growth.

Area of Outsourcing Advantage	Lean Principles and Potential Advantages
Able to focus on core competences	Leadership strategy: Outsourcing allows the client firm to focus on core competencies (what they do best), while the outsource provider improves the firm's noncore competencies, both of which can enhance supply chain performance.
	Agility strategy: Outsourcing frees assets to be reallocated to core competencies.
	Growth strategy: Unique market access can be gained through the business opportunities that the outsource provider brings with them (for example, provider has unique connections to natural resources).
	Leadership strategy: Client firms may find they have outsourcing capacities that they could sell to other firms (for example, spare trucks).
	Leadership strategy: Lean orientation provides the client firm with a discipline to identify and learn what their core competencies are and, in doing so, aids strategic planning.
	Growth strategy: Outsource provider brings their core competencies to the client to maintain state-of-the-art status in contrast to competitors.
Gain knowledge and use of advanced technology	Synchronized efficiency: Firms can outsource to state-of-the-art providers instead of retaining older legacy systems (that is, pick and choose newer technologies anytime needed, because the client firm does not have to invest in such technologies).
	Leadership strategy: Outsourcing can help client organizations learn newer technology.
Other advantages	Continuous improvement: Outsourcing changes the culture of a client firm to be more productive and embrace CI.
	Waste-elimination principle: Outsourcing can be used as a strategy for downsizing or reengineering the client firm.
	Synchronized efficiency: Improved risk mitigation because the efficiency problems with human resources, technology, and systems can be given over to the outsource provider.
	Synchronized efficiency: Outsource provider can serve as a branch of operations for client firm, which can save the client firm from going international and thus avoid the complexity of dealing with multicurrency, multilingual issues, multinational accounting problems, and so on.
	Synchronized efficiency: Conserve capital for alternative investment in core competencies.

Source: Adapted from Schniederjans et al. (2005, Tables 2.1, 2.2, 2.3, 2.4, pp. 24–28); Schniederjans et al., 2010, pp. 287–289; Abu-Musa (2011); Boehe, (2010).

13.3 Other Topics in Strategic Planning in Outsourcing

13.3.1 Measuring Outsourcing Services

In the area of outsourcing services, it is important for the client firm to ensure compliance with its goals and directives on the part of the providers. The more attention given to the outsource provider's behavior in providing services, the more likely that desired results will ensue (Li and Choi, 2009). Li and Choi's research reported by Wade (2011) suggests employing a rating scale survey divided into two parts where a questions are designed to extract information on both outsourcing outcomes and customer satisfaction. The rating scale is set up on a 1 to 6 scale, where a rating of 1 means the outsource customer completely disagrees with the survey question the way it is stated, and a rating of 6 means they completely agree. For outsourcing outcome questions, Li and Choi suggested they be presented in terms of both negative statements (for example, for the outsourcing services we received, we believe we have paid more than expected) and positive statements (for example, the outsource provider provided timely service). Examples of customer satisfaction survey questions, likewise, should be structured both negatively (for example, our customers were concerned about the services they received) and positively (for example, our customers were pleased the services they received). These combinations help to ensure the rater is thinking about each question and giving an honest response.

Rating and scoring methods to evaluate outsource provider performance are very common methodologies in supply chain management (Schniederjans, 2005, pp. 77–80). When combined with gap analysis (see Chapter 3, "Staffing Supply Chains"), they can provide an ongoing monitoring system of the outcomes and satisfaction of customers with outsource provider performance (Schniederjans, 2005, pp. 84–86).

13.3.2 Outsourcing Benefits and Planning in the Product Life Cycle

As mentioned in several previous chapters, a supply chain life cycle is dependent on a firm's product life cycles. Operations planning for demand shifts in a product life cycle can be augmented by an outsourcing strategy (Tompkins, 2012; Benkler, 2010). That is, outsourcing activities can be applied to each phase of the product life cycle to enhance efficiency and effectiveness. Some of the potential benefits possible by using outsource providers at various stages in a product life cycle are presented in Table 13.8. Outsourcing at the right time during fluctuations in demand for a product's life cycle can help support a lean supply chain strategy by stabilizing the broad demand variation inherent in a product's life cycle by helping to smooth the demand cycle out.

Table 13.8 Potential Outsourcing Roles and Benefits in Supply Chain Product Life Cycle Planning

Product Life Cycle Stage	Outsource Provider Roles and Benefits
Introduction	Outsource provider allows resources to quickly be applied to aid in delivering new products to market increasing profitability and saving client firm from having to invest the capital.
	Allows client firm avoid start up risks by having provider handle the initial product and distribution activities for new products.
	Working with state-of-the-art outsource provider who can bring advanced technologies, processes, and other skills to innovate new products can results in a more successful product.
Growth	Allocating the rapid additional growth in demand to the provider allows the client firm more time to plan capital investment in logistic equipment rather than rushing out to acquire it in short term.
	Allocating the rapid demand to the provider allows the client firm to maintain a lean and stable operations level of services without having to respond to costly sudden increases in demand.
	Enhances agility and flexibility by being able to offer a wide variety of services whenever the client firm so chooses to engage providers.

Product Life Cycle Stage	Outsource Provider Roles and Benefits
Maturity	Being able to pick and choose outsource providers easily permits the client firm to reduce costs with outsourcing firms without need for discontinuation costs.
	Diversity of applications and experience of outsource providers can help bring new ideas on cost cutting that can keep profit margins up.
Decline	Helps to avoid legal or governmental regulation issues. A plant-closing law passed by the U.S. Congress in 1988 is called the *Worker Adjustment and Retaining Notification Act* (WARN) (Bohlman and Dundas, 2002, p. 705).
	A client firm can be contractually, require an outsource provider to deal with obsolete or end-of-life product at provider's expense.
	Helps client firm avoid capital investment write-offs and the accounting problems those cost when the product is discontinued.

Source: Adapted from Schniederjans et al. (2005, Tables 2.1, 2.2, 2.3, 2.4, pp. 24–28); Schniederjans et al., 2010, pp. 287–289; Abu-Musa (2011); Boehe, (2010).

13.3.3 Global Supply Chain Labor Standards in Outsourcing

With the increasing outsourcing to third parties around the world, many companies have taken an active interest in their conduct related to supply chain labor standards. A survey by *PricewaterhouseCoopers* (PwC) revealed that 59% of supply chain executives identified bad working conditions as the most significant risk to their supply chains ("Vulnerable to...," 2008). It was suggested that to mitigate this risk companies need to work in close partnership with suppliers to establish a set of clear expectations of what are acceptable working conditions and what are not. Developing a code of conduct is one way to initiate a risk management project. A research study by Singer (2012) examined the adoption of supplier codes of conduct and supply chain labor policies by major international organizations and governments. The United Nations Global Compact (www.unglobalcompact.org/) was found by Singer (2012) to offer a general framework that focused on labor working conditions and could aid in drafting a supplier code of conduct. In addition, the UN Global Compact offered a useful set of criteria for companies wanting to implement labor condition programs, including social and human rights issues. The UN Global

Compact outlined 28 criteria divided into 3 areas of concern that should be considered in negotiations with suppliers when developing codes of conduct ("Supply Chain...," 2010, p. 22). Useful as a guide for developing a code of supplier conduct, the areas of concern and criteria are presented in Table 13.9.

Table 13.9 Areas of Labor and Social Concern and Code of Conduct Criteria

Area of Labor or Social Concern	Criteria That Should Be Included in the Code of Conduct
Human rights and labor	Child labor
	Emergency preparedness
	Fire safety
	Forced labor
	Freedom of association and collective bargaining
	Humane treatment
	Industrial hygiene
	Machine safeguarding
	Nondiscrimination
	Occupational injury and illness
	Occupational safety
	Physically demanding work
	Wages and benefits
	Working hours
Environment	Air pollution
	Biodiversity
	Energy usage
	Greenhouse gas emissions
	Material toxicity and chemicals
	Raw material use
	Recyclability, obsolescence, and end-of-life of products
	Water use and wastewater treatment
Anticorruption	Accounting and business records
	Bribery and kickbacks
	Conflict of interest
	Gifts, meals, and entertainment
	Protecting information
	Reporting misconduct

Source: Adapted from Singer (2012); "Supply Chain...," (2010).

13.4 What's Next?

The future trends for the use of outsourcing seem to be mixed, depending on who is doing the forecasting. Freightgate (a logistics software company, www.freightgate.com/) forecast future increasing demand for better collaborative business processes and logistics procurement, coupled with the use of transportation rate management systems that will result in the need for greater execution capabilities, which are currently viewed beyond the knowledge base of most supply chain organizations ("Supply Chain...," 2012). They believe that response time and budgets of most in-house IT departments will drive a substantial increase in the growth of supply chain outsourcing to better fit the strategic requirements of client firms. The same forecast suggested that trends for increased use of *cloud computing* (that is, the delivery of computing and storage capacity as a service to end user who access cloud-based applications through a Web browser or mobile technology while other business software and the user's data are stored on servers at different locations) and mobile applications are creating faster collaborative sharing of information up and down the organization. This faster collaborative sharing is fostering teamwork synergies that improve processes, lessen carbon footprints, ensure adherence to security compliance regulations, reduce noncore costs, accelerate business value, aid in global environmental awareness, improve financial results, and speed up solutions/resolution discovery. Customers expect these outcomes, and so more outsourcing is required to find these capabilities.

Yet others looking to the future believe the outsourcing strategy is not necessarily as beneficial as it has been and therefore will decline. Albert (2011) reported on the KPMG's 3Q11 Sourcing Advisory Pulse (www.kpmg.com/) survey that disappointment with underachieving outsourcing efforts, changing economics, and a desire for greater control over strategic processes and sensitive data were reasons that firms struggle to make outsourcing work. In addition, the survey suggested client firms would continue to face challenges managing outsourcing transition processes and that their efforts would be hampered by a lack of skilled resources and by inadequate planning and procedures. This means failure in outsourcing transition efforts in terms of not being completed on time, within budget, or not achieving the required functionality. To compensate for the failures and to try to salvage some of the benefits of outsourcing, one trend noticed in the survey was that interest and adoption levels for shared services increased, due in part to disappointing outsourcing efforts and a wish to avoid overly aggressive outsourcing. The report stated that buyers had moderate success in achieving goals sought from shared service efforts, with cost savings being the most often cited goal (Albert, 2011).

Also, according to Leach (2011) and Beatty (2012), some of the most attractive countries (for example, India, China) are expected to have double-digit inflation going into the future. Given the main reason for outsourcing is low manufacturing and labor costs, inflation and local wage cost increases may end the growth and even mark a potential decline in offshoring. Although the current inflation rates and rising costs are yet to change the practice of outsourcing drastically, the next five years might see the disappearance of the term *offshoring*. In addition, it is clear that the business environment offered in foreign markets is altering. Global business services companies have become so effective in investing in technology that they are providing commercial-grade services. As a result, the old attitude that outsourcing overseas will cut costs but that a firm must accept poor quality has now changed. Firms are seeing improvement in quality from these same sources.

Most outsourcing decisions have been based on cost minimization, and many have failed. As the previously mentioned surveys reveal, the goal of cost minimization using the outsourcing strategy may not be as successful going forward. Regardless of the upward or downward trend of outsourcing in supply chain management, one constant should be followed to avoid the failure of projects. Moser (2012) suggests a new trend in evaluating outsourcing. Any outsourcing venture should be undertaken only with more extensive and inclusive analysis, bringing into consideration criteria that was until now excluded from consideration. Moser (2012) recommends a *total cost of ownership* (TCO) (Chapter 12, "Lean and Other Cost Reduction Strategies in Supply Chain Management") approach that includes the following:

- Costs of goods sold or landed costs, including price, packaging, duty, and planned freight costs
- Other costs, including factors affecting them, such as carrying costs for in-transit products, inventory onsite, prototyping, end-of-life or obsolescence, and travel costs
- Possible risk-related costs, including rework, quality, product liability, intellectual property, opportunity costs, brand impact, economic stability, governmental political stability, and recession
- Strategic costs, including impact on innovation, product differentiation, and mass customization
- Environmental costs, including those involved in going green

Moser suggests that by using inclusive analysis, which most firms in the past have not undertaken, not only will outsourcing failure rates be reduced but firms might also realize the TCO of outsourcing a current or future project is not in the best interest of the firm. What this means is that some firms currently involved in outsourcing might need to undertake a reshoring initiative to insource their supply chain and production activities.

14

Interview with Mr. Mike Orr of Genuine Parts Company

Introduction

This chapter consists of a series of questions and answers from an interview with a leading supply chain executive. The objective of this chapter is to provide a practitioner's perspective on the subject of life cycle issues in supply chain management. Other related subjects are also discussed in the interview.

About the Interviewee

Mr. Mike Orr is Senior Vice President of Operations & Logistics for Genuine Parts Company. Mike joined the company in 2005, and has more than 25 years of experience in global operations for industrial and consumer products companies. During his time with Genuine Parts Company, he has also served as Senior Vice President of Operations & Logistics for S.P. Richards Company, a GPC subsidiary.

Prior to joining Genuine Parts Company, he was Group Vice president of Operations for Newell Rubbermaid, where he had global operational responsibility, including manufacturing, safety, supply chain, and logistics. Before joining Newell Rubbermaid, he worked for Allied-Signal (Honeywell), in a variety of engineering and operation assignments.

Mike earned his Bachelor's degree in Mechanical Engineering from South Dakota State University and his Master's degree in Business Administration from Arizona State University.

"Automotive parts is a 30-minute business. If you can't deliver the part in 30 minutes, you won't get the order."

—*Mike Orr, 2011*

About Genuine Parts Company

Founded in 1928, *Genuine Parts Company* (GPC) is a service organization engaged in the distribution of automotive replacement parts, industrial replacement parts, office products, and electrical/electronic materials. Their products and services are offered through a network of more than 2,000 operations, geographically located across the United States, Canada, and Mexico. The regionally located distribution centers provide a unique ability to adapt product and service lines to better suit customer needs. GPC's commitment and reputation for *just-in-time* (JIT) service position us as a critical partner in our customers' success. GPC began to diversify its product lines over 30 years ago into several end markets with strong growth opportunities. The Automotive Parts Group, the largest Division of GPC, distributes over 380,000 products through its 58 NAPA distribution centers located across the United States. The Automotive Parts Group also consists of NAPA Canada/UAP Inc., Canada's leading automotive parts distributor, as well as Auto Todo, one of Mexico's largest automotive aftermarket organizations. In addition, we operate our heavy vehicle parts distribution business under the name TW Distribution and Traction, and our import parts distribution operations under the name Altrom. The Industrial Parts Group, which operates under the name Motion Industries, distributes over three million items from 500 operations located throughout the Unites States and Canada. Motion's rapid-delivery model provides customized product and technical expertise to customers in a JIT response, enabling clients to reduce production costs and free working capital. The Office Products group distributes over 50,000 business products from 45 distribution centers across the United States and Canada under the name S.P. Richards Company to thousands of office product resellers, including independent dealers, large contract stationers, national office supply superstores, mail-order distributors, Internet resellers, and college bookstores. The Electrical/Electronic Materials group is one of North America's leading distributors of process materials, production supplies, industrial MRO (*maintenance, repair, operations*), and value-added fabricated parts. Primary markets are the electrical OEM (*original equipment manufacturers*), apparatus repair, and assembly markets. The group distributes more than 100,000 items from 36 locations in the United States, Puerto Rico, Dominican Republic, Mexico, and Canada.

Interview Questions and Answers

How would you characterize your organization's supply chain?

GPC has complex supply chains across four distinct industries: automotive, industrial supplies, office supplies, and electrical supplies. The product offering and item count is extremely large: 32,000 office products, 400,000 automotive, 4 million industrial, and 25,000 electrical. Our supply chain spans from the source, a manufacturing facility, to the actual consumer of the product. GPC operates some of our own manufacturing sites, and we utilize contract manufacturing partners for selected categories. Of course, we also distribute national branded products that are sourced from parallel supply chains.

We are primarily a North American distribution company, but we ship goods all over the world. Our supply chain source is global. We do have production facilities outside of the United States. Although we ship goods all over the world, in our model we try to keep our inventory close to our customers and their consumption. That closeness is our *value proposition*. For example, NAPA stores are replenished via our internal supply chain system every night. If you go to a NAPA store today and can't find a part, we will have it to that stored by 7 a.m. the next day.

How do you deal with the Introduction Stage of a product or product line requiring a supply chain?

It depends on products or parts! Let's talk about new automotive parts. We *class* or identify every part or item used to assemble a car. We do this for every car made that is sold or distributed in North America, regardless of where it was manufactured. In essence, we know the future demand for replacement parts for each car that is sold in the United States. We know and keep track of where each part fits on each car, by make, model, and year. For example, a single spark plug "item" can be a replacement for multiple make and model cars and could be used for multiple years. That same spark plug unit may also be used by multiple manufacturers.

We know from our experience that the demand for spark plugs for a new car will be very minimal during the first several years. As we plan inventory deployment, the depth of inventory for that item would be minimized until the projected demand curve grows. In the replacement parts business, the "sweet spot" for demand creation is when a car has been in service six to nine years.

Establishing class is the first step in understanding demand patterns. The second phase is to collect current information for every car registered in the United States and where they are located. This information is readily available, and we categorize location by ZIP Code in the United States. Inventory is then deployed to individual store locations based on probability, age of vehicles, and items that would serve customers in that specific geographic area.

This comprehensive and data-driven information allows us to operate a highly efficient supply chain service for our customers and consumers. For example, we had a request from an individual for a specialized tail light assembly of a car that was more than 40 years old. Our supply chain network had the part, but not in this particular geographic area. We were able to deliver that part within 24 hours, and this is a routine process for our supply chain.

Through our supply chain network, we are able to deliver many types of standard or unique replacement auto parts to customers. Although we are proud of our supply chain performance, this is not a unique supply chain. A similar level of service is provided by companies like Caterpillar and John Deer because they have similar product complexity and need for our responsive customer service.

The challenge for our supply chain is product proliferation. When we get a new product or item in the supply chain, we have to make several assumptions or decisions for the item such as what the probability of product failure is going to be, what the timing (age) of failure will be, based on experience, what is likelihood of a repairs taking place, and finally, what replacement of an OEM or aftermarket substitution is likely to be used.

Historical data highlights the optimal vehicle age interval (six to nine years) for auto repair work in general. We know that the early interval age cars (before six years) tend not to need a repair or are under warranty repair, and late-cycle cars (after nine years) just don't get repaired. From these data and probabilities, we work up a demand forecast for new products. It is not a perfect science, but the process allows us to maximize our inventory investment across 6,000 locations.

In our business, parts need to be delivered to customers within half an hour or we lose the order. That dynamic drives inventory deployment, store count, and location. Generally, we place our facilities within 3- or 4-mile radius of our customers.

How do you know what to distribute to your customers given a new product?

In the case of a new car, we know some items are consumable and have specific service intervals. For example, a car will quickly need oil filters, a little later need air filters, even later brakes as they wear out. Of course, we factor the probability of *collision* demand for each part. Given that information we stock the inventory accordingly. We also look at the inventory items in terms of typical consumer good categories of *good, better, best*.

We have oil filters that are low cost with good performance, a little higher value (that is, better performance), and high end (that is, best performance). These factors are all depend on consumer behavior and can be associated with the kind of car purchased.

As a general observation, people who buy luxury sedans will buy the corresponding high-end products. People who buy pickup trucks or compact cars are more value conscience. Fewer customers will demand the high-end *best* quality, more the *better* quality, and considerably more the *good* quality products. We factor that into our algorithm for forecasting demand requirements to determine the stocking levels. We also use a hub-and-spoke model for stocking in locations. For example, if we have a city that has ten customer outlets for oil filters, we might stock one with the best quality filter, five with the better quality filter, and all ten with the good quality filter. The idea being that if demand for any filter existed in outlets that were not stocked, the item could be quickly transferred to that outlet like a spoke on wheel. This is a technique to have products in the correct geographic area, but not duplicate all items in every store.

How do you do your demand planning for totally new products?

I have worked at organizations where totally new products were being developed, so no frame of reference exists. When you invent something new or attempt to create a new category, you don't know for certain if or how strong demand will be.

For completely new items, a more rigorous analysis process is required. It starts with *sales and operations planning* (S&OP) and incorporates a financial pro forma analysis. The business assesses the market potential of the items, investment required to launch and most importantly the return on investment.

Before we even begin the planning process we would have an estimate for the size of the market for the new item. Sometimes you can go to your large retail partners or customers and they can provide some input on sales expectations. However, even with good information and due diligence, you can still end up with a dud of a product, a broken supply chain, and a write-off.

In cases of a less-than-successful product, with proper planning and communication most partners up- and downstream can recoup their investments. Marketing plays a role in successfully introducing new products and must contribute to the S&OP.

Statistical forecasting is useful in planning new products. Existing products or new products that are modeled after existing products can be more accurately forecast using historical data. New and unproven products require careful estimation effort. That is why an S&OP process is required.

We usually take marketing's estimates for really new products and adjust them down for any potential bias. Mathematically, forecast error is usually reasonable, but bias error can be very large. Marketing or any group trying to introduce a new item will be optimistic. That optimism can translate to *bias* that creates error in the forecast. Failure to recognize bias errors can prove costly to a supply chain.

For new items, the *groupthink* forecast can be extremely biased. In my experience, we have had to cut initial forecasts in half, knowing full well that it is better to chase growth in demand if a new product takes off than to deal with overproduction issues. Of course, we take into consideration the production lead times and how fast we could recover in the event of a rapid growth situation. There are many levers to pull if we see that demand is higher than forecast, such as expediting production with overtime. It is more difficult to address product that has no demand or sales potential.

We also protect our supply chain partners with robust and candid communication. They are advised with our initial demand, but we also let them know that forward demand could be erratic. Because uncertainty exists, we plan and discuss recovery actions such as expediting needed production. This helps to reduce some of the risk in the product Introduction Stage.

How do you deal with the Growth Stage of a product or product line requiring a supply chain?

Unplanned growth in demand is always a challenge. In very rapid growth, you have to protect your customers. Sometimes, the need for allocations, even for your very best customers and larger trading partners, is required. There is no real easy way to deal with growth other than chasing demand for a period of time. As an organization, we have a certain amount of surge capacity available to deal with surges in our supply chain. We might be able to use contract suppliers, overtime shifts, and other stretch capacity in our plants to deal with most cases of demand exceeding supply. The success of this depends on the industry you are in, the lead times, and how fast you can react.

For some explosive-growth situations where demand is substantially greater than existing production capacity, the solution is just a matter of working an extra weekend or adding a second or third shift. What is challenging is what I call *time-dependent explosive growth*.

An example is a seasonal product like Easter candy that has to be delivered before the season selling period. In this situation, you have to allocate what you can to your better customers (however *better* is defined). In a supply chain, we have retailers, wholesalers, and distributors. Basically you have to pick winners and losers based on their value to the firm. In the consumer products industry, Wal-Mart always wins. Generally, what we see is that the retailers are given the product first, then wholesalers, and then distributors. For untested new products, the allocation is the other way around. These are products that you can't seem to get a distribution channel for because potential partners don't want to take a risk on a really new product. For products that others don't want to take a chance on, you can sell them to wholesalers first. They will stock it, and they know that they can sell them to anyone (retailers, other wholesalers, distributors, or consumers).

How do you deal with the Maturity Stage of a product or product line requiring a supply chain?

Generally, our statistical forecasts will catch this kind of situation and adjust the demand level expectations, either higher or lower. It's best to let the forecasting models bring down the demand expectations. An interesting lesson here is to take the human element out of the forecasts. People have memories and get emotionally attached to certain products. As a result, they can input a natural bias to keep producing a product that is actually leveling off or declining in demand. When the statistics suggest a product's demand in softening, we have found it best to follow the data. Use the statistical forecasts in these situations without additional human adjustments being included. We try not to intervene with the demand forecasts for "golden zone" types of products that are steady sellers but are somewhat mature and have hit their apex of growth. The demand for these products follows a pattern, so the data speaks.

When your products become mature, do you seek to reduce the costs of their supply chains?

The need to take out costs for a product to make it completive is always present. The issue is how costs are taken out and the impact on the supply chain. Examples of cost reductions include changing from make or manufacturing to an outsource or contract manufacturer model. Firms also work on a raw materials supplier to lower their input costs. Other efforts to reduce costs include investing in automation, improving productivity in production, and reducing costs by reengineering a product and altering the composition of a product (for example, going from virgin plastic to recycled plastic). Cost reduction is a daily focus. However, you need to be aware of the product life cycle. The effort to reduce costs on a product line whose demand is declining might not produce a good return.

How do you deal with the Decline Stage of a product or product line requiring a supply chain?

Every year, we try to identify the products that are obsolete. At some point, you have to kill the product line. We try to be more proactive and place an end-of-life date on these products and communicate that to our supply chain. Sometimes this drives demand to depletion. Setting a fixed date can motivate a sellout, and that is a positive situation for the company.

We also measure GMROI (that is, *gross margin return on investment*). This is a standard industry measure for inventory productivity. As the inventory turns start to slow, we need a higher level of gross margin to make the product successful; otherwise, we seek to lower the inventory. When the GMROI is consistently below our threshold, it is an indication the product is nearing end-of-life stage. At that point, we sunset the product and put the notice out through our supply chain.

Sometimes, the supply chain is not successful at eliminating our inventory and we are stuck with some exit costs. When this happens, we have to make a choice of writing off the value or sending the product to a liquidation sale. To offset these costs, we establish an obsolescence financial reserve for each product during its life cycle. The method and cost of the reserve will vary based on a company's position in the supply chain.

A manufacturer will have a lower cost and is more willing to liquidate obsolete products than a distributor is. A manufacturer also has an advantage of not converting raw goods to finished product. Keeping material in the highest echelon or in raw material form is the most economical move for a supply chain. For example, a supply chain has more flexibility to recover cost when they have a piece of steel, because a piece of steel can be converted into a different product from the discontinued product that it was originally to be use in. By keeping materials in raw state, the manufacturer has greater options to reuse it in other products.

Do you have any concerns about the quality of your products coming out of different locations around the world?

In today's world market, it is a fallacy to question the quality of products, regardless of their country of origin. Today, product-quality expectations are fully vetted and completely qualified before the product is even shipped. There is much information and work put into qualifying suppliers, validating samples, and reviewing production processes. Most suppliers understand quality is fundamental to business. Some of the most sophisticated factories I have seen are in India and China.

A lot of technology has changed in the past ten years or so. What do you envision is the major impact of these technologies, and where will you be heading?

We are continually investing in supply chain system technology. This includes general communications technology. We have a fleet of more than 10,000 vehicles that deliver product every day. In the past, knowing the drivers and having them work for us was important. Now with common driver management systems we know where those trucks are every minute of the day. We know exactly when orders are delivered because of bar code scans and proof-of-delivery technology. Owning or even controlling the truck is not important because all we really need to know is whether the order was delivered on time and complete. This lets us know who has the best cost, whether it is our truck or someone else's. We have seen more investments in systems to manage inventory, processes, and supply chain transparency and visibility. This allows us to expand our breath of products and services. We are growing our SKU assortment and product mix and entering new product categories because systems can do a lot more work.

Do you have any additional comments you might like to share about your experiences in supply chain management?

The visibility of supply chains today is tremendous. We manage two supply chains: One is the physical product, and the other is information. The information can be more important than the product in some situations. If a retailer's information system does not recognize a product that is shipped to them, the product will often be returned. But if the product is recognized by the computer, even if it was not ordered, the retailer will often accept it and even pay for it.

The ever-present challenge that supply chain professionals face is this: What's next? Who or what will be introduced soon that will impact their supply chains? New technologies are being introduced almost weekly and can cause drastic changes in the flow of inventory and therefore supply chains. Supply chain managers must be aware of these coming changes and be prepared to embrace them.

15

Interview with Mr. Mark Holifield of The Home Depot

Introduction

This chapter consists of a series of questions and answers from an interview with a leading supply chain executive. The objective of this chapter is to provide a practitioner's perspective on the subject of life cycle issues in supply chain management. Other related subjects are also discussed in the interview.

About the Interviewee

Mr. Mark Holifield is the Senior Vice President of Supply Chain for The Home Depot. His responsibilities include the company's logistics, distribution, delivery, transportation, and inventory planning and replenishment operations. He has more than 30 years of experience in supply chain management, including serving as the Executive Vice President of Supply Chain Management for Office Depot, Director of Consulting Projects at Dallas Systems Corporation, and other supply chain positions at Frito-Lay North America Inc. and H.E. Butt Grocery Company. He earned his Bachelor's degree in Business Administration with honors from the University of Texas and his Master's degree in Business Administration from Baylor University.

"Our supply chain must deliver on all of our company's strategic imperatives. Our key supply chain deliverables are being in stock with the right products for our customers, driving inventory productivity, attaining low total logistics costs, and giving great service to our stores and customers."

—*Mark Holifield, 2012*

About The Home Depot

The Home Depot was founded in 1978, based on a vision of one-stop shopping for the home improvements do-it-yourselfer.

The Home Depot's strategy is based on answers to three key questions:

- What are we passionate about? We are passionate about providing outstanding service to our customers.
- What can we be best in the world at? We want to be the product authority in home improvement, bringing innovative products and great value to our customers.
- What drives our economic engine? We will be disciplined in our allocation of capital, always driving productivity and efficiency.

The Home Depot is able to offer the best customer service in the industry because its associates provide know-how to customers for their home improvement projects. This requires store associates to undergo rigorous product knowledge training. This training allows the firm to offer clinics for customers to learn how to do home improvements themselves. As a result of this approach, The Home Depot has become the fastest-growing retailer in U.S. history and is the world's largest home improvement retailer. The fourth quarter sales in 2011 were reported as $16 billion. The Home Depot has more than 2,200 retail stores in the United States, Puerto Rico, the territories of the U.S. Virgin Islands and Guam, Canada, Mexico, and China. They also operate procurement offices in the U.S., Canada, China, Mexico, and India. While principally a retailer, The Home Depot has committed to be the product authority in home improvement by bringing innovative products at great value to their customers. This often requires sourcing products globally and engaging in direct relationships with manufacturers to provide innovative products of high quality and great value.

Interview Questions and Answers

How do you manage your supply chain for products that are in the Introduction Stage of their product life cycle?

Bringing innovation and value to our customers requires us to work with our suppliers to develop new products and bring them to market. As a retailer, our suppliers provide the bulk of the product development. Our job as a retailer is to find the best products and bring them to market. New products are brought to us by vendors we have worked with for a long time or by new vendors we are just getting to know. Our merchant team is constantly looking for new ideas, and we source products from around the world. We operate sourcing offices in Asia, Latin America, and Europe, and the people that work in these offices work directly with manufacturers to develop products that will meet our customers' needs and desires.

From a supply chain perspective, we collaborate with our merchants and vendors to determine how best to flow product to our stores. This involves consideration of the handling characteristics of the product, and we evaluate the effectiveness of various paths through our supply chain network. Key determinants of the flow path are the expected sales velocity, the value of the product, and the handling characteristics. For example, lumber, large appliances, and power tools all flow through different parts of our supply chain network that are best suited for them.

We have a channel management team within our supply chain, and this team seeks to assign products and vendors to the optimal flow path through our supply chain from the manufacturer to our stores. Each time a new supplier and product are onboarded, this team works with the supplier to evaluate the various factors and choose an optimal flow path that will maximize our ability to be in-stock while having high inventory productivity and the lowest logistics cost.

How do you deal with the risk of newly introduced products?

We don't usually test a totally new product in 2,000 stores. We typically select a limited market to test and see how well products will meet our customers' needs and how well they will sell. We do attempt to forecast demand for new products with no sales history at The Home Depot, but obviously this is challenging. That is in part why we utilize test markets. We also look at similar products and use that demand behavior to forecast demand on a new product.

How do you manage your supply chain for products that are in the Growth Stage of their product life cycle?

We work to move the product as quickly as possible through our supply chain to meet the sales growth. We work closely with our suppliers to let them know what we are seeing in terms of demand growth. As we have built our distribution and logistics network, a key objective has been to build in flexibility, agility, and speed so that we can deal with challenges like scarcity in the most efficient manner. In that vein, we built our supply chain largely as a flow through model. Our recent efforts to rebuild our supply chain have largely focused on creating substantial capacity for fast flow and postponement, as these capabilities provide the needed flexibility, agility, and speed to handle our demand growth.

What if a product has a long lead time and growth strips the shelves empty?

We relentlessly focus on reducing cycle time in our supply chain so that we can quickly respond to changes in the business. We work with vendors to ensure they can handle the demand to our many stores. We work with them to reduce what we call VTT, or vendor turn time. This is the time it takes for a supplier to ship an order from the time we send them the order to the time it leaves their dock. We constantly evaluate transportation methods to optimize inventory needs and cost. If needed, we expedite transportation, but of course that adds cost. In any event, it can be a scramble to catch up with demand. We believe that we can never go wrong by having a supply chain that runs faster than others, and that's why we utilize more flow through than other hard-line retailers. Our point of view is that maximizing the use of flow-through logistics, rather than traditional warehouse storage, will drive a competitive advantage. This is a more challenging approach, requiring us to shorten our inventory decision time frames and speed up our logistics flow, but we think the extra effort is worth it. For example, utilizing flow-through distribution allows us to receive the product and send it right out to the stores immediately. To implement the flow model, we have *flow-through centers* that receive the goods from our suppliers and immediately send it on to our stores. About two thirds of our store SKUs are handled in the flow-through centers. We take the goods off of an inbound truck at a flow-through center, and they essentially move directly to an outbound truck destined for a store usually in just a few hours. These flow-through centers do not warehouse goods at all; the product simply passes through.

To augment the flow-through centers, we have stocking distribution centers that do engage in traditional distribution center practices of stock and pick. We use these facilities for product where it is most optimal to hold safety stock upstream. Our typical stocking distribution center holds in stock about 4,000 of our 35,000 store SKUs. Additionally, we operate lumber and bulk distribution centers that have a few hundred SKUs that are best distributed to stores on flatbed trucks.

What are the goods you are stocking? High volume goods or low volume goods?

Typically, these are goods that are high value, have low or unpredictable demand, or unreliable or long supply lines. A good example of these SKUs is seasonal SKUs that we might import. Specific examples might be lawn tractors or mowers, which are highly seasonal, and products with a very long supply chain like imported decorative Christmas lights.

How do you manage your supply chain for products that are in the Maturity Stage of their product life cycle?

Most of the products we sell fit this description and are handled through the rapid deployment flow-through centers. For these products, we would typically be on a weekly or more frequent order and delivery basis with our vendors. If a product is transitioning out of our assortment, we have to carefully manage the exit, utilizing effective clearance practices to move these goods out. A key challenge if there is a replacement product is to ensure that the new product is available when the older product is gone.

At the Maturity Stage of the life cycle, there is always the danger that a product can become a commodity, sold by any of your competitors. How do you keep your customers thinking of and coming back to The Home Depot for those mature products?

We constantly seek innovation from our suppliers. We carry the top brands, and we expect those brands to bring customers to us through their innovation and product relevancy. If the branded products are not doing that, or we think we need to create a distinct new product advantage, we do utilize private brands to drive innovation and competitive advantage. We have several brands that are sold only at The Home Depot for just this reason.

How do you manage your supply chain for products that are in the Decline Stage of their product life cycle?

Our quest for product authority in home improvement requires us to continually change our assortment to be relevant to our customers. When we see sales declining, we have to make tough decisions to rationalize our assortments to maximize the return on our investments in inventory and store square footage. That is not to say that we don't carry some slow moving goods. We are the kind of retailer that customers come to complete projects, not as much for one item at a time. So, customers come wanting a variety of items, and we keep that in mind when we look at a group of products that customers have come to associate with our business. We accept and are willing to allow slow moving inventory to maintain a customer base that needs a set or collection of products to complete a home improvement project. So, we try to balance our desire to satisfy our customers, and at the same time we expect all of our products to return a profit for our shareholders.

How do you deal with a discontinuation of a product?

Typically, we go to a markdown clearance process until it is gone. There is an art and a science to managing markdowns in retail, because you want not only to maximize return but also to move the goods out.

If end-of-life product won't sell at all, we end up destroying it, or we sometimes have to return it to vendor options, but with low-value products we usually don't want to handle the product too much. We also donate product to charities if they are products that can be used to meet a specific need.

Because our business is highly seasonal, we do have some unique challenges here. For example, think about Christmas decorations. After that holiday period is over, it takes a lot of space and labor to store the leftovers. Hence, we work hard to move these products quickly at the end of the season and give our customers a good deal on them.

How do you measure the performance of a product in your stores to know when to discontinue or manage products in general?

We use a variety of metrics, including sales per square foot and use those metrics to understand what is happening with our business and how to allocate space in our stores. Our merchandising staff handles most of this decision making.

What other unique features about understanding supply chain management at The Home Depot might you add to your interview comments?

Some key issues are important to understand The Home Depot supply chain, one of which is the seasonal nature of our business. If you are a retailer of toys, you know when Christmas comes and can plan for it. If you are in the home gardening business, you don't know when the first day of spring is going to come, because of the weather, but you have to be ready for it when it comes. Although the calendar marks the first day of spring, it comes at different times in different geographic locations. Predicting the weather is difficult. Predicting the impact on our inventory management is even more difficult!

In addition to seasonal variation, macroeconomic variations have to be factored into our forecasts and planning. The economy of the past several years, with the downturn in housing investment and housing turnover, has had a big impact on our business.

How do you deal with reverse logistics for return items?

When products are damaged or problems with products exist, they need to be returned to vendors. We have created *return logistic centers* where we collect the products from the stores and return the products to their disposition source.

How do you deal with packaging goods that are delivered to the stores?

We have a group that focuses on packaging for our private brand goods that we develop and merchandise. We also work with our vendors to partner with us to ensure packaging meets all our requirements. We are always working to improve our packaging and to meet the many demands on packaging for product protection, customer information, and sustainability.

16

Interview with Mr. Yadi Kamelian of Lincoln Industries

Introduction

This chapter consists of a series of questions and answers from an interview with a leading supply chain executive. The objective of this chapter is to provide a practitioner's perspective on the subject of life cycle issues in supply chain management. Other related subjects are also discussed in the interview.

About the Interviewee

Mr. Yadi Kamelian is the Vice President of Materials and Customer Service for Lincoln Industries. In his 23 years with Lincoln Industries, Kamelian has been instrumental in the development of the company's first quality department; the management of the company's technical services department, including the environmental and waste management programs; and the development of a business model that allowed the company to move from a traditional finishing role to the supplier of complex parts that required complex finishing. In his current role, Kamelian is responsible for the company's supply management, including the qualification and selection of suppliers on a global level, supplier performance, production planning and inventory control, and the development and integration of new products into the organization. Kamelian holds a Bachelor's degree in

Industrial Engineering, a Master's degree in mathematics and statistics and a Master's degree in Manufacturing Engineering—all from the University of Nebraska.

> "We select suppliers for the long term. We call this a *partners-for-life* relationship. Selecting suppliers for the long term involves a process that ensures that we and the supplier have shared values. This means our values for fairness, honesty, growth, profitability, people, and a passion for serving customers must be matched by our suppliers. This win-win situation has created an environment that is very collaborative. At the outset of a project, we know that no one knows everything. Yet with strong supplier relationships, we have found that great things are possible by coming together and combining our resources. This has allowed us to differentiate ourselves in the marketplace and strengthened our relationship with customers, ultimately creating *customers for life* for Lincoln Industries."

—*Yadi Kamelian, 2011*

About Lincoln Industries

Celebrating its sixtieth year in business, Lincoln Industries, located in Lincoln, Nebraska, is a national leader as supplier of products requiring high-performance metal finishing. We are the largest finishing company in North America. Lincoln Industries sells its products to original equipment manufacturers, distributors, and other customers throughout the nation, including the power sports, heavy duty truck, automotive, gaming, and agricultural industries. Selected five times as one of the best companies to work for in America, Lincoln Industries has also been nationally recognized for its workplace wellness program.

Interview Questions and Answers

How would you characterize your organizational role in supply chain management?

We manage the entire supply chain. Part of the area of my responsibility is leading and managing what we call our supply management organization; others call it purchasing and or materials management. Our strategy involves the development of a supply base at global level that will provide a competitive advantage to Lincoln Industries and support our growth and profitability strategies. I also am responsible for the architecture of a supply chain for each product. The objective is to provide best cost while meeting the critical criteria for quality, delivery, and flexibility. In our firm, this entails three primary functions:

- **Global sourcing:** Identifying and qualifying potential suppliers, writing supplier agreements, sourcing jobs to suppliers, and monitoring supplier viability and capacity.
- **Supplier performance:** Performance is based on quality, delivery, and costs. We develop and suggest new engineered ways of improving supplier performance and reducing costs.
- **Production planning and customer service:** We take the demand from customers and convert to a schedule for the supply base, prepare a production schedule, and determine what needs to be processed to fulfill customer needs.

Another responsibility I have is the development and integration of new products into our organization. Our integration team is a group of engineers who have responsibility for developing processes and documentation necessary to move a project from concept to production.

How do you deal with the Introduction Stage of a product or product line requiring a supply chain?

The Introduction Stage begins when we work with our customer on a potential new project. At Lincoln Industries, we begin by identifying the best supply chain for the project. We also work with our customers' engineers to ensure that the product has been designed with consideration for optimal manufacturability, including finishing. Internally, the integration team develops the finishing process. This, at times, might require a significant capital investment. We will not undertake this investment unless we have a commitment from the customer.

Are the contracts open ended or do they set very definable limits?

The contracts are open ended. Before we begin the work on the project, we determine the volume and longevity. We will not make a capital investment unless there is payback for the capital investment.

How do you determine which new product projects you will consider? What strategy do you use to select product projects?

We have a unique strategy that differentiates us from other competitors. First, we look for products that are complex in nature from a manufacturing and finishing standpoint. Second, we look for projects that will require a significant capital investment upfront. Third, our strategy is to work on projects that are high volume and where finishing is a significant portion of the overall part cost and performance.

How do you deal with the Growth Stage of a product or product line requiring a supply chain?

Capacity and consumption is monitored on a regular basis. When capacity reaches 85%, investments are made to increase capacity where needed. We also monitor our suppliers' capacity on a regular basis to ensure our supply needs are not in jeopardy. It is important to note that we communicate strongly with our suppliers regarding future needs. This ensures our suppliers are well prepared in advance of an increase in volume. Contingency plans are also developed for situations when a supplier may not be able to meet our growth requirements. I have had several instances where I have had to call the owner or a president of a company and ask them to put on an extra shift over the weekend to meet our growth in demand needs. And almost without exception, our suppliers have stepped forward to solve the problem. This demonstrates the value of our strategic initiatives that emphasizes strong relationships with our supply base.

What happens if your outside supplier reaches their capacity limitation?

Having several qualified and approved suppliers to choose from for each of the products we produce allows us to redistribute and shift work among them as needed to meet growth demands.

What forward planning efforts do you use to anticipate growth in demand and then deal with?

There is no way to better predict future growth than through constant communication with the customer. Understanding our customers' business and working with them to receive extended forecasts, sometimes as long as 52 weeks, allows us to best predict the future growth of our business. Based on this information, the necessary plans are put into place to ensure performance.

How do you communicate this type of information to your suppliers?

We provide our suppliers extended purchase orders. In addition, if needed, we hold daily and weekly calls with suppliers to keep them informed with current and future demand needs.

How is your supply chain advisory council established?

Our Supplier Advisory Council was formed after we identified a need to better communicate and solicit feedback from the strategic supply base on new initiatives within our company, especially those issues that impact the supply base. This council is composed of high-level individuals from our strategic supply base. Membership is based on two criteria: first, the dollar value of the products they provide; and second, the strategic nature of product the supplier provides.

How do you manage the Supplier Advisory Council?

The advisory council meets twice a year. Meetings are held at our facility, or in certain cases a supplier may host a meeting. These meetings are preceded with a dinner the night before where suppliers have an opportunity to network with one another and representatives of our company. The following day, a business meeting is held. Agenda items are published in advance, and most topics are strategic in nature. We also include members from within our company, including our CEO, president, vice president of materials, director of supplier performance and global sourcing and director of production planning and customer service, and various members of the teams led by these people. Their role is to provide our strategic suppliers with an update on our business (present and future) long-term strategic plans and new initiatives, especially those that impact our strategic suppliers. In addition, we, including our suppliers, share best practices on a variety of topics. We also get an update from every supplier on their status of their business and their views on what they see in the future for their respective industries.

How do you deal with the Maturity Stage of a product or product line requiring a supply chain?

As the products mature, we seek to maximize our efficiency. This is accomplished by continually working with the entire supply chain to eliminate waste and scrap and minimize inventory. For example, we have a product we have been providing one of our customers for the past 20 years. Our plating price today is less than when the project began. This has been accomplished while most of the costs associated with plating a part have increased. Throughout the life of the product, we have worked with our suppliers to identify innovative ways to reduce all costs associated with producing a part, including a significant investment in automation. This is an example of how we have been able to fine-tune the process to make a project more efficient for the entire supply chain without compromising on the performance of a part and any increase in price to our customer.

As you continually improve, how do you deal with production problems that may be costly or problem solving in general?

In cases like this, we form a cross-functional team. Members of this team are selected based on their background and expertise. They are fully trained to use quality tools that include fishbone diagrams and problem-solving techniques. This team meets on a regular basis and continues to work until the problem is solved. There are times when we will ask suppliers to participate in this process. We believe that problem solving is a core competency of our organization.

Do you put a manager on the problem or do you use a team approach?

If the problem gets to the point where the person experiencing the problem is not capable of solving it alone, a team is formed to solve the problem. The important thing when solving a problem is to make sure that the changes are communicated correctly and the people responsible for implementing the changes understand that a change has taken place. This follow-through is critical for the successfully solving the problem and maintaining the solution.

How do you deal with the Decline Stage of a product or product line requiring a supply chain?

We usually have at least three months notice from the customer when a product is being phased out. When this occurs, we notify the entire supply chain and plans are put into place to ensure that we do not produce more parts than what is needed.

Do you have any additional comments you might like to share about your experiences in supply chain management?

- You need suppliers who are partners and have the same values as you do and can meet your needs.

- What works for others may not work for you. You cannot just go out and copy another firm's business model. You have to be able to develop unique approaches to your unique problems.

- We do our best to be our suppliers' best customer and our customers' best supplier.

- To grow you must perform. To perform, you must have a reliable supply base. Do not select a supplier based only on their price.

17 ────────────────────────────

Interview with Mr. Eddie Capel of Manhattan Associates

Introduction

This chapter consists of a series of questions and answers from an interview with a leading supply chain executive. The objective of this chapter is to provide a practitioner's perspective on the subject of life cycle issues in supply chain management. Other related subjects are also discussed in the interview.

About the Interviewee

Mr. Eddie Capel is the Manhattan Associates Executive Vice President and Chief Operating Officer. He previously served as Executive Vice President of their global operations. Mr. Capel is responsible for worldwide strategic direction and quality execution across solution strategy, research and development, product management, professional services, and customer support. He also leads Manhattan's EMEA and APAC regional operations. Mr. Capel brings more than 20 years of experience to overseeing supply chain organization strategy and operations. Prior to joining Manhattan Associates in 2000, he held various positions at Real Time Solutions (RTS), including Chief Operations Officer and Vice President of Operations, where he led teams that supported the supply chain strategies of companies such as Wal-Mart, Amazon.com, and J.C. Penney. He also served as Director of Operations, with Unarco Automation, an industrial automation/robotics systems integrator. Prior to joining Unarco, Mr. Capel worked as a Project Manager and System Designer for ABB Robotics in the United Kingdom.

> "At Manhattan Associates, we provide sophisticated supply chain solutions to those who see providing exemplary service to their customers at a highly competitive cost a priority"

—*Eddie Capel, 2012*

About Manhattan Associates

Manhattan Associates, Inc. (www.manh.com/) is a best-in-class global solutions provider for supply chain leader-organizations intent on leveraging their supply chains. Their software solutions enable Fortune 500 and other organizations to create customer experiences consistent with their brand values; improve relationships with suppliers, customers, logistics providers, and other organizations in their supply chain ecosystems; leverage investments across supply chain functions; effectively manage costs; and meet dynamically changing market requirements. They are the only vendor exclusively focused on a platform-based approach to supply chain management. This enables organizations that view their supply chains strategically to execute more effectively and achieve competitive advantage. Platform thinking combines technology, principles, and practices to create Whole Chain Awareness—unified insight and execution across all organizational and market dimensions that yields more integrated, agile, and responsive supply chains.

Interview Questions and Answers

How would you characterize your organization's support role in supply chain management?

Our firm supplies software solutions for supply chain experts. So we facilitate and support the movement, distribution, forecasting, and so forth of finished products through our client's supply chains. We don't provide broad software like *material requirements planning* (MRP) or *enterprise resource planning* (ERP) manufacturing software. We are 100% focused on the supply chain and getting their goods throughout their supply chain to whoever the consumer may be.

Does your software just provide the information on which a supply chain functions?

Our software provides more than just information. We actually help execute supply chain transactions. For example, suppose we dropped into a large *distribution center* (DC) for a very large firm with, say, $50 million in inventory, a million-square-feet DC, 500,000 products, and 600 people performing a number of primary distribution functions (for example, receiving, storage or put-away, inventory control, processing orders, shipping). What our software does is that it knows what products will be received, which will fit into the facility, where they will be located; and our software takes orders from customers and manages and directs the staff to efficiently utilize their time by telling them where to pick stock. In addition, supporting the outbound logistics functions, our software coordinates the right shipping carrier going from the right source to the right destination with the right service level. It also provides the right bar code shipping labels to go through the complex FedEx shipping centers, if they ship that way. So, our software manages the entire symphony of actions to optimize the firm's supply chain operations. Now, imagine a firm like The Home Depot, which has 75 DCs. What our software will do is coordinate all these activities in the network of DCs for this firm. We management all of these transactions throughout the firm's network in the most cost-efficient way. My point here is that we are about executing, operating, and running supply chains, not just providing information.

You offer a full range of products that support, among other things, the product life cycles that your supply chain customers have to deal with. Don't some of those software products focus on the development phase or Introduction Stage of the product life cycle for your customers?

In our portfolio of software products, we provide companies with software that deals with nearly all phases of product life cycles in supply chain management. We provide companies first of all with forecasts of the demand for their goods. We look at anything from historical patterns to projected or predicted seasonal patterns to help firms know when and where their demand will be. That starts the process in supply chain. We are going to seed the forecast with the most similar products that we can find—so that new products will be picked up and be modeled with the same kind of attributes, whether they be product attributes or sales history attributes based on geo-location and any other demographics.

For the software products that you create to solve your client's needs, are their features or add-ons that you modify your software products as your clients' firms supply chain changes in size?

Yes, is the easy answer! Our products have to match the developing needs of our clients, and this goes beyond simply size issues. Whole strategies have to be modified as their environments change. For example, as diesel fuel prices change, the strategic use of logistics often has to change rapidly as well. If diesel fuel becomes cheaper than it normally is, there will be more transportation, resulting in less inventory and more frequent trips. This impacts inventory and logistics planning strategies, which in turn requires alteration of software applications. We seek to build in to our software applications some of the flexibility and agility needed to satisfy customers demands (that is, our customers and theirs) for our supply-chain-intensive firms.

Does your firm offer your customers the flexibility to adjust their needs as their products go through the Introduction, Growth, Maturity, and Decline Stages of a product life cycle?

Sure! We do not have a *product life cycle* (PLC) software application per se, as it is usually used for product design. But in terms of execution, we certainly offer our customers software applications that permit them to deal with all phases of their PLCs.

How do you help your supply chain customers manage products that are in the Growth Stage of their product life cycle?

Building a system to deal with growth is not hard to do, but here is the problem. A system can work well for 360 days a year, but on the other days, like Black Friday, Cyber Monday, Mother's day, Valentine's day, and some other one-day special yearly events, we need a system that can handle ten times the volume of business than the other 360 days of the year. But here is the challenge: Our customers don't want to pay for a system that can handle ten times the need for the other 360 days. There are number of different approaches that we can use to deal with this kind of service-level demand for those five extreme growth days of the year. Of course, it depends on the type of business. There are simple solutions like provisioning flexible hardware where additional servers and staff would be available on those five busy days to keep systems from slowing down during high demand. That is the easy part of dealing with growth spurts. A different demand situation that could be in any phase of the product life cycle is where a customer shifts the service level from, say, delivering goods in three or four days to an overnight delivery service level. This would take an entirely new execution service process because you are receiving goods, staging goods, and calling transportation carriers to achieve the new service level.

Growth in demand can also cause inventory problems, as well, since demand outstrips supply. This leads to issues of how you should prioritize customers and which customers you decide you will satisfy. Often times, the decision is made based on profit margin.

All the factors previously mentioned are relevant and important to helping our customers deal with the Growth Stages of their products. Sudden growth is something that is fairly predictable. We know the days of the year when growth will occur and we can fairly well predict the amount of demand but there are other situations, like natural disasters that cause disruptions in supply chains that are not always predictable and cause a variety of supply chain challenges (for example, inventory outages, wasted labor effort, lost sales). Without agile and flexible software, a firm will not be able to respond in a timely manner to deal with those unexpected types of situations. Our software is design to provide that type of agility and flexibility.

How do you help your supply chain customers manage products that are in the Maturity or Decline Stages of their product life cycle?

In these stages, a firm tries to minimize the inventory they have to avoid carrying costs and minimize transportation costs. Firms are looking for much more economic ways to transport goods to customers. Reducing the costs generally means longer lead times to customers. Using our software, employees can dial in the number of days they are willing to allow for delivery to a customer (for example, one day, two days, three days, or more), and the software will optimize their choice of shipping methods and carriers to reduce the costs of shipping. The longer the lead time, the more opportunities exist to reduce the transportation costs.

As your software products age because of new innovations and technologies, even your product goes through a product life cycle. How do you deal with these changes within the context of supply chain management changes?

Yes, this happens, but to deal with it we are spending millions of dollars every year in research and development. We do this to either build new products or continue to innovate products in a certain form. Twenty-five years ago it was common for DCs to be screwed onto manufacturing factories for supply chain purposes. Today, things have changed, and there are very few DCs/factory combinations, so this evolution process has changed and our software systems have changed, as well, to match these industry changes. These changes have required us to spend tens of millions of dollars to upgrade and enhance our software applications. In this regard, our software applications go through the same kind of product life cycle stages that our customers experience with their products. It is the nature of our firm to have to stay ahead of the changes in supply chain management, so our software will be more than current, but ahead of the needs of our customers. The software solutions we are building this year are designed to solve what we perceive to be the supply chain problems of next year and the year after.

Let me give you an example of one issue of how supply chains are changing and how our organization tries to help to deal with it. The workforce in the United States is graying. There are about 500,000

DC workers in the United States, and they are all getting older. We are exploring what that means to the needs of the firms that have DCs. Related and even more acute is the graying of truck drivers for supply chain truck-oriented firms. The market for drivers today has changed, and not as many younger drivers are entering that career. As a result, the cost of truck drivers is going up. This shortage is causing a whole number of other challenges in supply chain management. We don't have a magic wand to solve this problem completely, but we can help solve some of these issues. By using software that optimizes transportation, such as minimizing miles and improve driver utilization, you need fewer truck drivers, which in turn helps to reduce their costs and other human resource problems. To develop software to deal with this kind of issue, we are looking at age patterns, demographic patterns, commodity prices, and fuel prices and making some of our bets on product development investments around those real macro issues.

Are there any additional points you might like to add about supply chain management?

At every turn, supply chain management is becoming more complicated. The macro-economic downturn that started in 2009 has heightened the need for minimizing the capital investment in, among other things, inventory. Trying to drive down inventory within a supply chain makes the need for optimization much greater than it ever was before. During a downturn in the economy, orders tended to become smaller, requiring us all to be more responsive to customers' needs. Smaller orders tend to translate into an increased frequency of orders. On top of that, we are facing an ever-expanding number of new products entering the market. So, a combination of focusing on inventory, a higher level of customer support, orders becoming smaller, and millions of products being introduced into the market has made supply chain management more complicated every day. This becomes even more complicated when adding in the globalization aspects from a sourcing perspective and the consumer markets. Of course, we love complication because the more complicated the supply chain world is, the more demand for sophisticated software solutions such as ours.

18

Interview with Mr. Ron Robinson of LI-COR Biosciences

Introduction

This chapter consists of a series of questions and answers from an interview with a leading supply chain executive. The objective of this chapter is to provide a practitioner's perspective on the subject of life cycle issues in supply chain management. Other related subjects are also discussed in the interview.

About the Interviewee

Mr. Ronald D. Robinson is the Director of Supply Chain Management for LI-COR Biosciences, with 15 years of experience in this field. In addition, he supported Brunswick Corporation's aerospace and defense Division (later Lincoln Composites) as a Senior Contracts Administrator for over 12 years, with an additional 4 years in the position of production/material control specialist. He graduated from the University of Nebraska - Lincoln, with a Bachelor of Science degree in Business Administration, with additional education received through the American Graduate University - Marketing, Pricing, and Management, and Dale Carnegie Associates - Effective Speaking, and Human Relations. He is a current member of *Institute for Supply Management - Nebraska* (ISM–NE), and most recently served on their Board. He is also a member of the *Midwest*

International Trade Association (MITA) and the Lincoln Employer's Coalition. Other groups that he has previously had affiliation with include *National Contracts Management Association* (NCMA), *American Production and Inventory Control Society* (APICS), and Dream It, Do It.

> "Working with engineers, manufacturing personnel, or scientists may require an individual to go well beyond the realms of business knowledge. Many individuals today entering the supply chain arena want to quickly attain high wages but don't understand the progression of on-the-job learning needed to attain this."

—*Ron Robinson, 2011*

About LI-COR

For more than 40 years, LI-COR has been in business in Lincoln, Nebraska. LI-COR designs, manufacturers, and markets instrument systems for plant biology, environmental, and biotechnology research. LI-COR has subsidiaries in Bad Homburg, Germany, and in Cambridge, United Kingdom. LI-COR instruments are used in more than 100 countries worldwide in studies ranging from global climate change to cancer research. It is a privately held company and is ISO certified. LI-COR has received awards in the United States and Germany for their contributions to business and science. In 2010, they received the Quantum Workplace's Employee Voice Award for exceptional employee engagement.

Interview Questions and Answers

How would you characterize your organizational role in supply chain management?

Organizationally, I report to the Vice President of Business Operations Management. Our supply chain management team consists of expeditors, ISO specialists, internal auditing specialists, and other supply chain specialists. LI-COR is somewhat unique in that we do not have a formal quality-control department. As a result, our supply chain department has to perform quality-control functions and logistics functions and serves as the focal point for transportation for the organization. We work with all the transportation carriers and negotiate transportation rates. We also get involved with the disposition of products. Instead of having a quality-control manager and quality-control engineer, we work as a team. We work with manufacturing, production, engineering, and our supply chain partners to make decisions about products that might be discrepant or have a quality problem. We wear a lot of hats and make a lot of decisions, but it puts us closer to the product. Our organization is fairly flat. We don't have a lot of layers. We also don't have a lot of distinct departments that other organizations have. That permits everyone in the supply chain team to know what is happening, and the people who need to know have visibility to the information they need. It helps us to make quick decisions. To augment our decision making, we use SharePoint technology for communication purposes. (Microsoft SharePoint is software that aids people working together. It permits people to set up Web sites to share information with others, manage documents from start to finish, and publish reports to help make better decisions.)

With the team approach and the changes in the way the purchasing industry and organizations like the *Institute of Supply Management* (ISM) have gone, we reorganized job titles to permit a more updated representation of what we are now doing in terms of supply chain staff positions and their titles. We have gone away from designating junior or senior titles, like a junior buyer title. Yet people wanted to be recognized in their career advancement. To deal with this situation, we redesigned the staff position titles. We used to have a senior buyer level, but once you hit that, there was no place to go, except for a management position. Not everyone wants to be a manager, and not everyone is management material. We went to a more open-ended title designation where we can change their title with a number system (that is, supply chain specialist levels 1, 2, 3, and so on) that could go on forever.

So, you are achieving both an integration and collaboration of functional departments?

Absolutely! That is what is happening today in supply chain management. Classic department functionality is being replaced. Blending the functions together has a positive impact on our supply chain partners. We are able to combine input from our internal functional areas and work out problems that might have taken countless meetings with the supplier. By our blending of functions into one group (that is, supply chain group), they can see we are going to bat for them in other areas within our organization. We are giving them an opportunity to have the benefit of all the internal discussions (concerning these other areas) before we come back to them with questions about a part or a problem. This saves everyone time and effort, and they appreciate it. As a result, this organizational approach has lead to having great relationships with our suppliers.

A part of the training for our supply chain specialists is to understand the entire supply chain role in our organization. While most of our supply chain people become specialists in several types of products (for example, electrical, mechanical, optics, computers, commodities, expediting, auditing), they have to understand the entire supply chain process more than just buying products. Getting the product here, transportation of the product, how the product flows through the manufacturing floor, and what the impact the product has in the supply chain and organization are all important components of what we do. They also are expected to understand the supplier side. One of the many expanding roles of supply chain management that is changing is that engineering expects the supply chain to provide them with the knowledge of who can make the parts needed for new products. Consequently, we must be able to identify which suppliers can best make the part. This results in much more interaction with engineering in the design of products today.

Given the expanded role of the supply chain, does your staff ever go out to inspect suppliers as a means of qualifying them to provide parts or work?

Oh, yes! We do a number of onsite visits. Supplier evaluation is a significant part of our supplier qualification process. Typically, we do a supplier evaluation and qualification process for all of our suppliers. We also must deal with a number of government guidelines, ISO requirements, and the *Restriction of Hazardous Substances* (RoHS) directive.

RoHS is a restriction on the use of certain hazardous substances that came into force across European Union member states on July 1, 2006. From that date, producers of eight categories of electrical and electronic equipment were not able to place on the market products that contain six banned substances (for example, including lead, mercury, hexavalent chromium, cadmium) unless specific exemptions apply.

A lot of our customers are international. We have to work closely with engineering to bring our knowledge of governmental guidelines and restrictions to bear on our product development efforts. We have to learn and train our staff on these regulations, particularly since businesses in the European Union, China, and South Korea are requiring more consideration of these kinds of governmental directives and regulations.

Do the government regulations impact your operations very much?

Yes. They add substantially to the cost of our products. For example, when RoHS was implemented, it required us to completely redesign all of our products that we intended to keep selling. RoHS requires a unique temperature when soldering electronic components to our equipment and PC boards. Changing the temperature meant reviewing every component in the bill of material and assessing the impact to the current design. In some cases, complete redesign was required. In addition, our manufacturing process also needed to be altered to allow both RoHS and non-RoHS products, because we had customers for both types of products. An added complication in dealing with this regulation was that some of the suppliers stopped making non-RoHS-certified parts because of dwindling demand. So, new suppliers had to be researched and found, with many of the new suppliers now charging exorbitant prices for parts based on limited supplies. All of this has added millions of dollars to our product costs.

How do you feel the role of supply chain management adds value to your organization?

Let me give you one small example. We had an engineer call me and say they needed a particular type of foam-rubber tubing and it had to be RoHS compliant. The engineer called a firm thinking they were the production source for the tubing, but they were really just a

distributor, not the manufacturer. He was unable to get needed information for ordering the material and handed the assignment to me.
I called the engineer back in 30 minutes after I talked with the same
distributor so that they could provide the information to place the
order. Why could I get the information but the engineer couldn't? It's
the approach you go in with, how you explain to the people why you
need it and why it has to be a certain way. If you treat a distributor
like you just want to cut them out of the picture so as to cut costs, they
won't divulge their manufacturing sources. Sometimes you have to
be able to reach down to the second-, third-, or fourth-tier suppliers
on issues, and that is possible only if you have cooperation from first-
tier suppliers. Sharing information and working with our suppliers as
partners is our approach.

How do you deal with the Introduction Stage of a product or product line requiring a supply chain?

It depends on the product. We are experiencing this type of situation presently with a new product. We had been planning to introduce a new product for about a year. Normally we plan to allocate
one unit of a new product to each of our distributors for their use as a
demonstrator. This product was designed to replace an older product,
so we factored in the potential demand on the new product based
partly on older product sales. The older product was a "bread and but-
ter" product, which represented a considerable important sales base;
so, to avoid a loss of customers, we had to keep producing the older
product while we were launching the new product. What we did was
to overlap the manufacturing of both the older and newer products.
Given our policy of sharing information with our supply chain partners, we had notified them we would be discontinuing the older product. That cut off the pipeline of supplies needed for the older product
more rapidly than expected, causing a need to find additional parts.
In addition, it resulted in more sales on the new product as customers
quickly shifted over from the older one. When we had a monthly sales
analysis meeting, we found this unexpected spike in demand for this
new product. These things happen all the time at the Introduction
Stage of a new product.

In another situation for a really new product that was expected
to have high volume due to the cost being considerably less than our
competition, we ran into some marketing problems. The distributor's

sales force sells the items based their commission on sales price. They thought that they could make more money selling a more-expensive unit that performs essentially the same task versus selling a less-expensive unit. The sales force also felt the value of the new product was greater than the price being suggested and that it should be raised. We listened to them and pushed up the price. Now here is where the supply chain is impacted in this alteration of pricing. This product was designed to be sold at a higher volume, but the higher price pushed this product's sales down. We had previously gone out to the supply chain partners and obtained pricing quotes from them for 1,000 to 2,500 of units of parts. Now the lower volume resulted in a demand of only 25, 50, or 100 units of parts. The suppliers who had previously given lower unit costs because of the higher volume of units now increased those bill of material costs by over 50%, resulting in profit margins and overhead structures changing. These are things that can happen when you are developing products for distribution within supply chains.

In situations where the expected market demand might exceed our projections, we establish buffer stocks. In situations where the marketing forecasts might be a little too optimistic, we work together with everyone to tamp down such forecasts. It is a part of our role to look at demand history and share our judgment on the viability of future demand requirements for supply chain needs. Unfortunately, we are not always accurate ourselves. When that occurs, we use contingency planning. For new products, we look at the lead times for parts and buffer those. Even during prototyping stages, many times we purchase the very long lead time components for development and initial production at the same time. We are finding that this helps improve our ability to introduce products more quickly to the market. Although there is some risk with this approach, the gains have certainly outweighed the losses.

In "ramp-up" situations for new products that don't make it, the damage control efforts are difficult but an expected part of our job. We had a product that didn't make it a couple of years ago. Everyone was ramped up, we had a lot of inventory, and it didn't make it in the market. What could be done? It's painful, but we just did what we could to unload the inventory. Also, we pushed back the delivery dates for incoming inventory. This way the inventory does not tie up a lot of capital or space in our facilities. We eventually consumed the remaining inventory.

How do you deal with the Growth Stage of a product or product line requiring a supply chain?

We buffer inventory on some items, usually the long lead time items to deal with unexpected demand growth. We also use outsourcing from qualified suppliers.

A part of our strategy is that we are right sized for our distribution channels with a level production approach to manufacturing. We don't jump around a lot with demand or demand expectations. Our distributors know what to expect from us, and they value the consistency of our level production and distribution expectations. We produce to stock, not to order! This allows us to be very stable in our production efforts and in the supply chain that supports them. We seek to have a 30-to-60-day supply of all parts on hand. We are very careful in the selection of our distributors, and so we know their capacity. We might start out being a supplier's largest customer, but over time we might become or end up a smaller customer. This happens! But, because our need for their capacity is so steady and consistent, they can count on us, and we find we can count on them regardless of the volume of the business.

How do you deal with the Maturity Stage of a product or product line requiring a supply chain?

We have a lot of products in this stage. The ordering process for materials when dealing with these types of products is very different from others. We sometimes have to buy an entire year's supply of parts for these products just to make minimum cost objectives. Sometimes we even have to buy excessive amounts to hit the minimums for price discounts. We inventory these items longer because of reduced demand, and this adds cost. Also, we see an increase in materials cost because we (and others) are buying small quantities, resulting in increased cost per unit.

An interesting aspect to this product stage concerns competition. Some of our products in this stage become the only source for customers. That is, competitors start leaving a mature market to avoid the inevitable Decline Stage in product demand. Less competition helps maintain prices even if the costs go up.

How do you deal with the Decline Stage of a product or product line requiring a supply chain?

One of our strategies here is to do a *lifetime buy*. A lifetime buy is where we go out and determine how many more years we want to sell a particular product. We then purchase inventory equaling the total number parts needed to meet that lifetime demand. Once it is used up, that is the end of that product and its life cycle. It is common for some of our suppliers to contact us when they are going to discontinue a part we need and allow us one last purchase.

Many of the products that are in a Decline Stage are considered obsolete and discontinued. In some cases, they are completely retooled into a new or newer product. The interesting cost behavior of suppliers is completely opposite of the way you might think it should be in this situation. Most people think a discontinued item should be cheaper because suppliers want to rid themselves of inventory that will not be saleable in the future. So while we might expect the price to go down, the current trend is for them to be more expensive. For example, we have one environmental product that is not RoHS compliant, and we plan on phasing it out in June 2013. Unfortunately, one of our suppliers is phasing out their electronic part very soon. So, we looked around to find a replacement part. We think we have it, but the price to us is going from $400 per unit to over $600. What is happening is that some suppliers are buying up discontinued parts and becoming sole suppliers of these parts, increasing the price to their customers. Some very shrewd suppliers actually buy these items from production overruns for pennies on the dollar. Then they store it for future sales at very high prices. They only need to sell a few of these items to make a profit. For this reason, cost cutting in some areas is essential to keep our product prices as low as possible during a demand decline or phasing out of products.

Compliance with government regulations can also lead to the discontinuance of a product and its supply chain. One of the trends today is for supplier firms to really look at the bottom line on investments they make. For example, we have been doing business with a plating company for many years. When the RoHS directive became mandatory, we needed to have our suppliers become RoHS compliant. The plating company undertook a cost analysis and found it too expensive to change their operations to become RoHS compliant. So, that meant we not only stopped doing most of our business with them but also that we had to redo the supply chain by finding new suppliers at a greater distance, which increased the amount of transportation and costs. Also it meant increased production lead times from days to weeks because of the distance the parts had to travel.

Do you have any additional comments you might like to share about your experiences in supply chain management?

The field of supply chain management has been changing in the past few years to become much more contractual. Many more agreements are being written than in the past covering things like intellectual property rights and nondisclosure agreements. In the past, buyers were not expected to know a lot about these things, but today they are.

One of the major topics that is critical to supply chain management today is business-interruption planning. For most supply chain managers, it is second nature to use contingency planning in all areas of our supply chains to deal with interruptions. We can use safety stock as a buffer to address long lead times or risky suppliers. If we were to lose a major supplier, we plan to know where we will turn next. We actually have a business-interruption contingency program to deal with catastrophes like a natural disaster or pandemic flu. We know exactly what we will do if such disasters befall us. For example, we have plans for employees to work at home or at a distance. We also have backups in software to co-generate support as a contingency to system failure. Some of our planning is very detailed. We actually have plans if we lose power to our laptop computers, to have backup batteries so that we don't miss a beat. We have crisis situations hitting our supply chains all the time. Part of our planning effort is to create zones in the United States with manufacturing capacity capabilities identified. What we did was to identify producers with redundant production capacity in these zones that we can geographically turn to if we need additional capacity due to an interruption of our business.

We have been in business for 40 years. Some of our supply chain relationships with suppliers have been that long. These kinds of relationships represent one of our strengths.

19

Interview with Mr. James Chris Gaffney of The Coca-Cola Company

Introduction

This chapter consists of a series of questions and answers from an interview with a leading supply chain executive. The objective of this chapter is to provide a practitioner's perspective on the subject of life cycle issues in supply chain management. Other related subjects are also discussed in the interview.

About the Interviewee

Mr. James Chris Gaffney has been with the Coca-Cola system for 17 years. He began his career at Coca-Cola in the fountain business before taking leadership roles with the Coca-Cola North America Supply Chain team and Logistics and Planning team. Mr. Gaffney was promoted to the President of Coca-Cola Supply in December 2008. In 2010, he was selected as the strategy lead for the Coca-Cola Refreshments Product System Supply Business Integration. At the conclusion of the integration, he was appointed as the Senior Vice President Product Supply System-Strategy for Coca-Cola Refreshments. Before joining the Coca-Cola Company, he worked for with AJC International, a global food trader, as Global Operations Manager. He started his career with Frito-Lay and held various roles in distribution and logistics. He received his Bachelor's degree and Master's degree in Industrial and Systems Engineering from Georgia Tech.

> "We recognize that our success depends on the sustainability of the communities where we operate. For this reason, we are dedicated to having positive economic, social, and environmental impacts on local communities. It is also the right thing to do in a world of growing population."

—*James Chris Gaffney, 2012*

About The Coca-Cola Company

The Coca-Cola Company (NYSE: KO) is the world's largest beverage company, refreshing consumers with more than 500 sparkling and still brands. Led by Coca-Cola, the world's most valuable brand, the company's portfolio features 15 billion-dollar brands, including Diet Coke, Fanta, Sprite, Coca-Cola Zero, vitaminwater, Powerade, Minute Maid, Simply, Georgia, and Del Valle. Globally, we are the number one provider of sparkling beverages, ready-to-drink coffees, and juices and juice drinks. Through the world's largest beverage distribution system, consumers in more than 200 countries enjoy our beverages at a rate of 1.8 billion servings a day. With an enduring commitment to building sustainable communities, our company is focused on initiatives that reduce our environmental footprint, support active and healthful living, create a safe and inclusive work environment for our associates, and enhance the economic development of the communities where we operate. Together with our bottling partners, we rank among the world's top ten private employers with more than 700,000 system employees. For more information, visit www.thecoca-colacompany.com or follow us on Twitter at http://twitter.com/CocaColaCo.

Interview Questions and Answers

How would you characterize your organization's supply chain?

We have a large, national end-to-end supply chain. I would characterize it as increasingly complex in just the past couple of years. We have a multi-echelon supply chain with multiple product class points and multiple routes to markets.

How would you characterize you role in your supply chain?

My team and I set out long-term supply chain strategy and lay out plans to build the capability to deliver the strategy. We also prioritize capital and people resources to support initiatives within the business that deliver end-year results and multiyear capability.

How do you manage your supply chain for products that are in the Introduction Stage of their product life cycle?

We use a formal stage-gate process for product innovation and commercialization. A traditional stage-gate process for the supply chain is a cross-functional process with primary ownership on the commercialization side of the business. Supply chain participation begins early in the product development process and at a very intentional stage to help with the assessment of high-level value-added supply chain capacity needs. This helps to inform decision makers in early product-gating decisions moving from ideation to preliminary development. We also have supply chain involvement at late stages in the development to provide more detail on actual product packaging cost and actual manufacturing and distribution cost to go into the final value chain. During the execution phase, the supply chain area applies formal detail program management tools and processes to bring the product to the market, typically 60 to 90 days post-market introduction.

Sometimes, a product in the Introduction Stage doesn't make it in the market. How does your supply chain handle this type of situation?

We have a formal process to manage a product during its life cycle, including the Introduction, Growth, Maturity, and Decline Stages. We have a traditional SKU optimization process that manages an exit strategy, and we are adding an additional step in the process that manages product recovery before we toss everything out the window for a less-than-successful product. We try to get a midlife assessment for products to help us understand whether a product is not performing as expected. We are interested to know if it is a distribution gap or a marketing gap that is the problem. We try to close the gap by either injecting additional resources to gain the proper distribution so that the plan has its appropriate setting or we try to invest incremental additional marketing to be able to drive consumer pull against the existing distribution. That is a global best practice for us that we are striving to add to our processes to resolve the gaps. Finally, we typically provide a post-audit of product launches that reexamines the products that were less than successful to provide information on a cost-corrective action.

How do you manage your supply chain for products that are in the Growth Stage of their product life cycle?

We have a formal process that plans new launches and that is used to gauge new product success. We have a lot of bullwhip effects that gives us false positives (that is, suggesting a successful product when in fact it is not) that potentially might cause us to overreact. We are changing things to a more demand-driven view. We are providing insights to understand how a product is performing at retail and make the appropriate decisions to reinvest incremental raw materials, package ingredients, and line times, as well as revising an inventory plan to manage real consumer demand. We then go back into our infrastructure process, and if we, say, launch a product that is justified to have four production locations in the initial plan, and if it goes from 15 million cases to 20 million, then we would have a case to justify additional incremental production capacity. Also, in some situations, we identify some precandidate production facility locations and identify the capital requirements so that if the product performs well it will trigger the business case to accomplish the needed growth support.

Do you ever have situations where the growth of a product takes off such that supply chain demand greatly exceeds supply chain capacity?

Yes, we have dealt with this in the past, particularly with some of our newest beverages, vitaminwater and Simply Orange. These situations certainly sound promising, but they can also be a real challenge because we are a consumable and our cycle time gap to putting production capacity on the ground is typically a long period of time. We also have had products that boom and bust. We have a brand of products called Simply Orange that has been capped (that is, growth exceeded capacity) three or four times in its life and has always been up, but the upside has not always been smooth. The production-capacity additions are more discrete, so you have to manage that through supply and demand balancing. Typically, we get ahead of the game and manage through a limited supply for a time prior as incremental investment is brought on. Given that new product capacity temporarily exceeds demand, some concern is expressed about underutilizing the investment, which typically lasts for less than a year, and a year later we are thankful we made the investment. We then start all over again as growth in demand starts exceeding capacity. Simply Orange is a brand that went from $0 to a billion dollars in ten years but has been through three growth-capacity loop cycles. You are never perfect. You are either early or late on the infrastructure investment, and people either moan and groan because you place too much depreciation on them or they moan and groan that you're losing profits because of net sales loss.

How do you manage your supply chain for products that are in the Maturity Stage of their product life cycle?

There are some things we do in this stage. We have a company philosophy around continuous improvement that there are always opportunities for improvement. At the Maturity Stage, the emphasis will be on improving overall profits, stabilizing core process performance, and on reducing inventory. At this stage, we are looking to improve the overall operations and ultimately deliver the product with less effort. We look for opportunities to improve service in the business. We try to reduce all lost sales and seek zero defects on service. In summary, we stabilize the process, increase the demand, take out all nonvalued activities and waste from the process, and drive continuous improvement. We have seen some decent leverage with this approach. Reducing all lost sales, for example, even if it is only a half a point in growth, will make a difference.

How do you manage your supply chain for products that are in the Decline Stage of their product life cycle?

This comes down to an assortment strategy. The commercial group (as opposed to the supply chain group) really owns the decision on this stage of the product life cycle. We are a company of brands. The brand teams in the commercial group would say a larger assortment and even complexity in an assortment is a good thing. From the supply chain perspective, we would advocate a balanced view. We need to be very thoughtful in identifying the portfolio that we need to meet the vast majority of customer needs and then manage the portfolio to that point. We are not as balanced as we would like to be. We have to deal with the acute gaps where customers will no longer order a product or give us shelf space. When we have lost distribution of a product, it then falls into an SKU deletion process, and we eventually clean it out. We are continuing to be more proactive to quicken the product-deletion process that best practices would suggest. So as it turns out, the supply chain group is on one end of this balancing continuum and the commercial group on the other.

Are there any additional points you might like to add about supply chain management?

One of the big priorities for us in recent years the is recognition that for every dollar of raw materials we buy and every case of product that we physically produce less than 100% of what we produce results in a revenue producing sale. The reality is you put a lot of cost into something that did not produce any revenue. That can be caused by some kind of product breakage or expired shelf life that results in revenue loss. Actually focusing on the yield of maximizing all of your assets that you have at your command is required in our business. Doing the best that we can on these cost issues has added $100 million to the bottom line by looking at the root causes on the controllable variables and dealing with them. We continue to say there are controllable impacting variables that keep some of our product from making it to market at full price that we can reduce. How you handle and get the most of every dollar you buy is a bigger opportunity than some people realize. The real discipline to process is a relentless focus on every single case and every dollar. This discipline is a real benefit to us every single day.

How does your firm value the new technologies coming out?

We did not historically make the best use of technology because we were enamored with technology for the sake of technology. Our focus was on the use of technology and not on the process around it. Today, we do not earn the right to apply technology until we have gotten a very clear understanding and effective use of our business processes. In addition, we need to clearly demonstrate pain points in the process where there is no technology or lesser technology. Given this, it provides a clear case to justify the introduction of new technology. We use a lot more feedback mechanisms and continuous improvement processes to get what we need. If we are getting what we expect, let's keep doing it. If not, let's correct what we are doing and reduce the cycle path of feedback so that we can correct things quickly to minimize the path-correction efforts. This allows us to spend most of our efforts in the right direction.

How has Coca-Cola's new delivery technology impacted its supply chain?

Our new Coca-Cola Freestyle system of delivering our products is impacting our supply chain. The machine has the ability to generate a replenish order to the customer so that they can tell the distributor to create a replenish order to replace the cartridges needed. The machine knows when it has reached an economic order quantity. The suggested order can go directly to their distributor and in parallel back to our production facility to inform scheduling. It has turned out to be the first truly customer-driven supply chain. Consumption at the outlet is tracked every single day, in detail at the drink level off of every machine. It is communicated every night back into our supply chain. We even know when they should have ordered, and that permits us to call them and ask about it. In addition, we have telemetry in the machine to tell us if it is sick and needs fixing. This and other types of technology are leading our strategic planning to move to a more demand-driven firm. They create demand signal visibility that can be the engine helping move the rest of our legacy businesses into a demand-driven process—whether they are vending machines that will let you know what you need to load it up with so that when the driver shows up the machine knows exactly how many cans of each product the driver should bring, or a traditional grocery model where we are connected to the point of sale and drive it back into a demand signal for inventory. Instead of making an *information technology* (IT) investment for one business, our investment in Coca-Cola Freestyle will allow us to accelerate our maturity in technology a lot faster.

What does your firm do in sustainability?

If we are not focused on sustainability, we will go out of business. Sustainability is not just a nice thing to do, it is an essential thing to do. We have made public, long-term commitments around the primary resources we use to stay in business: water, packaging, agriculture ingredients, and energy. Our chairman made it clear that the Coca-Cola Company has to deliver on these commitments, and so sustainability is an important part of our overall supply chain strategy. We track and publish our own scorecard on our progress on the Web (good, bad, or ugly). One of our goals is to replenish every drop of water we use in our products. We are also looking for a dramatic decrease in our packaging that hits landfills and a huge increase in the recapture of every bottle we use. All of our plants are striving to have 100% landfill diversion, and some have already achieved that goal. Trucks at these plants are no longer taking away trash, but just recycling materials. Sustainability for us is a part of our having permission to do business in the communities where we operate. You can track our progress on these things on our website: www.thecocacolacompany.com/citizenship/index.html.

One final point can be added about our core strategy and our supply chain. Our business, as big as it is, is not an *or* business, it's an *and* business. We have to do everything. We have to deliver great service, we have to provide perfect-quality products that consumers want to buy and are a part of a consumer's healthy lifestyle. We have to do it at an affordable price and drive out waste every year. We have to be a sustainable player, we have to be an attractor of capital for our business, and we don't get an out on anything. If we don't do this, it's tough luck. It's not an or business, we have to do everything *and* we have to be good at it.

20

Interview with Mr. Brent Beabout of Office Depot

Introduction

This chapter consists of a series of questions and answers from an interview with a leading supply chain executive. The objective of this chapter is to provide a practitioner's perspective on the subject of life cycle issues in supply chain management. Other related subjects are also discussed in the interview.

About the Interviewee

Mr. Brent Beabout is currently serving as the Senior Vice President, Supply Chain at Office Depot, leading all facets of the supply chain for the $11.5 billion, multichannel global retailer. Prior to joining Office Depot, he served as Vice President of Engineering at DHL Express and Director, Operations Engineering at Amazon.com. He holds degrees from the Pennsylvania State University and MIT, including an MBA from the Sloan School of Management. He is a member of IIE, INFORMS, and CSCMP, and has been a frequent lecturer and collaborator at numerous academic forums on the intersection of supply chain and technology in today's globalized economy. He began his professional career as a naval officer while serving over a decade on nuclear-powered submarines.

"Nature favors the nimble. Get excited by change... it's coming one way or another."

—*Brent Beabout, 2012*

About Office Depot

Office Depot was founded in 1986 with its first store in Fort Lauderdale, Florida. Today, Office Depot provides office supplies and services through 1,677 worldwide retail stores, e-commerce sites, and a dedicated sales force. Office Depot has annual sales of approximately $11.5 billion, and employs about 39,000 associates in 60 countries around the world.

Interview Questions and Answers

How would you characterize your organization's supply chain?

Our supply chain is rapidly evolving. During our short history, we've evolved from a wholesale-type of operation where we placed product on pallets and watched it fly out the door to a more specialized retail operation. We're also continuing to evolve from the traditional retail model to that of a more consumer-driven, customized operation... more like an e-commerce type of supply chain. So what you're seeing is a much different type of supply chain than what we were even a few years ago.

How would you characterize you role in your supply chain?

I am currently responsible for all aspects of the supply chain at the enterprise level. In my previous role at Office Depot, I had three main areas of responsibility: global transportation, global network design strategies (building locations, sizes, and so on), and engineering (inside building design).

How do you manage your supply chain for products that are in the Introduction Stage of their product life cycle?

Any new product in our assortment is assumed to have an inaccurate demand forecast until a sales "run rate" can be firmly established. We try our best to forecast with similar existing SKUs, but those tend to be hit or miss at best. So, we like to do a couple of things with new products. We tend to source them domestically rather than from overseas. There are usually some cost disadvantages to this approach (that is, given cheaper labor overseas), but it minimizes the amount of working capital investment in these new products that might not take off with the customers and that might therefore become quickly obsolete. Additionally, domestically supplied products have a much shorter lead time and can be quickly switched off in the case of an inaccurate demand forecast.

A second thing we often do with Introductory Stage products is to move them to an "eaches pick" type of fulfillment strategy (that is, a selective distribution) instead of immediately dispersing them to over 1,100 retail stores. That being said, we make exceptions for the few "blockbuster" SKUs that we know will be big sellers, and we immediately ship these products to our retail stores. We also store the majority of stock in our *distribution centers* (DCs) and employ a "pull" strategy for supplying demand to the retail stores in a *just-in-time* (JIT) fashion. This strategy minimizes the inventory carried in the retail stores and places the remaining inventory where it's needed. So if a store in Texas can't sell the new product but a store in Florida can, we can quickly divert the product to serve the customer demand in Florida.

We can also regularly reevaluate the SKU based on sales velocity. We then convert that SKU into a flow product (based on a real-time store allocation model) where we will send it directly to the retail stores; otherwise, we store it at the DC level and allocate as we need it later down the road.

Do you ship directly from the manufacturer to your retail stores, bypassing the DCs?

We are no longer a pallet type of operation where we just drop off a large amount of inventory at one time. Instead, we use an intelligent "cross-dock" approach at our supply chain facilities. For items that are designated as "flow," we receive them from the manufacturer and allocate them to each retail store according to a JIT allocation model based on near-term customer demand and forecasts. These products flow out the same day they are received so that they can be delivered to the retail stores the next day. For slow-moving (low-velocity) products or new SKUs, we retain those units in the DC section of the buildings, as I mentioned earlier. These items get picked in a normal warehousing setting and are eventually merged with the flow type of traffic outbound. We review inventory frequently and SKUs regularly get reclassified as flow or pull depending on their current attributes and forecast accuracy.

How do you manage your supply chain for products that are in the Growth Stage of their product life cycle?

We have a number of explosive growth SKUs, and in those cases sourcing becomes the major focus. There are two parts to this strategy depending on the manufacturer. First we want to get a volume-based price break to increase the gross margin because we're selling a significant amount of the item. More important, we want to confirm that we can continue to receive the fast-moving product in a timely fashion. We measure the timeliness and accuracy of the vendor inbound deliveries using specific metrics, and we watch it very closely so that we don't stock out of fast-moving items. Additionally, we're now moving toward a much tighter vendor collaboration model with our manufacturers using cloud-based tools to ensure they have the visibility and capabilities to satisfy our future customer demand. Finally, since we're talking about fast-moving SKUs, we expect to use our cross-dock flow approach to move them quickly along in our supply chain and out to the retail stores as rapidly as possible.

How do you manage your supply chain for products that are in the Maturity Stage of their product life cycle?

For this subset of items, these items are typically steady sellers but not rapidly growing. This dynamic moves the sourcing discussion further upstream, most likely overseas to be manufactured under our own brands. SKUs in this category generally become a gross margin play, and since we have good forecasting data, we feel comfortable sitting on the extra lead time coming across the ocean and making the additional investment in inventory (that is, longer lead time requires a larger inventory purchase), knowing we will be able to sell it.

What about SKUs that require you to use their brand name products rather than produce under your brand names?

For nationally branded name products that our customers expect us to carry, we purchase them from domestic sources, but there are also many SKUs where you try to source overseas. We also try to grow our own brand portfolio to offer products that our customers want and expect. While some of these products are not the Office Depot brand name, they provide our customers with a choice and attractive price points. Some of these provide us with the opportunity to utilize our overseas margin enhancing strategy, while still carrying other domestically manufactured products for our customers.

How do you manage your supply chain for products that are in the Decline Stage of their product life cycle?

Dealing with end-of-life products which will eventually become discontinued is always a constant struggle since these could end up as an unwanted write-off if not properly managed. To manage these properly, we try to gracefully remove the remaining inventory in our system by either moving the remaining inventory upstream to the pull DC environment or use store-to-store transfers to put these older SKUs in high-traffic stores. If well executed, we will sell the remaining inventory before customer demand drops to zero.

How do you deal with a product that is a part of a plan-a-gram **(that is, a display of multiple products, usually from a single manufacturer and often offered as a full line of products)?**

Almost everything we sell in the retail channel is part of a larger plan-a-gram. Some of these displays are made up of SKUs from a single manufacturer, whereas others are based on SKU type or classification. There is a carefully choreographed plan to constantly replace old or slower selling SKUs in each plan-a-gram with newer ones to ensure the best customer presentation and sales rates.

Do you use sales per square foot as criteria for measuring sales performance of products?

Yes, sales per square foot is one of the many criteria we use to evaluate product sales.

How does this type of measurement impact core suppliers and their plan-a-grams? Is there a threshold on this metric that might be used to determine which manufacturers you continue to allow display space in your stores?

Yes, there are sales expectations for our suppliers that must be met or they risk our stores offering their competitors' products.

When a product is in decline, do you have any difficulties in bringing a product to an end with your suppliers when you decide to discontinue a product?

In any merchandising environment, you want to work with your vendors to be able to make the right decision regarding when and how to discontinue a product or a particular SKU. Sometimes it's hard for both parties to discontinue a product that used to be a hot seller but no longer is. Part of the issue is finding a replacement SKU, and sometimes it is hard to find a good replacement. Also, if you still have a lot of inventory in that particular SKU, you have to be aware of the possibility of writing off a lot of the inventory (liquidation) for a discontinued product.

Are there any additional points you might like to add about supply chain management?

One key point concerns the future, and I mentioned the desire to increase the gross margins on our products. I believe that fuel costs are going to continue to increase in the long term, and this may change the current vendor dynamic with Asia-based suppliers, particularly China. As Chinese labor and fuel costs continue to climb, this will likely change the cost/benefit advantage China currently enjoys and increasingly will place greater pressure on retailers to nearshore. Consequently, sourcing will become even more global, and continents such as Africa and South America are likely to see an uptick in sourcing into the United States. Additionally, as countries like China become more affluent, there will be a greater need to export goods into China to meet their domestic demands, so their production efforts will be diverted over time from export-focused to domestic consumption.

How does your firm deal with *reverse logistics* (that is, reversing the flow from the consumer back to the manufacturer) in any phase of their product life cycle?

We have a complete reverse logistics network using facilities in the United States that are designed to handle reverse logistics from all of our retail stores. Some of our products are recycled, some are sold for liquidation, and some items get returned back to our shelves for resale.

Do you use a "milk run" between the stores to pick up the items for reverse logistics or how do you handle this part of your supply chain activities?

No, we use a different approach. For our retail operations, we service over 1,100 stores in the United States using a five-days-per-week delivery schedule. We do this to take full advantage of our DC's eaches pick operations for the slow-moving SKUs, keeping store (SKU) outages and overall inventory levels to an absolute minimum. This delivery frequency allows us to conveniently backhaul the reverse logistics items (including recycling waste) to the cross-docks on a regular schedule, and eventually these items make their way to one of our three reverse logistics consolidation centers or recycling vendors (as appropriate).

Do you use your own trucks or common carriers for the logistics?

We are completely asset free from a transportation perspective. We have an extensive network of third-party carriers that provides the assets and drivers to deliver to over 1,100 retail stores daily and well over 1 million packages a week to our "last mile" customers. In many markets, the retail and direct delivery assets are dual-utilized each day to ensure maximum efficiency.

Do you run your containers through the flow centers?

We are currently in the middle of optimizing our global inbound operations. We utilize a number of inbound (container) deconsolidation centers in the United States operated by third-party providers (*third-party logistics* [3PLs]) to optimize transportation costs. Most of our large cube items (for example, furniture) run through these facilities, while the remainder typically gets shipped directly from overseas to one of our regional DCs. For containers that contain a heavy mix of product destined for many regions of the country, these containers get deconsolidated, and the import product is commingled with domestic shipments to give full truckload quantities to our destination

DCs. To enable this process, we use sophisticated decision support tools to ensure lowest total landed cost.

You mentioned the reverse logistics program. Do you have a sustainable program that is related?

Yes, we have and continue to expand our sustainability programs. We currently recycle most waste streams from our retail stores using the same reverse logistics network I described earlier. Office Depot has been recently recognized as the "greenest" retailer in the United States in an annual assessment by *Newsweek* magazine.

Do you practice any lean principles in the supply chain?

Yes! We are in the beginning stages of a multiyear "lean journey" with a focus on elevating all of our operations to a world-class level. We're currently building a team of experts both from the corporate level and in the field to ensure we shift our culture toward a lean way of thinking. I firmly believe lean is *the* path toward operational excellence in any endeavor.

21

Novelette: So You Want to Build a Plant in a Foreign Country

The decision to locate a plant in a foreign country can be triggered for many reasons. Most of them are cost related or to maintain or increase market share of sufficient sales to justify the plant in the first place. Whereas the decision to build the plant in a foreign country is made by a board of directors, operations people make it happen.

A conversation took place between our CEO and the President of a not-so-small South American country. We currently have 80% of the market share of all engines and parts imported into that country. A threshold of $50 million in sustainable business was reached last year and was used to determine whether we should build a plant there. The engines we export to them are used extensively for the country's farming equipment and automobile industries and impact their two primary exportable food and automobile products. In addition, these products are highly taxed by the government and are viewed as strategically important to the nation. As a result, the president of the country informed our CEO that because of high unemployment rates, the government preferred the engines be produced in their own country to provide employment opportunities. The CEO was also informed they would give huge financial incentives to both automobile and farming industries to produce more products. Those dollars are the "carrot" for us, because when production increases, our engines and parts will be are used. However, the "stick" was clearly defined by the president in the form of new protectionist policies directed against all importers of these strategic industries. There are only three very small manufacturers that we compete against in the country. What the protectionism policies mean to us is that a small local manufacturer in the country with 1% or less of the market share of any products we export

429

to them could issue a complaint, effectively ending our entire market in that country for those products. The president knows our firm has contributed substantially to the government's bottom line, tax-wise, and knows the quality of our products is desired by this nation's firms, who currently use the engines and parts in their vehicle-assembly operations. Recognizing our joint willingness to work together, the President of the country contacted our CEO to explain things well ahead of any public announcements. The CEO believed that for the continued successful long-term nature of our relationship we need to build a manufacturing facility in this nation and have it up and running within two years. The CEO also saw how operating a plant here could work out for the benefit of the organization. If we became a local producer, we could file complaints about other importers, who currently are our competition, and as a result gain more market share. So, the CEO promised the President that the facility would be up and running in two years. Like any typical CEO, she turned the matter over to her VP of Operations, me.

I have worked on other facility location projects before and know what needs to be done. Like any major project, developing a plan for the location and building of a new plant requires assembling a team to manage the project. In addition to the VPs of the Divisions who are impacted and their staff, I called upon the corporation-level VP of International Sales and staff to be brought into the process to make sure there are sustainable sales, to identify barriers to entrance in the country, and other risk factors. They have to determine what the pricing is going to be, if we have a current dealer distribution system in place, and whether it will change. The marketing plan has to be well articulated to show the market what the competition is going to do when we build the plant. We also have to have lawyers to deal with necessary contracts. Other decisions involving the CEO and Board will have to be made concerning identification of investors. Operations people will have to determine who will run the plant. We must also have the local real estate help us in procuring land, aligning contractors to build the plant, and completing necessary documents. Negotiations must take place with local people regarding who is going to buy the land, design the building, see to construction, and determine the project manager. During that effort, local employees have to be hired. Typically, the first person hired is the plant manager;

the second person is the human resource (HR) director. Some would argue the HR person should be hired first; after all, the HR person might not like the project manager the operations people recommend.

The entire supply chain must be set up. Which staff members will come from local talent and which will be from other countries? Are *third-party logistics* (3PLs) going to help with logistics or will it be insourced completely? To set up the supply chain, I turned to the director of international operations, who is under our VP of International Operations, and will have a production control person and a procurement person comprising the team to handle setting up the facility. In the United States, we would call this Director a *Manager*, but to better aid in global communications, the term *Director* is a better title. The Director's team will travel to the foreign country to begin planning and recruitment efforts. They will be aided by corporate procurement and will establish sourcing for the supply chain. There will be some commodity items that we don't need to spend much time on to validate their quality level, but for other items that are strategically important to the nature and structure of our product, we will handle this locally in the foreign country. We will bring those materials back to our U.S. facilities to test them in a *production part approval process* (PPAP). This will ensure our engineered design and specifications are properly understood by the suppliers of the new facility. PPAP is commonly used in the automotive supply chain to establish confidence in component suppliers and their production processes. There should be no resistance to using this approach to validate quality. After the products and parts have successfully gone through the PPAP tests, we will certify the foreign local suppliers. We will also implement a quality control plan to monitor quality over a period of time after the facility comes online to ensure both the suppliers and the new facility maintain quality. We have seen that some firms from China show the best pieces and then what they deliver on a regular basis is just not comparable in quality. Some suppliers like to substitute the materials without informing the purchaser. They think nothing of changing specifications on materials used in products or parts. It looks the same, but the performance is much less than expectations. Based on my experience, China just doesn't yet have the kind of quality controls in commodities necessary for our products.

After I delivered the initial orientation on where and why the organization was going to build a new plant, Tyler, the Corporate VP of International sales, asked, "Bill, this is one of those situations where we are going in regardless of the sales. You explained what our CEO believed were good reasons. What additional factors can you share with me about reasons why we need this plant?"

"Tyler, while your ongoing research shows the local sales have recently grown to meet our normal triggering level of sustainable sales, there are other cost-related reasons why building a plant in this country is a smart move. First, the cost of shipping our metal-intensive parts to that country for assembly is very expensive. Containers to ship goods there run $4,000 to $5,000 per container. That puts us at a competitive disadvantage to any home-grown manufacturer; and while we don't have many yet, it would be best for us to maintain and even grow our market share by having that cost reduction show up in reduced prices for our customers. With government incentives, the home-grown manufacturers will seek to grow at our expense unless we soak up most of the incentives ourselves. Another important point is the opportunity to leverage our currency against their currency, which is relatively weak. We can gain substantially by the exchange rates as things stand now. Also, although we normally go into a country to reduce our total cost of products, sometimes there are economic factors that we can take advantage of. The government's plan to give our customers incentives to spend money on our products is a great opportunity for us to cash in. Their government knows this and wants us there to do just that. If we get in with our current market share, we could end up putting protectionism on other importing competitors who might want to come in and compete against us. We could actually pick up 90% or more of the market," I explained.

"Bill, why haven't we gone into this country before this?" asked Tyler.

Not wanting to state the obvious, I replied, "Tyler, several years ago there was an explosion that killed the President and other important officials in the government. At that time, it was a very unstable country in which to run a business. In the last year, things have calmed down politically and socially, and our board of directors believes it has recently become stable enough to warrant the risk of opening a production facility. Another factor is the promised, but not yet delivered, government incentives program the CEO was told about by the country's president. A similar program was announced in an Asian country where we have a facility. The announcement had the effect of our customers not buying anything for several years while they waited for the incentive. Why should they buy something now when the government is going to give them money and free interest rates in the future? So, most of the big-ticket sales stopped in anticipation of the purchases being offset by the government's incentive program. A couple of years went by before the incentive showed up. The loss in sales during that period so negatively impacted our facility that we almost closed it. We learned, as a result, not to be motivated by the promise of a government to put money in our pockets. However, we started up a plant in China because the government put in place protectionist policies of a 30% import duty. We were sending our product into the country and found we were competing against ten other local manufacturers. The increased duty motivated us to open a plant to avoid it. Fortunately, the volume of sales increased, because we didn't face the duty other importers did, and it justified the plant economically. The longer term outlook for this plant is continued growth as we meet the growing market in China."

"Bill, will we have any local barriers to entrance? As a marketing person, I have run into those big time, and they are really costly after the fact," Tyler stated.

"Yes Tyler, I agree with you, but in this case we have a disadvantage that we will turn into an advantage by eliminating barriers to entrance. There is one person who owns exclusive rights to all the engines and parts that are shipped into the foreign country. He is very politically connected and owns all the distribution centers in the country to house all the import products. Now, as you know, we use lean management principles in our operations and supply chain. As such, we don't even use distribution centers; we ship directly to the customers. Because we will have a manufacturing plant right in the country, it will render this distribution monopolist redundant; but given how politically connected he is, we have to include him in the business. So we are planning on giving him some of the ownership in the production facility. He, in turn, will be asked to help use his connections to get the necessary licenses with the government and to help us set up our supply chain without the use of distribution centers," I said.

"Bill, I have been involved in plant locations where we have sold ownership in our facilities, but is it normal that we give away ownership rights to individuals in the foreign counties?" asked Tyler.

"Without this distribution monopolist, we would not be able to do anything in the country. In terms of ownership, we have plant in Colombia. It's a 90/10% arrangement, where we own 90%. Some of the people down there own 10% of the plant, because we need them for their relationships with the government or businesses in Colombia. We will do the same for this new plant being built in the foreign country. Of course, we will take precautions to ensure we maintain control. We will set up a board of directors who understands the country very well. The board will consist of key stakeholder owners, including lawyers who have a vested interest in the plant and will perform legal services for us, bankers who help fund and maintain the registered capital that needs to be available for the operation, and the plant manager representing our organization. We have to put our team in there. They will understand our need for reporting structures and understand the ownership responsibilities. We have learned to be careful in allowing locals to hire important or key employees. For example, we would want to have the comptroller from the United States so that we can be assured of reporting the financials in a timely and accurate manner. This is an ethics situation, as well. You don't want a person from the foreign country reporting to another person from the same country, where backdoor deals could pop up and the plant manager gets cut out of the information flow. We don't want to set up conflicts of interest. To help monitor all of this, we will we do board meetings through video conferencing to our U.S. corporation headquarters with our CEO and comptroller in the room. Ultimately, we have the final say on board of director decisions."

22

Novelette: So You Want to Eliminate a Plant in a Foreign Country

Not all production facilities turn a profit for their stakeholders. When they start losing money, they are at risk of being discontinued. Usually, decisions to eliminate a plant are at the executive level in an organization, but who actually eliminates it are the same people who generally created the plant in the first place: the operations management people. Just as they can engineer a plant that does not work, so too can they fix it to work!

The Executive VP whom I work under came to my office to inform me of a decision he had made. "Hi, Bill. As you know, we bought a facility in Korea eight years ago to produce our medium-sized automobile engines that we sell to the car manufacturers, principally in Japan, but also throughout Asia. I know they have been a pain to work with in terms of late deliveries and quality issues with regard to your overall supply chain efforts for many years. They have also been in the red for all eight years we have owned them. I have pitched the closing of this plant to the CEO, and she has given me permission to begin the process. Because this type of operation falls under your area of responsibility, I am asking you to begin closing the plant now in combination with our VP of Global Operations. Because of the complexity of the paperwork and the general activities required in closing a plant in Korea, you will have a year to phase down the operation and reorganize your global supply chain operations to take the closing into consideration. I personally want to see this as a done deal in a year, since I was against purchasing this plant in the first place. It helps me validate my original opinion of this purchase," he stated.

As the VP of Operations for the entire organization, I was aware of the troubles in the Korean facility, but was not really allowed to do much about it because it fell under the responsibility of the VP of Global Operations, who is in charge of the success of all foreign global operations we operate. That being said, I was now given full responsibility from the Executive VP to get an operations management team from the Medium-Sized Engine Division into the Korean plant and see what was going on that actually led to the Executive VP's desire to shut it down. I called in Barack, our VP of Operations for Medium-Sized Engines, and had him create a project team for this phasing down job. The project team was made up of a director of project management or project director (since it was an international job, we used the title *director* rather than *manager* as would be done in the United States), the current plant manager of the Korean facility, the director of procurement and materials, and a small team of Six Sigma-trained industrial engineers.

A month into the project, Barack called me to say, "Bill, we have an interesting situation in the Korean plant shutdown project."

As I anticipated the usual foreign project outcome of trouble, I said, "Okay, but don't surprise me with anything that is going to cost more money."

Barack in a laughing tone added, "No, nothing like that, but based on what the project manager is telling me, I think we can turn this plant around to turn it into a moneymaker."

Thinking, but still remembering the Executive VP's desires, I said, "Barack, that was not what you were sent out to do. The Executive VP really wants to kill this plant. The corporate people are in the process of drafting the paperwork to officially end the plant."

Barack replied, "What we have learned is that the people in the plant really didn't know how to manage inventory, their supply chains, or even their production processes. It is like we bought this plant and then just ignored it. Also, they have too many people, and some don't have the skills to do their jobs."

Never wanting to turn down a challenge, while at the same time not wanting to go against the Executive VP, I suggested the following course of action, "Okay, you have what you need in a team out there, so there won't be any additional costs that I would have to hide. So, have fun for the next eight or nine months training people and changing systems as you want. But remember, in about 11 months we will be closing the plant down. In the meanwhile, your training efforts will benefit the employees by enriching their skills and, in turn, helping them to be more prepared in their next jobs. We can write this off as a new job training program, or at least that is what I will call it if I am pressed by anyone here."

The project director worked closely with the plant manager. During this time, the Plant Manager was told that everything would be fine for him, just to hang in there (as the firm was going to give him an umbrella when they announced the closing of the plant). Basically, they would continue his employment to further manage the elimination of the plant and its assets after the closing date. This would provide employment for as long as it took to sell the plant and equipment.

The project director then launched into programs to identify production problems and explained. "Hi, Barack, you asked me to keep you informed about what we are doing on the Korean project, and I just wanted to let you know that we have implemented an education program for those who have the skills the plant needs. Others are being retrained for new jobs, and some employees are being let go because they were just not needed. The industrial engineers have set up Six Sigma training programs to help employees find problems and come up with solutions to correct them. The plant people and the plant manager are working very hard to learn and turn the facility around. They were easily schooled in lean and other quality-improvement methods. We also provided them with some additional training in supply chain management and logistics effectiveness. We are all working diligently with the supply chain to lower the costs and improve the logistics, but we need all the help we can get. We are using lean and Six Sigma methodologies to assemble the engines with the least labor possible. We got rid of all the waste and will continue to look for more."

The project director asked Barack for help in finding additional supply chain cost reductions that might be beyond the plant's scope of control. Barack had Todd, the Head of the Supply Chain Department, come up with some ideas. After investigation, Todd suggested the following, "Barack, it appears this plant was left all on its own to do a lot of its supply chain activities since we purchased it eight years ago. For example, we found that they were not bundling orders within our Division or with any of our other Divisions to obtain quantity discounts, even on standardized parts that are interchangeable on our other small and large engines. So, they were paying full price on parts and materials, where we could easily have reduced the cost by 40%."

Surprised, Barack asked, "What does that add to their bottom line?"

"Barack, just this one area of cost reduction will add $10,000 in monthly savings, and we are not done yet. It turns out they haven't ever used our database on suppliers to find the best suppliers or the least cost for services, materials, and parts. That will save thousands over the year."

"Todd, as you know, we are scheduling this plant to be discontinued within the year, so short-term cost reductions will be a greater value to us."

Todd, being quick to reply, said, "Yep, I know that, so I also brought in some of my expert procurement buyers to reverse what they do best and find sources to sell off obsolete materials this plant has accumulated and didn't know what to do with. As you know, culturally, Koreans are very frugal. They don't waste things, so they had piled up a lot of unneeded goods that they had purchased over the years, but the goods had become obsolete or useless. Just the space in warehouses they were renting to store them will save thousands more each month. In addition, the plant had accumulated logistics equipment that was either in disrepair or no longer used. Like the obsolete inventory, they were just collecting dust. We will have some of our buyers help sell off these and other assets that we have nearly or fully depreciated to help shore up the bottom line of this plant."

"Todd, is there anything else you might want to share with me about this facility and our supply chain in a final report that I am preparing for the VP of Operations?" asked Barack.

"Barack, it should be noted that the location of the Korean facility is important to our supply chain network. We use it as a distribution breakout center. Basically, we ship engines from our U.S. and Chinese facilities to distribute through this center, where we stage and sort the products going to our Japanese customers, who are major consumers of our automobile engines and parts. Without the facility in Korea, we will have to start up a distribution center in Japan, which could be very expensive, given land and building costs. Also, the facility acts as a conduit for access to rare metals from China that we use in our products. Our connections in Korea have made possible our access and licenses to procure the rare metals from China. Without that Korean contact, we may lose this arrangement and have to have a more costly route to obtain them. I join others in suggesting that the positives of operating this plant supporting our supply chain outweigh the negatives. I hope the board changes its mind on the plant closing," implored Todd.

"Todd, that is a good point, and I will include it in my final report. As it stands now, we will be closing the plant in a few months. I appreciate your continued hard work in getting what you can out of the facility and helping them improve their supply chain efficiency."

As the VP of Operations charged with the responsibility of handling this plant's discontinuance, I review monthly the organization financial-performance information. As the year went on, I was pleasantly surprised to see the financials from the Korean plant had started improving on same/similar sales levels. Costs were going down and profit was going up without an increase in sales, which was clearly a contribution of the operations people. The paperwork indicated that we had started making a profit. Obviously, the project team was having a significant impact on plant operations. Unfortunately, none of this had any effect on the corporate plans to discontinue the operation. Time had finally run out, and the showdown at the Board of Directors meeting was imminent.

Like most board meetings, the CEO, Executive VP, other corporate VPs (myself included), the comptroller, corporate lawyer, and Division VPs, whose areas were impacted by board decisions in this meeting, as well as some of their subordinates who had prepared applicable reports, were all present. Those of us connected to the Korean plant closing project were there: I, as the VP of Operations; the VP of Global Operations in charge of all international operations; Barack, the VP of the Medium-Sized Engine Division; his Supply Chain Department Head, Todd; and the Project Manager who prepared the operations report. Everyone in the meeting had access to the financial reports on the Korean project, and there was dissension among the VPs on whether to close the plant. The Executive VP was still determined to close the plant, for personal reasons if nothing else. We started the meeting with a review of general business and market conditions for the organization as a whole, discussing a few insignificant items on the agenda. Then, we brought up the Korean facility closure item. Our CEO was well respected by all. She had been very successful for the organization, and she did not like losing money on any projects or facilities. We handed her the paperwork and documents to close down the plant for her final signature. These had been drafted over the past year by the Executive VP, lawyers, and other international experts who specialize in Korean government policy on plant closing legalities. A lot of work went into drafting the documents, and they had already been countersigned by all the appropriate authors, except our CEO. Like any new project, you need a capital authorization or statement of capital expenditures at the head the document so that it can be weighed in the final decision. If you are going to close something, as were planning to do here, you also need to have a capital authorization. This document serves that purpose. The document was placed in front of the CEO, who, with pen in hand, looked at it with disgust given the losses of this facility during the eight prior years.

She looked upset, and wanting to be angry one more time, she asked me, as the VP of Operations, "Bill, how much money did we lose this ninth year of the operation?

Happily I replied, "We are not going to lose any money this year."

The CEO sat back, put her pen on the table, and started tapping her fingers on the document that awaited her signature and asked, "Bill, how much money will we make from this facility this year?"

I quickly replied, "We are going to make a $1 million."

The CEO, in shock, said, "$1 million! Really? Haven't we lost money here for the last eight years?"

I replied, "Yes."

She then asked, "What happened? I know we didn't have that much more in sales, so what happened?"

And with glee that only an operations person can have in such a situation, I replied, "Well, the operations people got in there and fixed a lot of things that were going wrong and found things could be done with fewer people."

The CEO, still a bit puzzled, asked, "How much money are we going to making in this facility during the next timing horizon?"

"I am happy to inform you, that if we continue down this path, we should make about $8 million during the next timing horizon."

The CEO started looking at the discontinuance document in front of her asked, "Who brought me this paperwork today?"

Afterword

Like all the novelettes in this book, this is based on true events, with only names, locations, and some identifiers changed to avoid proprietary conflicts. This plant, plan, and the Board actions really took place. The plant was not closed and continues operating to this day. It is one of the most profitable facilities owned by the corporation that operates it.

References

Abo-Hamad, W., Arisha, A., (2011). Simulation-optimization methods in supply chain applications: A review. *Irish Journal of Management.* Vol. 30, No. 2, pp. 95–124.

Abu-Musa, A. A. (2011). Exploring information systems/technology outsourcing in Saudi organizations: An empirical study. *Journal of Accounting, Business & Management.* Vol. 18, No. 2, pp. 17–73.

Accounting rule wipes billions from outsourcers' profits. (2003). Global Computing Services. October 17, pp. 2–3.

Agarwal, A., Shankar, R., Tiwari, M. K. (2007). Modeling agility of supply. *Industrial Marketing Management.* Vol. 36, No. 4, pp. 443–457.

Albert, A. (2011). Buyers find transition to outsourcing a challenge. *Supply Management.* November 4, 2011. Retrieved January 15, 2012. www.supplymanagement.com/news/2011/buyers-find-transition-to-outsourcing-a-challenge/

Allen, C. (2011). The value of taking time off. *Inside Supply Management,* Vol. 22, No. 8, p. 44.

Altschuller, S.A. (2011). Trafficking in supply chains. *Inside Supply Management.* Vol. 22, No. 8, pp. 38–40.

Amini, M., Li, H. (2011). Supply chain configuration for diffusion of new products: An integrated optimization approach. *Omega.* Vol. 39, No. 3, pp. 313–322.

Amir, F. (2011). Significance of lean, agile and leagile decoupling point in supply chain management. *Journal of Economics and Behavioral Studies*. Vol. 3, No. 5, pp. 287–295.

A new era of sustainability: UN global compact-accenture. (2010) Accenture Institute for High Performance. June 2010, pp. 1–66.

Anderson, L. (2011). Develop the entrepreneurial spirit. *Inside Supply Management*. Vol. 22, No. 6, pp. 38–39.

Araujo, L., Dubois, A., Gadde, L. E. (1999). Managing interfaces with supplier. *Industrial Marketing Management*. Vol. 28, No. 5, pp. 497–506.

Arnseth, L. (2011a). Core competencies for strategic leadership. *Inside Supply Management*. Vol. 22, No. 5, pp. 32–35.

Arnseth, L. (2011b). Finding the push-pull balance. *Inside Supply Management*. Vol. 22, No. 8, pp. 22–25.

Arnseth, L. (2012a). Lessons in supplier relationship management. *Inside Supply Management*. Vol. 23, No. 2, pp. 24–27.

Arnseth, L. (2012b). Sharing value with suppliers. *Inside Supply Management*. Vol. 23, No. 4, pp. 26–29.

Arnseth, L. (2012c). The rise of global ethics. *Inside Supply Management*. Vol. 23, No. 5, pp. 30–33.

Arnseth, L. (2012d). Transforming traditional lean principles. *Inside Supply Management*. Vol. 22, No. 6, pp. 20–23.

Atasu, A., Guide, Jr., V. D. R., Van Wassenhove, L. N. (2010). So what if remanufacturing cannibalizes my new product sales? *California Management Review*. Vol. 52, No. 2, pp. 56–76.

Axelrod, R., 1984. *The Evolution of Cooperation*, Basic Books, New York, NY.

Badasha, K. (2012). Manufacturers try 'near shoring' to mitigate supply chain risk. *Supply Management*. June 17, 2012.

Retrieved July 4, 2012. www.supplymanagement.com/news/2012/manufacturers-try-near-shoring-to-mitigate-supply-chain-risk/

Bandfield, E. (1999). *Harnessing Value in the Supply Chain.* Wiley and Sons, New York, NY.

Beatty, A. (2012). Rising Chinese wages a headache for U.S. firms. Industry Week.com. March 26, 2012. Retrieved July 7, 2012. www.industryweek.com/articles/rising_chinese_wages_a_headache_for_u-s_firms_26931.aspx

Benkler, M. (2010). Co-operation and innovation cut life-cycle costs. *Railway Gazette International.* Vol. 166, No. 11, pp. 37–40.

Beth, S., Burt, D. N., Copacino, W., Gopal, C., Lee, H. L., Lynch, R. P., Morris, S. (2011). Supply chain challenges: building relationships. In *Harvard Business Review: Managing Supply Chains.* Harvard Business School Publishing, Boston, MA.

Blanchard, D. (2007). *Supply Chain Management Best Practices.* Wiley & Sons, New York, NY.

Boehe, D. (2010). Captive offshoring of new product development in Brazil. *Management International Review (MIR).* Vol. 50, No. 6, pp. 747–773.

Bohlman, H. M., Dundas, M. J. (2002). *The Legal, Ethical and International Environment of Business, 5th ed.* West, Cincinnati, OH.

Borgstrom, B., Hertz, S. (2011). Supply chain strategies: changes in customer order-based production. *Journal of Business Logistics.* Vol. 32, No. 4, pp. 361–373.

Bowersox, D. J., Closs, D. J., Cooper, M. B. (2007). *Supply Chain Logistics Management, 2nd ed.,* McGraw-Hill/Irwin, Boston, MA.

Brown, M. T., Ulgiati, S. (1999). Emergy evaluation of natural capital and biosphere services. *AMBIO.* Vol. 28, No.6, pp. 31-42

Butner, K. (2011). A commanding view. *CSCMP's Supply Chain Quarterly.* Vol. 5, No. 3, pp. 28–32.

Byrne, P. M. (2007). Impact and ubiquity: Two reasons to proactively manage risk. *Logistics Management.* Vol. 46, No. 4, pp. 24–25.

Carter, J. R., Choi, T. Y. (2008). *Foundation of Supply Chain Management.* Institute of Supply Management, Tempe, AZ.

Carter, P. L., Giunipero, L. C. (2010). Supplier financial and operational risk management. CAPS Research, Tempe, AZ.

Casemore, S. (2012). Social media and the coming supply-chain revolution. CFO. February 29, 2012. Retrieved July 7, 2012. www3.cfo.com/article/2012/2/supply-chain_supply-chain-innovation-social-media-casemore-ghg?currpage=1

Cavusgil, S. T., Ghauri, P. N., Agarwal, M. R. (2002). *Doing Business in Emerging Markets.* Sage Publications, Thousand Oaks, CA.

Cecere, L. (2012a). S&OP planning improves supply chain gility. Supply Chain Insights LLC Research Reports May 2012. Retrieved June 18, 2012. http://www.slideshare.net/loracecere/sop-planning-improves-supply-chain-agility

Cecere, L. (2012b). How S&OP drives agility. Supply Chain Insights LLC Research Reports May 2012. Retrieved June 18, 2012. http://www.slideshare.net/loracecere/how-sop-drives-agility

Choi, T. Y., Krause, D. R. (2005). The supply base and its complexity: Implications for transaction costs, risks, responsiveness, and innovation. *Journal of Operations Management.* Vol. 24, No. 5, pp. 637–652.

Chopra, S., Meindl, P. (2001). *Supply Chain Management: Strategy, Planning, and Operation.* Prentice Hall, Upper Saddle River, NJ.

Christopher, M. (2011). *Logistics & Supply Chain Management, 4th ed.* Pearson, Harlow, England.

Christopher, M. (2000). The agile supply chain: Competing in volatile markets. *Industrial Marketing Management.* Vol. 29, No. 1, pp. 37–44.

Clients to blame for outsourcing failure. (2003). Global Com[ ]ing Services, Computerwire, Inc., June 27, p. 4, www.computerw[ ]com.

Cohen, S. G., Bailey, D. E. (1997). What makes teams work: Group effectiveness research from the shop floor to the executive suite. *Journal of Management*. Vol. 23, No. 3, pp. 239–290.

Colicchia, C., Dallari, F. Melacini, M. (2011). A simulation-based framework to evaluate strategies for managing global inbound supply risk. In*ternational Journal of Logistics: Research & Applications*. Vol. 14, No. 6, pp. 371–384.

Cooke, J. A. (2011). Wehkamp.nl takes it one day at a time. *CSCMP's Supply Chain Quarterly*. Vol. 5, No. 3, pp. 34–37.

Correll, S. (2011). How to sidestep supply chain hiccups before they happen. Business Finance Magazine.com, August 31, 2011. Retrieved January 1, 2012. http://businessfinancemag.com/article/ how-sidestep-supply-chain-hiccups-they-happen-0831

Cullen, S., Willcocks, L. (2003). *Intelligent IT Outsourcing*. Butterworth-Heinemann, London.

Davis, M. (2011). Toolkit: Frameworks to design and enable supply chain segmentation. Gartner. May 19, 2011. Retrieved June 18, 2012. http://my.gartner.com/portal/server.pt?open=512&objID=249 &mode=2&PageID=864059&resId=1691114&ref=Browse

Day, A. (2011). How to be a customer of choice. CPO Agenda. Autumn. Retrieved January 20, 2012. www.cpoagenda.com/previous-articles/ autumn-2011/features/how-to-be-acustomer-of-choice/

Digman, L. (2003). Outsmarting outsourcers. *Baseline*. July, pp. 20–21.

Dolcemascolo, D. (2006). *Improving the Extended Value Stream: Lean for the Entire Supply Chain*. Productivity Press, New York, NY.

Dunphy, D., Bryant, B. (1996). Teams: Panaceas or prescriptions for improved performance. *Human Relations*. Vol. 49, No. 5, pp. 677–699.

ⅎ). Trust, perceived importance of praise and
⌐erformance: An examination of feedback in the
England. *Journal of Management.* Vol. 12, No. 4,

⌐ees ignored in outsourcing deals, says report. (2002).
⌐gram Weekly. (Nov. 5), p. 5.

⌐llram, L. M. (2000). The supplier alliance continuum. *Purchas-*
⌐ Today. Vol. 11, No. 2, p. 8.

Elmuti, D., Kathawala, Y. (2000). The effects of global outsourcing strategies on participants' attitudes and organizational effectiveness. *International Journal of Manpower.* Vol. 21, Nos. 1&2, pp.
112–129.

Fox, M. S., Huang, J. (2005). Knowledge provenance in enterprise information. *International Journal of Production Research.* Vol.
43, No. 20, pp. 4471–4492.

Evans, R. (2011). Taking the alternative route. CPO Agenda.
Autumn. Retrieved October 4, 2011. www.cpoagenda.com/
current-issue/features/taking-the-alternative-route/

Farasyn, I., Humair, S., Kahn, J., Neale, J., Ruark, J., Tarlton, W.,
Van de Velde, W., Wegryn, G., Willems, S. (2011). Inventory optimization at Procter & Gamble: Achieving real benefits through user
adoption of inventory tools. *Interfaces,* Vol. 41, No. 1, pp. 66–78.

Fawcett, S. E., Ellran, L. M., Ogden, J. A. (2007). *Supply Chain
Management.* Pearson/Prentice Hall, Upper Saddle River, NJ.

Fitzgerald, M. (2011). Five common lean maintenance missteps.
Business Week.Com. August 17, 2011. Retrieved July 1, 2012. http://
industryweek.com/articles/five_common_lean_maintenance_mis-
steps_25313.aspx

Fixon, S. K. (2005). Product architecture assessment: A tool to
link product, process, and supply chain design decisions. *Journal of
Operations Management.* Vol. 23, No. 3/4, pp. 345–369.

Flynn, A. E. (2008). *Leadership in Supply Management.* Insti for Supply Management, Tempe, AZ.

Ford, R. C., Randolph, W. A. (1992). Cross-functional structure A review and integration of matrix organization and project management. *Journal of Management,* Vol. 18, No. 2, pp. 267–294.

Fulmer, R., Bleak, J. (2011). How to succeed at succession. *Inside Supply Management.* Vol. 22, No. 7, pp.14–16.

Gabbard, E. G. (2007). Building relationships. *Inside Supply Management.* Vol. 18, No. 4, p. 12.

Ganeshan, R., Jack, E., Magazine, M. J., Stephans, P. (1998). A taxonomic review of supply chain management research. In Tayur, S., Ganeshan, R., Magazine, M. J. *Quantitative Models for Supply Chain Management.* Springer-Verlag, New York, NY.

Global Manufacturing Outlook. (2011). KPMG International Cooperative. September 20, 2011. Retrieved July 4, 2012. www.kpmg.com/Global/en/IssuesAndInsights/ArticlesPublications/global-manufacturing-outlook/Pages/growth-while-managing-volatility.aspx

Global Risks 2011, 6th ed., (2011). World Economic Forum. Retrieved January 12, 2012. http://reports.weforum.org/wp-content/blogs.dir/1/mp/uploads/pages/files/global-risks-2011.pdf

Globalization and global trade drive renewed focus on supply chain visibility. (2011). Aberdeen Group, September 2011. Retrieved January 14, 2012. www.aberdeen.com.

Goldman, S. L., Nagel, R. N., Preiss, K. (1995). *Agile Competitors and Virtual Organizations.* Van Nostran Reinhold, New York, NY.

Gold, S. (2012). Providing 21st-century skills for 21st-century manufacturing. Industrweek.com. March 14, 2012. Retrieved July 7, 2012. http://industryweek.com/articles/providing_21st-century_skills_for_21st-century_manufacturing_26800.aspx?Page=2

Gouge, I. (2003). *Shaping the IT Organization.* Springer, London.

ute

.9). *Strategic Outsourcing.* American Manage-
w York, NY.

., A. (1998). Agile manufacturing: enablers and imple-
.nework. *International Journal of Production Research.*
. 5, pp. 1223–1247.

.aasekaran, A., Lai, K-H., Cheng, E. (2008). Responsive supply
.t: A competitive strategy in a networked economy. *Omega.* Vol.
., No. 4, pp. 549–564.

Goldratt, E. M., Cox, J. (1984). *The Goal.* North River Press, Cro-
ton-on-Hudson, NY.

Haklik, J. E. (2012). ISO 14001 and Sustainable Development.
February. Retrieved February 12. www.trst.com/sustainable.htm

Harrison, A., Van Hoek, R. (2008). *Logistics Management and
Strategy: Competing through the supply chain, 3rd ed.* Prentice Hall.
London.

Hyndman, R., Koehler, A. B., Ord, J. K., Snyder, R. D. (2008).
Forecasting with Exponential Smoothing. Springer Publishing, New
York, NY.

Institute of Supply Management. (2012). Metrics and Indices:
Sustainability and Social Responsibility Metrics and Performance
Criteria. Retrieved April 2012. www.ism.ws/SR/content.cfm?ItemN
umber=16738&navItemNumber=16739

Intelligence agent. (2012). *CSCMP's Supply Chain Quarterly.*
Vol. 6, No. 2, pp. 20–21.

Ito, T., Zhang, M., Robu, V., Matsuo, T. eds. (2012). *New Trends
in Agent-Based Complex Automated Negotiations.* Springer, New
York, NY.

Jacobs, F. R., Berry, W. L., Whybark, D. C., Vollmann, T. E.
(2011) *Manufacturing Planning and Control for Supply Chain Management.* McGraw-Hill, New York, NY.

Jennings, R.J. (2011). Talent issues arise once more. *Inside Supply Management.* Vol. 22, No. 8, p. 42.

Jensen, K. (2011). Delay tactics: When to stall and how to recognize when someone is giving you the run-around. September 29, 2011. Retrieved January 20, 2012. http://keldjensen.wordpress.com/2011/09/29/delay-tactics-when-to-stall-and-how-to-recognize-when-someone-is-giving-you-the-run-around/

Johnson, B. (2012). Succeed: How We Can Reach Our Goals. February. Retrieved February 11, 2012. http://experiencelife.com/article/succeed-how-we-can-reach-our-goals/

Journal of Commerce. (2012). Supply chain synchronicity. *Journal of Commerce.* February 13, 2012. Retrieved April 20, 2012. www.joc.com

Kaye, S. (2011). Achieving a Truly Green Supply Chain. IFW-net.com. September 1, 2011. Retrieved January 20, 2012. www.ifw-net.com/freightpubs/ifw/index/achieving-a-truly-green-supply-chain/20017900492.htm

Kerbe, B., Dreckshage, B. J. (2011). *Lean Supply Chain Management Essentials.* CRC Press, Boca Raton, FL.

Kilger, C., Wagner, M. (2008). Demand planning. In Stadtler, H., Kilger, C. *Supply Chain Management and Advanced Planning.* Springer-Verlag, New York, NY.

Knemeyer, A. M., Zinn, W., Eroglu, C. (2009). Proactive planning for catastrophic events in supply chains. *Journal of Operations Management.* Vol, 27, No. 2, pp. 141–153.

Kogut, B. (1985). Designing global strategies: profiting from operational flexibility. *Sloan Management Review.* Vol. 27, pp. 27–38.

Komoto, H., Tomiyama, T., Silvester, S., Brezet, H. (2011). Analyzing supply chain robustness for OEMs from a life cycle perspective using life cycle simulation. *International Journal of Production Economics.* Vol. 134, No. 2, pp. 447–457.

ıp.

ₔman, L. P., Malhotra, M. K. (2013). *Opera-
th ed.*, Pearson, Boston, MA.

₁2). Making the Grade in Supplier Sustainability
₃4th Annual International Supply Management Con-
y 2009. Retrieved February 22, 2012, www.ism.ws/files/
ₑedings/09ProcFB-Kuhn.pdf

ₐmar, S. K., Tiwari, M. K., Babiceanu, R. F. (2010). Mini-
ation of supply chain cost with embedded risk using computa-
ₒnal intelligence approaches. *International Journal of Production
Research.* Vol. 48, No. 13, pp. 3717–3739.

Leach, A. (2011). The cost of global inflation. CPO Agenda.
Autumn 2011. Retrieved January 20, 2012. www.cpoagenda.com/
previous-articles/autumn-2011/features/the-cost-of-global-inflation/

Leach, A. (2011). More than a third of supply chain disruptions are the result of problems with indirect suppliers, research
has found. Supply Management. November 4, 2011. Retrieved
January   15,   2012.   www.supplymanagement.com/news/2011/
beware-of-risk-at-lower-tier-suppliers/

Lee, H. L. (2011). Don't Tweak Your Supply Chain-Rethink It
End to End. In *Harvard Business Review: Managing Supply Chains.*
Harvard Business Review Press, Boston, MA.

Le Merle, M. (2011). How to prepare for a black swan.
Strategy+Business.com, Issue 64, Autumn 2011. Retrieved January
20, 2012. www.strategybusiness.com/media/file/sb64_11303.pdf

Leong, J. (2012). Risk management in real time. *Inside Supply
Management.* Vol. 23, No. 1, pp. 22–25.

Li, M., Choi, T. Y. (2009). Triads in services outsourcing: Bridge,
bridge decay and bridge transfer. *Journal of Supply Chain Management.* Vol. 45, No. 3, pp. 27–39.

Lussier, R. N., Achua, C. F. (2004). *Leadership: Theory, Application, Skill Development, 2nd ed.* Thomson/South-Western, Australia.

McBeath, B. (2011). Demanding times: Part three-aligning supply and demand. ChainLink Research. October 4. Retrieved October 13, 2011. www.clresearch.com/research/detail.cfm?guid=B250BF1E-3048-79ED-9963-EA9982C6A4EE

Mangan, J., Lalwani, C., Butcher, T. (2008). *Global Logistics and Supply Chain Management.* John Wiley & Sons, New York, NY.

Martin, J. W. (2007). *Lean Six Sigma for Supply Chain Management.* McGraw-Hill, New York, NY.

Martin, J. W. (2008). *Operations Excellence.* Auerbach Publications, Boco Raton, FL.

Matthews, D. L., Stanley, L. L. (2008) Effective Supply Management Performance. Institute for Supply Management, Tempe, AZ.

Miles, T. (2012). Supply Chain Agility: If you know it when you see it, do you need to define it? Kinaxis.com. March 15, 2012. Retrieved June 18, 2012. http://blog.kinaxis.com/2012/03/supply-chain-agility-if-you-know-it-when-you-see-it-do-you-need-to-define-it/

Milgate, M. (2001). *Alliances, Outsourcing, and the Lean Organization.* Quorum Books, Westport, CT.

Miller, J. (2012). Supply chain industry predictions for 2012. *Industry Leaders Magazine,* January 4, 2012. Retrieved on June 20, 2012. www.industryleadersmagazine.com/supply-chain-industry-predictions-for-2012/

Mitchell, L. K. (2012). Calling it quits. *Inside Supply Management.* Vol. 22, No. 9, pp. 14–15.

Mollenkoft, D. A., Tate, W. L. (2011). Green and lean supply chains. *CSCMP Explores.* Vol. 8, pp. 1–17.

Moncza, R. M., Choi, T. Y., Kim, Y., McDowell, C. P. (2011). *Supplier Relationship Management: An Implementation Framework.* CAPS Research, Tempe, AZ.

Monczka, R. M. Petersen, K. J. (2011). *Supply Strategy Implementation: Current and Future Opportunities 2011.* CAPS Research, Tempe, AZ.

Moser, H. (2011). Time to come home? *CSCMP's Supply Chain Quarterly.* Vol. 4, No. 5, pp. 38–44.

Mullan, J. (2011). Market intelligence matters. *Inside Supply Management.* Vol. 22, No. 7, pp. 22–25.

Multi-Sourcing Just a Red Herring? (2003). Global Computing Services. July 4, pp. 3–4.

Myerson, P. (2012). *Lean Supply Chain and Logistics Management.* McGraw-Hill Professional, New York, NY.

Nagel, R., Dove, R. (1991). *21st Century Manufacturing Enterprise Strategy.* Incocca Institute, Leigh University.

Nassimbeni, G., Sartor, M., Dus, D. (2012). Security risks in service offshoring and outsourcing. *Industrial Management & Data Systems.* Vol. 112, No. 3, pp. 405–440.

Nicholas, J. (2011). *Lean Production for Competitive Advantage.* CRC Press, New York, NY.

Nirenburg, I. (2012). Model for sustainability. *Inside Supply Management.* Vol. 23, No. 1, pp. 30–31.

O'Connor, J. O. (2008). *Supply Chain Risk Management.* Cisco Systems, Inc., New York, NY.

Outlook on the Logistics & Supply Chain Industry 2012. (2012). World Economic Forum. June 2012. Retrieved January 14, 2012. www.weforum.org/reports/

Patton, J. (2011). Leveraging RFID. *Inside Supply Management.* Vol. 22, No. 8, pp. 12–13.

Pint, E. M., Baldwin, L. H. (1997). *Strategic Sourcing: Theory and Evidence from Economics and Business Management.* Rand, Santa Monica, CA.

Polansky, M. (2012). Exploring sustainability. *eSide Supply Management,* Vol. 3, No. 2, March/April 2010. Retrieved January 15, 2012. www.ism.ws/pubs/eside/esidearticle.cfm?ItemNumber=20133

Quariguasi, J., Walther, G., Bloemhof, J., van Nunen, J. A. E. E., Spengler, T. (2010). From closed-loop to sustainable supply chains: The WEEE case. *International Journal of Production Research.* Vol. 48, No. 15, pp. 4463–4481.

Reducing Overall Supply Chain Costs is #1 Priority Among Manufacturers, Survey Finds. (2012). SupplyChainBrain.com, June 25, 2012. Retrieved June 26, 2012. www.supplychainbrain.com/content/nc/industry-verticals/industrial-manufacturing/single-article-page/article/reducing-overall-supply-chain-costs-is-1-priority-among-manufacturers-survey-finds/

Rimiené, Kristina. (2011). Supply chain agility concept evolution (1990-2010). *Economics & Management.* Vol. 16, pp. 892–899.

Ring, P. S., Van de Ven, A. H. (1994). Developmental process of cooperative interorganizational relationships. *Academy of Management Review.* Vol. 19, No. 1, pp. 90–118.

Roach, Q. (2011). Make mentoring a priority. *Inside Supply Management.* Vol. 22, No. 6, pp. 28–30.

Roberts, K. H., O'Reilly, C. A., III. (1974). Failures in upward communication in organizations: Three possible culprits. *Academy of Management Journal.* Vol. 17, No. 2, pp. 205–215.

Robinson, W. M., Harkness, K. (2011). Flex your negotiating muscle. *Inside Supply Management,* Retrieved September 8, 2012. www.ism.ws/pubs/ISMMag/ismarticle.cfm?ItemNumber=22056

Sako, I. M. (1992). Price, *Quality and Trust: Inter-organization Relations in Britain and Japan.* Cambridge University Press. Cambridge, UK.

Sampath, K., Saygin, C., Grasman, S. C., Leu, M. C. (2006). Impact of reputation information sharing in an auction-based job allocation model for small and medium-sized enterprises. *International Journal of Production Research.* Vol. 44, No. 9, pp. 1777–1798.

Schniederjans, M. J. (1998). *Operations Management in a Global Context.* Quorum Books, Westport, CT.

Schniederjans, M. J. (1999). *International Facility Acquisition and Location Analysis.* Quorum Books, Westport, CT.

Schniederjans, M. J., Schniederjans, A. M., Schniederjans, D. G. (2010). *Topics in Lean Supply Chain Management.* World Scientific Press, Singapore.

Schniederjans, M. J., Schniederjans, A. M., Schniederjans, D. G. (2005). *Outsourcing and Insourcing in an International Context.* M. E. Sharpe, Armonk, NY.

Schniederjans, M. J., (1993). *Topics in Just-In-Time Management.* Allyn & Bacon, Needham Heights, MA.

Schniederjans, M. J., Olson, J. R. (1999). *Advanced Topics in Just-In-Time Management.* Quorum Books, Westport, CT.

Schniederjans, M. J., Schniederjans, A. M. and Schniederjans, D. G. (2005). *Outsourcing and Insourcing in an International Context.* M. E. Sharpe, Armonk, NY.

Schonberger, R. J., (2010). *Building a Chain of Customers.* Free Press, New York, NY.

Schonberger, R. J., (1982). *Japanese Manufacturing Techniques.* Free Press, New York, NY.

Schutt, J., Moore, T. (2011). Are You a Candidate for Produce-to-Demand? *CSCMP's Supply Chain Quarterly,* Vol. 5, No. 3, pp. 54–60.

Seuring, S. (2009). The product-relationship-matrix as framework for strategic supply chain design based on operations theory. *International Journal of Production Economics.* Vol. 120, No. 1, pp. 221–232.

Shaw, H. (2006). The trouble with COSO. CFO Magazine. March 15. Retrieved October 24, 2011. www.cfo.com/article.cfm/5598405/1/c_5620756

Sheffi, Y. (2005). *The Resilient Enterprise: Overcoming Vulnerablity for Competitive Advantage.* MIT Press, Cambride, MA.

Shell, R. G. (2006). *Bargaining for Advantage.* Penguin Books, New York, NY.

Sherer, S. A., Kohli, R., Yao, Y., Cederlund, J. (2011). Do cultural differences matter in IT implementation? A multinational's experience with collaborative technology. *Journal of Global Information Management.* Vol. 19, No. 4, pp. 1–17.

Siegfried, M. (2011). Aligned for success. *Inside Supply Management.* Vol. 22, No. 6, pp.25–27.

Siegfried, M. (2012). Building a resilient supply chain. *Inside Supply Management.* Vol. 23, No. 5, pp. 24–25.

Siegfried, M. (2012b) Collaborating with the competition. *Inside Supply Management.* Vol. 23, No. 2, pp. 20–23.

Siegfried, M. (2011). Tracing through the supply chain. *Inside Supply Management.* Vol. 22, No. 5, pp. 36–39.

Simchi-Levi, D. (2010). *Operations Rules: Delivering Customer Value through Flexible Operations.* MIT Press, Cambridge, MA.

Simchi-Levi, D., Kaminsky, Simchi-Levi, E. (2008). *Designing and Managing the Supply Chain, 3rd ed.* McGraw-Hill, Boston, MA.

Singer, T. (2012). Global supply chain labor standards. The Conference Board. Retrieved June 15, 2012. https://www.conference-board.org/retrievefile.cfm?filename=TCB-DN-V4N10121.pdf&type=subsite

Sirkin, H. L. (2011). How to prepare your supply chain for the unthinkable. Harvard Business Review/HBR Blog Network. March 28, 2011. Retrieved January 14, 2012. http://blogs.hbr.org/cs/2011/03/why_are_supply_chains_eternall.html

Skills gap report, 2011. (2011). The Manufacturing Institute. Retrieved July 7, 2012. www.themanufacturinginstitute.org/Research/Skills-Gap-in-Manufacturing/2011-Skills-Gap-Report/2011-Skills-Gap-Report.aspx

Slaybaugh, R. (2010) Sustainable production's star performers. *eSide Supply Management*. Vol. 3, No. 1. Retrieved January 13, 2012. www.ism.ws/pubs/eside/esidearticle.cfm?ItemNumber=19978

Slone, R. E. (2011). Leading a Supply Chain Turnaround. In *Harvard Business Review: Managing Supply Chains*. Harvard Business Review Press, Boston, MA.

Slone, R. E., Dittmann, J. P., Mentzer, J. T. (2010). *The New Supply Chain Agenda*. Harvard Business Press, Boston, MA.

Smith, D. (2004). Outsourcing: Will utilities plug in? *Electric Perspectives*. Vol. 29, No. 2, pp. 22–32.

Smith, G. A. (2011). Leveraging private section practices in the public sector. *CSCMP's Supply Chain Quarterly*. Vol. 5, No. 3, pp. 38–45.

Supply Chain 2020. (2012). Supply chain 2020: The agile supply chain. *MHD Supply Chain Solutions*. Vol. 42, No. 1, pp. 10–11.

Supply chain and logistics outsourcing set to grow in 2012. (2012). January 11, 2012. Retrieved January 15, 2012. www.procurementleaders.com/news/latestnews/0111-supply-chain-and-logistics/

Supply chain sustainability: A practical guide for continuous improvement. (2010). United Nations Global Compact and Business for Social Responsibility. 2010. Retrieved July 1, 2012. www.unglobalcompact.org/docs/issues_doc/supply_chain/SupplyChainRep_spread.pdf

Strategic Sourceror. (2011). How do supply chain management experts FedEx and UPS prepare for the holiday season? December 14. Retrieved January 14, 2012. www.strategicsourceror.com/2011/12/how-do-supply-chain-management-experts.html

Svendsen, A., Boutilier, R. G., Abbott, R. M., Wheeler, D. (2001). Measuring the business value of stakeholder relationships. *CA Magazine*. August, pp. 29–36.

Tompkins, J. A. (2012). Creating value. *Industrial Engineer*. Vol. 44, No. 7, p. 24.

Trebilcock, B. (2011). Skechers tones up distribution center. www.mmh.com. December 1. Retrieved January 14, 2012. www.mmh.com/article/skechers_tones_up_distribution_center.

Trowbridge, M. (2011). Building superheroes. *Inside Supply Management.* Vol. 22, No. 5, pp.12–13.

Trowbridge, M. (2012). How to prep for a winning negotiation. *Supply Chain Management Review.* January/February, pp. 46–51.

Tuel, K. (2011). Think laterally. *Inside Supply Management.* Vol. 22, No. 5, p. 48.

Turbide, D. (2011). Logistics, supply-chain mastery play key roles in achieving success. Seacoastonline.com. November 28. Retrieved January 15, 2012. www.seacoastonline.com/apps/pbcs.dll/article?AID=/20111128/BIZ/111280323/-1/NEWSMAP

Van Arnum, P. (2011). Achieving cross-functional supplier integration: a case study. *Pharmaceutical Technology.* August, pp. 54–58.

Verner, J. M., Abdullah, L. M. (2012). Exploratory case study research: Outsourced project failure. *Information & Software Technology.* Vol. 54, No. 8, pp. 866–886.

Vickery, S. K., Droge, C., Setia, P., Sambamurthy, V. (2010). Supply chain information technologies and organizational initiatives: Complementary versus independent effects on agility and firm performance. *International Journal of Production Research.* Vol. 48, No. 23, pp. 7025–7042.

Vulnerable to valuable: How integrity can transform a supply chain. (2008). PwC, December 2008. Retrieved May 7, 2012. www.pwc.com/en_US/us/supplychain-management/assets/pwc-sci-112008.pdf

Wade, D. S. (2011). Measuring services outsourcing. *Inside Supply Management.* Vol. 22, No. 6, pp. 36–37.

Wakolbinger, T., Cruz, J. M. (2011). Supply chain disruption risk management through strategic information acquisition and sharing and risk-sharing contracts. *International Journal of Production Research.* Vol. 49, No. 13, pp. 4063–4084.

Wang, G., Huang, S. H., Dismukes, J. P. (2004). Product-driven supply chain selection using integrated multi-criteria decision-making methodology. *International Journal of Production Economics.* Vol. 91, No. 1, pp. 1–15.

Wetterauer, U., Meyr, H. (2008). The implementation process. In Stadtler, H., Kilger, C. eds. (2008). *Supply Chain Management and Advanced Planning, 4th ed.,* Springer, Berlin, GE., pp. 325–346.

Wincel, J. P. (2004). *Lean Supply Chain Management.* Productivity Press, New York, NY.

Yang, S. L., Li, T. F. (2002). Agility evaluation of mass customization product manufacturing. *Journal of Materials Processing Technology.* Vol. 129, Nos. 1–3, pp. 640–644.

Yusuf, Y. Y., Sarhadi, M., Gunasekaran, A. (1999). Agile manufacturing: The drivers, concepts and attributes. *International Journal of Production Economics.* Vol. 62, No.1, pp. 33–43.

Yuva, J. (2011). Share and share alike. *Inside Supply Management.* Vol. 22, No. 7, pp. 30–33.

Zylstra, K.D. (2006). *Lean Distribution.* John Wiley & Sons. New York, NY.

INDEX

M

MAD (mean average deviation), defined, 172

management by exception, defined, 239

manager (supply chain), described, 66

Manhattan Associates, about, 396

Manufacturers Alliance for Productivity and Innovation (MAPI), 91

The Manufacturing Institute, 91

market intelligence (MI), monitoring customer demand with, 117-118

market research, defined, 171

master planning in supply chain synchronization, 241

materials requirement planning (MRP), defined, 54

matrix organizational structure design
explained, 40
for supply chains, 41-43

maturity stage (life cycle)
Brent Beabout interview, 424-425
defined, 13
demand planning in, 167
Eddie Capel interview, 400
forecasting methods, 171
James Chris Gaffney interview, 417
Mark Holifield interview, 383-384
Mike Orr interview, 374
outsourcing in, 361
Ronald Robinson interview, 410
strategy opportunities and, 20
Yadi Kamelian interview, 392

maximum supportable solution (MSS), 216

mean average deviation (MAD), defined, 172

mean square error (MSE), defined, 172

mediation, 139-140

mediators, described, 140

mentoring, defined, 111

mentoring programs, described, 110-111

metrics. *See* performance metrics

MI (market intelligence), monitoring customer demand with, 117-118

migration, defined, 352

milestones, defined, 228

mission statement, explained, 10

mixed model scheduling, defined, 315

monitoring
customer demand, 117-118
defined, 115
future of, 120-121
outsourcing projects, 344-345
performance metrics for, 115
systems for, 115-117

MRP (materials requirement planning), defined, 54

MSE (mean square error), defined, 172

MSS (maximum supportable solution), 216

multi-agent systems, 219

multisourcing outsourcing, defined, 336

N

near field communications (NFC), defined, 55

nearshore outsourcing, defined, 336

negotiation
best practices, 210-212
defined, 194
executive-level support in, 213-214
future of, 216-219
preparation for, 215-217
process overview, 200
stalling tactics, 214-215
strategies for, 206-209
styles of, 203-207
tactics for, 210-211
winning agreements, 203-204

negotiation strategy worksheet, 217

netsourcing, defined, 336

network complexity, 99

network design
explained, 43-45
phases of, 49-52

Network for Business Innovation and Sustainability, 163

new product demand planning. *See* demand planning

new product distribution, Mike Orr interview, 371-372

new product risk management, Mark Holifield interview, 382

NFC (near field communications), defined, 55

nonequity strategic alliances, defined, 181

FT Press

FINANCIAL TIMES

In an increasingly competitive world, it is quality
of thinking that gives an edge—an idea that opens new
doors, a technique that solves a problem, or an insight
that simply helps make sense of it all.

We work with leading authors in the various arenas
of business and finance to bring cutting-edge thinking
and best-learning practices to a global market.

It is our goal to create world-class print publications
and electronic products that give readers
knowledge and understanding that can then be
applied, whether studying or at work.

To find out more about our business
products, you can visit us at www.ftpress.com.